£8.80

Introduction to Control Syst

PUES-18

**Pergamon Unified
Engineering Series**

Pergamon
Unified Engineering
Series

GENERAL EDITORS

Thomas F. Irvine, Jr.
State University of New York at Stony Brook
James P. Hartnett
University of Illinois at Chicago Circle

EDITORS

William F. Hughes
Carnegie-Mellon University
Arthur T. Murphy
Widener College
Daniel Rosenthal
University of California, Los Angeles

SECTIONS

Continuous Media Section
Engineering Design Section
Engineering Systems Section
Humanities and Social Sciences Section
Information Dynamics Section
Materials Engineering Section
Engineering Laboratory Section

Introduction to Control Systems

D. K. Anand
Professor of Mechanical Engineering
University of Maryland, College Park, Maryland

Pergamon Press

Oxford · New York · Toronto · Sydney · Paris · Frankfurt

U.K.	Pergamon Press Ltd., Headington Hill Hall, Oxford, OX3 0BW, England
U.S.A.	Pergamon Press Inc., Maxwell House, Fairview Park, Elmsford, New York 10523, U.S.A.
CANADA	Pergamon of Canada, Suite 104, 150 Consumers Road, Willowdale, Ontario M2J 1P9, Canada
AUSTRALIA	Pergamon Press (Aust.) Pty. Ltd., P.O. Box 544, Potts Point, N.S.W. 2011, Australia
FRANCE	Pergamon Press SARL, 24 rue des Ecoles, 75240 Paris, Cedex 05, France
FEDERAL REPUBLIC OF GERMANY	Pergamon Press GmbH, 6242 Kronberg-Taunus, Pferdstrasse 1, Federal Republic of Germany

Copyright © 1974 Pergamon Press Inc.

All Rights Reserved. No part of this publication may be reproduced, stored in a retrieval system or transmitted in any form or by any means: electronic, electrostatic, magnetic tape, mechanical, photocopying, recording or otherwise, without permission in writing from the publishers.

First edition 1974

Reprinted 1979

Reprinted (with corrections) 1980

Library of Congress Cataloging in Publication Data

Anand, Davinder K
Introduction to control systems.

(Pergamon unified engineering series, 18)
Includes bibliographical references.
1. Automatic control. 2. Control theory.
I. Title
TJ213.A45 1973   629.8   72-12834
ISBN 0 08 019005 7 flexicover
ISBN 0 08 017104 4 hardcover

Printed in Great Britain by Biddles Ltd, Guildford, Surrey

To
My Friends and Teachers
and the memory of
Bibi Hem Kaur

Contents

Preface

This book is written for use as a text in an introductory course in control systems. The classical as well as the state space approach is included and integrated as much as possible. The overall organization, somewhat different from the current books, is based upon my experience teaching the material to a fairly interdisciplinary group of students. The first part of the book deals with analysis in the time domain. Then all the graphical techniques are presented in one chapter. Finally, the latter part of the book deals with some advanced material. It is intended that the student be already familiar with Laplace transforms and have had an introductory course in circuit analysis or vibration theory. Although some familiarity with matrix algebra would be helpful, there is an adequate coverage of this material in the appendixes. Throughout the text care was taken to avoid the appearance of cookbook formulas but at the same time to avoid an excessive amount of mathematics. Derivations were included only where it was felt that this would aid the student.

After a brief introduction in Chapter 1, the modeling of physical systems is presented in Chapter 2. Here the transfer function representation as well as a set of first-order linear differential equations are used to describe an idealized system. Chapter 3 considers control system representation. Again the transfer function as well as state space representation is considered. It is stressed that these two representations may be directly related and is done so at the outset.

Chapters 4 and 5 dwell upon the response in the time domain. Here we consider the transient and steady state behavior and then introduce the Routh–Hurwitz criterion. Again the analysis is carried out via classical as well as the modern approach. The performance and design specifications are then discussed in Chapter 6.

Whereas the material up to this point considers only analytical methods, Chapter 7 is devoted to graphical techniques. These include the Bode plot, Nyquist plot, and the root locus. The stability criterion due to Nyquist is also covered here. I have found in my experience that the students are very receptive to this method of presentation. The availability of time sharing and plotting routines has greatly enhanced the attraction of these methods. This too, I believe, should be stressed. The design of systems is discussed in Chapter 8. Here, the concept of using feedback gain using state variables is introduced.

Discrete systems are covered in Chapters 9 and 10. The former is based upon classical, whereas the latter is based upon state space methods. Generally I have covered Sections 9-1 to 9-4 and then gone to Chapter 10 thereby omitting the sampled systems at this level. I have included this material for completeness. Finally, small nonlinearities are discussed in Chapter 11. Here the stability criterion of Lyapunov is also introduced. I have avoided the problem of the construction of Lyapunov functions since this is too advanced for the students at this level.

The major parts of this book were used to teach my students at the University of Maryland for the last seven years. To them, my sincere thanks. Acknowledgment is due George Bush of The Applied Physics Laboratory for providing some problems, and to Professor P. C. Cunniff of the University of Maryland for reading parts of the manuscript. Mr. J. M. Whisnant read the entire manuscript and made many suggestions for which I am most appreciative. The entire manuscript and its drafts were patiently reviewed and critiqued by Dean Arthur T. Murphy to whom I owe a very special thanks. It is a pleasure to acknowledge the assistance of Mary Jane O'Neill who expertly and patiently typed the manuscript. Finally, for their patience and understanding, I am greatly indebted to Asha, Anita, and Dilip.

Silver Spring, Maryland   D. K. ANAND

About the Author . . .

Davinder K. Anand (D.Sc., The George Washington University) is Professor of Mechanical Engineering at the University of Maryland, College Park and a consultant at The Applied Physics Laboratory of the Johns Hopkins University, Silver Spring, Maryland. His main interests lie in the fields of Systems Analysis and Dynamics and he is the holder of a U.S. Patent on Heat Pipe Control. Dr. Anand has published many papers in technical journals and conference proceedings and has published two other books on Introductory Engineering. He is a member of ASME, Sigma Tau, Pi Tau Sigma, and Sigma Xi.

1

Introduction

1-1 HISTORICAL PERSPECTIVE

The desire to control the forces of nature has been with man since early civilizations. Although many examples of control systems existed in early times, it was not until the mid-eighteenth century that several steam operated control devices appeared. This was the time of the steam engine, and perhaps the most noteworthy invention was the speed control flyball governor invented by James Watt.

Around the beginning of the twentieth century much of the work in control systems was being done in the power generation and the chemical processing industry. Also by this time, the concept of the autopilot for airplanes was fairly well developed.

The period beginning about twenty-five years before World War Two saw rapid advances in electronics and especially in circuit theory, aided by the now classical work of Nyquist in the area of stability theory. The requirements of sophisticated weapon systems, submarines, aircraft and the like gave new impetus to the work in control systems before and after the war. The advent of the analog computer coupled with advances in electronics saw the beginning of the establishment of control systems as a science. By the mid-fifties, the progress in digital computers had given the engineers a new tool that greatly enhanced their capability to study large and complex systems. The availability of computers also opened the era of data-logging, computer control, and the state space or modern method of analysis.

Finally, the sputnik began the space race and large governmental expenditures in the space as well as military effort. During this time, circuits became miniaturized and large sophisticated systems could be put together very compactly thereby allowing a computational and control advantage coupled with systems of small physical dimensions. We were now capable of designing and flying minicomputers and landing men on the moon. The post sputnik age saw much effort in system optimization and adaptive systems.

Today control systems is a science with the art still playing an important role. Much mathematical sophistication has been achieved with considerable interest in optimal control systems. The modern approach, having been established as a science, is being applied not only to the traditional control systems, but to newer problems like urban analysis, econometrics, transportation, biomedical problems, and a host of similar problems that affect modern man.

1-2 BASIC CONCEPTS

Control system analysis is concerned with the study of the behavior of dynamic systems. The analysis relies upon the fundamentals of system theory where the governing differential equations assume a cause-effect relationship. A physical system may be represented as shown in Fig. 1-1,

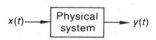

Fig. 1-1 A physical system.

where the excitation or input is $x(t)$ and the response or output is $y(t)$. A simple control system is shown in Fig. 1-2. Here the output is compared to the input signal, and the difference of these two signals becomes the excitation to the physical system, and we speak of the control system as having feedback. The *analysis* of a control system, such as described in

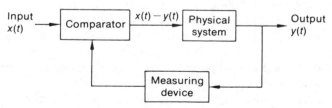

Fig. 1-2 A simple control system.

Fig. 1-2, involves the obtaining of $y(t)$ given the input and the characteristics of the system. On the other hand, if the input and output are specified and we wish to design the system characteristics, then this is known as *synthesis*.

A generalized control system is shown in Fig. 1-3. The *reference* or *input variables* $r_1, r_2, \ldots, r_m$ are applied to the *comparator* or *controller*. The *output variables* are $c_1, c_2, \ldots, c_n$. The signals $e_1, e_2, \ldots, e_p$ are *actuating* or *control variables* and are applied by the controller to the *system* or *plant*. The plant is also subjected to *disturbance inputs* $u_1, u_2, \ldots, u_q$. If the output variable is not measured and fed back to the controller, then the total system consisting of the controller and plant is an *open loop system*. If the output is fed back, then the system is a *closed loop system*.

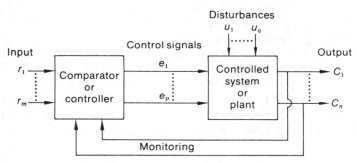

Fig. 1-3   A general control system.

1-3 SYSTEMS DESCRIPTION

Because control systems occur so frequently in our lives, their study is quite important. Generally, a control system is composed of several subsystems connected in such a way as to yield the proper cause-effect relationship. Since the various subsystems can be electrical, mechanical, pneumatic, biological, etc., the complete description of the entire system requires the understanding of fundamental relationships in many different disciplines. Fortunately, the similarity in the dynamic behavior of different physical systems makes this task easier and more interesting.

As an example of a control system consider the simplified version of the attitude control of a spacecraft illustrated in Fig. 1-4. We wish the satellite to have some specific attitude relative to an inertial coordinate system. The actual attitude is measured by an attitude sensor on board the satellite.

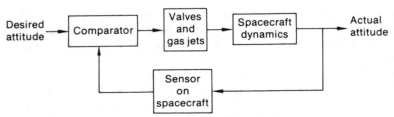

Fig. 1-4   Control of satellite attitude.

If the desired and actual attitudes are not the same, then the comparator sends a signal to the valves which open and cause gas jet firings. These jet firings give the necessary corrective signal to the satellite dynamics thereby bringing it under control. A control system represented this way is said to be represented by block diagrams. Such a representation is helpful in the partitioning of a large system into subsystems and thereby allowing the study of one subsystem at a time.

If we have many inputs and outputs that are monitored and controlled, the block diagram appears as illustrated in Fig. 1-5. Systems where several variables are monitored and controlled are called *multivariable* systems. Examples of multivariable systems are found in chemical processing, guidance and control of vehicles, the national economy, urban housing growth patterns, the postal service, and a host of other social and urban problems.

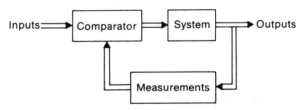

Fig. 1-5   Representation of a multivariable system.

As another example consider the system shown in Fig. 1-6. The figure shows an illustration of the conceptual design of a proposed Sun Tracker. Briefly, it consists of an astronomical telescope mount, two silicon solar cells, an amplifier, a motor, and gears. The solar cells are attached to the polar axis of the telescope so that if the pointing direction is in error, more of the sun's image falls on one cell than the other. This pair of cells, when connected in parallel opposition, appear as a current source and act as a positional error sensing device. A simple differential input transistor

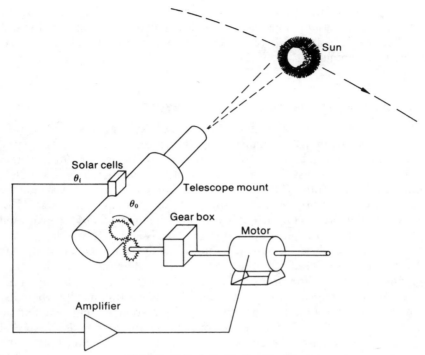

Fig. 1-6   Schematic of a Sun Tracker.

amplifier can provide sufficient gain so that the small error signal produces an amplifier output sufficient for running the motor. This motor sets the rotation rate of the polar axis of the telescope mount to match the apparent motion of the sun. This system is depicted in block diagram form in Fig. 1-7.

The number of control systems that surround us is indeed very large. The essential feature of all these systems is in general the same. They all

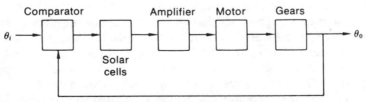

Fig. 1-7   Block diagram of the Sun Tracker.

have input, control, output, and disturbance variables. They all describe a controller and a plant. They all have some type of a comparator. Finally, in all cases we want to drive the control system to follow a set of pre-conceived commands.

1-4   DESIGN, MODELING, AND ANALYSIS

Prior to the building of a piece of hardware, a system must be designed, modeled, and analyzed. Actually the analysis is an important and essential feature of the design process. In general, when we design a control system we do so conceptually. Then we generate a mathematical model which is analyzed. The results of this analysis are compared to the performance specifications that are desired of the proposed system. The accuracy of the results depends upon the quality of the original model of the proposed design. The Sun Tracker proposed in Fig. 1-6 is a conceptual design. We shall show, in Chapter 8, how it is analyzed and then modified so that its performance satisfies the system specifications. The objective then may be considered to be the prediction, prior to construction, of the dynamic behavior that a physical system exhibits, i.e. its natural motion when disturbed from an equilibrium position and its response when excited by external stimuli. Specifically we are concerned with the speed of response or transient response, the accuracy or steady state response, and the stability. By stability we mean that the output remains within certain reasonable limiting values. The relative weight given to any special requirement is dependent upon the specific application. For example, the air conditioning of the interior of a building may be maintained to $\pm 1°C$ and satisfy the occupants. However, the temperature control in certain cryogenic systems requires that the temperature be controlled to within a fraction of a degree. The requirements of speed, accuracy, and stability are quite often contradictory and some compromises must be made. For example, increasing the accuracy generally makes for poor transient response. If the damping is decreased, the system oscillations increase and it may take a long time to reach some steady state value.

It is important to remember that all real control systems are nonlinear; however, many can be approximated within a useful though limited range as linear systems. Generally, this is an acceptable first approximation. A very important benefit to be derived by assuming linearity is that the superposition theorem applies. If we obtain the response due to two different inputs, then the response due to the combined input is equal to the sum of the individual responses. Another benefit is that operational mathematics can be used in the analysis of linear systems. The operational method allows us to transform ordinary differential equations into algebraic equations which are much simpler to handle.

Traditionally, control systems were represented by higher-order linear differential equations and the techniques of operational mathematics were employed to study these equations. Such an approach is referred to as the *classical method* and is particularly useful for analyzing systems characterized by a single input and a single output. As systems began to become more complex, it became increasingly necessary to use a digital computer. The work on a computer can be advantageously carried out if the system under consideration is represented by a set of first-order differential equations and the analysis is carried out via matrix theory. This is in essence what is referred to as the *state space* or state variable approach. This method, although applicable to single input-output systems, finds important applications in the multivariable system. Another very attractive benefit is that it enables the control system engineer to study variables inside a system.

It is perhaps interesting to note that much of the work in the classical theory of dynamics rests on the state variable viewpoint. In writing the equations of motion of a system using Lagrange's principle it is necessary to use linearly independent variables or generalized coordinates. The number of these coordinates is equal to the number of degrees of freedom. Hamilton, however, showed that the use of generalized momentum coordinates lead to greatly simplified equations of motion. What this meant was that the state of a second-order system, for example, could be represented by the independent variable and its time derivative. Therefore, the system under consideration is represented by first-order differential equations.

Since this is an introductory course, it is our intention to expose you to both the classical and state space viewpoints. We must note however that although the easier route is to initially begin with the classical viewpoint, it is the state approach that is more natural for the more complex and interesting problems. At this level, a thorough study should necessarily include both viewpoints.

Regardless of the approach used in the design and analysis of a control system, we must at least follow the following steps:

(1) Postulate a control system and state the system specifications to be satisfied.
(2) Generate a functional block diagram and obtain a mathematical representation of the system.

(3) Analyze the system using any of the analytical or graphical methods applicable to the problem.
(4) Check the performance (speed, accuracy, stability, or other criterion) to see if the specifications are met.
(5) Finally, optimize the system parameters so that (1) is satisfied.

Whatever the physical system or specific arrangement, we shall see that there are only a few basic concepts and analytical tools that are pivotal to the prediction of system behavior. The fundamental concepts that are learned here and applied to a few examples have therefore a much wider range of applicability. The real range will only be clear when you start working with the ideas to be developed here.

1-5 TEXT OUTLINE

With the assumption that the student is familiar with Laplace transforms, Chapter 2 introduces mathematical modeling of analogous physical systems. Various systems are represented in operational form as well as by a set of first-order differential equations. Representation of control systems by classical as well as state space techniques is introduced in Chapter 3. It is seen that in the classical approach a system is represented by its transfer function, whereas in the state space approach it is represented by a vector-matrix differential equation.

Response in the time domain is discussed using classical methods in Chapter 4. This development relies on operational mathematics, with which prior familiarity is assumed. The state space method of analysis is discussed in Chapter 5. Some fundamentals of matrix theory to support this chapter are given in Appendix C and should be reviewed at this time. Performance and specifications of control systems in the time domain are discussed in Chapter 6.

Complementing the time domain analysis, several graphical procedures are presented in Chapter 7. It is stressed that the utility of these procedures is greatly enhanced if a digital computer is used.

Once system performance is obtained, methods for altering it are introduced next in Chapter 8. This chapter includes the Sun Tracker problem we spoke about in the previous section. Here we also show how state space methods may be used to design systems and optimize performance.

Whereas the first eight chapters are introductory, the last three are more advanced. Chapters 9 and 10 dwell on discrete systems. Again both the classical as well as state space method of analysis are introduced.

Finally, the effect on system behavior due to small nonlinearities is discussed in Chapter 11. In this chapter we also introduce Lyapunov's stability criterion. This is a method of ascertaining system stability via energy considerations.

2

Physical Systems

2-1 INTRODUCTION

Before analyzing a control system it is necessary that we have a mathematical model of the system. The analysis of the mathematical model gives us insight into the behavior of the physical system. Naturally, the accuracy of the information obtained depends upon how well the system has been mathematically modeled.

The behavior of real systems is nonlinear in nature and often quite difficult to analyze. As a first step we can, however, construct models that are linear over a satisfactory range of operating conditions. When this is done, we gain two important advantages. The first is the property of superposition. This means that the system initially at rest responds independently to different inputs applied simultaneously. If $r_1(t)$ and $r_2(t)$ are two inputs applied separately to a system, then the outputs may be represented as

$$r_1(t) \rightarrow x_1(t); \qquad r_2(t) \rightarrow x_2(t)$$

Now if $r_1(t)$ and $r_2(t)$ are applied together, then the property of superposition allows us to represent the output as

$$[r_1(t) + r_2(t)] \rightarrow [x_1(t) + x_2(t)]$$

The second property of linearity is concerned with proportional response. This implies that if the input is multiplied by a factor K, then the output is multiplied by the same factor, i.e.

$$[K_1 r_1(t) + K_2 r_2(t)] \rightarrow [K_1 x_1(t) + K_2 x_2(t)]$$

Although many mechanical and electrical systems do indeed behave in a linear fashion over fairly large useful ranges, fluid and thermal systems frequently do not exhibit this behavior. Also, active network elements such as diodes and transistors exhibit nonlinear characteristics. When the elements under investigation are nonlinear, they may be linearized over a specified operating point. Consider the nonlinear mechanical spring whose behavior is shown in Fig. 2-1. The force F is given by

$$F = f(x)$$

where $f(x)$ is some nonlinear function of x. Let us assume that we wish to use the spring about point x_1 so that a Taylor series expansion about this point yields

$$F = f(x) = f(x_1) + (x - x_1)\left(\frac{df(x)}{dx}\right)_{x=x_1} + \cdots$$

If we assume that $(df(x)/dx)_{x=x_1}$ is a good estimate of the slope of the curve about x_1 and denote this by k, then

$$F \cong f(x_1) + k(x - x_1)$$

or

$$F - F_1 \cong k(x - x_1)$$

which is the necessary linear approximation to the nonlinear element provided we restrict the application of this equation about the operating point x_1.

In addition to the property of linearity it sometimes simplifies work if we assume that the signals flowing in the control system are incremental

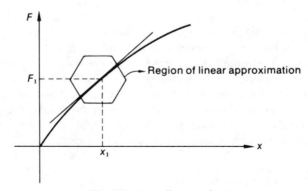

Fig. 2-1   A nonlinear spring.

values. This can be best understood by an example. Consider a mechanical system to which a torque $T(t)$ is applied,

$$T(t) = \frac{d}{dt}(I\omega(t))$$

$$\frac{d\omega(t)}{dt} = \frac{T(t)}{I} \tag{2-1}$$

where I is the constant moment of inertia and $\omega(t)$ is the angular velocity. If we define $\Omega(s)$ as the output signal and $T(s)$ as the input signal in the Laplace† domain, then the ratio $\Omega(s)/T(s)$ becomes

$$\frac{\Omega(s)}{T(s)} = \frac{1}{Is} \tag{2-2}$$

This is known as the *transfer function* of the system. Now let us vary the torque by $q(t)$ which causes a variation in the angular velocity by $\theta(t)$, then

$$T(t) + q(t) = I\frac{d}{dt}(\omega(t) + \theta(t))$$

which may be simplified, by taking the Laplace transform and using the previous result, to

$$\frac{\Theta(s)}{Q(s)} = \frac{1}{Is}$$

We note that now although the input signal is $Q(s)$ and output is $\Theta(s)$ the right-hand side of the equation is the same, i.e. the same transfer function. Comparison with the previous case shows that the input and output values have been replaced by their *incremental values*. It is customary in the analyses of control systems to employ incremental values. These values are variations about some operating conditions. This operating condition is sometimes referred to as a quiescent point of operation.

Our object, in the remainder of this chapter, will be to show how a system can be represented by its transfer function or a set of first-order differential equations of the type shown in Eq. (2-1). Also, we shall restrict our considerations to systems that can be characterized by linear ordinary differential equations. As examples we shall include some very fundamental components, commonly used in control systems.

---

†It is assumed you are familiar with Laplace transforms. Here $\Omega(s)$ and $T(s)$ are the Laplace transforms of $\omega(t)$ and $T(t)$. We will use capital letters throughout to denote variables in the Laplace domain. A table of commonly used expressions appears in Appendix A.

2-2 ANALOGOUS SYSTEMS

Mathematical models can be found for a system by the application of one or more fundamental laws peculiar to the physical nature of the system or component. For example, electrical circuit problems use Kirchhoff's and Ohm's laws; mechanical translational and rotational problems use Newton's law and the d'Alembert principle; thermal systems employ the Fourier heat conduction equation and Newton's law; and finally, Darcy's law for flow and the continuity equation can be used to describe hydraulic systems. Regardless of the nature of the system however, the application of any of these laws yields differential equations that have the same basic form. This leads us to consider them as analogous systems. The units and symbols used in these systems appear in Appendix B.

The balance of this section should be considered as a review since the equations we derive have been encountered before. The object here shall be to derive the system equations and either represent them as transfer functions or systems of first-order differential equations. The former is necessary for classical analysis while the latter for modern or state space analysis.

Electrical Systems

Equations representing the behavior of electrical systems can be obtained by the application of Kirchhoff's laws. They are: (1) the sum of the voltage drops is equal to the sum of the voltage rises in any given loop, and (2) the sum of currents flowing into a node equals the sum of currents flowing out of the node. The method employing the first law is referred to as the loop method and that employing the second is referred to as the node method. Either of the two methods are used, in conjunction with the laws that describe the physical nature of each component in a system, to derive the governing equations.

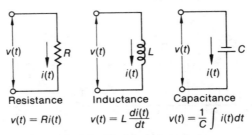

Resistance	Inductance	Capacitance
$v(t) = Ri(t)$	$v(t) = L\dfrac{di(t)}{dt}$	$v(t) = \dfrac{1}{C}\int i(t)dt$

Fig. 2-2   Electrical elements.

Elements used in electrical networks are shown in Fig. 2-2. If we apply a voltage $v(t)$ across a resistance, then from Ohm's law $v(t) = Ri(t)$. Similarly, if voltage is applied across an inductor and capacitor, we have $v(t) = L\,di(t)/dt$ and $v(t) = 1/C \int i(t)dt$ from Faraday's and Coulomb's laws. Resistance is the energy dissipating device, inductance stores kinetic energy, whereas capacitance stores potential energy.

Consider the network shown in Fig. 2-3a. For deriving the necessary differential equation using the loop method, we observe that there are two loops. Summing the voltage drop across R, L, and C, we have the following two equations corresponding to the two loops,

$$R_1 i_1(t) + L\frac{di_1(t)}{dt} + \frac{1}{C}\int i_1(t)dt - \frac{1}{C}\int i_2(t)dt = 0 \qquad (2\text{-}3a)$$

$$\frac{1}{C}\int i_2(t)dt - \frac{1}{C}\int i_1(t)dt + R_2 i_2(t) = -v_2(t) \qquad (2\text{-}3b)$$

Taking the Laplace transform, assuming zero initial conditions, and rearranging, we obtain

$$I_1(s)\left[R_1 + Ls + \frac{1}{Cs}\right] - I_2(s)\left[\frac{1}{Cs}\right] = 0$$

$$-I_1(s)\left[\frac{1}{Cs}\right] + I_2(s)\left[\frac{1}{Cs} + R_2\right] = -V_2(s)$$

Solving these simultaneous equations and noting that $V_1(s) = R_1 I_1(s)$, we obtain $\qquad V_1(s) = -R_1 I_1(s)$

$$\frac{V_1(s)}{V_2(s)} = \frac{R_1}{LCR_2 s^2 + s(R_1 R_2 C + L) + (R_1 + R_2)} \qquad (2\text{-}4)$$

where $V_1(s)/V_2(s)$ is the transfer function for the network. This is sometimes denoted by $G(s)$ as shown in Fig. 2-3b.

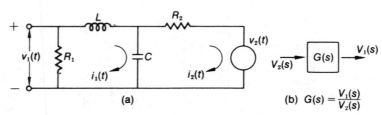

(a)

(b) $G(s) = \dfrac{V_1(s)}{V_2(s)}$

Fig. 2-3 An electrical network.

As an alternate mathematical representation, we define

$$x_1(t) = i_1(t); \qquad x_2(t) = \frac{1}{C}\int i_1(t)\,dt - \frac{1}{C}\int i_2(t)\,dt \qquad (2\text{-}5a)$$

Substituting these into Eqs. (2-3a) and (2-3b)

$$R_1 x_1(t) + L\dot{x}_1(t) + x_2(t) = 0 \qquad (2\text{-}5b)$$

$$-x_2(t) + R_2 i_2(t) = v_2(t) \qquad (2\text{-}5c)$$

The second equation can be rewritten as

$$-x_2(t) + R_2(-C\dot{x}_2(t) + x_1(t)) = v_2(t)$$

Rearranging this and Eq. (2-5b) we obtain two first-order differential equations describing the network,

$$
\begin{aligned}
\dot{x}_1(t) &= -\frac{R_1}{L}x_1(t) - \frac{x_2(t)}{L} \\
\dot{x}_2(t) &= -\frac{x_1(t)}{C} + \frac{x_2(t)}{R_2 C} - \frac{v_2(t)}{R_2 C}
\end{aligned}
\qquad (2\text{-}6)
$$

It is perhaps proper to note here that:

(1) State variables can always be chosen as current through inductances and voltage across capacitances, provided they have independent connections. This is also true of energy storage variables in other systems.

(2) The order of the system is equal to the order of the characteristic equation. This is the same as the minimum number of state variables needed for the systems that we shall consider.

We shall formalize this procedure in the next chapter. Here we are content to show how a system is represented by a set of first-order differential equations. The nodal and loop method of analysis may be generalized to include active networks. The study of active networks is very important since most feedback control systems include some active elements. Although such elements are not completely linear, they may be treated over a limited range of operation as mentioned earlier. Consider the transistor, used in the common-emitter connection, for a single stage amplifier shown in Fig. 2-4a. The equivalent circuit is shown in Fig. 2-4b. Employing the loop equations we obtain,

$$(R_g + r_b + r_e)i_1(t) - r_e i_2(t) = v_1(t)$$

$$-r_e i_1(t) + [r_e + r_c(1-\alpha) + R_L]i_2(t) = -r_m i_b(t)$$

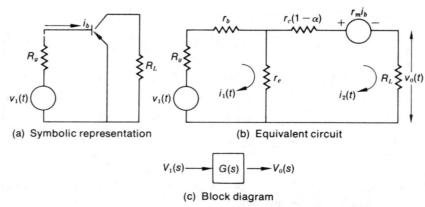

(a) Symbolic representation   (b) Equivalent circuit

$$V_1(s) \longrightarrow \boxed{G(s)} \longrightarrow V_0(s)$$

(c) Block diagram

Fig. 2-4 Single stage amplifier.

Here r_e is the emitter resistance, r_c is collector resistance, r_b is base resistance, and r_m is mutual resistance. Since the output voltage $v_0(t)$ is $R_L i_2(t)$ and $i_b(t) = i_1(t)$ we have

$$(R_g + r_b + r_e)i_1(t) - \left(\frac{r_e}{R_L}\right)v_0(t) = v_1(t)$$

$$(r_e - r_m)i_1(t) + \frac{(r_e + r_c(1-\alpha) + R_L)}{R_L} v_0(t) = 0$$

The transfer function $V_0(s)/V_1(s)$ may now be obtained. This is often referred to as the amplifier gain and is seen to be constant.

Transformers are often needed as coupling or matching devices in electrical networks. When a transformer is present in an electrical network, then any current change in the primary side causes an induced voltage in the secondary side and vice versa. This phenomenon is referred to as "mutual inductance." Consider the circuit shown in Fig. 2-5a, where the dots indicate that mutual inductance is negative.† Using the loop method, we have

$$R_1 i_1(t) + L_1 \frac{di_1(t)}{dt} + \frac{1}{C}\int i_1(t)\,dt - M\frac{di_2(t)}{dt} = v_1(t) \qquad (2\text{-}7a)$$

$$R_2 i_2(t) + (L_2 + L_3)\frac{di_2(t)}{dt} - M\frac{di_1(t)}{dt} = 0 \qquad (2\text{-}7b)$$

---

†If i_1 and i_2 both flow in or out of the dots, then the fluxes aid and the mutual inductance treated as a voltage drop has the same sign as self-inductance, i.e. positive. If i_1 were flowing into the dot whereas i_2 were flowing out of the dot, then mutual inductance is negative.

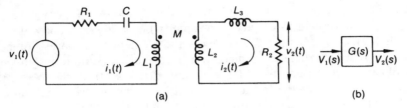

Fig. 2-5 An electric circuit with a transformer.

The transfer function may now be obtained by Laplace transforming and solving the equations simultaneously as we did before. In order to represent the system by first-order equations, we can define

$$x_1(t) = \frac{1}{C} \int i_1(t)\,dt; \qquad x_2(t) = i_1(t); \qquad x_3(t) = i_2(t)$$

and obtain a set of first-order differential equations. We leave this as an exercise for you.

Mechanical Systems

Mechanical systems may be classified into two categories, viz. translational and rotational. Although the method of analysis is the same in both cases, the appearance of gears tends to make rotational systems somewhat more complex.

The equations of mechanical systems are formulated generally by the application of Newton's law, i.e. the sum of the applied forces is equal to the change of momentum. Since the systems we consider here have fixed mass, this law is equivalent to the celebrated $F = ma$ relationship.

The translational mode refers to motion along a straight path. The physical elements employed to describe translation problems are mass, spring, and damper. These are schematically shown in Fig. 2-6. Also shown is the relationship of force, displacement, and the physical property of the element. Mass is the element that stores kinetic energy. When a

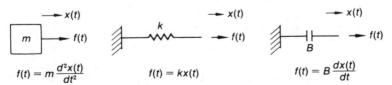

Fig. 2-6 Mechanical elements.

body of weight W is in the gravitational field, then $m = W/g$, where g is the acceleration due to gravity. If a force $f(t)$ is acting on a body of mass m, then $f(t) = md^2x(t)/dt^2$. A spring is the element that stores potential energy. If a force $f(t)$ is applied to a linear spring (sometimes called a Hookean spring), then from Hooke's law, $f(t) = kx(t)$. A damper is the element that creates the frictional force. In general, the frictional force in moving bodies consists of static friction (striction), coulomb friction, and viscous or linear friction. We shall concern ourselves only with linear friction. When a force $f(t)$ is applied to a linear damper, then $f(t) = Bdx(t)/dt$. Consider the mechanical system shown in Fig. 2-7a and its equivalent shown in Fig. 2-7b. If initially the system is assumed to be under static equilibrium and the mass m is then perturbed, a free body diagram showing all the forces is drawn as shown in Fig. 2-7c. If the mass is stretched by $x(t)$, then the spring plus damper force is equal to the inertial force,

$$\Sigma F = -(f_s + f_D) = m\frac{d^2x(t)}{dt^2}$$

Substituting for the spring and damper force we have,

$$m\frac{d^2x(t)}{dt^2} + B\frac{dx(t)}{dt} + kx(t) = 0$$

Now if we also apply a force $f(t)$, an input force, then

$$m\frac{d^2x(t)}{dt} + B\frac{dx(t)}{dt} + kx(t) = f(t) \qquad (2\text{-}8)$$

We now define

$$x_1(t) = x(t); \qquad x_2(t) = \frac{dx(t)}{dt}; \qquad r(t) = f(t)$$

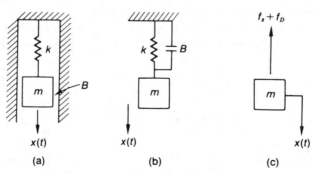

(a)   (b)   (c)

Fig. 2-7   Schematic of a mechanical system.

then substitution into Eq. (2-8) yields two first-order differential equations,

$$\frac{dx_1(t)}{dt} = x_2(t) \qquad (2\text{-}9a)$$

$$\frac{dx_2(t)}{dt} = -\frac{B}{m}x_2(t) - \frac{k}{m}x_1(t) + \frac{1}{m}r(t) \qquad (2\text{-}9b)$$

which completely describes our system. The transfer function representation is obtained by Laplace transforming Eq. (2-8), assuming zero initial conditions, and rearranging

$$\frac{X(s)}{F(s)} = \frac{1}{ms^2 + Bs + k} \qquad (2\text{-}10)$$

Notice that we obtained only one second-order differential equation for the system shown in Fig. 2-7. This is so because the system has only one degree of freedom. The number of degrees of freedom is equal to the number of masses in motion of this type. If there were two masses, the system would have two degrees of freedom and we would require two coordinates to describe the position of the masses.

EXAMPLE 2-1

Obtain the transfer functions for the double mass problem shown in Fig. 2-8.

Assuming $x > y > z > 0$, $dy(t)/dt > 0$, $dz(t)/dt > 0$, we note that the two springs are in tension. Summing the forces on each mass,

$$\Sigma F_1 = m_1 \frac{d^2y(t)}{dt^2} = k_1[x(t) - y(t)] - k_2[y(t) - z(t)] - B_1 \frac{dy(t)}{dt}$$

$$\Sigma F_2 = m_2 \frac{d^2z(t)}{dt^2} = k_2[y(t) - z(t)] - B_2 \frac{dz(t)}{dt}$$

Rearranging these equations we obtain

$$m_1 \frac{d^2y(t)}{dt^2} + B_1 \frac{dy(t)}{dt} + (k_1 + k_2)y(t) - k_2z(t) = k_1x(t)$$

$$m_2 \frac{d^2z(t)}{dt^2} + B_2 \frac{dz(t)}{dt} + k_2z(t) - k_2y(t) = 0$$

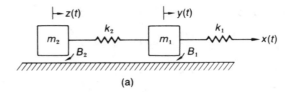

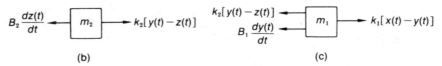

(b)   (c)

Fig. 2-8   Two degrees of freedom mechanical system.

The Laplace transform for zero initial conditions yields,

$$[m_1s^2 + B_1s + (k_1 + k_2)]Y(s) - k_2Z(s) = k_1X(s)$$
$$- k_2Y(s) + [m_2s^2 + B_2s + k_2]Z(s) = 0$$

Since there are two outputs, one for each mass, we expect to find two transfer functions. Solving the above equations simultaneously we obtain the two transfer functions,

$$\frac{Y(s)}{X(s)} = \frac{k_1[m_2s^2 + B_2s + K_2]}{\Delta} \tag{2-11a}$$

$$\frac{Z(s)}{X(s)} = \frac{k_1k_2}{\Delta} \tag{2-11b}$$

$$\Delta = [m_1s^2 + B_1s + (k_1 + k_2)][m_2s^2 + B_2s + k_2] - k_2^2$$

If we had represented the system of Example 2-1 by a set of first-order differential equations we would find that the set contained four equations.

When the motion of the mechanical system is rotational, then Newton's law states that the sum of the torques is equal to the change of angular momentum. Since in most applications inertia is constant, this is identical to the statement that $T(t) = I\alpha(t)$ where $T(t)$ is torque, I is the moment of inertia, and $\alpha(t)$ is the angular acceleration. The physical elements employed to describe rotational problems are inertia, spring, and damper. The interpretation of these quantities is identical to those defined for translational motion.

Consider the single degree of freedom (one shaft position completely defines the position of the rotating element) rotational system shown in

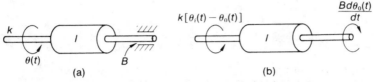

(a)   (b)

Fig. 2-9 Single degree of freedom rotational system.

Fig. 2-9a. The free body diagram is shown in Fig. 2-9b where $\theta_i(t)$ is the positive input displacement and $\theta_i > \theta_0$. The spring torque acts in the positive direction and the damping torque acts in the negative direction. Summing the torques we have

$$\Sigma T = I\frac{d^2\theta_0(t)}{dt^2} = k(\theta_i(t) - \theta_0(t)) - B\frac{d\theta_0(t)}{dt}$$

Rearranging, taking the Laplace transform for zero initial conditions, we obtain the transfer function,

$$\frac{\Theta_0(s)}{\Theta_i(s)} = \frac{k}{Is^2 + Bs + k} \tag{2-12}$$

Rotational mechanical systems are quite common in control systems and are often used in conjunction with gears. The use of gears in control systems helps attain torque magnification and speed reduction. Gear trains are used as matching devices just like transformers are used in electrical systems. A gear train system is shown in Fig. 2-10. The gear with N_1 teeth is the primary gear and that with N_2 teeth is the secondary gear. When two or more gears are in contact we observe that:

(1) The work done by one gear is equal to that of the other gear, i.e. $T_1\theta_1 = T_2\theta_2$.
(2) The linear distance traveled by one gear is equal to that of the other, i.e. $\theta_1 r_1 = \theta_2 r_2$.
(3) The number of teeth on the surface of a gear is proportional to the radius of the gear, i.e. $r_1/r_2 = N_1/N_2$.

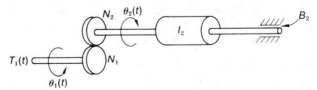

Fig. 2-10 A simple gear train.

Incorporating these three ideas, we have

★
$$\frac{T_1}{T_2} = \frac{\theta_2}{\theta_1} = \frac{N_1}{N_2} \tag{2-13}$$

These equations are correct only under idealized conditions. In practice, coupled gears have backlash and friction. If backlash is large, then the control system can get unstable. For our purposes, we shall consider idealized conditions. Referring now to Fig. 2-10, the rotational equation for the secondary side, when the inertia of shaft and gears is neglected, becomes

$$T_2(t) = I_2 \frac{d^2\theta_2(t)}{dt^2} + B_2 \frac{d\theta_2(t)}{dt}$$

where $T_2(t)$ is the torque developed by the secondary gear. We also know from Eq. (2-13) that

$$\frac{T_1(t)}{T_2(t)} = \frac{d^2\theta_2(t)/dt^2}{d^2\theta_1(t)/dt^2} = \frac{d\theta_2(t)/dt}{d\theta_1(t)/dt} = N_1/N_2$$

Substituting this result in the previous equation we obtain

$$T_1(t) = I_2\left(\frac{N_1}{N_2}\right)^2 \frac{d^2\theta_1(t)}{dt^2} + B_2\left(\frac{N_1}{N_2}\right)^2 \frac{d\theta_1(t)}{dt}$$

If we define

$$I = I_2\left(\frac{N_1}{N_2}\right)^2; \qquad B = B_2\left(\frac{N_1}{N_2}\right)^2$$

then the governing equation becomes

$$T_1(t) = I \frac{d^2\theta_1(t)}{dt^2} + B \frac{d\theta_1(t)}{dt} \tag{2-14}$$

We have essentially reflected the inertia and damping from the secondary side to the primary side. This procedure may be extended to systems containing several gear trains as shown in the next example.

EXAMPLE 2-2

For the multiple gear system shown in Fig. 2-11, obtain (a) the system transfer function and (b) a set of first-order differential equations.

(a) The inertia I_3 and damping B_3 may be reflected to shaft 2 and when added to I_2 and B_2 yields,

$$I_{2e} = I_2 + I_3\left(\frac{N_3}{N_4}\right)^2$$

$$B_{2e} = B_2 + B_3\left(\frac{N_3}{N_4}\right)^2$$

where I_{2e} and B_{2e} are the equivalent inertia and damping about shaft 2. This inertia and damping in turn is reflected to shaft 1 and

$$I_{1e} = I_1 + I_{2e}\left(\frac{N_1}{N_2}\right)^2$$

$$B_{1e} = B_1 + B_{2e}\left(\frac{N_1}{N_2}\right)^2$$

Finally, the rotational equation for this system becomes

$$T_1(t) = I_{1e}\frac{d^2\theta_1(t)}{dt^2} + B_{1e}\frac{d\theta_1(t)}{dt} \qquad (2\text{-}15)$$

Taking the Laplace transform for zero initial conditions, the transfer function becomes

$$\frac{\Theta_1(s)}{T_1(s)} = \frac{1}{s(I_{1e}s + B_{1e})}$$

(b) In order to represent the system by a set of first-order differential equations we define

$$x_1(t) = \theta_1(t); \qquad x_2(t) = \frac{d\theta_1(t)}{dt}; \qquad r(t) = T_1(t)$$

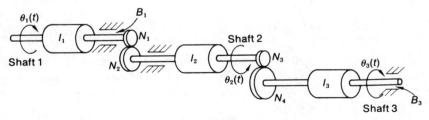

Fig. 2-11   A multiple-gear system.

and substitute in Eq. (2-15) to obtain

$$\frac{dx_1(t)}{dt} = x_2(t)$$

$$\frac{dx_2(t)}{dt} = -\frac{B_{1e}}{I_{1e}} x_2(t) + r(t)$$

which are the required equations governing the behavior of the rotational system.

Thermal Systems

Modeling of thermal systems by linear differential equations is generally not as common as the other systems since thermal systems tend to be generally nonlinear. However, in order to obtain a first approximation we shall linearize the systems about an appropriate operating point. Often this results in the assumption that the physical system under consideration be characterized by one uniform temperature.

The fundamental concept used for deriving the thermal system equation is that the difference of heat coming into and leaving a body is equal to the increase of the thermal energy of the system. The physical properties used are mass, specific heat, thermal capacitance, conductance, and resistance. Temperature is the driving potential and heat is the quantity which flows. Generally, thermal resistance is defined as

$$R = \frac{\Delta T}{q}$$

where ΔT is the temperature difference and q the heat flow. Depending upon the system, R may include the contributions of thermal conduction, convection, and radiation. The thermal capacitance C is the product of mass and specific heat and

$$q(t) = mc\frac{dT(t)}{dt} = C\frac{dT(t)}{dt}$$

Consider a mass m dropped into an oil bath at temperature T_h. We shall assume that the temperature is uniform inside the mass at any given time and also that the oil bath temperature is constant. The heat entering the mass from the oil at any time is

$$q_{in}(t) = \frac{(T_h(t) - T_m(t))}{R} \tag{2-16}$$

where T_m is the temperature of the mass. Here $R = 1/hA$ where A is the surface area of mass in contact with the oil and h is the heat transfer coefficient due to convection. This heat entering the mass goes to increase the heat content (or internal energy) of the system, i.e.

$$q(t) = mc\frac{dT_m(t)}{dt} \tag{2-17}$$

Equating Eq. (2-16) to Eq. (2-17) we have

$$mc\frac{dT_m(t)}{dt} = \frac{(T_h(t) - T_m(t))}{R}$$

Defining $T(t) = T_m(t) - T_h(t)$ we obtain

$$\frac{dT(t)}{dt} = -\frac{1}{Rmc}T(t) \tag{2-18}$$

which is a first-order differential equation. For obtaining the transfer function we assume that the initial temperature of the mass is T_{0m}. Letting $T_0(t) = T_{0m} - T_h(t)$, Laplace transforming yields the transfer function

$$\frac{T(s)}{T_0(s)} = \frac{1}{s - \tau} \tag{2-19}$$

where

$$\tau = 1/Rmc$$

EXAMPLE 2-3

A satellite of mass m kg and surface area A m^2 is subjected to solar heating. Assuming that the satellite exhibits some average temperature T_m, obtain the equation governing the temperature of the satellite. Linearize the result about an equilibrium temperature T_0 of the satellite and obtain the system transfer function.

The thermal input from the sun is

$$q_s = A\alpha E(t)$$

where A is the outer area of the satellite, α is the coefficient of absorptivity, and $E(t)$ is the incident energy of the sun at time t. The satellite is simultaneously loosing heat† at the rate of

$$q_L = A\epsilon\sigma T_m{}^4$$

†This is the Stefan–Boltzmann law which states that a body at temperature T (in °Kelvin) radiates energy at the rate of $\epsilon\sigma T^4$. For ideal radiation $\epsilon = 1$. σ is 8.1274×10^{-10} Kcal/min m^2 °K^4. If T is in °R, then T is given by 0.1714×10^{-8} BTU/hr ft^2 °R^4.

where ϵ is the emissivity of the body, and σ is the Stefan–Boltzmann constant. Since the difference between the incoming and outgoing energy increases the energy of the system, we have

$$q_s - q_L = q_{\text{increase}} = mc \frac{dT_m(t)}{dt}$$

Substituting for q_s and q_L,

$$mc \frac{dT_m(t)}{dt} = A\alpha E(t) - A\epsilon\sigma T_m{}^4 \qquad (2\text{-}20)$$

which is a nonlinear differential equation. In order to linearize, we assume

$$T_m = T_0 + T(t); \qquad T_0 \text{ is constant, } T(t) \text{ is small}$$

$$E(t) = E_0 + e(t); \qquad E_0 \text{ is constant, } e(t) \text{ is small}$$

Substituting these into Eq. (2-20) and expanding $T_m{}^4$ we obtain

$$mc \frac{dT(t)}{dt} = A\alpha E_0 - A\epsilon\sigma T_0{}^4 + A\alpha e(t) + 4A\epsilon\sigma T_0{}^3 T(t)$$

Under equilibrium conditions, $A\alpha E_0 = A\epsilon\sigma T_0{}^4$ so that

$$mc \frac{dT(t)}{dt} = A\alpha e(t) + 4A\epsilon\sigma T_0{}^3 T(t)$$

We set

$$C_1 = \frac{A\alpha}{mc}; \qquad C_2 = \frac{4A\epsilon\sigma T_0{}^3}{mc}$$

then the governing equation becomes

$$\frac{dT(t)}{dt} - C_2 T(t) = C_1 e(t)$$

which is a first-order linear differential equation. The transfer function is

$$\frac{T(s)}{E(s)} = \frac{C_1}{s - C_2}$$

Hydraulic Systems

Hydraulic systems have wide application in the fluid power and chemical processing industries. In fluid power applications there are two types of hydraulic servomechanisms: the displacement controlled systems and the valve controlled systems. Although the former has better efficiency, the latter has high gain and quick response. Since it is the more popular of the two we consider the valve controlled systems in this section.

The fundamental relation in hydraulic systems is

$$q = C_d A v \qquad (2\text{-}21)$$

where q is volume flow rate, A is cross sectional area, v is velocity, and C_d is coefficient of discharge. In valve applications the flow of fluid is achieved by varying the area of the control orifice as shown in Fig. 2-12.

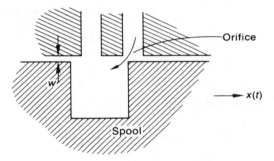

Fig. 2-12   Configuration of a valve port.

The velocity through the orifice is given by

$$v = \sqrt{2\Delta P/\rho} \qquad (2\text{-}22)$$

where ΔP is the pressure drop across the orifice and ρ is density of the working fluid. If the spool moves a distance x and the orifice is characterized as having width w (port width), then $A = wx$ and substitution in Eq. (2-21) gives the flow rate as

$$q(t) = C_d w \sqrt{\frac{2\Delta\rho}{\rho}}\, x(t) \qquad (2\text{-}23)$$

Consider the valve shown in Fig. 2-13. If the spool moves by $x(t)$, then the flow into the main cylinder is given by Eq. (2-23). This flow causes the piston to move with a velocity $dy(t)/dt$. Using Eqs. (2-21) and (2-22) we get

$$q(t) = C_d w \sqrt{\frac{2\Delta P}{\rho}}\, x(t) = A\,\frac{dy(t)}{dt}$$

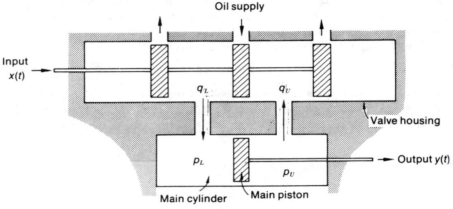

Fig. 2-13   Hydraulic valve actuator.

where the coefficient of discharge for the main cylinder is unity. Assuming constant ΔP,

$$\frac{dy(t)}{dt} = K_v x(t)$$

where

$$K_v = \frac{C_d w}{A} \sqrt{\frac{2\Delta P}{\rho}}$$

The transfer function becomes

$$\frac{Y(s)}{X(s)} = \frac{K_v}{s} \tag{2-24}$$

In this case, the amount of liquid that leaks has been neglected. The analysis of hydraulic systems is not complete unless this component is considered. The effects of fluid compressibility is another item that must be reckoned with.

EXAMPLE 2-4

For the hydraulic actuator shown in Fig. 2-13, derive the governing equation if compressibility effects are included. Obtain the system transfer function and show that it reduces to $1/As$ if compressibility and leakage are zero. The storage due to compressibility effects is $(v/\beta)(dP/dt)$ where β is the bulk modulus. Assume that the output shaft is connected to a mass of m kg.

The flow into or out of the actuator is a linear combination of the following:

(1) Flow resulting from the motion across the actuator. This is $A \, dy(t)/dt$ where $y(t)$ is the actuator rod displacement.
(2) Storage due to compressibility effects. This is given by $(v \, dP/dt)/\beta$ where β is bulk modulus of hydraulic fluid.
(3) Finally, flow resulting from leakage across the actuator piston. This is $C_L(P_L - P_U)$ where C_L is the leakage coefficient and P_L, P_U represents pressures at the lower and upper chambers.

The flow out of the upper chamber is q_U and lower is q_L where

$$q_U(t) = A \frac{dy(t)}{dt} - \frac{v}{\beta} \frac{dP_U}{dt} + C_L(P_L - P_U)$$

$$q_L(t) = A \frac{dy(t)}{dt} + \frac{v}{\beta} \frac{dP_L}{dt} + C_L(P_L - P_U)$$

Now if we consider the average flow q to be $(q_U + q_L)/2$, then

$$q = A \frac{dy(t)}{dt} + \frac{v}{2\beta} \left(\frac{dP_L}{dt} - \frac{dP_U}{dt} \right) + C_L(P_L - P_U)$$

In addition to this equation, we have a force equation, i.e. the force generated by the actuator rod equals the inertia force,

$$A(P_L - P_U) = m \frac{d^2y(t)}{dt^2}$$

Substituting this into the previous equation yields

$$q = A \frac{dy(t)}{dt} + \frac{vm}{2\beta A} \frac{d^3y(t)}{dt^3} + \left(\frac{C_L m}{A} \right) \frac{d^2y(t)}{dt^2} \qquad (2\text{-}25)$$

Taking the Laplace transform of Eq. (2-25) and assuming zero initial conditions we obtain the necessary transfer function

$$\frac{Y(s)}{Q(s)} = \frac{1}{\dfrac{vm}{2\beta A} s^3 + \left(\dfrac{C_L m}{A} \right) s^2 + As} \qquad (2\text{-}26)$$

For a simplified analysis it is often assumed that the fluid is incompressible ($\beta = \infty$) and leakage is zero, so that the transfer function reduces to

$$\frac{Y(s)}{Q(s)} = \frac{1}{As}$$

If the flow rate through the valve could be controlled, then any desired output can be obtained.

2-3   SYSTEM COMPONENTS

Most control systems and components consist of a combination of the systems we have been discussing in the previous section. For example, an electrical amplifier may be used to amplify an electrical signal that drives a motor which may be coupled to an inertia and a gear train. Clearly, we need to apply the method developed for analyzing electrical systems as well as Newton's law for mechanical systems in order to obtain the transfer function of the complete system.

In this section we consider systems that combine some of the concepts developed previously. We shall derive the differential equations and the transfer functions. Since you have been introduced to the representation of systems by a set of first-order differential equations, we shall not attempt to do so in each case here. Instead, we shall agree that such a representation can be obtained when necessary. Additionally, we need to note that the components considered here are very fundamental. Indeed, modern systems contain many other components that are far more complex. Here we are content with more common as well as simpler examples of control system components.

Potentiometers

Potentiometers are devices that produce a signal directly proportional to a physical quantity. This signal may be mechanical, electrical, or whatever form is convenient. By far the most important type of potentiometer is the resistance potentiometer shown in Fig. 2-14. The transfer function is given by

$$\frac{E(s)}{\Theta(s)} = \frac{E}{\theta_{max}} = \text{constant} \tag{2-27}$$

The actual transfer function deviates from this constant when the potentiometer is loaded. This departure from linearity is very small however.

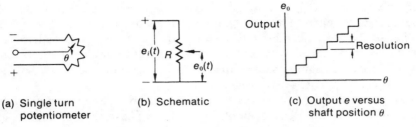

(a) Single turn
    potentiometer

(b) Schematic

(c) Output e versus
    shaft position θ

Fig. 2-14   A Potentiometer.

Since most potentiometers are wire wound, the sliding brush contact touches the wires only discretely as the potentiometer shaft is rotated. This causes the output voltage, instead of being a continuous function of shaft position, to be discontinuous as shown in Fig. 2-14c.

The minimum change in output voltage obtained by rotating the shaft, divided by total applied voltage is called the resolution of a potentiometer.

$$\text{Resolution} = \Delta e/E$$

If the potentiometer has n turns, then $\Delta e = E/n$ and the resolution is $1/n$. This resolution determines the accuracy of a control system. More modern potentiometers have helical resistance elements and also have many turns. This tends to smooth out the staircase effect of Fig. 2-14c.

Linear Variable Differential Transformer (LVDT)

This device is used as a displacement transducer and is shown in Fig. 2-15a. It consists of a primary winding, energized with a fixed a-c voltage,

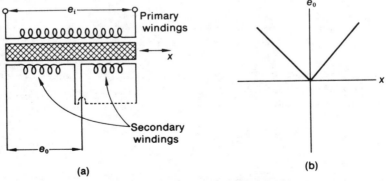

(a)

(b)

Fig. 2-15   Linear variable differential transformer.

and two secondary windings. A movable magnetic core provides the necessary coupling. The secondary windings are wired to oppose each other. If the core is centered, there is no voltage and if it is moved, there is an increased induced voltage in one and a decrease in the other. The net increase has the same phase as the secondary with the increased voltage. This is graphically shown in Fig. 2-15b.

The output of the LVDT therefore not only provides an output voltage proportional to the displacement, but yields a phase relationship dependent upon the direction of displacement. The transfer function is

★
$$\frac{E_0(s)}{X(s)} = \text{constant} \tag{2-28}$$

Accelerometer

As the name implies, this device measures the acceleration of a system. Basically this instrument measures the motion of a restrained mass when it is subjected to an acceleration. The instrument consists of a mass, spring, and damper as shown in Fig. 2-16.

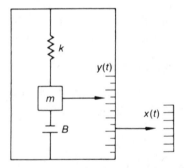

Fig. 2-16   Schematic of an accelerometer.

The mass position is given by $y(t)$ whereas $x(t)$ is the displacement of the frame with respect to the body whose acceleration is to be measured. The transfer function may be obtained using Newton's law and is

★
$$\frac{Y(s)}{s^2 X(s)} = \frac{1}{s^2 + \dfrac{B}{m}s + \dfrac{k}{m}} \tag{2-29}$$

The output of the accelerometer is $y(t)$ and is generally measured with a potentiometer. If the values of m, k, and B are selected properly, a fairly linear device, over given operating conditions, is obtained.

Synchros

These devices are used as torque transmitters or position indicators. They are generally used in pairs. When they are used to transmit torques, one synchro is used to generate an electrical signal corresponding to a shaft position. This signal is introduced into the receiver which assumes the same shaft position as the transmitter. Because of system losses the power at the receiver is less than that transmitted, therefore the angle at the receiver does depend upon the electrical efficiency. Synchros used in this mode are useful for presenting display information like dial readings.

When synchros are used as position indicators they become error detecting devices. The output is equal to the sine of the difference between the input and output voltage. When the error is small it is approximately equal to the difference of the shaft position. This is shown in Fig. 2-17.

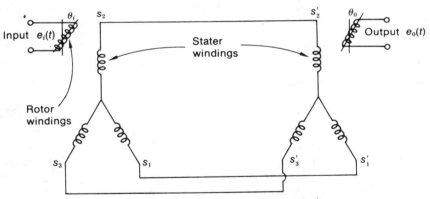

Fig. 2-17   Synchro pair as error detecting device.

The error equation is given by

$$e_0(t) = K(\theta_i(t) - \theta_0(t)) \qquad (2\text{-}30)$$

Tachometers

Tachometers are used as velocity pickoff devices since they generate an output voltage proportional to the shaft angular velocity. A very important use of a tachometer is for damping position servomechanisms in the feedback loop as will be shown in a later chapter. Of the many types of velocity pickoff devices, the a-c and d-c tachometers are the most widely used.

An a-c tachometer is shown schematically in Fig. 2-18. A known sinusoidal voltage $e_i(t)$ is applied, to the primary winding, setting up flux. Since the secondary winding is at 90°, the output voltage $e_0(t)$ is zero, or very

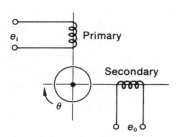

Fig. 2-18 Schematic of an a-c tachometer.

close to it, if the rotor is not moving. When the rotor moves the output voltage is proportional to $d\theta(t)/dt$

$$e_0 = K \frac{d\theta(t)}{dt}$$

and the transfer function becomes

$$\frac{E_0(s)}{\Theta(s)} = Ks \qquad (2\text{-}31)$$

where K is the sensitivity of the tachometer. When the control system is a d-c system, then it is necessary to use a d-c tachometer. Since these devices have brushes, they are generally less accurate and have drift. They are very similar to d-c motors. The transfer function of a d-c tachometer is the same as that shown in Eq. (2-31).

a-c Control Motors

Control motors are employed for obtaining the necessary torque in control systems. Both a-c and d-c motors are used. The a-c motors generally have two phases and are similar to a-c tachometers. The two phases are "excitation," or fixed, and "control," or variable. A reference voltage is applied to the fixed part and an error voltage to the variable phase. If the control or variable phase is shorted, there is no torque. This torque increases directly as a function of the error voltage. These motors produce a damping torque proportional to velocity and also one proportional to control voltage.

Consider an a-c motor having the following characteristics

$$T = b - m\omega$$

where T is torque, ω is angular velocity, while m and b are constants. The constant b depends upon control voltage v,

$$b = Kv$$

therefore

$$T = Kv - m\omega$$

Now if $T = 0$, then

$$m = \frac{Kv}{\omega}$$

and if we further assume that the torque speed curves are linearized as shown in Fig. 2-19, then

$$m = \frac{\text{stall torque (rated voltage)}}{\text{no-load speed (rated voltage)}}$$

If the motor has moment of inertia I, and viscous damping B, then the torque becomes

$$T(t) = I\frac{d^2\theta(t)}{dt^2} + B\frac{d\theta(t)}{dt}$$

Equating this torque to the previous expression yields

$$kv(t) - m\frac{d\theta(t)}{dt} = I\frac{d^2\theta(t)}{dt^2} + B\frac{d\theta(t)}{dt} \tag{2-32}$$

Rearranging and taking the Laplace transform for zero initial conditions

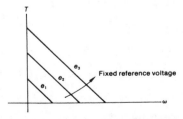

Fig. 2-19   Linearized speed torque curves for 2-phase a-c motor.

we obtain the transfer function

$$\frac{\Theta(s)}{V(s)} = \frac{K}{s(Is + m + B)}$$

or

★
$$\frac{\Theta(s)}{V(s)} = \frac{K_m}{s(\tau s + 1)} \qquad (2\text{-}33)$$

where

$$K_m = \frac{K}{m + B}; \qquad \tau = \frac{I}{m + B}$$

This then is the transfer function of a two-phase induction motor.

d-c Control Motors

d-c motors have speed torque characteristics that depend upon excitation, i.e. series or shunt. They have generally more complicated transfer functions owing to the inclusion of armature inductance and winding time lags. Generally, they produce large power output for small size.

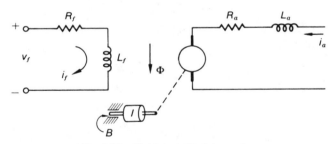

Fig. 2-20   Field controlled d-c motor.

Consider the field controlled d-c motor shown schematically in Fig. 2-20. The armature current i_a is constant and the air gap flux Φ is given by

$$\Phi(t) = K_f i_f(t)$$

where K_f is constant. The developed torque T is

$$T(t) = K_1 i_a \Phi(t) = (K_1 K_f i_a) i_f(t) = K_2 i_f(t)$$

The field voltage is

$$v_f(t) = R_f i_f(t) + L_f \frac{di_f(t)}{dt}$$

and the mechanical torque is

$$T(t) = I\frac{d^2\theta(t)}{dt^2} + B\frac{d\theta(t)}{dt}$$

Assuming zero initial conditions and Laplace transforming,

$$T(s) = K_2 I_f(s)$$
$$V_f(s) = (L_f s + R_f) I_f(s)$$
$$T(s) = (Is^2 + Bs)\Theta(s)$$

Substitution yields

★

$$\frac{\Theta(s)}{V_f(s)} = \frac{K_2}{s(\tau_m s + 1)(\tau_f s + 1)} \tag{2-34}$$

where

$$\tau_m = \frac{I}{B} = \text{time constant of motor}$$

$$\tau_f = \frac{L_f}{R_f} = \text{time constant of field}$$

$$K = \frac{K_2}{BR_f}$$

For a d-c motor that is armature controlled the schematic diagram is shown in Fig. 2-21. The torque becomes

$$T(t) = K_1 \Phi i_a(t) = K_2 i_a(t)$$

The back electromotive force v_b is proportional to motor speed,

$$v_b(t) = K_3 \frac{d\theta(t)}{dt}$$

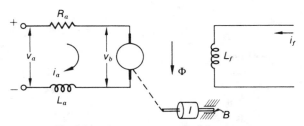

Fig. 2-21 Armature controlled d-c motor.

The armature circuit is then governed by

$$v_a(t) - v_b(t) = R_a i_a(t) + L_a \frac{di_a(t)}{dt}$$

Again assuming zero initial conditions and Laplace transforming,

$$T(s) = K_2 I_a(s)$$
$$V_b(s) = K_3 s \Theta(s)$$
$$V_a(s) = R_a I_a(s) + L_a s I_a(s) + V_b(s)$$
$$T(s) = s(Is + B)\Theta(s)$$

Combining these equations yields the transfer function

★
$$\frac{\Theta(s)}{V_a(s)} = \frac{K}{s(\tau_m s + 1)(\tau_a s + 1) + bs} \tag{2-35}$$

where

$$K = K_2 / BR_a \qquad \tau_a = L_a / R_a$$
$$b = K_2 K_3 / BR_a \qquad \tau_m = I / B$$

In general $\tau_m > \tau_a$. Note that we have introduced damping in the system equation.

Hydraulic Pump

The source of all fluid power is the hydraulic pump. The pump that we consider here has positive but variable displacement. A schematic of a hydraulic pump is shown in Fig. 2-22. Such pumps are motor driven. The amount of fluid pumped is a function of the pump stroke $x(t)$ for a fixed motor speed. The direction of stroke dictates the flow direction. The flow rate is given by

★
$$q(t) = Kx(t) \tag{2-36}$$

where K is a characteristic of the pump.

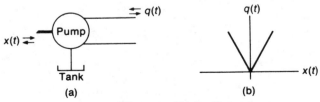

Fig. 2-22   Schematic of hydraulic pump.

Hydraulic Actuator

A hydraulic actuator and valve arrangement is shown in Fig. 2-13. The transfer function for the idealized system is given by Eq. (2-24).

Error Detecting Devices (Subtractors)

Besides using a pair of synchros for obtaining positional error, there are several other devices commonly used as error sensing devices. Potentiometers and linear variable differential transformers when used in pairs are displacement error detecting devices. The hydraulic valve as well as a bevel and gear differential are commonly used error sensors in hydraulic and gear train systems. Some of these devices are shown in Fig. 2-23.

For a-c control systems transformers may be used as error sensors. Another attractive method to difference or add signals is to use resistances

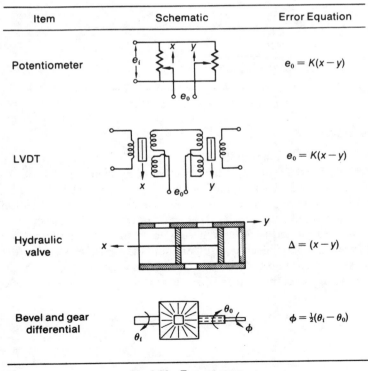

Item	Schematic	Error Equation
Potentiometer		$e_0 = K(x - y)$
LVDT		$e_0 = K(x - y)$
Hydraulic valve		$\Delta = (x - y)$
Bevel and gear differential		$\phi = \tfrac{1}{2}(\theta_i - \theta_0)$

Fig. 2-23 Error sensors.

in conjunction with a high gain amplifier. Consider the network of Fig. 2-24. Writing the nodal equations at node N,

$$\frac{e_i(t) - v(t)}{R_1} + \frac{e_f(t) - v(t)}{R_2} + \frac{e_0(t) - v(t)}{R_f} = 0$$

Since the amplifier has high gain, $v(t)$ is small so the above equation may be written as

★ $$e_0(t) = -\frac{R_f}{R_1} e_i(t) - \frac{R_f}{R_2} e_f(t) \qquad (2\text{-}37)$$

Since $e_i(t)$ may be biased to be positive or negative, Eq. (2-37) may be used for summing or differencing. This technique is quite common in analog computation.

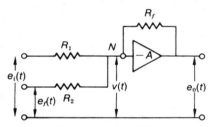

Fig. 2-24   Resistance differencing.

Gyroscopes

The gyroscopes (commonly called a gyro) is a basic element in many instruments for guidance and control of moving vehicles. A gyro is shown in Fig. 2-25. The inner gimbal supports the spinning wheel and is restrained by a spring or damper depending upon the application. The z-axis is the input axis and x-axis is the output axis. Assume the outer gimbal is rigidly fixed to a moving vehicle. If the vehicle turns at a rate of $d\psi/dt$, then the rate of change of angular momentum is $I\omega(d\psi/dt)$. This gives rise to a moment about the output axis. If the outer gimbal has a spring of stiffness k, then the moment is $k\theta$ and

$$k\theta(t) = I\omega \frac{d\psi(t)}{dt}$$

or

★ $$\frac{\Theta(s)}{\Psi(s)} = \frac{I\omega s}{k} \qquad (2\text{-}38)$$

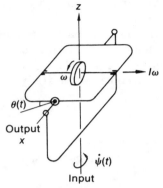

Fig. 2-25   Single degree of freedom gyro.

When the output is proportional to the input rate $d\psi(t)/dt$, the gyro is called a rate gyro.

If the torsional spring is replaced by a torsional damper having a damping coefficient B, then the moment about the output axis is $B\,d\theta(t)/dt$ and

$$B\frac{d\theta(t)}{dt} = I\omega\frac{d\psi(t)}{dt}$$

or

$$\frac{\Theta(s)}{\Psi\cdot(s)} = \frac{I\omega}{B} \qquad (2\text{-}39)$$

Here the output angle is proportional to the integral of the input angular rate, or the input angle. When this happens the gyro is called an integrating gyro. Whether the gyro is an integrating or rate gyro, we need to obtain the angle θ. This angle may be obtained by a potentiometer. A special potentiometer used for this is called an E-pickoff potentiometer.

SUMMARY

We have shown how a linearized mathematical model of a physical system may be developed by using certain fundamental laws describing the behavior of the physical system. This mathematical model was seen to reduce to the form of an integro-differential equation.

From the integro-differential equation, the system transfer function was obtained. This is the ratio of the output to the input when the output and input are expressed as Laplace transforms and the initial conditions are zero. As an alternate representation, the system was described by a set of first-order differential equations.

It is important to note however that many complex components and real problems can often not be characterized by linear models and represented by linear equations. Nevertheless, linear models serve as very powerful tools for first approximations in studying system behaviors over useful ranges.

PROBLEMS

2-1. Obtain the transfer functions for the circuits shown in Fig. P2-1.

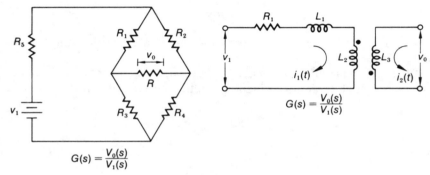

Fig. P2-1

2-2. Obtain the transfer function for the single stage amplifier shown in Fig. 2-4.

2-3. Obtain $G(s)$ for the system shown in Fig. 2-5.

2-4. Obtain a set of first-order differential equations for each of the systems shown in Fig. P2-4.

2-5. Represent the system of Fig. 2-8 by a set of first-order differential equations.

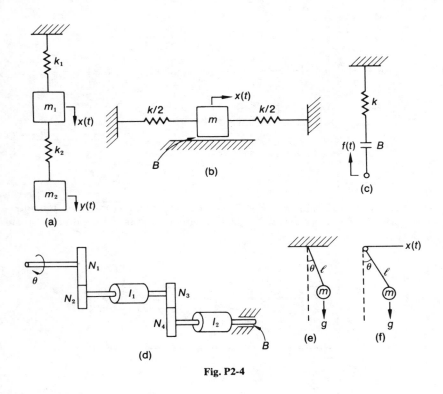

Fig. P2-4

2-6. Obtain the transfer function $\Theta(s)/X(s)$ for the system shown in Fig. P2-6.

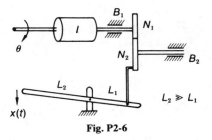

Fig. P2-6

2-7. For the two fluid systems of Fig. P2-7, obtain $Q_0(s)/Q_1(s)$. Do these systems differ? How? Assume these are two cylindrical tanks of radius R in each case.

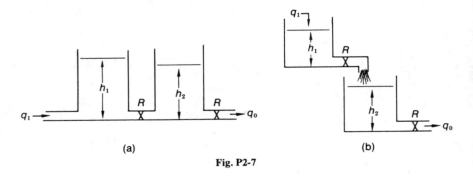

(a)   (b)

Fig. P2-7

2-8. A shaker table is shown in Fig. P2-8. The potentiometer measures the difference between the two masses. Neglecting gravity and initial conditions obtain $E_0(s)/Y(s)$.

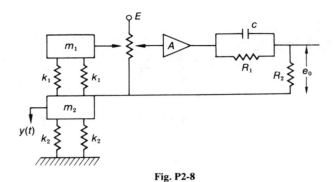

Fig. P2-8

2-9. A simple integrating servomechanism is shown in Fig. P2-9. Derive the transfer function $V_0(s)/V_1(s)$ and discuss all your assumptions.

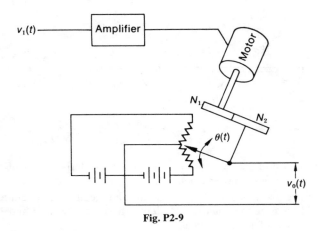

Fig. P2-9

2-10. Obtain $X(s)/E(s)$ for the system of Fig. P2-10.

2-11. Represent the system of Fig. P2-10 by a set of first-order differential equations.

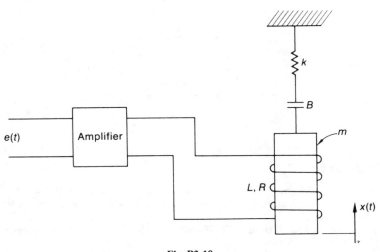

Fig. P2-10

2-12. Obtain $\Theta_2(s)/E(s)$ for the system of Fig. P2-12.

2-13. Obtain a set of first-order differential equations to represent the system of Fig. P2-12.

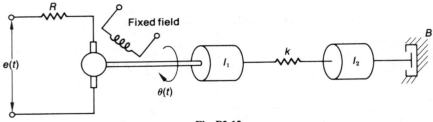

Fig. P2-12

2-14. For the hydraulic actuator shown in Fig. 2-13, derive a set of first-order differential equations governing its behavior.

2-15. Obtain the equations of motion of the cart and the inverted pendulum shown in Fig. P2-15. Linearize the equations under the assumption that x and θ are small and $m_1 \gg m_2$. Neglect frictional forces.

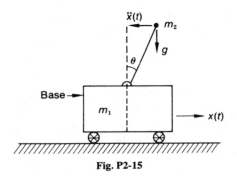

Fig. P2-15

REFERENCES

1. Cannon, R. H., *Dynamics of Physical Systems*, New York, McGraw-Hill, 1967.
2. Sutherland, R. L., *Engineering Systems Analysis*, Reading, Mass., Addison-Wesley, 1958.
3. D'Azzo, J. J., and C. H. Houpis, *Feedback Control System Analysis and Synthesis*, 2nd Edition, New York, McGraw-Hill, 1966.
4. Reswick, J. B., and C. K. Taft, *Introduction to Dynamic Systems*, Englewood Cliffs, N.J., Prentice-Hall, 1967.
5. Takahashi, T., *Mathematics of Automatic Control*, New York, Holt, Rinehart and Winston, 1966.
6. Kuo, B. C., *Automatic Control Systems*, 2nd Edition, Englewood Cliffs, N.J., Prentice-Hall, 1968.

7. Morse, A. C., *Electrohydraulic Servomechanism*, New York, McGraw-Hill, 1963.
8. Davis, S. A., and B. K. Ledgerwood, *Electromechanical Components for Servomechanism*, New York, McGraw-Hill, 1961.
9. Harrison, H. L., and J. G. Bolinger, *Introduction to Automatic Control*, 2nd Edition, Scranton, International Textbook, 1969.
10. Gehmlich, D. K., and S. B. Hammond, *Electromechanical Systems*, New York, McGraw-Hill, 1967.
11. Toro, V. Del, and S. R. Parker, *Principles of Control System Engineering*, New York, McGraw-Hill, 1959.
12. Churchill, R. V., *Operational Mathematics*, 2nd Edition, New York, McGraw-Hill, 1958.
13. LePage, W. R., *Complex Variables and the Laplace Transform for Engineers*, New York, McGraw-Hill, 1961.
14. Dorf, R. C., *Modern Control Systems*, Reading, Mass., Addison-Wesley, 1967.
15. Ruzicka, J. E., "Active vibration and shock isolation," *SAE Transactions*, paper 6807 47, 1968.

3

Control System Representation

3-1 INTRODUCTION

In the previous chapter we saw how a system may be represented by linear ordinary differential equations with constant coefficients. By defining a single input and single output in Laplace transform notation, we managed to obtain the transfer function of the system under consideration. We shall now begin with the transfer function of individual components and show how they can be combined in a systematic way to obtain the transfer function of the entire control system. The analysis of this overall transfer function constitutes the classical method.

As an alternate way of system representation in the last chapter we also obtained a set of first-order differential equations. Later in this chapter we shall use such a set to show how a control system can be compactly represented in matrix notation. Such a representation is also called state space representation and the variables used are known as state variables. We will show that such a representation is directly related to the governing first-order differential equations as well as the system transfer function. The analysis of control systems using the state space representation constitutes what is referred to as the modern method.

3-2 THE TRANSFER FUNCTION

The transfer function of a block diagram is defined as the output divided by its input when represented in the Laplace domain with zero initial conditions. The transfer function $G(s)$ of the block diagram shown in Fig. 3-1 is

★
$$\frac{X(s)}{Y(s)} = G(s) \tag{3-1}$$

Here the path of the signals $X(s)$ and $Y(s)$ is a forward path.

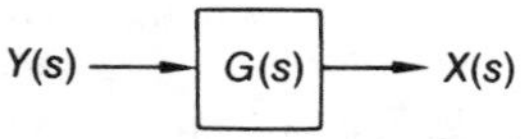

$$Y(s) \longrightarrow \boxed{G(s)} \longrightarrow X(s)$$

Fig. 3-1   Transfer function of a block diagram.

We have seen how the transfer function of an individual component can be obtained in the previous chapter. Owing to the occurrence of many transfer functions in series (or cascade) and parallel connections it is necessary that we have rules to combine them systematically. Consider the block diagram of cascaded elements shown in Fig. 3-2a. From the definition of a transfer function we have

$$\frac{X_2(s)}{X_1(s)} = G_1(s)$$

$$\frac{X_3(s)}{X_2(s)} = G_2(s)$$

$$\frac{Y(s)}{X_3(s)} = G_3(s)$$

or

$$X_2(s) = G_1(s)X_1(s)$$
$$X_3(s) = G_2(s)X_2(s)$$
$$Y(s) = G_3(s)X_3(s)$$

and substitution yields

$$Y(s) = G_3(s)X_3(s) = G_3(s)\left[G_2(s)X_2(s)\right] = G_3(s)G_2(s)G_1(s)X_1(s)$$

which can be written as

$$\frac{Y(s)}{X_1(s)} = G_3(s)G_2(s)G_1(s) = G(s) \tag{3-2}$$

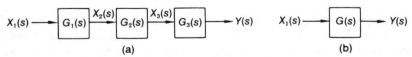

Fig. 3-2   Cascaded elements.

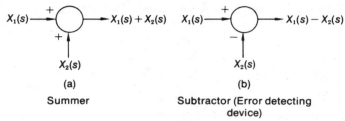

(a)

Summer

(b)

Subtractor (Error detecting device)

Fig. 3-3   Addition or subtraction of signals.

The overall transfer function then is simply the product of individual transfer functions as shown in Fig. 3-2b.

For applications where it is required to generate a signal which is the sum of two signals we define a summer or summing junction as shown in Fig. 3-3a. If the difference is required, then we define a subtractor as shown in Fig. 3-3b. Subtractors are often called error detecting devices since the output signal is the difference between two signals of which one is usually a reference signal. Examples of several components used for summing and subtracting signals were given in the previous chapter.

The combination of block diagrams in parallel is shown in Fig. 3-4a. From the definition of the transfer function we have

$$Y_1(s) = G_1(s)X(s)$$
$$Y_2(s) = G_2(s)X(s)$$
$$Y_3(s) = G_3(s)X(s)$$

and the summer adds these signals,

$$Y(s) = Y_1(s) + Y_2(s) + Y_3(s)$$

or

$$Y(s) = [G_1(s) + G_2(s) + G_3(s)]X(s)$$

The overall transfer function shown in Fig. 3-4b is

$$\frac{Y(s)}{X(s)} = G(s) \tag{3-3}$$

where

$$G(s) = G_1(s) + G_2(s) + G_3(s)$$

In summary, we observe that for cascaded elements the overall transfer function is equal to the product of the transfer function of each element, whereas the overall transfer function for parallel elements is equal to the sum of the individual transfer function.

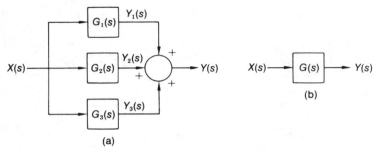

Fig. 3-4   Parallel combination of elements.

When a control system is represented in block diagram form we have not only forward paths but feedback paths as well. By giving due consideration to the direction of the signals we can derive a single transfer function to represent the entire system. This overall transfer function will be seen to be the ratio of the input and the output of the entire system.

3-3 CLOSED LOOP SYSTEMS

Although control systems having a single input and output can be represented by a single block diagram and one transfer function, it is advantageous to show the individual elements since their transfer functions may be generally determined independently.

A single loop control system is shown in Fig. 3-5. The individual signals and blocks are identified as follows:

$$R(s) = \text{Reference input}$$
$$B(s) = \text{Feedback signal}$$
$$E(s) = \text{Error or actuating signal}$$
$$C(s) = \text{Output signal}$$
$$G_c(s) = \text{Transfer function of controller}$$
$$A(s) = \text{Transfer function of amplifier}$$
$$G_p(s) = \text{Transfer function of system to be controlled}$$
$$\text{(commonly referred to as the plant)}$$
$$H(s) = \text{Transfer function of feedback element}$$
$$C(s)/E(s) = G(s) = G_c(s)A(s)G_p(s) = \text{Forward loop transfer}$$
$$\text{function}$$
$$G_c(s)G_p(s)A(s)H(s) = \text{Open loop transfer function}$$
$$C(s)/R(s) = \text{Closed loop transfer function}$$

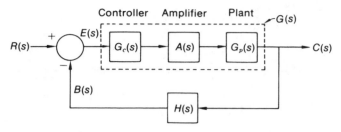

Fig. 3-5 Block diagram of simple closed loop system.

If the system does not have any feedback, $H(s) = 0$, and we have an open loop system. This system consists of three cascaded transfer functions. If however we do have feedback, then the closed loop transfer function may be obtained by first defining the error equation

★
$$E(s) = R(s) - B(s) \tag{3-4}$$

In addition, the following transfer functions may be written,

$$C(s) = G(s)E(s)$$
$$B(s) = H(s)C(s)$$
$$G(s) = G_c(s)A(s)G_p(s)$$

Substituting for $E(s)$ and $B(s)$,

$$\frac{C(s)}{G(s)} = R(s) - H(s)C(s)$$

$$C(s)\left[\frac{1}{G(s)} + H(s)\right] = R(s)$$

and the overall transfer function becomes

★
$$\frac{C(s)}{R(s)} = \frac{G(s)}{1 + G(s)H(s)} \tag{3-5}$$

The error-input transfer function may be derived using Eq. (3-5),

★
$$\frac{E(s)}{R(s)} = \frac{1}{1 + G(s)H(s)} \tag{3-6}$$

When a control system consists of a feedback path where $H(s) = 1$, then it is referred to as a *unity feedback control system*. In general, $H(s)$ need not be unity and also the control system may consist of many feedback loops. The technique to obtain the overall transfer function for multiloop systems is identical to the previous method except that additional error equations are generally necessary.

EXAMPLE 3-1

Derive the overall transfer function for the control system shown in Fig. 3-6.

$$E_1(s) = R(s) - B_2(s)$$
$$E_2(s) = C_1(s) - B_1(s)$$
$$C_1(s) = G_1(s)E_1(s)$$
$$C_2(s) = G_2(s)E_2(s)$$
$$C(s) = G_3(s)C_2(s)$$
$$B_1(s) = H_1(s)C(s)$$
$$B_2(s) = H_2(s)C_2(s)$$

Substituting the transfer functions into the second error equation we obtain

$$E_2(s) = C(s)\frac{[1 + G_2(s)G_3(s)H_1(s)]}{G_1(s)G_2(s)G_3(s)}$$

Substituting the transfer functions into the first error equation,

$$E_1(s) = R(s) - [H_2(s)C(s)/G_3(s)]$$

Finally, equating these two equations we obtain the overall transfer function

$$\frac{C(s)}{R(s)} = \frac{G_1(s)G_2(s)G_3(s)}{1 + G_1(s)G_2(s)H_2(s) + G_2(s)G_3(s)H_1(s)} \tag{3-7}$$

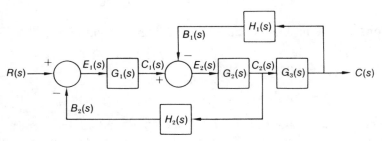

Fig. 3-6   Block diagram for transfer function given in Eq. (3-7).

If we define $G(s) = G_1(s)G_2(s)G_3(s)$ and $H(s) = H_1(s)/G_1(s) + H_2(s)/G_3(s)$, then

$$\frac{C(s)}{R(s)} = \frac{G(s)}{1 + G(s)H(s)} \tag{3-8}$$

which has a form identical to Eq. (3-6).

The method used is straightforward but very cumbersome. It can be greatly simplified if we employ some shortcuts which we consider next.

Block Diagram Reduction

When the block diagram representation gets complicated, it is advisable to *reduce* the diagram to a simpler and more manageable form prior to obtaining the overall transfer function. We shall consider only a few rules for block diagram reduction. We have already two rules, viz. cascading and parallel connection.

Consider the problem of moving the starting point of a signal shown in Fig. 3-7a from behind to the front of $G(s)$. Since $B(s) = R(s)$ and $R(s) = C(s)/G(s)$, then $B(s) = C(s)/G(s)$. Therefore if the takeoff point is in front of $G(s)$, then the signal must go through a transfer function $1/G(s)$ to yield $B(s)$ as shown in Fig. 3-7b.

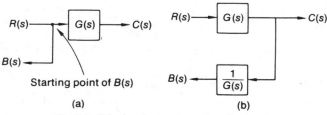

Fig. 3-7   Moving the starting point of a signal.

Consider the problem of moving the summing point of Fig. 3-8a. Since

$$E(s) = [M(s) + C(s)]G(s) = M(s)G(s) + C(s)G(s)$$
$$E(s) = M_1(s) + C_1(s)$$

where

$$M_1(s) = M(s)G(s); \qquad C_1(s) = C(s)G(s)$$

The generation of the signals $M_1(s)$ and $C_1(s)$ and adding them to yield $E(s)$ is shown in Fig. 3-8b. A table of the most common reduction rules is given in Table 3-1.

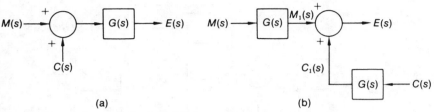

(a)   (b)

Fig. 3-8   Moving a summing junction.

Table 3-1   Some rules for block diagram reduction.

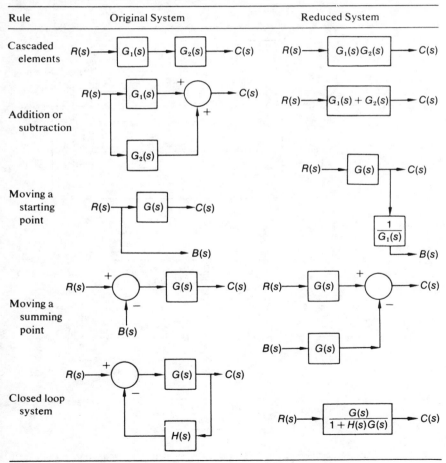

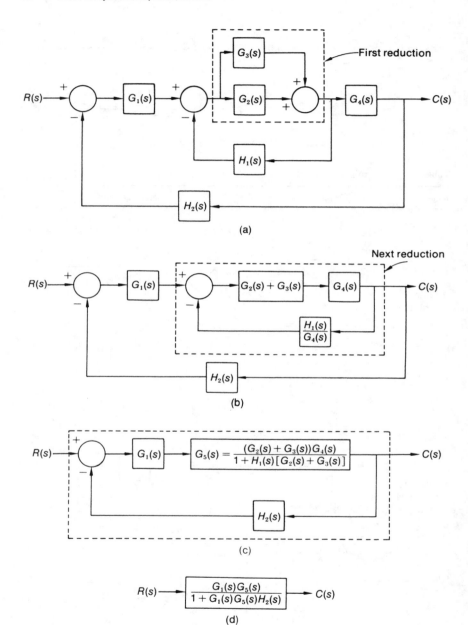

Fig. 3-9 Obtaining transfer function by block diagram reduction.

Consider the transfer function of the system shown in Fig. 3-9a. The final transfer function is shown in Fig. 3-9d. Note that the first reduction involves a parallel combination; the second involves a cascade combination as well as the use of Eq. (3-6). The last reduction again involves the use of Eq. (3-6).

Before we continue, let us stop and consider a few examples of complete systems and derive their overall transfer function.

EXAMPLE 3-2

An electromechanical servomechanism is shown in Fig. 3-10. This is a simple position servomechanism employing a d-c motor. The error detector measures the difference between the input θ_i and output θ_0,

$$\theta_e(t) = K_1(\theta_i(t) - \theta_0(t))$$

and feeds this signal to the amplifier. The signal then goes to the d-c motor whose transfer function is $G(s)$. The output, after being modified

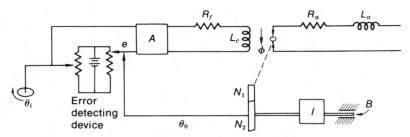

Fig. 3-10 Schematic of positional servomechanism.

by the gear ratio $N = N_1/N_2$, is the feedback signal. The block diagram is shown in Fig. 3-11.

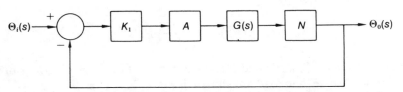

Fig. 3-11 Block diagram of a positional servomechanism.

Since all the transfer functions in the forward loop are cascaded, the overall transfer function becomes

$$\frac{\Theta_0(s)}{\Theta_i(s)} = \frac{K_1 AG(s)N}{1 + K_1 AG(s)N}$$

Substituting for $G(s)$ from Eq. (2-34) we obtain

$$\frac{\Theta_0(s)}{\Theta_i(s)} = \frac{K_1 ANK}{s(1 + s\tau_m)(1 + s\tau_f) + K_1 ANK}$$

or

$$\frac{\Theta_0(s)}{\Theta_i(s)} = \frac{K_2}{s(1 + s\tau_m)(1 + s\tau_f) + K_2} \tag{3-9}$$

where $K_2 = K_1 ANK$ and τ_m, τ_f are the motor and field time constants.

EXAMPLE 3-3

We shall derive the governing equations and transfer functions of a gas turbine. It will be assumed that the turbine behavior is linear about some operating condition.

The following variables are first defined:

$q(t)$ The variation of fuel input
$\omega_R(t)$ Speed setting of the turbine
$\omega(t)$ Actual speed of the turbine (must be controlled)
$T(t)$ Variation in driving torque
$T_l(t)$ Variation of torque disturbance

Assuming linear behavior we note that

$$q(t) = K_1[\omega_R(t) - \omega(t)]$$

$$T(t) = K_2 q(t) = K_1 K_2[\omega_R(t) - \omega(t)]$$

where K_1 is gain of the governor and constant, whereas K_2 is a constant property of the turbine design. The rotational motion of the turbine is related to the torque by

$$T(t) - T_l(t) = I\frac{d\omega(t)}{dt} + B\omega(t)$$

where I is the load inertia and B is the damping. The block diagrams of the governor, turbine, and load are shown in Fig. 3-12.

Writing these equations in Laplace transform notation and setting

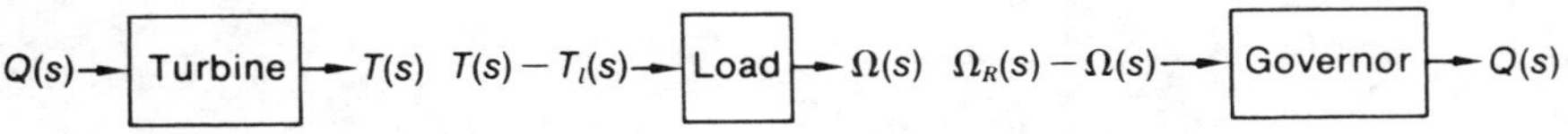

$Q(s)$→|Turbine|→$T(s)$ $T(s) - T_l(s)$→|Load|→$\Omega(s)$ $\Omega_R(s) - \Omega(s)$→|Governor|→$Q(s)$

Fig. 3-12   Transfer function of turbine, load, and governor.

$K = K_1K_2,$

$$T(s) = K\,[\Omega_R(s) - \Omega(s)]$$
$$T(s) - T_l(s) = (Is + B)\Omega(s)$$

Substituting the first into the second we obtain

$$\Omega(s) = \frac{K}{Is + B + K}\,\Omega_R(s) - \frac{1}{Is + B + K}\,T_l(s) \qquad (3\text{-}10)$$

The entire block diagram is shown in Fig. 3-13. We note that one transfer function is not obtained. This is due to two inputs.

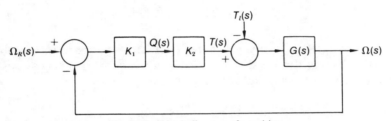

Fig. 3-13   Block diagram of a turbine.

EXAMPLE 3-4

As our last example we consider a stable platform. The function of a stable platform is to maintain a fixed angular reference using the property of a gyroscope, i.e. a torque about an input axis produces an angular velocity about the orthogonal axis. Naturally, the input axis must not be the spin axis of the gyro. (Why?) Consider a single axis platform shown in Fig. 3-14 where the y-axis is the input and the x-axis is the output axis. A disturbing torque $T_y(t)$ about the y-axis causes the spin axis direction to rotate through θ. We wish to obtain $\Theta(s)/T_y(s)$ for the platform. Noting that the angular momentum of the wheel is h, we balance the torques,

$$T_y(t) - J_y\frac{d^2\Phi_y(t)}{dt^2} = h\frac{d\theta(t)}{dt}$$

where J_y is the platform, gyro, and frame moment of inertia about the

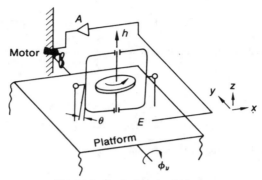

Fig. 3-14   A single axis platform.

y-axis. The torque $T_y(t)$ gives rise to $\dot\theta$ (called precession) which causes a torque about the x-axis of

$$T_x(t) = h\frac{d\Phi_y(t)}{dt} - I_x\frac{d^2\theta(t)}{dt^2} = 0$$

We have set $T_x(t)$ to zero since there is actually no applied torque about the x-axis. Taking the Laplace transform of the above two equations for zero initial conditions and substituting yields

★

$$\frac{\Theta(s)}{T_y(s)} = \frac{h/I_xJ_y}{s(s^2 + h^2/I_xJ_y)} \tag{3-11}$$

The second term in the denominator is generally quite small and as a first approximation is neglected. This term is referred to as the *nutation frequency*. Neglecting this yields

$$\frac{\Theta(s)}{T_y(s)} = \frac{1}{J_ys^2}\cdot\frac{h}{I_xs} = G_p(s)G_G(s) \tag{3-12}$$

The block diagram representation for this is shown in Fig. 3-15a. Now since it is necessary to counteract the torque $T_y(t)$, we sense θ and use this signal to drive a motor and gears in order to apply a torque T_s about the y-axis. The difference between this torque T_s and T_y is the error that drives the platform as shown in Fig. 3-15b. Denoting the transfer function of the motor and amplifier as G_m and A, we obtain

$$\frac{\Theta(s)}{T_y(s)} = \frac{G_p(s)G_G(s)}{1 + G_p(s)G_G(s)AG_m(s)} \tag{3-13}$$

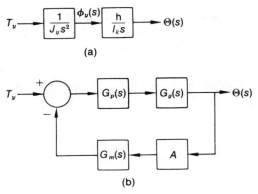

(a)

(b)

Fig. 3-15   Stable platform.

If $G(s) = G_p(s)G_G(s)$ and $H(s) = AG_m(s)$, then Eq. (3-13) reduces to

$$\frac{\Theta(s)}{T_y(s)} = \frac{G(s)}{1 + G(s)H(s)}$$

3-4 SIGNAL FLOW GRAPHS

Although the block diagram representation is a very convenient way of symbolizing a control system, an alternate method is the signal flow diagram or signal flow graph. Once a signal flow diagram of a control system is constructed, the application of a gain formula† yields the overall transfer function. This representation is also useful when casting the system in state space form as we shall see in the next section.

A signal flow diagram of a system is like a network consisting of junction points called nodes and directed line segments called branches. These nodes are connected by branches that have prescribed directions. A signal traveling along this branch does so only in the prescribed direction. Each branch has associated with it a gain or transmittance. The construction of a signal flow diagram involves the following of the cause and effect relations. Consider the flow diagram for $C(s) = G(s)R(s)$ as shown in Fig. 3-16. Generally, $C(s)$, $G(s)$, and $R(s)$ are replaced by C, G, and R for brevity. The output node is C, input node is R, and the direction of the branch is from R to C. The transmittance or gain is G and is

---

†This is popularly called Mason's gain formula since it was derived by S. J. Mason and reported in 1953.

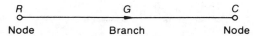

Fig. 3-16   Signal flow diagram for $C = GR$.

indicated on the branch. Consider the following set of error and transfer function equations:

$$x_1 = R - H_1x_3$$
$$x_2 = G_1x_1 - H_2C$$
$$x_3 = G_2x_2$$
$$C = G_3x_3$$

where x_1, x_2, and x_3 are the nodes. Construction of the signal flow diagram proceeds as shown in Fig. 3-17. The first equation (*see* Fig. 3-17a) states that the signal x_1 depends upon the signals R and x_3. The signal x_3 is multiplied by gain $-H_1$ as it comes into the node x_1. The gain $-H_1$ is indicated on the branch $x_3 \rightarrow x_1$. Similarly, the other three equations are included in the signal flow diagram and the final diagram is shown in Fig. 3-17d. In

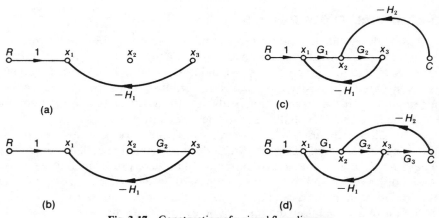

Fig. 3-17   Construction of a signal flow diagram.

order to facilitate the drawing of a signal flow diagram we give the following basic properties:

(1) The nodes represent variables of a system and are arranged following a succession of causes and effects through the system.

(2) Signals travel along a branch only in the prescribed direction.

(3) A signal transmitted along any branch is multiplied by the gain of that branch.

(4) The value of the variable represented by any node is equal to the sum of the signals entering the node.

(5) The value of the variable represented by a node is transmitted on all branches leaving that node.

(6) The forward path is the path from the input node to the output node without passing through any node twice.

(7) A feedback path is a path originating and terminating on the same node.

(8) Nontouching feedback paths or loops are those that have no nodes in common.

(9) The gain of any path is equal to the product of all the gains on that path.

With these rules in mind, let us consider as an example the block diagram of a feed forward system shown in Fig. 3-18. The following equations may be written by inspection,

$$x_1 = R - H_1 C$$
$$x_2 = G_1 x_1$$
$$x_3 = x_2 + G_3 x_1$$
$$C = G_2 x_3$$

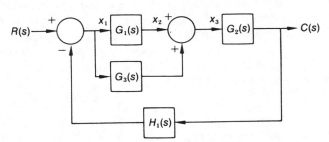

Fig. 3-18 A feedforward control system.

The signal flow diagram is shown in Fig. 3-19. Note that it is not necessary to have the block diagram representation at all. If we had the equations we could have directly constructed the signal flow diagram.

Once the signal flow diagram is constructed, the overall gain may be

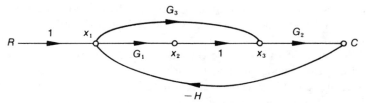

Fig. 3-19   Signal flow diagram of a feedforward system.

derived by using Mason's gain formula,

★
$$M = \frac{1}{\Delta} \sum_k G_k \Delta_k \qquad (3\text{-}14)$$

where

M = overall gain (usually $C(s)/R(s)$)
G_k = gain of kth forward path
L_i = gain of ith feedback loop

$$\Delta = 1 - \sum_i L_i + \left[\sum_{i,j} L_i L_j - \sum_{i,j,p} L_i L_j L_p + \cdots \right]_{\text{Nontouching loops}}$$

Δ_k = value of Δ excluding all terms which touch the kth forward path

The value of G_k is equal to the product of the gains between the input node and the output node for the kth forward path; L_i is the ith loop gain, i.e. the product of all the gains appearing in the ith feedback loop; $\Sigma L_i L_j$ is the sum of the product of the gains of all possible combinations of two loops that are nontouching. Similarly, the sum of the product of the gains of all possible combinations of three loops that are nontouching and then four loops and so on until there is no higher combination of nontouching loops. Finally, if the terms involving loops touching the kth forward path in Δ are eliminated, then Δ_k results.

EXAMPLE 3-5

The block diagram shown in Fig. 3-20a has its signal flow diagram shown in Fig. 3-20b. We wish to obtain the overall gain by Mason's formula.

We begin by observing that there are three touching loops, and one forward path ($k = 1$). Therefore we have

$$M = [G_k \Delta_k / \Delta]_{k=1}$$

$$\Delta = 1 - (L_1 + L_2 + L_3) + (L_1 L_2)$$

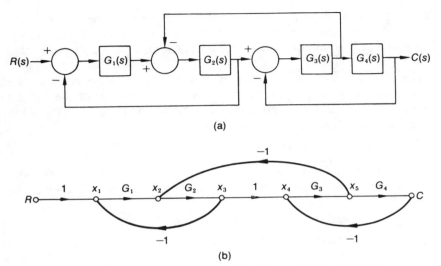

Fig. 3-20 Block diagram and signal flow diagram for Example 3-5.

Substituting values for the gains,

$$L_1 = -G_1G_2; \qquad L_2 = -G_3G_4; \qquad L_3 = -G_2G_3$$

Noting that $[G_k]_{k=1} = G_1G_2G_3G_4$ and $\Delta_1 = 1$ and substituting in the previous equation

$$M = \frac{C(s)}{R(s)} = \frac{G_1G_2G_3G_4}{1 + G_1G_2 + G_2G_3 + G_3G_4 + G_1G_2G_3G_4}$$

which is the necessary overall transfer function.

3-5 STATE REPRESENTATION

When a system is represented by its transfer function we are able to study the behavior of the system in terms of its input and output. The state variable method of system representation, however, allows us to investigate the behavior internal to the system as well. In such a representation the state of a system is characterized by a collection of variables called *state variables*. Given the input they must be specified at any time in order to uniquely predict the behavior of the system, for $t \geq t_0$. The state of the system is a function of the input for $t \geq t_0$ and the state at t_0 but independent of the state and input before t_0. If there are n variables $x_1, x_2, \ldots, x_n$ to describe the state, then the vector $\mathbf{x}$ of n components is the *state vector*. The space defined by the state variables as coordinates is called the *state space*.

The idea central to state representation is clarified if we consider the system shown in Fig. 3-21. We can ascertain the state of the system uniquely at any time if we know the angular position and velocity of the pendulum, i.e. $\theta(t)$ and $\dot{\theta}(t)$. Let us define

$$x_1(t) = \theta(t); \qquad x_2(t) = \dot{\theta}(t)$$

where $x_1(t)$ and $x_2(t)$ are the state variables of this system. If we consider θ to be small so that the governing equations are linear, then we can establish

$$\dot{x}_1(t) = x_2(t)$$

$$\dot{x}_2(t) = -\frac{g}{l}x_1(t)$$

which are the state equations. We have already shown how the mathematical model of a system may be written in this way in Chapter 2. It should be emphasized here that although the state of a dynamic system is uniquely determined from a specified set of state variables, the set itself is not unique. We can therefore select a variety of such sets. The particular one chosen is dictated often by convenience or the type of information desired.

In general, then, when we represent a system in terms of state variables we do so by a set of first-order linear differential equations of the form,

$$
\begin{aligned}
\dot{x}_1(t) &= a_{11}x_1(t) + a_{12}x_2(t) + \cdots + a_{1n}x_n(t) + b_1r(t) \\
\dot{x}_2(t) &= a_{21}x_1(t) + a_{22}x_2(t) + \cdots + a_{2n}x_n(t) + b_2r(t) \\
&\vdots \qquad \vdots \qquad \vdots \qquad \qquad \vdots \qquad \vdots \\
\dot{x}_n(t) &= a_{n1}x_1(t) + a_{n2}x_2(t) + \cdots + a_{nn}x_n(t) + b_nr(t)
\end{aligned}
\tag{3-15}
$$

where $x_1(t), x_2(t), \ldots, x_n(t)$ are the state variables. The output of the system is expressed as a linear combination of the state variables,

$$y(t) = c_1x_1(t) + c_2x_2(t) + \cdots + c_nx_n(t) \tag{3-16}$$

Equations (3-15) and (3-16) can be written compactly as

$$\dot{\mathbf{x}}(t) = \mathbf{A}\mathbf{x}(t) + \mathbf{b}r(t) \tag{3-17}$$

$$y(t) = \mathbf{c}\mathbf{x}(t) \tag{3-18}$$

Fig. 3-21   A simple pendulum.

where

$$\mathbf{x}(t) = \begin{bmatrix} x_1(t) \\ x_2(t) \\ \vdots \\ x_n(t) \end{bmatrix} \qquad \mathbf{A} = \begin{bmatrix} a_{11} & a_{12} & \cdots & a_{1n} \\ a_{21} & a_{22} & \cdots & a_{2n} \\ \vdots & \vdots & & \vdots \\ a_{n1} & a_{n2} & \cdots & a_{nn} \end{bmatrix} \qquad \mathbf{b} = \begin{bmatrix} b_1 \\ b_2 \\ \vdots \\ b_n \end{bmatrix}$$

$$\mathbf{c} = \begin{bmatrix} c_1 & c_2 & \cdots & c_n \end{bmatrix}$$

Here $\mathbf{x}(t)$ is the *state vector*, $\mathbf{A}$ is the *coefficient matrix* which is assumed constant, $\mathbf{b}$ is the *input vector* and it essentially weighs the effect of $r(t)$ which is the system input or forcing function, and $\mathbf{c}$ is the *output vector* and is constant. The vector-matrix differential equation shown in Eq. (3-17) is the *state equation* and that given by Eq. (3-18) is the *output equation*. When the input is zero in Eq. (3-17), the resulting equation becomes a *homogeneous equation*.

Before we continue, it is important that we establish the relationships between the state equation, system transfer function, and the governing differential equation of the system. This can be understood very easily as follows. We first assume zero initial conditions and take the Laplace transform of Eq. (3-17) and Eq. (3-18).

$$s\mathbf{X}(s) = \mathbf{A}\mathbf{X}(s) + \mathbf{b}R(s)$$

$$Y(s) = \mathbf{c}\mathbf{X}(s)$$

Solving for $\mathbf{X}(s)$ in the first equation and substituting into the second,

$$\mathbf{X}(s) = (s\mathbf{I} - \mathbf{A})^{-1}\mathbf{b}R(s)$$

and

$$Y(s) = \mathbf{c}(s\mathbf{I} - \mathbf{A})^{-1}\mathbf{b}R(s)$$

so that

$$\frac{Y(s)}{R(s)} = \mathbf{c}[s\mathbf{I} - \mathbf{A}]^{-1}\mathbf{b} \qquad (3\text{-}19)$$

★

Therefore $\mathbf{c}(s\mathbf{I} - \mathbf{A})^{-1}\mathbf{b}$ is the transfer function of a system whose output is $Y(s)$ and input is $R(s)$.

An interesting form of Eq. (3-17) and Eq. (3-18) occurs when

$$\mathbf{A} = \begin{bmatrix} 0 & 1 & \cdots & 0 \\ 0 & 0 & 1 & \cdots & 0 \\ \vdots & & & \\ -a_1 & -a_2 & \cdots & -a_n \end{bmatrix} \qquad \mathbf{b} = \begin{bmatrix} 0 \\ \vdots \\ 0 \\ 1 \end{bmatrix} \qquad \mathbf{c} = [c_1 \quad c_2 \quad \cdots \quad c_n]$$

so that

$$\begin{aligned} \dot{x}_1(t) &= x_2(t) \\ \dot{x}_2(t) &= x_3(t) \\ &\vdots \qquad \vdots \\ \dot{x}_{n-1}(t) &= x_n(t) \\ \dot{x}_n(t) &= -a_1 x_1(t) - a_2 x_2(t) \quad \cdots \quad -a_n x_n(t) + r(t) \\ y(t) &= c_1 x_1(t) + c_2 x_2(t) + \cdots + c_n x_n(t) \end{aligned} \qquad (3\text{-}20)$$

The signal flow graph for this is shown in Fig. 3-22. The overall transfer function may be obtained using Mason's formula and is

$$\frac{Y(s)}{R(s)} = \frac{c_n s^{n-1} + c_{n-1} s^{n-2} + \cdots + c_1}{s^n + a_n s^{n-1} + \cdots + a_1} \qquad (3\text{-}21)$$

This shows that the system whose transfer function is given by Eq. (3-21) has a state representation given by Eq. (3-20). We can additionally see

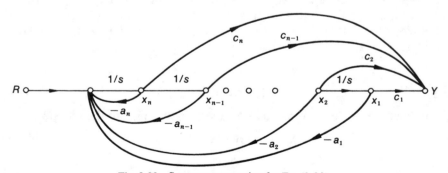

Fig. 3-22 State representation for Eq. (3-20).

that Eq. (3-21) corresponds to the differential equation

$$\frac{d^n y(t)}{dt^n} + a_n \frac{d^{n-1} y(t)}{dt^{n-1}} + \cdots + a_1 y(t) = c_n \frac{d^{n-1} r(t)}{dt^n} + \cdots + c_1 r(t) \qquad (3\text{-}22)$$

We see therefore how the governing differential equation, transfer function, and state representation are related. They are, in fact, all equivalent but alternate ways of looking at the mathematical model of the same system.

In the remaining section we shall consider several methods for obtaining the state representation of a control system. In obtaining the state representation we shall use the signal flow graphs (also called state variable diagrams) discussed in the previous section. It is however not necessary that these diagrams be constructed. They are used because they systematize the obtaining of state equations. Indeed, with experience the state equations can often be written directly from the transfer function or the differential equation.

State Equations from Differential Equations

If the differential equation of a system is available, it may be directly represented in state variable form. Consider, for example, the equation of a harmonic oscillator,

$$\ddot{\theta}(t) + k\theta(t) = f(t)$$

This equation may be written by the following system of equations,

$$\ddot{\theta}(t) = f(t) - k\theta(t)$$

$$\dot{\theta}(t) = \int \ddot{\theta}(t)\, dt$$

$$\theta(t) = \int \dot{\theta}(t)\, dt$$

Now let us define two state variables,

$$x_1(t) = \theta$$
$$x_2(t) = \dot{\theta}$$

These definitions combined with the previous equation yield

$$\dot{x}_1(t) = x_2(t)$$
$$\dot{x}_2(t) = -kx_1(t) + f(t)$$

which are two first-order linear differential equations replacing the original second-order differential equation. In matrix notation the above equations are written as,

$$\begin{bmatrix} \dot{x}_1(t) \\ \dot{x}_2(t) \end{bmatrix} = \begin{bmatrix} 0 & 1 \\ -k & 0 \end{bmatrix} \begin{bmatrix} x_1(t) \\ x_2(t) \end{bmatrix} + \begin{bmatrix} 0 \\ 1 \end{bmatrix} f(t)$$

or abbreviated as

$$\dot{\mathbf{x}}(t) = \mathbf{A}\mathbf{x}(t) + \mathbf{b}r(t)$$

where

$$\dot{\mathbf{x}}(t) = \begin{bmatrix} \dot{x}_1(t) \\ \dot{x}_2(t) \end{bmatrix} \qquad \mathbf{b} = \begin{bmatrix} 0 \\ 1 \end{bmatrix} \qquad \mathbf{A} = \begin{bmatrix} 0 & 1 \\ -k & 0 \end{bmatrix} \qquad r(t) = f(t)$$

The coefficient matrix is seen to be constant. If the previous differential equation had damping so that

$$\ddot{\theta}(t) + B\dot{\theta}(t) + k\theta(t) = f(t)$$

then the constant coefficient matrix becomes

$$A = \begin{bmatrix} 0 & 1 \\ -k & -B \end{bmatrix}$$

We can now easily generalize our observations and consider an nth-order differential equation,

$$\frac{d^n x(t)}{dt^n} + a_{n-1} \frac{d^{n-1} x(t)}{dt^{n-1}} + \cdots + a_0 x(t) = f(t) \qquad (3\text{-}23)$$

Again we employ the previous method of solving for the highest derivative,

$$\frac{d^n x(t)}{dt^n} = -a_{n-1} \frac{d^{n-1} x(t)}{dt^{n-1}} - \cdots - a_0 x(t) + f(t)$$

$$\frac{d^{n-1} x(t)}{dt^{n-1}} = \int \frac{d^n x(t)}{dt^n} \, dt$$

$$\vdots$$

$$x(t) = \int \frac{dx(t)}{dt} \, dt$$

The signal flow graph for the above case will consist of $n+1$ nodes and one input node as shown in Fig. 3-23. As before, the output of each integrator is defined as a state variable,

$$x_1(t) = x(t)$$
$$x_2(t) = \dot{x}(t)$$
$$x_3(t) = \ddot{x}(t)$$
$$\vdots$$

etc.

Substitution yields

$$\dot{x}_1 = x_2$$
$$\dot{x}_2 = x_3$$
$$\dot{x}_3 = x_4$$
$$\vdots$$
$$\dot{x}_n = -a_{n-1}x_n - a_{n-2}x_{n-1} - \cdots + f(t)$$

In matrix notation the $n \times n$ coefficient matrix and the $1 \times n$ input matrix become

$$\mathbf{A} = \begin{bmatrix} 0 & 1 & 0 & 0 & \cdots & 0 \\ 0 & 0 & 1 & 0 & \cdots & 0 \\ & & 0 & & & \\ \vdots & & \vdots & & & \\ -a_0 & -a_1 & & & \cdots & -a_{n-1} \end{bmatrix} \qquad \mathbf{b} = \begin{bmatrix} 0 \\ 0 \\ 0 \\ \vdots \\ 1 \end{bmatrix}$$

where the matrix differential equation is defined by Eq. (3-17). The examples considered so far have involved only one differential equation. In many situations it is necessary to study simultaneous equations that are coupled. The approach is the same as above and illustrated in the next example.

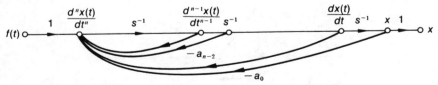

Fig. 3-23 Signal flow graph for an nth-order differential equation.

EXAMPLE 3-6

Obtain state equations for a system described by

$$\ddot{\phi}(t) + k_1\phi(t) + B_1\dot{\psi}(t) = f_1(t)$$
$$\ddot{\psi}(t) + k_2\psi(t) + B_2\dot{\phi}(t) = f_2(t)$$

We first write the governing equations as

$$\ddot{\phi} = -k_1\phi - B_1\dot{\psi} + f_1(t)$$
$$\ddot{\psi} = -k_2\psi - B_2\dot{\phi} + f_2(t)$$
$$\dot{\phi} = \int \ddot{\phi}dt; \qquad \phi = \int \dot{\phi}dt$$
$$\dot{\psi} = \int \ddot{\psi}dt; \qquad \psi = \int \dot{\psi}dt$$

which can be represented by the signal flow diagram of Fig. 3-24. This signal flow diagram is slightly different from the previous cases since the two second-order equations are coupled. As before, we define the following state variables,

$$x_1 = \phi$$
$$x_2 = \dot{\phi}$$
$$x_3 = \psi$$
$$x_4 = \dot{\psi}$$

From the signal flow diagram and the state variable definitions, the state

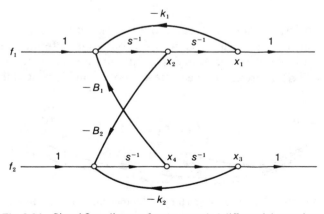

Fig. 3-24   Signal flow diagram for two coupled differential equations.

equations become

$$\dot{x}_1 = x_2$$
$$\dot{x}_2 = -k_1 x_1 - B_1 x_4 + f_1$$
$$\dot{x}_3 = x_4$$
$$\dot{x}_4 = -k_2 x_3 - B_2 x_2 + f_2$$

The coefficient matrix and the input matrix can now be written by inspection as

$$\mathbf{A} = \begin{bmatrix} 0 & 1 & 0 & 0 \\ -k_1 & 0 & 0 & -B_1 \\ 0 & 0 & 0 & 1 \\ 0 & -B_2 & -k_2 & 0 \end{bmatrix} \quad \mathbf{br}(t) = \begin{bmatrix} 0 \\ f_1(t) \\ 0 \\ f_2(t) \end{bmatrix}$$

and again the matrix differential equation is given by Eq. (3-17). We note that the procedure followed is identical to the case of the uncoupled problem.

State Equations from Transfer Functions

It is often necessary to form the state equations directly from the transfer functions themselves. Here we shall consider three techniques to achieve this.

Direct Programming

Consider the transfer function

$$\frac{Y(s)}{R(s)} = \frac{(s+1)(s+2)}{s(s+3)(s+4)} \tag{3-24}$$

Multiplying the factored form and obtaining a polynomial and then dividing the numerator and denominator by the highest power of s, which is 3 in this case,

$$\frac{Y(s)}{R(s)} = \frac{s^{-1} + 3s^{-2} + 2s^{-3}}{1 + 7s^{-1} + 12s^{-2}}$$

from which we form

$$E(s) = R(s) - (7s^{-1} + 12s^{-2})E(s) \tag{3-25a}$$
$$Y(s) = (s^{-1} + 3s^{-2} + 2s^{-3})E(s) \tag{3-25b}$$

where $E(s)$ is a convenient variable used to relate the two equations. The state variable diagram is formed by considering the equation for $E(s)$ and $Y(s)$ and is shown in Fig. 3-25. Once the state variable diagram is formed we may use the convention that the output of each integrator be considered a state variable. This leads to three state variables $x_1(t), x_2(t)$, and $x_3(t)$. By inspection the equations may be written as

$$\dot{x}_1(t) = x_2(t)$$
$$\dot{x}_2(t) = x_3(t)$$
$$\dot{x}_3(t) = -7x_3(t) - 12x_2(t) + r(t)$$

If the state equation is written in vector form, then

$$\dot{\mathbf{x}}(t) = \mathbf{A}\mathbf{x}(t) + \mathbf{b}r(t)$$

where

$$\mathbf{A} = \begin{bmatrix} 0 & 1 & 0 \\ 0 & 0 & 1 \\ 0 & -12 & -7 \end{bmatrix} \qquad \mathbf{b} = \begin{bmatrix} 0 \\ 0 \\ 1 \end{bmatrix}$$

Sometimes it is desirable to consider the input as an additional state variable. This is simply done for convenience. If this is done, and assuming that the input is a step function, the state equation becomes

$$\dot{\mathbf{x}}(t) = \mathbf{A}\mathbf{x}(t) \tag{3-26}$$

where

$$\mathbf{x}(t) = \begin{bmatrix} x_1(t) \\ x_2(t) \\ x_3(t) \\ x_4(t) \end{bmatrix} \qquad \mathbf{A} = \begin{bmatrix} 0 & 1 & 0 & 0 \\ 0 & 0 & 1 & 0 \\ 0 & -12 & -7 & 1 \\ 0 & 0 & 0 & 0 \end{bmatrix}$$

where $x_4(t) = r(t)$.

We notice that the output does not correspond to any of the state variables. However, it is obtained by a linear algebraic combination of the state variables,

$$y(t) = 2x_1 + 3x_2 + x_3$$

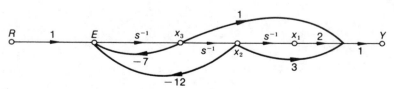

Fig. 3-25   State variable diagram for Eq. (3-24).

so that

$$\mathbf{c} = [2 \quad 3 \quad 1]$$

Parallel Programming

This technique is preferred when the transfer function appears in partial fraction form. Consider a transfer function that has been expanded in partial fraction form,

$$\frac{Y(s)}{R(s)} = \frac{1}{6s} - \frac{2}{3(s+3)} + \frac{3}{2(s+4)} \tag{3-27}$$

The state diagram is generated for each factor and then added as shown in Fig. 3-26. The state variables are defined using the convention of the previous section and including $r(t)$ as a state variable we have

$$\dot{x}_1(t) = x_4(t)$$
$$\dot{x}_2(t) = -\tfrac{2}{3}x_4(t) - 3x_2(t)$$
$$\dot{x}_3(t) = \tfrac{3}{2}x_4(t) - 4x_3(t)$$
$$\dot{x}_4(t) = \dot{r}(t) = 0$$

where $r(t)$ is assumed to be a step input. The coefficient matrix and the state vector becomes

$$\mathbf{x}(t) = \begin{bmatrix} x_1(t) \\ x_2(t) \\ x_3(t) \\ x_4(t) \end{bmatrix} \qquad \mathbf{A} = \begin{bmatrix} 0 & 0 & 0 & 1 \\ 0 & -3 & 0 & -\tfrac{2}{3} \\ 0 & 0 & -4 & \tfrac{3}{2} \\ 0 & 0 & 0 & 0 \end{bmatrix}$$

Iterative Programming

This method deals directly with the transfer function of individual components of a system.

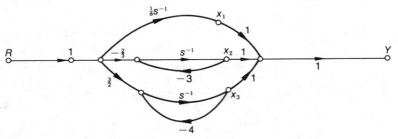

Fig. 3-26   State variable diagram for Eq. (3-27).

Consider the transfer function

$$\frac{Y(s)}{R(s)} = \frac{(s+1)(s+2)}{s(s+3)(s+4)} \tag{3-28}$$

Now let

$$Y(s) = N_3(s+2) \tag{3-29a}$$

$$N_3 = \frac{N_2}{s+4} \tag{3-29b}$$

$$N_2 = N_1(s+1) \tag{3-29c}$$

$$N_1 = \frac{R(s)}{s(s+3)} \tag{3-29d}$$

The state variables diagrams are first constructed for N_1, N_2, N_3, and Y and then combined to form the overall diagram as shown in Fig. 3-27. Considering $r(t)$ as a state variable and also a step input, the coefficient matrix becomes

$$\mathbf{A} = \begin{bmatrix} -4 & -2 & 1 & 0 \\ 0 & -3 & 1 & 0 \\ 0 & 0 & 0 & 1 \\ 0 & 0 & 0 & 0 \end{bmatrix}$$

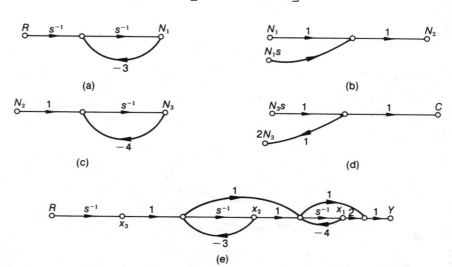

Fig. 3-27   State variable diagrams for the system of equations shown in Eq. (3-29).

The output $y(t)$ is again a linear combination of the state variables,

$$y(t) = -4x_1 + 2x_1 + x_2 + x_3 - 3x_2$$
$$y(t) = -2x_1 - 2x_2 + x_3$$

The output is written as

$$y(t) = \mathbf{cx}(t)$$

where

$$\mathbf{x}(t) = \begin{bmatrix} x_1(t) \\ x_2(t) \\ x_3(t) \end{bmatrix} \qquad \mathbf{c} = [-2 \quad -2 \quad 1]$$

EXAMPLE 3-7

The angular attitude motion θ_x, θ_y, and θ_z of an artificial satellite are given by the following three equations,

$$\ddot{\theta}_x(t) + \delta_1\dot{\theta}_y(t)\dot{\theta}_z(t) = f_x(t)$$
$$\ddot{\theta}_y(t) + \delta_2\dot{\theta}_x\dot{\theta}_z + \delta_4\dot{\theta}_z = f_y(t)$$
$$\ddot{\theta}_z(t) + \delta_3\dot{\theta}_x(t)\dot{\theta}_y(t) - \delta_5\dot{\theta}_y = f_z(t)$$

where it is assumed that $\dot{\theta}_y$, $\dot{\theta}_z$ are small and $\dot{\theta}_x = \omega + \dot{\phi}_x$ where ω is constant but $\dot{\phi}_x$ is small, and $\delta_1, \delta_2, \delta_3$, and δ are all constants. Obtain the state representation for these equations involving $\dot{\phi}_x$, $\dot{\theta}_y$, and $\dot{\theta}_z$.

We first linearize the equations. Since $\dot{\theta}_y$, $\dot{\theta}_z$, $\dot{\phi}_x$ are small their products can be neglected, so that

$$\ddot{\phi}_x(t) = f_x(t)$$
$$\ddot{\theta}_y(t) + \alpha\dot{\theta}_z(t) = f_y(t)$$
$$\ddot{\theta}_z(t) - \beta\dot{\theta}_y(t) = f_z(t)$$

where

$$\alpha = \delta_4 + \delta_2\omega \quad \text{and} \quad \beta = \delta_5 - \delta_3\omega$$

The state equation becomes

$$\dot{\mathbf{x}}(t) = \mathbf{A}\mathbf{x}(t) + \mathbf{b}r(t)$$

where

$$\mathbf{x}(t) = \begin{bmatrix} \dot{\phi}_x(t) \\ \dot{\theta}_y(t) \\ \dot{\theta}_z(t) \end{bmatrix} \qquad \mathbf{A} = \begin{bmatrix} 0 & 0 & 0 \\ 0 & 0 & -\alpha \\ 0 & -\beta & 0 \end{bmatrix} \qquad \mathbf{b}r(t) = \begin{bmatrix} f_x(t) \\ f_y(t) \\ f_z(t) \end{bmatrix}$$

Note this yields three first-order differential equations since we are solving for the rates only.

SUMMARY

In this chapter we have been concerned with various ways of representing control systems.

Each block diagram was characterized by its own transfer function, i.e. the ratio of the output over the input signal when the signals are represented in the Laplace domain. This transfer function contains all the information we require about the behavior of the physical system represented by the block diagram. By a systematic handling of the transfer functions we were able to reduce complicated systems to a single overall transfer function. As an alternate method to block diagram representation we introduced the signal flow diagram. The use of Mason's gain formula was found to be a handy tool for obtaining the overall gain from the signal flow diagram.

The state representation involved the characterization of the entire system in matrix notation. It was seen that although the number of state variables is unique, any particular set is not. We described how the differential equation, transfer function, and the state equations of a system are related.

PROBLEMS

3-1. Draw a functional block diagram of the working of the national economy. Assume that the input is the money spent by the government and the output is the national income. Comment on the validity of your assumptions.

3-2. Draw a functional block diagram of the behavior of your car. Consider the input to be the displacement of your accelerator and the output the velocity of your car.

3-3. Obtain $C(s)/R(s)$ and $E(s)/R(s)$ for the following control systems shown in Fig. P3-3.

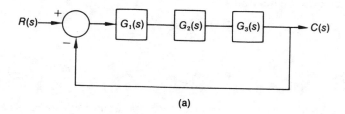

(a)

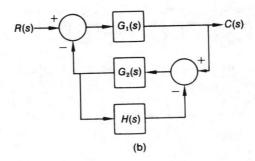

(b)

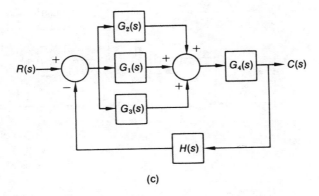

(c)

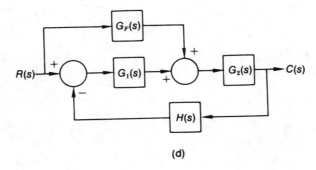

(d)

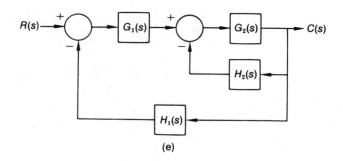

(e)

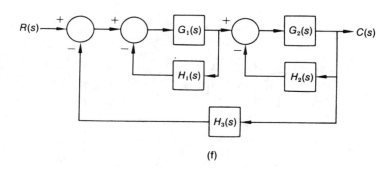

(f)

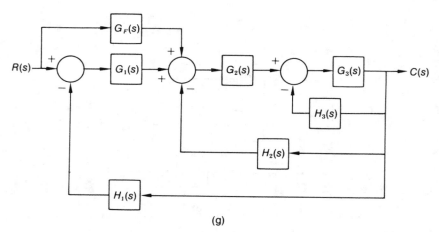

(g)

Fig. P3-3

3-4. Obtain the output $C(s)$ and error $E(s)$ for the control systems shown in Fig. P3-4.

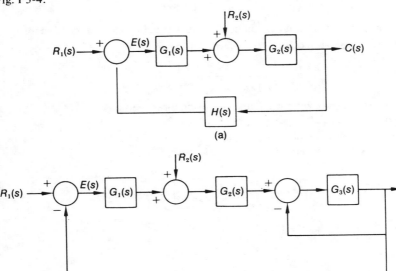

(a)

(b)

Fig. P3-4

3-5. Represent the systems of Problem 3-3 in signal flow diagram notation obtaining the output $C(s)$ using Mason's formula.

3-6. Using a signal flow graph show that

$$\frac{C(s)}{R(s)} = \frac{G_1 G_2 G_3}{1 + (G_1 H_1 + G_2 H_2 + G_3 H_3) + G_1 G_3 H_1 H_3)}$$

for the control system of Fig. P3-6.

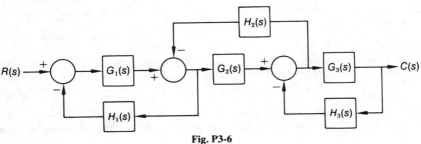

Fig. P3-6

3-7. The differential equation of a linear system is given by

$$\dddot{x}(t) + 6\ddot{x}(t) + 11\dot{x}(t) + 6x(t) = f(t)$$

Using the highest derivative method, obtain the equation in state variable form.

3-8. For a closed loop transfer function

$$\frac{C(s)}{R(s)} = \frac{s+1}{s^3 + 3s^2 + 5s + 3}$$

(a) Determine the dynamical equations using three methods.
(b) Discuss the relative advantages of each.

3-9. A feedback control system is shown in Fig. P3-9. Assuming $r(t)$ to be a step input and a state variable, obtain the state equations.

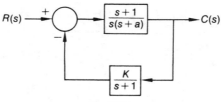

Fig. P3-9

3-10. After obtaining **A**, **b**, and **c** for Problem 3-8, verify Eq. (3-19).

3-11. Obtain the state equations for the electromechanical servomechanism of Fig. 3-10. Having obtained **A**, **b**, and **c** verify Eq. (3-19).

3-12. Obtain the coefficient matrix **A** for the stable platform described by Eq. (3-11).

REFERENCES

1. Kuo, B. C., *Automatic Control Systems*, Englewood Cliffs, N.J., Prentice-Hall, 1962.
2. Dransfield, P., *Engineering Systems and Automatic Controls*, Englewood Cliffs, N.J., Prentice-Hall, 1968.
3. Chow, Y., and E. Cassignol, *Linear Signal-Flow Graphs and Applications*, New York, Wiley, 1962.
4. D'Azzo, J. J., and C. H. Houpis, *Feedback Control System Analysis and Synthesis*, 2nd Edition, New York, McGraw-Hill, 1966.
5. DeRusso, P. M., R. J. Roy, and C. M. Close, *State Variables for Engineers*, New York, Wiley, 1965.
6. Dorf, R. C., *Modern Control Systems*, Reading, Mass., Addison-Wesley, 1967.
7. Klir, G. J., *An Approach to General Systems Theory*, New York, Van Nostrand Reinhold, 1969.

8. Greenwood, D. T., *Principles of Dynamics*, Englewood Cliffs, N.J., Prentice-Hall, 1965.
9. Saucedo, R., and E. E. Schiring, *Introduction to Continuous and Digital Control Systems*, New York, Macmillan, 1968.
10. Zadeh, L. A., and C. A. Desoer, *Linear System Theory*, New York, McGraw-Hill, 1963.
11. Melsa, J. L., and D. G. Schultz, *Linear Control Systems*, New York, McGraw-Hill, 1969.
12. Harrison, H. L., and J. G. Bollinger, *Introduction to Automatic Controls*, 2nd Edition, Scranton, Pa., International Textbook, 1969.

4

Response – Classical Method

4-1 INTRODUCTION

Having represented control systems using block diagrams as well as state variables, we turn our attention to system response, i.e. how does a system respond as a function of time when subjected to various types of stimuli? Here we are interested in the system output without regard to the behavior of variables inside the control system. This can be most readily achieved by investigating the system transfer function employing operational techniques. Such an approach is referred to as the classical method.

In general, the input excitation to a control system is not known ahead of time. However, for purposes of analysis it is necessary that we assume some simple types of excitation and obtain system response to at least these types of signals. In general, there are three types† of excitations used in obtaining the response of linear feedback control systems. They are the step input, ramp input, and the parabolic input. These are typical test or reference inputs. In practice, the input is generally never exactly specifiable.

Step Input

A step input consists of a sudden change of reference input at $t = 0$.

---

†In many control systems the input may be a sinusoidally varying signal. When this is so, and we know the system is linear, then the output also consists of a sinusoidally varying signal but having a different magnitude and a phase shift which may be functions of the input frequency. We shall consider this in more detail in a later chapter.

Mathematically it is

$$r(t) = A \qquad (t > 0)$$
$$r(t) = 0 \qquad (t < 0)$$

The function shown in Fig. 4-1a is not defined for $t = 0$. The Laplace transform of the step input is A/s.

Ramp Input (Step Velocity)

A ramp input is a constant velocity and is represented as

$$r(t) = At \qquad (t \geqslant 0)$$
$$r(t) = 0 \qquad (t < 0)$$

The function is shown in Fig. 4-1b and has a Laplace transform of A/s^2.

Parabolic Input (Step Acceleration)

In this case the input is a constant acceleration,

$$r(t) = At^2 \qquad (t \geqslant 0)$$
$$r(t) = 0 \qquad (t < 0)$$

The function is shown in Fig. 4-1c and has a Laplace transform of $2A/s^3$.

In studying the system response of a feedback control system there are three things we wish to know, viz. the *transient response*, the *steady state* or forced response, and the *stability* of the system. The transient solution yields information on how much the system deviates from the input and the time necessary for the system response to settle to within certain limits. The steady state or forced response gives an indication of the

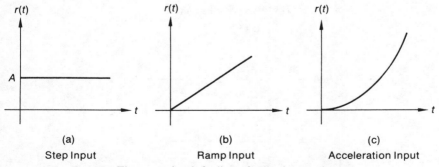

| (a) | (b) | (c) |
| Step Input | Ramp Input | Acceleration Input |

Fig. 4-1   Three test signals for linear feedback control systems.

accuracy of the system. Whenever the steady state output does not agree with the input, the system is said to have a steady state error. By stability we mean that the output does not get uncontrollably large.

4-2 TRANSIENT RESPONSE

Consider a closed loop system shown in Fig. 4-2. The output and the error transfer functions are

$$\frac{C(s)}{R(s)} = \frac{G(s)}{1+G(s)H(s)} \tag{4-1a}$$

$$\frac{E(s)}{R(s)} = \frac{1}{1+G(s)H(s)} \tag{4-1b}$$

The transient response of the system, be it the error E or the output C, depends upon the roots (also called zeros) of the *characteristic equation*

★ $$1+G(s)H(s) = 0 \tag{4-2}$$

The zeros of the characteristic equation are also the poles of the transfer functions given by Eqs. (4-1a) and (4-1b). These poles are known as the closed loop poles. It is interesting to note that the transient response does not depend upon the kind of input but depends only on the zeros of the characteristic equation. Now if the forward and feedback transfer functions are defined as

$$G(s) = \frac{P(s)}{Q(s)}; \qquad H(s) = \frac{A(s)}{B(s)}$$

then the characteristic equation becomes

$$\frac{Q(s)B(s)+P(s)A(s)}{Q(s)B(s)} = 0$$

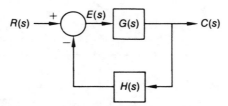

Fig. 4-2   A closed loop system.

and the zeros are obtained from

$$Q(s)B(s) + P(s)A(s) = 0$$

which correspond to the poles of

$$\frac{C(s)}{R(s)} = \frac{P(s)B(s)}{Q(s)B(s) + P(s)A(s)}$$

The right-hand side of the above equation is a ratio of two polynomials where the degree of the denominator is equal to or higher than the order of the numerator. Let us assume that the degree of the denominator is n and of the numerator is ν, then if we factorize Eq. (4-1a) it can be written as

$$\frac{C(s)}{R(s)} = \frac{K \prod\limits_{i=1}^{\nu} (s + z_i)}{\prod\limits_{i=1}^{n} (s + p_i)} \tag{4-3}$$

Note that we began with the system transfer function to obtain this expression. It is perhaps interesting to observe that had we begun with a state representation, then

$$\frac{C(s)}{R(s)} = \mathbf{c}[\,s\mathbf{I} - \mathbf{A}]^{-1}\mathbf{b}$$

which would have been factored to obtain the right-hand side of Eq. (4-3). Returning to Eq. (4-3) we now assume that the input† $r(t)$ is a unit step, then $R(s) = 1/s$ and the output becomes

★
$$C(s) = \frac{K \prod\limits_{i=1}^{\nu} (s + z_i)}{s \prod\limits_{i=1}^{n} (s + p_i)} \tag{4-4}$$

Let us now assume that of the n distinct poles, $2k$ poles are complex‡ and the remaining poles are real. If we denote the conjugate of s_m and K_m by $\bar{s}_m$ and $\bar{K}_m$, then Eq. (4-4) may be expanded in partial fractions and written as

$$C(s) = \frac{K_0}{s} + \sum_m \frac{K_m}{(s + s_m)} + \sum_m \frac{\bar{K}_m}{(s + \bar{s}_m)} + \sum_i \frac{K_i}{(s + s_i)} \tag{4-5}$$

†Sometimes it is assumed that $r(t)$ is an impulse at $t = 0$ so that $R(s) = 1$. When the output is obtained in the time domain, we obtain the transient part that goes to zero for well-behaved systems. However, using a step input we obtain not only this same transient response but in addition a constant term.
‡Complex poles appear as conjugates.

where

$$K_0 = \lim_{s \to 0} sC(s)$$

$$K_m = \lim_{s \to -s_m} (s + s_m)C(s)$$

$$K_i = \lim_{s \to -s_i} (s + s_i)C(s)$$

If we denote $s_m = \sigma_m + j\omega_m$, then the output in the time domain is obtained by taking the inverse Laplace transform of Eq. (4-5),

$$c(t) = K_0 + \sum_m K_m e^{(-\sigma_m + j\omega_m)t} + \sum_m \bar{K}_m e^{(-\sigma_m - j\omega_m)t} + \sum_i K_i e^{-s_i t}$$

$$= K_0 + \sum_m |K_m| e^{-\sigma_m t} \cos(\omega_m t + \phi_m) + \sum_i K_i e^{-s_i t} \qquad (4\text{-}6)$$

where ϕ_m is the phase contribution of the constant K_m. Notice the second term of Eq. (4-6) is obtained by combining two terms.

If $C(s)$ has m poles that are equal (i.e. repeat), then

$$C(s) = \frac{K_0}{s} + \sum_\alpha \frac{K_\alpha}{(s + s_\alpha)^\alpha} \qquad (4\text{-}7)$$

where

$$K_\alpha = \lim_{s \to -s_\alpha} \frac{1}{(m - \alpha)!} \frac{d^{(m-\alpha)}}{ds^{(m-\alpha)}} [(s + s_\alpha)^m C(s)]$$

and

$$c(t) = K_0 + \sum_\alpha \frac{K_\alpha t^{\alpha-1}}{(\alpha-1)!} e^{-s_\alpha t} \qquad (4\text{-}8)$$

where α goes from 1 to m. In general, the response of a system contains terms of the type given in Eq. (4-6) as well as Eq. (4-8).

The important fact here is that the form of the transient response is a function of the location of the closed loop poles, which are identical to the zeros of the characteristic equation, on the s-plane.

For real, simple poles the time response is simply an exponential which decays if the pole is in the left half s-plane and increases with time if the pole is in the right half s-plane. The rate of this decay or increase is dependent upon the magnitude of pole. Poles closer to the imaginary axis are referred to as *dominant poles* since the decay due to them takes longer.

For complex poles the response is oscillatory with the magnitude varying exponentially with time. Again, if the real part is in the left half s-plane,

Location of closed loop
poles on *s*-plane

Transient response

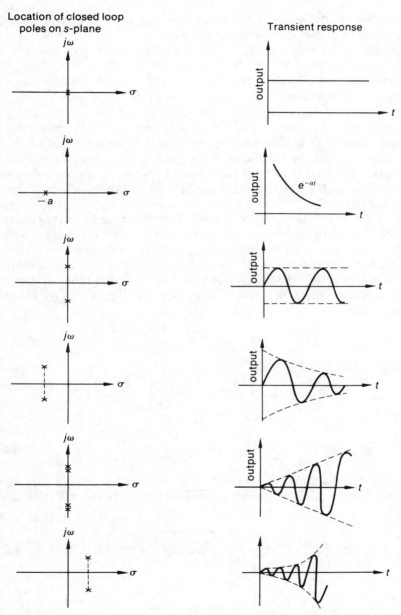

Fig. 4-3 Transient response as a function of the closed loop poles on the *s*-plane.

the magnitude decreases with time. If the real part is positive, then the magnitude increases exponentially with time.

Finally, if the poles are real and of multiplicity m, then the time response is of the form $t^m e^{-s_\alpha t}$. We have not shown the response if the poles are multiple and complex. It is left for you to show that for complex multiple poles the response is of the form $(t^m/m!)e^{-\sigma m t}|K_m|\cos(\omega_m t + \phi_m)$.

Our ideas of this section are consolidated and shown graphically in Fig. 4-3. We note that for well-behaved systems, i.e. systems exhibiting a stable response, it is reasonable to require that the closed loop poles of the control system be located in the left half s-plane. If the poles exist on the imaginary axis they must be simple. Otherwise, the control system responds in such a way that the magnitude of the output becomes uncontrollably large.

We observe that the number of closed loop poles is equal to the order of the characteristic equation. Although many control systems possess higher-order characteristic polynomials, the second-order polynomial is most abundant and consequently plays a very fundamental role in the physical world. We shall therefore dwell on a second-order system and analyze it a bit more thoroughly. Consider the system of Fig. 4-4. The output becomes

$$C(s) = \frac{KR(s)}{As^2 + Bs + K}$$

and, if we define

$$\omega_n^2 = \frac{K}{A}; \qquad \delta = \frac{B}{2\sqrt{KA}}$$

then

$$\frac{C(s)}{R(s)} = \frac{\omega_n^2}{s^2 + 2\delta\omega_n s + \omega_n^2} \tag{4-9}$$

Here ω_n is the *natural frequency* and δ is the *damping ratio* of the control system. The transient response is dependent upon the roots of the charac-

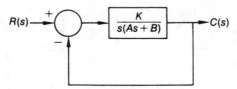

Fig. 4-4 A second-order unity feedback system.

teristic equation

$$s^2 + 2\delta\omega_n s + \omega_n{}^2 = 0 \qquad (4\text{-}10)$$

The roots, for nonnegative δ, are

$(\delta < 1)$ $s_1, s_2 = -\delta\omega_n \pm j\omega_n\sqrt{1-\delta^2}$ (Underdamping)

$(\delta = 1)$ $s_1, s_2 = -\omega_n$ (Critical damping)

$(\delta > 1)$ $s_1, s_2 = -\delta\omega_n \pm \omega_n\sqrt{\delta^2-1}$ (Overdamping)

$(\delta = 0)$ $s_1, s_2 = \pm j\omega_n$ (No damping)

The term $\omega_n\sqrt{1-\delta^2}$ is often referred to as the damped natural frequency and denoted by ω_d. If we assume that δ is positive, then the system has positive damping and the roots of the characteristic equation exist in the left half s-plane only. This means that this system shall always exhibit a stable time response. The migration of the closed loop poles as a function of the damping ratio for this system is shown in Fig. 4-5 for constant natural frequency.

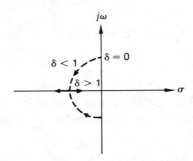

Fig. 4-5   Closed loop migration as a function of damping ratio for a second-order system.

Let us assume the input to be a unit step so that $R(s) = 1/s$. The time response of the output may be obtained by the techniques already discussed or read directly from tables. For the underdamped case the time response to a unit step is

$$c(t) = 1 - \frac{e^{-\delta\omega_n t}}{\sqrt{1-\delta^2}}\sin(\omega_d t + \phi) \qquad (4\text{-}11)$$

where

$$\phi = \tan^{-1}\frac{\sqrt{1-\delta^2}}{\delta}; \qquad \omega_d = \omega_n\sqrt{1-\delta^2}$$

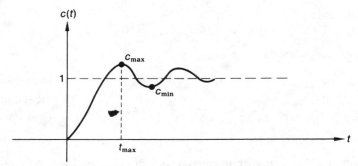

Fig. 4-6 Underdamped response of a second-order system.

Here ω_d is referred to as the *damped frequency*. A plot of $c(t)$ is shown in Fig. 4-6. We note that an underdamped system exhibits an overshoot. The amount of this overshoot may be obtained by solving $dc(t)/dt = 0$. The first maximum value occurs at

$$t_{\max} = \frac{\pi}{\omega_n\sqrt{1 - \delta^2}} \tag{4-12}$$

The amount of overshoot is obtained by substituting $t_{\max}$ in Eq. (4-11) which yields

$$c(t)_{\max} = 1 + e^{-\pi\delta/\sqrt{1-\delta^2}} \tag{4-13}$$

and is seen to be a function of the damping ratio only. This is shown in Fig. 4-7. As the damping ratio is decreased to zero the output becomes

$$c(t) = 1 - \cos \omega_n t$$

and we obtain pure oscillations. If we had increased the damping ratio to

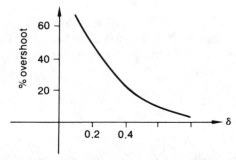

Fig. 4-7 Overshoot as a function of damping ratio for a unit step input.

$\delta = 1$, we obtain double roots of the characteristic equation and

$$C(s) = \frac{\omega_n^{\,2}}{s(s+\omega_n)^2}$$

the inverse Laplace transform of which is

$$c(t) = 1 - e^{-\omega_n t}(1 + \omega_n t)$$

and is seen not to exhibit any oscillations. Note the appearance of the term $\omega_n t\, e^{-\omega_n t}$ due to the multiplicity of the pole at $s = -\omega_n$. This system damps to the input without any overshoot.

The last case, overdamping, has two unequal but real poles. Again we expect to see no oscillatory behavior. The response for different values

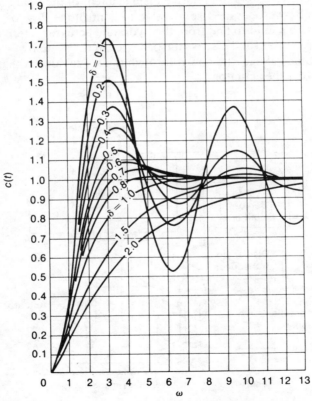

Fig. 4-8 Transient response of a second-order system subjected to a unit step input.

of δ is shown in Fig. 4-8. We observe that as δ becomes small the system has larger overshoots and is faster acting.

As δ is increased the system overshoot decreases and then vanishes as we approach critical damping and $\delta > 1$. In this case the system is sluggish. It is a characteristic of second-order physical systems that sluggish systems are overdamped, whereas fast acting systems are underdamped.

EXAMPLE 4-1

Consider the electrohydraulic† vibration isolation system shown in Fig. 4-9. The system essentially consists of a rigid mass m vibrating as a result of the excitation input $y(t)$. The mass m is connected to a hydraulic actuator rod having a negligible cross sectional area. By considering the acceleration, velocity, and relative displacement of the rigid body as feedback signals, we operate a servovalve to control the flow of a relatively incompressible fluid to and from the hydraulic actuator. Derive the equations of this system and discuss the behavior of the system.

Neglecting leakage, the flow q through the servovalve is that due to the motion across the actuator

$$q(t) = A(\dot{x} - \dot{y})$$

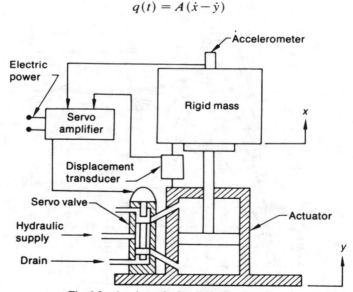

Fig. 4-9   An electrohydraulic isolation system.

†*See* Reference 14.

By processing the acceleration, relative displacement, and relative velocity signals, the flow through the valve can be made proportional to $\ddot{x}$, $(\dot{x} - \dot{y})$, and $(x - y)$,

$$q(t) = -[C_a\ddot{x} + C_v(\dot{x} - \dot{y}) + C_d(x - y)]$$

where C_a, C_d, and C_v are proportionality constants. Equating the two equations for the flow and taking the Laplace transform, we obtain

$$\frac{X(s)}{Y(s)} = \frac{C_d + (C_v + A)s}{C_a s^2 + (C_v + A)s + C_d}$$

where the initial conditions are assumed to be zero. If we define the natural frequency ω_n as $\sqrt{C_d/C_a}$ and the damping ratio δ as $(C_v + A)/2\sqrt{C_a C_d}$, then

$$\frac{X(s)}{Y(s)} = \frac{\omega_n^2 + 2\delta\omega_n s}{s^2 + 2\delta\omega_n s + \omega_n^2} \qquad (4\text{-}14)$$

The characteristic equation is recognized as being identical to the second-order equation already discussed. Since the values of ω_n and δ are dependent upon the feedback signals C_a, C_v, and C_d, we have the ability of obtaining vibration isolation over a wide range of frequencies. In conventional passive isolation this is not possible since the properties of a passive isolator for any given system are fixed. Note also that since the mass m does not appear in the equations of motion, the isolation system performance characteristics are independent of the weight of the isolated body. Examination of the natural frequency and damping ratio definitions indicate that the relative velocity feedback effects only the damping ratio. This provides us with the facility of varying the damping ratio but with fixed natural frequency. In this problem if we employ only acceleration feedback gain, then the resulting characteristic equation becomes a polynomial of order one, i.e. the transient response exhibits an exponential decay. Another special case is obtained if in addition to acceleration, velocity, and displacement gains we have integral feedback of the displacement. In this case the characteristic equation becomes a third-order system.

EXAMPLE 4-2

Consider the third-order servomechanism shown in Fig. 4-10a. Such a closed loop system can be used for positioning a large antenna or a mass

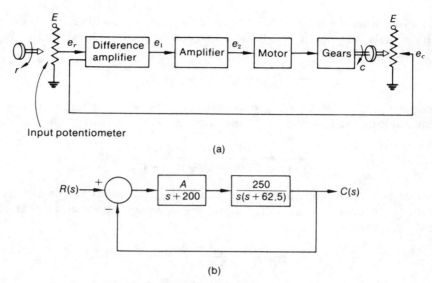

Input potentiometer

(a)

(b)

Fig. 4-10 A position servomechanism.

having a large moment of inertia. The output potentiometer measures the output shaft position and converts this to voltage,

$$e = K_0 c$$

where K_0 has units of volts per radian and is the transfer function of the potentiometer. A particular position servo with known speed torque characteristics of the servomotor is shown in Fig. 4-10b and it is assumed that the gear ratio is unity. Derive the overall transfer function and obtain $c(t)$ for (a) $A = 2.625 \times 10^5$ and (b) $A = 9375$. Assume a unit step input. The output transfer function becomes

$$\frac{C(s)}{R(s)} = \frac{250A}{s(s+200)(s+62.5) + 250A} \qquad (4\text{-}15)$$

where the characteristic equation is a third-order polynomial.

(a) The transfer function for an amplifier gain A of 2.625×10^5 is

$$\frac{C(s)}{R(s)} = \frac{6.56 \times 10^7}{s^3 + (2.625 \times 10^2)s^2 + (1.25 \times 10^4)s + 6.56 \times 10^7}$$

Factoring the characteristic equation and substituting $R(s) = 1/s$ for a unit step,

$$C(s) = \frac{6.56 \times 10^7}{s(s+500)(s^2-237.5s+(1.312\times10^6))} \qquad (4\text{-}16a)$$

The output in the time domain becomes

$$c(t) = K_0 - K_1 e^{-500t} - K_2 e^{118.7t} \sin(1140t+\phi) \qquad (4\text{-}16b)$$

Examination of this equation indicates that the first two terms of $c(t)$ are well behaved but the last term becomes large, i.e. the magnitude of the oscillations increase exponentially with time. It is clear that this is an undesirable characteristic and must be avoided. Actually when this happens we speak of the system as being *unstable*.

(b) The transfer function for $A = 9375$ becomes

$$C(s) = \frac{2.34 \times 10^6}{s(s+250)(s^2+12.5s+(9.375\times10^3))} \qquad (4\text{-}17a)$$

and the output in the time domain becomes

$$c(t) = B_0 - B_1 e^{-250t} - B_2 e^{-6.25t} \sin(96.6t+\phi) \qquad (4\text{-}17b)$$

The last term now is a positively damped sinusoid. The output of the position servomechanism now exhibits exponentially decaying oscillations, about a constant value B_0 which corresponds to some input constant. We speak of such a system as being *stable*.

Impulse Response of a Transfer Function

We have seen that the output $C(s)$ of an open loop linear system represented as a block diagram is related to the input by

$$C(s) = G(s)R(s)$$

where $G(s)$ is the transfer function. If the input is specified, then the output $c(t)$ is

★ $$c(t) = \mathcal{L}^{-1}[G(s)R(s)] \qquad (4\text{-}18)$$

If however we assumed that the input is a unit impulse $\delta(t)$, then $R(s) = 1$ and $C(s) = G(s)$. The output now becomes

★ $$c(t) = \mathcal{L}^{-1}[G(s)] = g(t) \qquad (4\text{-}19)$$

where $g(t)$ is the inverse Laplace transform of $G(s)$. The function $g(t)$ is called the *impulse response* of the control system which is identical to the transient response minus the term which is in the image of the excitation.

We can say then, that when a unit impulse is applied to a control system the output is the impulse response of the system. More important, the Laplace transform of the impulse response gives the transfer function $G(s)$ of the system under consideration. Theoretically, the measurement of the impulse response of a system provides a complete description of the control system. Since a true impulse is not practical, a pulse of very narrow width is an acceptable approximation for such analysis.

Although theoretically for any $r(t)$ the output $c(t)$ may be obtained as indicated by Eq. (4-18), the procedure becomes quite complex if not impossible if $R(s)$ is not readily available. This may happen if $r(t)$ is a very complex function and not easily Laplace transformable. When this happens we employ the complex convolution integral method. Consider the input $r(t)$ given by Fig. 4-11. Since $r(t)$ is approximated by a series of small

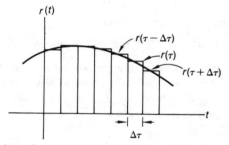

Fig. 4-11   Input $r(t)$ approximated by rectangular pulses.

rectangular pulses of width Δr, it may be approximated by the average value of the pulse in that interval, i.e. $r(\tau)$. The output c_1 due to one impulse is the strength of the impulse multiplied by the system response,

$$c_1 = g(t-\tau)r(\tau)\Delta\tau$$

and since the system is linear, the superposition theorem allows us to add up all the responses so that

$$c(t) \cong g(t-\tau+\Delta\tau)r(\tau-\Delta\tau)\Delta\tau + g(t-\tau)r(\tau)\Delta\tau$$
$$+ g(t-\tau-\Delta\tau)r(\tau+\Delta\tau)\Delta\tau + \cdots \qquad (4\text{-}20)$$

As $\Delta\tau \to 0$, the number of pulses increase and we have

$$c(t) = \int_{-\infty}^{t} g(t-\tau)r(\tau)d\tau$$

Defining $p = t - \tau$ and noting that $dp = -d\tau$, we have

★
$$c(t) = \int_0^\infty g(p)r(t-p)dp \qquad (4\text{-}21)$$

This is the convolution integral and is generally written as

$$c(t) = g(t) * r(t) \qquad (4\text{-}22)$$

With Eq. (4-22), the output may be obtained even for cases where $r(t)$ is a non-Laplace transformable function.

4-3 STEADY STATE RESPONSE

In addition to the transient response, we are interested in the steady state response, i.e. the character of the system after a very long time has elapsed. The steady state value of the error can be obtained by using the final value theorem,

★
$$e(t)\Big|_{t\to\infty} = \lim_{s\to 0} sE(s) \qquad (4\text{-}23)$$

provided a final value exists. Note that if a system is purely oscillatory, this theorem cannot be used. The steady state error, shown in Eq. (4-23), is important since it tells us how accurate the idealized system is. The steady state performance of a system is best defined in terms of *error constants* when the inputs are simple aperiodic inputs. These error constants for a unity feedback system are defined as

★
$$\left.\begin{array}{l} K_0 = \lim_{s\to 0} G(s) \\[4pt] K_1 = \lim_{s\to 0} sG(s) \\[4pt] K_2 = \lim_{s\to 0} s^2 G(s) \end{array}\right\} \qquad (4\text{-}24)$$

where K_0 is referred to as the positional error constant, K_1 as the velocity error constant, and K_2 as the acceleration error constant. The relationship between the steady state error and error constants may be readily shown.

The error for a unity feedback control system shown in Fig. 4-12 is

$$E(s) = \frac{R(s)}{1 + G(s)}$$

If the input is a unit step, then the steady state error becomes

$$e_{ss}(t) = \lim_{s\to 0} sE(s) = \lim_{s\to 0} s\left[\frac{1}{s}\frac{1}{1+G(s)}\right] = \frac{1}{1+K_0}$$

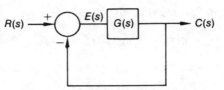

Fig. 4-12   Feedback control system.

If the input is a ramp input, then $R(s) = 1/s^2$ and

$$e_{ss}(t) = \lim_{s \to 0} s \left[\frac{1}{s^2} \frac{1}{1 + G(s)} \right] = \frac{1}{K_1}$$

For a parabolic input $R(s) = 1/s^3$ and

$$e_{ss}(t) = \lim_{s \to 0} s \left[\frac{1}{s^3} \frac{1}{1 + G(s)} \right] = \frac{1}{K_2}$$

We conclude then that K_0, K_1, and K_2 are measures of the system error in following a step, ramp, or parabolic input.

EXAMPLE 4-3

The open loop transfer function of the unity feedback control system shown in Fig. 4-12 is given by

$$G(s) = \frac{K}{s(As + B)}$$

Derive the steady state error and error coefficients for a step, ramp, and parabolic input. For a step input,

$$K_0 = \lim_{s \to 0} G(s) = \infty$$

$$e_{ss}(t) = \frac{1}{1 + K} = 0$$

which suggests that such a system can follow a step input without any steady state error.

If the input is a ramp, $R(s) = 1/s^2$, then

$$K_1 = \lim_{s \to 0} sG(s) = \lim_{s \to 0} \frac{sK}{s(As + B)} = \frac{K}{B}$$

and the steady state error becomes

$$e_{ss}(t) = \frac{B}{K}$$

Since K cannot be increased without bound, there is a physical limitation as to how small the steady state error may become.

Finally, if the input to this control system is parabolic, $R(s) = 1/s^3$, then $K_2 = 0$ and

$$e_{ss}(t) = \infty$$

i.e. this control system cannot follow a parabolic input as time becomes large.

The physical interpretation of the steady state error for different inputs is illustrated in Fig. 4-13. It is interesting to see how we can modify the control system of Example 4-3 so that it can follow, even with finite error, a parabolic input. A quick look at $G(s)$ indicates that if we introduce another pole at $s = 0$, then

$$G(s) = \frac{K}{s^2(As+B)}$$

and $K_2 = K/B$. This achieves two things. First, the error due to a ramp input goes to zero. Second, the error due to a parabolic input becomes finite. We may conclude, therefore, that the value of a specific error constant and the steady state error are dependent upon the number of poles

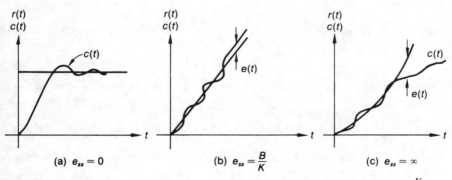

Fig. 4-13 Steady state error for a step, ramp, and parabolic input, $G(s) = \dfrac{K}{s(As+B)}$, $H(s) = 1$.

at the origin of the open loop transfer function. The rest of the polynomial does not contribute anything except of course the constant term.

The number of open loop poles for a unity feedback system is often used to classify control systems as to their type. A system having no open loop poles is a type 0 system; a system having one open loop pole is classified as a type 1 system and so on. The error constants as a function of system type are shown in Table 4-1.

Table 4-1   Error constants and steady state error, $e_{ss}(t)$.

Open Loop Poles at $s = 0$	System Type	Error Constants			Steady State Error, $e_{ss}(t)$		
		K_0	K_1	K_2	Position	Velocity	Acceleration
0	0	F	0	0	F	∞	∞
1	1	∞	F	0	0	F	∞
2	2	∞	∞	F	0	0	F
3	3	∞	∞	∞	0	0	0
	F – Nonzero and finite						

Error Series

When the inputs are not simple aperiodic signals, the steady state error can be expressed as a function of more general error coefficients. These error coefficients are meaningful for unity feedback systems or more general systems that can be represented as equivalent unity feedback systems.

Consider a unity feedback control system where the error in the Laplace domain is

$$E(s) = W(s)R(s)$$

and $W(s)$ is defined as

$$W(s) = \frac{1}{1 + G(s)}$$

From the theory of the convolution integral, we may write the error in the time domain as

$$\star \qquad e(t) = \int_{-\infty}^{t} w(\tau)r(t-\tau)d\tau \qquad (4\text{-}25)$$

where $w(\tau)$ is the inverse Laplace transform of $W(s)$ and τ is a dummy variable. Expressing $r(t-\tau)$ in a Taylor's series,

$$r(t-\tau) = r(t) - \tau\dot{r}(t) + \frac{\tau^2\ddot{r}(t)}{2!} - \frac{\tau^3\dddot{r}(t)}{3!} + \cdots$$

and recalling that $r(t) = 0$ for $t < 0$, Eq. (4-25) becomes

$$e(t) = \int_0^t w(\tau) \left[r(t) - \tau \dot{r}(t) + \frac{\tau^2 \ddot{r}(t)}{2!} + \cdots \right] d\tau$$

$$e(t) = \int_0^t w(\tau) r(t) \, d\tau - \int_0^t w(\tau) \tau \dot{r}(t) \, d\tau + \cdots$$

Now if we take the limit of $e(t)$ as t approaches infinity, we obtain the steady state error,

$$e_{ss}(t) = r(t) \int_0 w(\tau) \, d\tau - \dot{r}(t) \int_0 \tau w(\tau) \, d\tau + \cdots$$

Defining

$$C_0 = \int_0^\infty w(\tau) \, d\tau$$

$$C_1 = -\int_0^\infty \tau w(\tau) \, d\tau$$

$$C_n = \int_0^\infty (-1)^n \tau^n w(\tau) \, d\tau$$

the steady state error becomes

★
$$e_{ss}(t) = C_0 r(t) + C_1 \dot{r}(t) + C_2 \ddot{r}(t) + \cdots \qquad (4\text{-}26)$$

where $C_0, C_1, \ldots, C_n$ are the *generalized error coefficients* and Eq. (4-26) is referred to as the *error series*. We note that given any input, the steady state error, i.e. the difference between the steady state input and the steady state output, may be obtained *without* solving the complete system equation. For example, if the input is a step, then all the derivatives of $r(t)$ go to zero and the error series becomes

$$e_{ss}(t) = C_0 A$$

where $r(t) = A$. If the input $r(t) = At$, then $\dot{r}(t) = A$ and $\ddot{r}(t) = \dddot{r}(t) = \cdots = 0$ and

$$e_{ss}(t) = C_0(At) + C_1 A$$

We note that for this control system the steady state error goes to infinity as t goes to infinity if C_0 has any finite positive value. If the error is to be contained, i.e. stay within finite limits, then C_0 must go to zero. Since C_0 is determined by $\omega(\tau)$, its value is a characteristic of the control system.

Let us for a moment return to the definition of the generalized error coefficients. From the definition of the Laplace transform,

$$W(s) = \int_0^\infty w(\tau) e^{-s\tau} d\tau \qquad (4\text{-}27)$$

and taking the limit of Eq. (4-27) as $s \rightarrow 0$ we have

$$\lim_{s \to 0} W(s) = \int_0^\infty w(\tau)\,d\tau$$

But this is identical to the definition of the error coefficient C_0 so that

$$C_0 = \lim_{s \to 0} W(s)$$

Next we form $dW(s)/ds$

$$\frac{dW(s)}{ds} = -\int_0^\infty \tau w(\tau)\,e^{-s\tau}d\tau$$

Again taking the limit as $s \rightarrow 0$,

$$\lim_{s \to 0} \frac{dW(s)}{ds} = -\int_0^\infty \tau w(\tau)\,d\tau$$

and this defines C_1. We can see by now that in general,

★
$$C_n = \lim_{s \to 0} \frac{d^n W(s)}{ds^n} \tag{4-28}$$

which is certainly a lot simpler than the previous definition.

EXAMPLE 4-4

Obtain the error series for the second-order control system with the following transfer function:

$$\frac{E(s)}{R(s)} = W(s) = \frac{s^2}{s^2 + 2\delta\omega_n s + \omega_n^2}$$

From the definition of the error coefficients, we have

$$C_0 = \lim_{s \to 0} W(s) = 0$$

$$C_1 = \lim_{s \to 0} \frac{dW(s)}{ds} = 0$$

$$C_2 = \lim_{s \to 0} \frac{d^2 W(s)}{ds^2} = \frac{2}{\omega_n^2}$$

$$C_3 = \lim_{s \to 0} \frac{d^3 W(s)}{ds^3} = -\frac{12\delta}{\omega_n^3}$$

Substituting the error coefficient in Eq. (4-26), the steady state error becomes

$$e_{ss}(t) = \left(\frac{1}{\omega_n^2}\right)\ddot{r}(t) - \left(\frac{2\delta}{\omega_n^3}\right)\dddot{r}(t) + \cdots$$

Since the steady state error is a function of the second and higher derivatives of $r(t)$, the only way the steady state error can be zero or constant is if the input is at *most* parabolic.

The error series is seen to be a fairly general expression capable of yielding the steady state error for *any* class of inputs.

Since the error constants are a subset of the more general error coefficients, it is only natural that we see how they are related. For a type 0 system and unit step input, the error series yields

$$e_{ss}(t) = C_0$$

and since we established that the steady state error is related to the position error constant as

$$e_{ss}(t) = \frac{1}{1 + K_0}$$

we have

$$C_0 = \frac{1}{1 + K_0}$$

Similarly, for a type 1 system and a ramp input

$$e_{ss}(t) = C_1$$

and again since

$$e_{ss}(t) = \frac{1}{K_1}$$

we have

$$C_1 = \frac{1}{K_1}$$

Following this procedure we may relate as many of the error coefficients to the error constants as we desire. Substituting for the error coefficients in Eq. (4-26),

$$e_{ss}(t) = \frac{1}{1 + K_0}r(t) + \frac{1}{K_1}\dot{r}(t) + \frac{1}{K_2}\ddot{r}(t) + \cdots$$

Although this series looks general enough, we must caution ourselves with the understanding that its utility depends upon its convergence properties.

4-4   STABILITY VIA ROUTH–HURWITZ

We have seen how the response of a system is dependent upon the characteristic equation zeros. If the order of the characteristic polynomial is small, then it is generally not too difficult to obtain the zeros. However, if the order of the characteristic equation becomes large, then obtaining the zeros becomes nontrivial. The problem gets worse if some of the coefficients of the polynomial can vary and thereby cause some of the roots of the characteristic equation to move to the right half s-plane, as in the case of the positional servomechanism example considered in Section 4.2. It is therefore necessary that we have some means of knowing the admissable values of the coefficients of the characteristic equation that would insure system stability, i.e. to avoid roots that have real parts in the right half s-plane or multiple zeros on the imaginary axis. In this section we consider this problem and introduce a stability criteria that allows us to say whether the characteristic equation roots lie in the right half s-plane.

The Routh–Hurwitz stability criterion is a method for determining system stability from the characteristic equation.

Consider the characteristic polynomial† of a control system

★
$$a_n s^n + a_{n-1} s^{n-1} + \cdots + a_0 = 0 \qquad (4\text{-}29)$$

where a_n is positive and we form the Routh array as shown below.

s^n	a_n	a_{n-2}	$\cdots$	
s^{n-1}	a_{n-1}	a_{n-3}	$\cdots$ a_0	
s^{n-2}	b_1	b_2	b_3 $\cdots$ 0	
s^{n-3}	c_1	c_2	$\cdots$ 0	
s^{n-4}	d_1	d_2	$\cdots$	
$\vdots$				
s^0	a_0			

where

$$b_1 = -\frac{\begin{vmatrix} a_n & a_{n-2} \\ a_{n-1} & a_{n-3} \end{vmatrix}}{a_{n-1}} \qquad b_2 = -\frac{\begin{vmatrix} a_n & a_{n-4} \\ a_{n-1} & a_{n-5} \end{vmatrix}}{a_{n-1}} \qquad b_3 = -\frac{\begin{vmatrix} a_n & a_{n-6} \\ a_{n-1} & a_{n-7} \end{vmatrix}}{a_{n-1}}$$

†From the theory of equations we know that if any coefficients a_i is negative, then there must be roots with positive real parts. Also if any coefficient except a_0 is zero, then we either have roots with positive real parts or roots exist on the imaginary axis.

$$c_1 = - \frac{\begin{vmatrix} a_{n-1} & a_{n-3} \\ b_1 & b_2 \end{vmatrix}}{b_1} \qquad c_2 = - \frac{\begin{vmatrix} a_{n-1} & a_{n-5} \\ b_1 & b_3 \end{vmatrix}}{b_1} \qquad \cdots$$

$$d_1 = - \frac{\begin{vmatrix} b_1 & b_2 \\ c_1 & c_2 \end{vmatrix}}{c_1} \qquad d_2 = - \frac{\begin{vmatrix} b_1 & b_3 \\ c_1 & c_3 \end{vmatrix}}{c_1} \qquad \cdots \qquad (4\text{-}30)$$

The coefficients in the first two rows of the array are obtained from the characteristic polynomial, whereas the other coefficients are evaluated as indicated. In the course of evaluating a row, the terms of any row may be multiplied or divided by a positive quantity without altering the results. The coefficients are evaluated until a zero is obtained in each row. Once the table is complete, the Routh criterion states that

the number of zeros of the characteristic equation with positive real parts is equal to the number of sign changes in the first column of the coefficients in the Routh array.

Consider the characteristic equation given by

$$F(s) = s^3 + 6s^2 + 12s + 8 = 0$$

The Routh array becomes

s^3	1	12
s^2	6	8
s^1	$\frac{32}{3}$	0
$3s^1$	32	0
s^0	8	

The coefficients in the first row are $1, 6, \frac{32}{3}, 8$ and since there are no sign changes, then $F(s)$ has no zeros with positive real parts.

As another example consider the characteristic equation

$$s^3 + 3s^2 + 3s + 11 = 0$$

The Routh array becomes

s^3	1	3
s^2	3	11
s^1	$-\frac{2}{3}$	0
s^0	11	

There are two sign changes in the first column, therefore the characteristic equation has zeros that do have positive real parts and the system will naturally be unstable. When there are sign changes, the stability criterion states that

the number of zeros having positive real parts is equal to the number of sign changes in the first column.

In this example therefore, the characteristic equation has two zeros that have positive real roots.

Since the coefficients are dependent upon control system parameters, the Routh test is very useful in ascertaining values of system parameters that would insure stability. We see that in the next example.

EXAMPLE 4-5

For the servomechanism in Example 4-2 we obtained the value of the amplifier gain A that insures a stable response. The characteristic equation was

$$F(s) = s^3 + 262.5s^2 + 12500s + 250A = 0$$

The Routh array becomes

$$
\begin{array}{c|cc}
s^3 & 1 & 12500 \\
s^2 & 262.5 & 250A \\
\hline
s^1 & b_1 & b_2 \\
s^0 & c_1 &
\end{array}
\qquad
\begin{aligned}
b_1 &= \frac{(12500)(262.5) - 250A}{262.5} \\
b_2 &= 0 \\
c_1 &= 250A
\end{aligned}
$$

Since b_1 and c_1 must be positive for stability, we know that A must be positive and

$$[(262.5)(12500) - 250A] > 0$$

or

$$A < 13125$$

which is why the first time around the response was unstable since we had selected $A = 26.25 \times 10^4$. The application of the Routh–Hurwitz criterion therefore yields the range of system parameters that insure stability.

In constructing the Routh array, there is one problem that is often encountered which prevents us from completing the array. Referring back to the original array we observe that if any of the coefficients in the first column goes to zero (except the last), then the next coefficient cannot be evaluated. Consider the following characteristic equation,

$$F(s) = a_6s^6 + a_5s^5 + a_4s^4 + a_3s^3 + a_2s^2 + a_1s + a_0 = 0$$

The Routh array is formed till we reach the fourth row where the first coefficient vanishes but $c_2 \neq 0$. We replace

s^6	a_6	a_4	a_2	a_0
s^5	a_5	a_3	a_1	
s^4	b_1	b_2	b_3	
s^3	$c_1 = 0$	c_2		
s^3	$c_1 \to \epsilon$	c_2		
s^2	d_1	d_2		
s^1	e_1	e_2		
s^0	f_1			

c_1 by $\epsilon > 0$ and continue,

$$d_1 = \frac{\epsilon b_2 - b_1 c_2}{\epsilon}; \qquad d_2 = \frac{\epsilon b_3 - 0}{\epsilon} = b_3$$

As an example, consider the characteristic equation

$$F_4 = s^4 + 2s^3 + 4s^2 + 8s + 10 = 0$$

The array becomes

s^4	1	4	10
s^3	2	8	
s^2	0	10	
	ϵ	10	
s^1	b_1	b_2	
s^0	c_1		

$$b_1 = \frac{8\epsilon - 20}{\epsilon} \quad b_2 = 0 \quad c_1 = 10$$

Since ϵ is very small and positive, $(8\epsilon - 20)/\epsilon$ is negative. This means that there are two sign changes in the first column and therefore $F(s)$ has two roots with positive real parts.

The previous method of replacing the coefficient cannot be used if *all* the coefficients of a row go to zero. Let us assume that the unfinished

Routh array looks like

$$
\begin{array}{c|cccc}
s^6 & a_6 & a_4 & a_2 & a_0 \\
s^5 & a_5 & a_3 & a_1 & \\
\hline
s^4 & b_1 & b_2 & b_3 & \\
s^3 & 0 & 0 & 0 &
\end{array}
$$

The presence of such a row indicates the existence of two roots having the same magnitude but opposite sign. A pair of purely imaginary roots or four roots symmetrically located about the origin of the s-plane would cause a vanishing row. We proceed with the construction of the Routh array by forming what is known as the *auxiliary equation*,

$$A_1(s) = b_1 s^4 + b_2 s^2 + b_3$$

Notice that b_1, b_2, and b_3 are constants appearing in the row above the zero row. The derivative of $A(s)$ is used to form a new s^3 row,

$$
\begin{array}{c|ccc}
s^4 & b_1 & b_2 & b_3 \\
\hline
s^3 & 0 & 0 & 0 \\
 & 4b_1 & 2b_2 & \\
\hline
s^2 & c_1 & \cdots &
\end{array}
\qquad
\begin{aligned}
\frac{dA_1(s)}{ds} &= (4b_1)s^3 + (2b_2)s \\[2mm]
c_1 &= \frac{4b_1 b_2 - 2b_1 b_2}{4b_1} = \tfrac{1}{2}b_2
\end{aligned}
$$

and the procedure is continued as before. If no additional rows go to zero and the first column has no sign changes, the system is stable. However, if another row goes to zero as indicated,

$$
\begin{array}{c|ccc}
s^4 & b_1 & b_2 & b_3 \\
\hline
s^3 & 0 & 0 & 0 \\
 & (4b_1) & (2b_2) & \\
\hline
s^2 & c_1 & c_2 & 0 \\
s^1 & 0 & 0 &
\end{array}
$$

then we not only have another pair of roots that are negative of each other but they are also equal to the previous roots. The auxiliary equation now becomes

$$A_2(s) = c_1 s^2 + c_2$$

The array is completed as follows

$$
\begin{array}{c|cc}
s^2 & c_1 & c_2 \\
\hline
s^1 & (2c_1) & 0 \\
s^0 & c_2 &
\end{array}
\qquad
\frac{dA_2(s)}{ds} = (2c_1)s
$$

Although there are no sign changes we do have repeating roots. The roots of the characteristic equation may be obtained by solving the auxiliary equation,

$$A_2(s) = c_1 s^2 + c_2 = 0$$

$$s = \pm j\sqrt{\frac{c_2}{c_1}}$$

The two sets of roots, that are negative of each other, are $+j\sqrt{c_2/c_1}$, $-j\sqrt{c_2/c_1}$, and $+j\sqrt{c_2/c_1}$, $-j\sqrt{c_2/c_1}$. When roots like this appear, then we expect to see response in the time domain having the form $t \sin (\sqrt{c_2/c_1}\, t)$, i.e. oscillatory motion whose magnitude increases linearly. Clearly this is an unstable phenomena. We therefore modify our Routh criterion to state that *a stable system requires no sign changes in the first column and at most one vanishing row.*

EXAMPLE 4-6

A control system has the following characteristic equation

$$F(s) = s^7 + 2s^6 + s^5 + 2s^4 - s^3 - 2s^2 - s - 2 = 0$$

Construct the Routh array and determine system stability.
The Routh array becomes

$$
\begin{array}{c|cccc}
s^7 & 1 & 1 & -1 & -1 \\
s^6 & 2 & 2 & -2 & -2 \\
\hline
s^6 & 1 & 1 & -1 & -1 \\
s^5 & 0 & 0 & 0 & 0
\end{array}
\qquad \text{(Dividing by 2)}
$$

The auxiliary equation and its derivative are

$$A_1(s) = s^6 + s^4 - s^2 + 1; \qquad \frac{dA_1(s)}{ds} = 6s^5 + 4s^3 - 2s$$

The array is continued as

s^6	1	1	-1	-1
s^5	6	4	-2	(New row)

s^5	3	2	-1	(Divide by 2)
s^4	$\frac{1}{3}$	$-\frac{2}{3}$	-1	
s^4	1	-2	-3	(Multiply by 3)
s^3	8	8		
s^2	-3	-3		(Divide by 1)
s^2	-1	-1		
s^1	0	0		

we have another vanishing row indicating a set of equal and opposite roots. Again forming the auxiliary equation

s^2	-1	-1	$A_2(s) = -1s^2 - 1$
s^1	(-2)	0	$\dfrac{dA_2(s)}{ds} = -2s$
s^0	$-\frac{1}{2}$		

The roots that appear as a set may be obtained by solving the auxiliary equation

$$A_2(s) = -s^2 - 1 = 0; \qquad s = \pm j$$

All the roots of the polynomial are shown in Fig. 4-14. Since there was

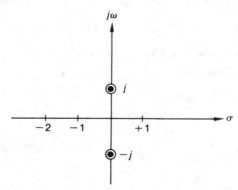

Fig. 4-14   Roots of $s^7 + 2s^6 + s^5 + 2s^4 - s^3 - 2s^2 - s - 2$.

one sign reversal in the first column one root exists in the right half s-plane. The system is unstable.

SUMMARY

This chapter has dwelt upon the analysis of control systems in the time domain via the classical method.

The transient response was seen to depend upon the roots of the characteristic equation, or the closed loop poles, and not on the type of input. The form of response was directly related to the location of these poles on the complex s-plane. It was seen that the response became uncontrollably large if the poles were in the right half s-plane or repeated on the imaginary axis.

The steady state response was studied using error constants.

System stability was analyzed via Routh–Hurwitz which is a criteria that determines if, and how many, roots of the characteristic equation exist in the right half s-plane. This criterion can also be used for ascertaining the range of system parameters that insure stability.

PROBLEMS

4-1. Obtain $c(t)$ for a step input to the control system shown in Fig. P4-1. Assume system is underdamped.

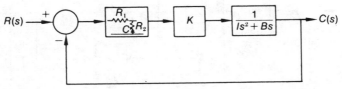

Fig. P4-1

4-2. The overall transfer function for a control system is given by

$$\frac{C(s)}{R(s)} = \frac{s^2 + 2}{(s+1)^2(s^2 + 2s + 4)}$$

Obtain $c(t)$ if $r(t) = 2$. What is the maximum value of $c(t)$?

4-3. The block diagram of a simplified servo is shown in Fig. P4-3. Obtain $c(t)$ if $r(t) = 1$ and $K = 2$. At what time does $c(t)$ reach its first peak? What is the percent overshoot of the response?

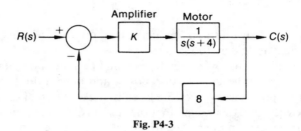

Fig. P4-3

4-4. Obtain $c(t)$ for the positional servo shown in Fig. 4-10b if $A = 13,100$.

4-5. A d-c positional servomechanism is shown in Fig. P4-5. Derive the overall transfer function if

$$T_1 \approx 0$$
$$K_f = 1.0$$
$$K_1 = 0.5$$
$$T_2 = 0.04$$

Obtain $\theta(t)$ if $\theta_i(t)$ is a unit step input. Obtain the peak overshoot.

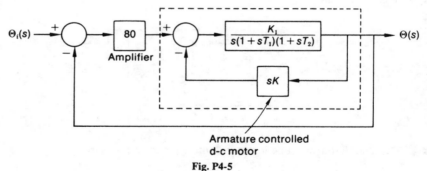

Fig. P4-5

4-6. Find the partial fraction expansion for

(a) $F(s) = \dfrac{1}{(s+1)(s+2)(s+3)}$

(b) $F(s) = \dfrac{1}{s(s+1)^2}$

4-7. Obtain $f(t)$ for the following,

(a) $F(s) = \dfrac{1}{(s^2+s+3)^2}$

(b) $F(s) = \dfrac{6s^2+1}{s^2(s+3)(s^2+2s+3)}$

(c) $F(s) = \dfrac{s^2+s+1}{s^2+3s+8}$

4-8. Apply the Routh–Hurwitz criterion to the following characteristic polynomials, and determine for what range of the parameter K is the system stable.

(a) $s^3+s^2+Ks+2=0$
(b) $s^4+2s^3+2s^2+Ks+5=0$
(c) $s^5+s^4+Ks^3+8s^2+s+K=0$
(d) $s^3+22s^2+9s+K=0$
(e) $s^3+Ks^2+8s+200=0$

4-9. Under what conditions will the systems characterized by Problem 4-8d exhibit pure oscillations?

4-10. Obtain the value of K for which the system of Problem 4-8e exhibits pure oscillations. What is the frequency of these oscillations?

4-11. A closed loop unity feedback system has the following forward loop transfer function

$$G(s) = \frac{K}{s^2(s+A)}$$

What is the steady state value of the error and the output if the input is
(a) Ramp
(b) Step
(c) Sin ωt
If you cannot obtain the answer to any of the above three questions, explain why.

4-12. What is the steady state error and output for Problem 4-5?.

4-13. Show that the inverted pendulum and the cart of Problem 2-15 comprise an unstable system with characteristic roots at $0, 0, \sqrt{g/l}, -\sqrt{g/l}$.

4-14. The attitude stabilization for a vertical takeoff aircraft is shown in Fig. P4-14. Obtain the transient response to a unit step input. What is the steady state error to a constant disturbance? Let $a=0.5, b=10, c=3, K_A=1, K_B=17$, and $K_C=1$.

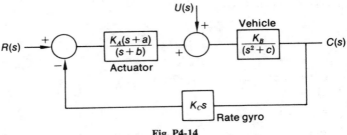

Fig. P4-14

4-15. How do changes in K_C effect the output of VTOL described in Problem 4-14?

4-16. A simplified control system for the speed setting of a gasoline engine is shown in Fig. P4-16. The lag τ_1 and τ_2 occur at the carburetor and the engine itself. The lag τ_3 is the time constant associated with the speed measurement. If the steady state error of 10% of the reference setting is desired, what must the gain be? Suggest some typical values of $\tau_1, \tau_2,$ and τ_3.

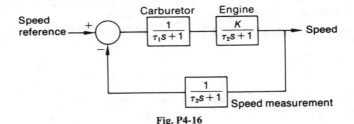

Fig. P4-16

4-17. A control system for controlling the temperature of a liquid container is shown in Fig. P4-17. The controller operates the solenoid valve which allows refrigerant to flow into the evaporator coil. Assume that the valve takes τ seconds to open fully and that the percentage opening varies linearly with time. Obtain the overall transfer function and obtain $T(t)$ if the desired temperature is suddenly *decreased* to T_L. State your assumptions. Does the response agree with the answer you arrive at intuitively?

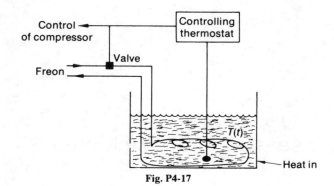

Fig. P4-17

REFERENCES

1. Cannon, R. H., *Dynamics of Physical Systems*, New York, McGraw-Hill, 1967.
2. Elgerd, O. I., *Control Systems Theory*, New York, McGraw-Hill, 1967.
3. Kuo, B. C., *Automatic Control Systems*, Englewood Cliffs, N.J., Prentice-Hall, 1962.
4. Harrison, H. L., and J. G. Bolinger, *Introduction to Automatic Controls*, 2nd Edition, Scranton, International Textbook, 1969.
5. Horowitz, I. M., *Synthesis of Feedback Systems*, New York, Academic Press, 1963.
6. Langill, A. W., *Automatic Control Systems Engineering*, Vol. I, Englewood Cliffs, N.J., Prentice-Hall, 1965.
7. Lewis, L. J., D. K. Reynolds, F. R. Bergseth, and F. J. Alexander, *Linear Systems Analysis*, New York, McGraw-Hill, 1969.
8. Koppel, L. B., *Introduction to Control Theory with Applications to Process Control*, Englewood Cliffs, N.J., Prentice-Hall, 1968.
9. Routh, E. J., *A Treatise on the Stability of a Given State of Motion*, London, Macmillan, 1877.
10. dePian, L., *Linear Active Network Theory*, Englewood Cliffs, N.J., Prentice-Hall, 1962.
11. Clark, R. N., *Introduction to Automatic Control Systems*, New York, Wiley, 1962.
12. Atkinson, P., *Feedback Control Theory for Engineers*, New York, Plenum Press, 1968.
13. Smith, O. J., *Feedback Control Systems*, New York, McGraw-Hill, 1958.
14. Ruzicka, J. E., "Active Vibration and Shock Isolation," *SAE Transactions*, paper 680747, 1968.
15. Gardner, M. F., and J. L. Barnes, *Transients in Linear Systems*, Vol. I, New York, Wiley, 1942.
16. Hildebrand, F. B., *Methods of Applied Mathematics*, Englewood Cliffs, N.J., Prentice-Hall, 1961.

5

Response — State Space Methods

5-1 INTRODUCTION

We have dealt with the analysis of systems that were represented by higher-order linear differential equations with constant coefficients. The response of the system was obtained via classical techniques that rely on operational mathematics. Such an approach is the direct growth of techniques developed in mechanical vibration theory and electrical network theory. It is very attractive when we study a single output of a system subjected to a single input. However, modern systems tend to get quite complex and it becomes not only necessary to study several inputs and outputs simultaneously but also the behavior of variables inside the control system. This can be most effectively achieved by the use of state space techniques where the system is represented by first-order differential equations and the analysis exploits matrix theory.† Since the characterization of systems in matrix form requires much computational time, the use of a digital computer becomes imperative. With the advent of faster computers the state space technique has enabled us to tackle some very complex but interesting systems.

The vector-matrix differential equation representation was introduced in Chapter 3 and it was also shown how it is related to the system transfer function. Here we shall be concerned with obtaining the response of the system represented in state space notation. We will also establish the stability of the system by investigating the nature of the eigenvalues of the coefficient matrix.

†A brief review of the fundamentals of matrix theory appears in Appendix C.

5-2 SOLUTION OF THE STATE EQUATION

The solution of the state equation will contain two parts, viz. the transient and steady state. Since the procedure is the same whether we seek the transient or steady state solution, we shall concern ourselves with the transient solution. There are several techniques of obtaining the solution of these equations. The technique using the Laplace transforms may be used to directly relate to the classical methods developed so far. The other methods involve the expansion of the state vector in Taylor's series.

The Laplace Transform Approach

The state equation was

★
$$\dot{\mathbf{x}}(t) = \mathbf{A}\mathbf{x}(t) + \mathbf{b}r(t) \tag{5-1}$$

Taking the Laplace transform of Eq. (5-1) and assuming $x(0)$ as the initial state vector (i.e. the initial condition) we obtain

$$s\mathbf{X}(s) - \mathbf{x}(0) = \mathbf{A}\mathbf{X}(s) + \mathbf{b}R(s) \tag{5-2}$$

where

$$\mathbf{x}(0) = \begin{bmatrix} x_1(0) \\ \vdots \\ x_n(0) \end{bmatrix} \quad \text{and} \quad \mathbf{X}(s) = \begin{bmatrix} X_1(s) \\ \vdots \\ X_n(s) \end{bmatrix}$$

Rewriting this,

$$[s\mathbf{I} - \mathbf{A}]\mathbf{X}(s) = \mathbf{x}(0) + \mathbf{b}R(s)$$

where $\mathbf{I}$ is the identity matrix. Solving the matrix equation,

★
$$\mathbf{X}(s) = [s\mathbf{I} - \mathbf{A}]^{-1}[\mathbf{x}(0) + \mathbf{b}R(s)] \tag{5-3}$$

The inverse Laplace transform of Eq. (5-3) yields

★
$$\mathbf{x}(t) = \left[\mathscr{L}^{-1}[s\mathbf{I} - \mathbf{A}]^{-1} \right]\mathbf{x}(0) + \mathscr{L}^{-1}\left[[s\mathbf{I} - \mathbf{A}]^{-1}\mathbf{b}R(s) \right] \tag{5-4}$$

The output for the system given by Eq. (5-1) is

★
$$y(t) = \mathbf{c}\mathbf{x}(t) \tag{5-5}$$

Taking the Laplace transform,

$$Y(s) = \mathbf{c}\mathbf{X}(s)$$

Substituting Eq. (5-3),

★
$$Y(s) = \mathbf{c}[s\mathbf{I} - \mathbf{A}]^{-1}\mathbf{x}(0) + c[s\mathbf{I} - \mathbf{A}]^{-1}\mathbf{b}R(s) \tag{5-6}$$

where the first term represents the transient or homogeneous part, whereas the second term represents the steady state part. Here we shall concern ourselves with the first part which can be rewritten if we observe that

$$[s\mathbf{I} - \mathbf{A}]^{-1} = \frac{\text{adj } [s\mathbf{I} - \mathbf{A}]}{\det [s\mathbf{I} - \mathbf{A}]} \tag{5-7}$$

where adj is the adjoint and det is the determinant. The homogeneous solution becomes

★
$$\mathbf{x}(t) = \mathscr{L}^{-1} \left[\frac{\text{adj } [s\mathbf{I} - \mathbf{A}]}{\det [s\mathbf{I} - \mathbf{A}]} \right] \mathbf{x}(0) \tag{5-8}$$

★
$$y(t) = \mathbf{c}\mathscr{L}^{-1} \left[\frac{\text{adj } [s\mathbf{I} - \mathbf{A}]}{\det [s\mathbf{I} - \mathbf{A}]} \right] \mathbf{x}(0) \tag{5-9}$$

Here the equation

★
$$\det [s\mathbf{I} - \mathbf{A}] = 0 \tag{5-10}$$

is the *characteristic equation* of the system.

EXAMPLE 5-1

A system is characterized by

$$\dot{x}_1(t) = 0$$
$$\dot{x}_2(t) = ax_1(t) - ax_2(t)$$

and the output vector is $\mathbf{c} = \begin{bmatrix} 1 & 2 \end{bmatrix}$. If $x_1(0) = 1$ and $x_2(0) = 2$, determine the output.

The coefficient matrix becomes

$$\mathbf{A} = \begin{bmatrix} 0 & 0 \\ a & -a \end{bmatrix}$$

and

$$[s\mathbf{I} - \mathbf{A}]^{-1} = \frac{1}{s(s+a)} \begin{bmatrix} s+a & 0 \\ a & s \end{bmatrix}$$

The characteristic equation is $s(s+a) = 0$. Therefore the above equation may be written as

$$[s\mathbf{I} - \mathbf{A}]^{-1} = \frac{1}{as} \begin{bmatrix} a & 0 \\ a & 0 \end{bmatrix} - \frac{1}{a(s+a)} \begin{bmatrix} 0 & 0 \\ a & -a \end{bmatrix}$$

so that

$$\mathbf{x}(t) = \mathscr{L}^{-1}[s\mathbf{I} - \mathbf{A}]^{-1}\mathbf{x}(0) = \begin{bmatrix} 1 & 0 \\ 1 - e^{-at} & e^{-at} \end{bmatrix} \begin{bmatrix} x_1(0) \\ x_2(0) \end{bmatrix}$$

Carrying out the matrix multiplication and letting $x_1(0) = 1, x_2(0) = 2$

$$\begin{bmatrix} x_1(t) \\ x_2(t) \end{bmatrix} = \begin{bmatrix} 1 \\ 1 + e^{-at} \end{bmatrix}$$

The output is

$$y(t) = \mathbf{c}\mathbf{x}(t) = x_1(t) + 2x_2(t)$$
$$y(t) = 3 + 2e^{-at}$$

EXAMPLE 5-2

Obtain the characteristic equation for the system characterized by the following set of differential equations,

$$\dot{x}_1(t) = x_2(t)$$
$$\dot{x}_2(t) = x_3(t)$$
$$\dot{x}_3(t) = -6x_1(t) - 11x_2(t) - 6x_3(t)$$

The coefficient matrix becomes

$$\mathbf{A} = \begin{bmatrix} 0 & 1 & 0 \\ 0 & 0 & 1 \\ -6 & -11 & -6 \end{bmatrix}$$

Forming $[s\mathbf{I} - \mathbf{A}]^{-1}$

$$[s\mathbf{I} - \mathbf{A}]^{-1} = \frac{1}{P(s)} \begin{bmatrix} s^2 + 6s + 11 & s + 6 & 1 \\ -6 & s^2 + 6s & s \\ -6s & -11s - 6 & s^2 \end{bmatrix}$$

where the characteristic equation $P(s)$ is

$$P(s) = s^3 + 6s^2 + 11s + 6$$

having zeros equal to $-1, -2$, and -3.

The procedure of taking the inverse Laplace transform may be formalized as we did for polynomials in Chapter 4. Let us define the matrix $\Phi(s)$ as

$$\Phi(s) = \frac{\text{adj } [s\mathbf{I} - \mathbf{A}]}{\det [s\mathbf{I} - \mathbf{A}]} = [s\mathbf{I} - \mathbf{A}]^{-1} \tag{5-11}$$

The characteristic equation here is $\det [s\mathbf{I} - \mathbf{A}] = 0$ and its roots are $-s_1$,

$-s_2, -s_3, \ldots, -s_n$. Therefore the $\Phi(s)$ matrix may be expressed as

$$\star \qquad \Phi(s) = \frac{[\mathbf{K}]_1}{s + s_1} + \frac{[\mathbf{K}]_2}{s + s_2} + \cdots \frac{[\mathbf{K}]_n}{s + s_n} \qquad (5\text{-}12)$$

where $[\mathbf{K}]_n$ is an undetermined coefficient matrix. If the roots of the characteristic equation $\det[s\mathbf{I} - \mathbf{A}] = 0$ are distinct, then the undetermined coefficient matrix may be determined by

$$[\mathbf{K}]_i = \lim_{s \to -s_i} \left[[s\mathbf{I} - \mathbf{A}]^{-1}(s + s_i) \right] \qquad (5\text{-}13)$$

If however there is a multiple root, then the matrix becomes

$$\star \qquad \Phi(s) = \frac{[\mathbf{K}]_1}{s + s_1} + \frac{[\mathbf{K}]_2}{s + s_2} + \frac{[\mathbf{K}]_3}{(s + s_2)^2} + \cdots + \frac{[\mathbf{K}]_n}{s + s_{n-1}} \qquad (5\text{-}14)$$

In this case all the matrices, except $[\mathbf{K}]_2$ and $[\mathbf{K}]_3$, may be evaluated using the previous method. $[\mathbf{K}]_2$ and $[\mathbf{K}]_3$ are evaluated from

$$[\mathbf{K}]_2 = \lim_{s \to -s_2} \frac{d}{ds} \left[[s\mathbf{I} - \mathbf{A}]^{-1}(s + s_2)^2 \right]$$

$$[\mathbf{K}]_3 = \lim_{s \to -s_2} \left[[s\mathbf{I} - \mathbf{A}]^{-1}(s + s_2)^2 \right]$$

This method is referred to as a generalization of Heaviside's expansion.

Once the constants in Eq. (5-12) or Eq. (5-14) are evaluated the inverse Laplace transform yields

$$\phi(t) = [\mathbf{K}]_1 e^{-s_1 t} + \cdots + [\mathbf{K}]_n e^{-s_n t} \qquad (5\text{-}15)$$

or for multiple roots it yields

$$\phi(t) = [\mathbf{K}]_1 e^{-s_1 t} + [\mathbf{K}]_2 e^{-s_2 t} + [\mathbf{K}]_3 t\, e^{-s_2 t} + \cdots \qquad (5\text{-}16)$$

Consider the mechanical system shown in Fig. 5-1. The governing differential equations are

$$\ddot{x}(t) + \frac{B}{m_1} \dot{x}(t) + \frac{k}{m_1} x(t) - \frac{m_2 g}{m_1} \theta(t) = 0$$

$$\ddot{\theta}(t) - \frac{B}{m_1 L} \dot{x}(t) - \frac{k}{m_1 L} x(t) + \frac{m_1 + m_2}{m_1 L} g\theta(t) = 0$$

We wish to obtain the state vector $\mathbf{x}(t)$. The state equation can be obtained by first defining the state variables,

$$x_1(t) = x(t); \qquad x_2(t) = \dot{x}(t); \qquad x_3(t) = \theta(t); \qquad x_4(t) = \dot{\theta}(t)$$

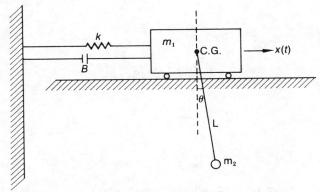

Fig. 5-1   A mechanical system.

and then substituting, we obtain

$$\dot{x}_1(t) = x_2(t)$$

$$\dot{x}_2(t) = -\frac{k}{m_1}x_1(t) - \frac{B}{m_1}x_2(t) + \frac{m_2 g}{m_1}x_3(t)$$

$$\dot{x}_3(t) = x_4(t)$$

$$\dot{x}_4(t) = \frac{k}{m_1 L}x_1(t) + \frac{B}{m_1 L}x_2(t) - \frac{m_1 + m_2}{m_1 L}g x_3(t)$$

which can be written as

$$\dot{\mathbf{x}}(t) = \mathbf{A}\mathbf{x}(t)$$

where

$$\mathbf{A} = \begin{bmatrix} 0 & 1 & 0 & 0 \\ -\dfrac{k}{m_1} & -\dfrac{B}{m_1} & \dfrac{m_2 g}{m_1} & 0 \\ 0 & 0 & 0 & 1 \\ \dfrac{k}{m_1 L} & \dfrac{B}{m_1 L} & -\dfrac{(m_1 + m_2)g}{m_1 L} & 0 \end{bmatrix}$$

The characteristic equation is

$$\det[s\mathbf{I} - \mathbf{A}] = 0$$

Substituting and carrying out the algebra we obtain

$$s^4 + \beta_3 s^3 + \beta_2 s^2 + \beta_1 s + \beta_0 = 0$$

where

$$\beta_3 = \frac{B}{m_1}$$

$$\beta_2 = \frac{(m_1 + m_2)g + kL}{m_1 L}$$

$$\beta_1 = \frac{Bg}{m_1 L}$$

$$\beta_0 = \frac{kg}{m_1 L}$$

The solution of the state equation depends upon the constants β_0, β_1, β_2, β_3. Let us assume that the physical system is such that the characteristic polynomial becomes

$$P(s) = s^4 + 5s^3 + 10s^2 + 10s + 4$$

The roots of this are

$$s = -1, -2, -1 - j, -1 + j$$

and the solution becomes

$$x(t) = \left[[K]_1 e^{-t} + [K]_2 e^{-2t} + [K]_3 e^{-t} \sin (t + \phi) \right] x(0)$$

where the constant matrices can be easily evaluated using the method shown previously.

EXAMPLE 5-3

A control system is characterized by the following coefficient matrix

$$A = \begin{bmatrix} 0 & 1 \\ 0 & -2 \end{bmatrix}$$

where the time response is $x(t) = \phi(t)x(0)$. Evaluate $\phi(t)$.

The roots of the characteristic equation $s(s + 2) = 0$ are

$$s = 0, -2$$

The $\Phi(s)$ matrix becomes

$$\Phi(s) = \frac{[K]_1}{s} + \frac{[K]_2}{s + 2}$$

and the undetermined coefficient matrices may be directly evaluated

$$[\mathbf{K}]_1 = \lim_{s \to 0} [s\mathbf{I} - \mathbf{A}]^{-1}s = \frac{1}{2}\begin{bmatrix} 2 & 1 \\ 0 & 0 \end{bmatrix}$$

$$[\mathbf{K}]_2 = \lim_{s \to -2} [s\mathbf{I} - \mathbf{A}]^{-1}(s+2) = -\frac{1}{2}\begin{bmatrix} 0 & 1 \\ 0 & -2 \end{bmatrix}$$

Substituting in the expression for $\Phi(s)$

$$\Phi(s) = \frac{1}{2s}\begin{bmatrix} 2 & 1 \\ 0 & 0 \end{bmatrix} - \frac{1}{2(s+2)}\begin{bmatrix} 0 & 1 \\ 0 & -2 \end{bmatrix}$$

Taking the inverse Laplace transform and adding we obtain $\phi(t)$

$$\phi(t) = \begin{bmatrix} 1 & \frac{1}{2}(1 - e^{-2t}) \\ 0 & e^{-2t} \end{bmatrix}$$

The Transition Matrix

If $\mathbf{x}(t)$ is expanded in a Taylor's series about $t = 0$, it can be shown that for a homogeneous equation

$$\mathbf{x}(t) = \left(\mathbf{I} + t\mathbf{A} + \frac{t^2}{2!}\mathbf{A}^2 + \cdots\right)\mathbf{x}(0) \tag{5-17}$$

where $\mathbf{A}$ is the coefficient matrix. The series in the bracket is the convergent infinite series of $e^{\mathbf{A}t}$, and therefore

$$\mathbf{x}(t) = e^{\mathbf{A}t}\mathbf{x}(0) \tag{5-18}$$

If we define a condition $\mathbf{x}(t_0)$ at $t_0 \neq 0$, then for a homogeneous equation

★ $$\mathbf{x}(t) = e^{\mathbf{A}(t-t_0)}\mathbf{x}(t_0) \tag{5-19}$$

The matrix exponential in the above equation is referred to as the *transition matrix* or the fundamental matrix $\phi(t - t_0)$,

★ $$e^{\mathbf{A}(t-t_0)} = \phi(t - t_0) \tag{5-20}$$

The state vector and the output in terms of the transition matrix becomes

★ $$\mathbf{x}(t) = \phi(t - t_0)\mathbf{x}(t_0) \tag{5-21}$$

★ $$y(t) = \mathbf{c}\phi(t - t_0)\mathbf{x}(t_0) \tag{5-22}$$

If the equation is not homogeneous, then

★
$$x(t) = \phi(t - t_0) x(t_0) + \int_{t_0}^{t} \phi(t - \alpha) \mathbf{b} r(\alpha) \, d\alpha \qquad (5\text{-}23)$$

★
$$y(t) = \mathbf{c}\phi(t - t_0) x(t_0) + \int_{t_0}^{t} \mathbf{c}\phi(t - \alpha) \mathbf{b} r(\alpha) \, d\alpha \qquad (5\text{-}24)$$

An examination of Eq. (5-20) indicates that the transition matrix transfers the state of the system from t_i to t_{i+1}. As a matter of fact this matrix contains all the information necessary to define the state of a system at any time. Indeed, if the transition matrix defined by Eq. (5-20) is obtained, then the system may be analyzed directly in the time domain. This is by far the most important reason why the transition matrix is particularly useful. Some of the more useful properties of the transition matrix are:

(1) The transition matrix is nonsingular and its inverse exists for all t.
(2) It is the solution to the matrix differential equation

$$\dot{\phi}(t - t_0) = \mathbf{A}\phi(t - t_0)$$

(3) It has the property that $\phi(t_0 - t_0) = \mathbf{I}$.
(4) It has a simple inverse, i.e. $\phi^{-1}(t) = \phi(-t)$. (Such matrices are called symplectic.)
(5) The transition matrix has a sequential property, i.e.

$$\phi(t_{i+2} - t_i) = \phi(t_{i+2} - t_{i+1})\phi(t_{i+1} - t_i)$$

This sequence of finite transitions will help when we make manipulations with $\phi(t - t_0)$.
(6) $\phi(t) = \mathscr{L}^{-1}[[s\mathbf{I} - \mathbf{A}]^{-1}]$.

Having obtained the solution of the matrix differential equation in terms of the transition matrix, let us see how we may evaluate this transition matrix.

The output in terms of the transition is

$$\mathbf{x}(t) = \phi(t)\mathbf{x}(0)$$

This equation may be expanded and written as

$$x_1(t) = \phi_{11} x_1(0) + \cdots + \phi_{1n} x_n(0)$$
$$x_2(t) = \phi_{21} x_1(0) + \cdots + \phi_{2n} x_n(0)$$
$$\vdots \qquad\qquad\qquad\qquad \vdots$$
$$x_n(t) = \phi_{n1} x_1(0) + \cdots + \phi_{nn} x_n(0)$$

where ϕ_{ij} are, in general, functions of time and $x_j(0)$ represent initial conditions. If $x_j(0)$ is unity, then ϕ_{ij} may be interpreted as a response to a unit initial condition. If a signal flow diagram were constructed, then ϕ_{ij} would be the response at the ith integrator (or node) for a unit input at the jth integrator (or node). This notion is identical to the transfer impedance or admittance characterization in vibration or network theory.

EXAMPLE 5-4

Obtain the transition matrix for the control system of Example 5-1. The state equation is expanded and written as

$$\begin{bmatrix} x_1(t) \\ x_2(t) \end{bmatrix} = \begin{bmatrix} \phi_{11}(t) & \phi_{12}(t) \\ \phi_{21}(t) & \phi_{22}(t) \end{bmatrix} \begin{bmatrix} x_1(0) \\ x_2(0) \end{bmatrix}$$

where each element $\phi_{ij}(t)$ of the transition matrix must be evaluated. Recalling that $\phi_{ij}(t)$ is the response at the jth node for a unit input at the ith node and referring to Fig. 5-2, we have

ϕ_{11} = response measured at 1 for unit input at 1
    = 1

ϕ_{12} = response measured at 1 for unit input at 2
    = 0 (direction of the signal flow tells us why)

ϕ_{21} = response measured at 2 for unit input at 1
    = $\mathscr{L}^{-1}[a/s(a+s)]$
    = $1 - e^{-at}$

ϕ_{22} = response measured at 2 for unit input at 2
    = $\mathscr{L}^{-1}[1/s+a]$
    = e^{-at}

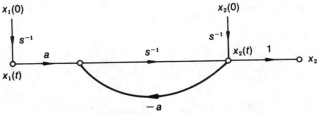

Fig. 5-2   State variable diagram for $a/(s+a)$.

In evaluating each $\phi_{ij}(t)$ we are simply evaluating the gain between the ith and jth node and then taking the inverse Laplace transform. Substituting the above results we obtain the transition matrix

$$\phi(t) = \begin{bmatrix} 1 & 0 \\ 1 - e^{-at} & e^{-at} \end{bmatrix}$$

which is identical to the result obtained in Example 5-1.

EXAMPLE 5-5

A control system has the following transfer function

$$\frac{C(s)}{R(s)} = \frac{1}{s(s+1)}$$

Obtain the transition matrix $\phi(t)$. Consider the input $r(t)$ as a state variable $x_3(t)$.

The state vector becomes

$$\mathbf{x}(t) = \begin{bmatrix} x_1(t) \\ x_2(t) \\ x_3(t) \end{bmatrix}$$

and the state variable diagram is shown in Fig. 5-3. From the flow of signals it may be immediately ascertained that

$$\phi_{32} = \phi_{31} = \phi_{21} = 0$$

The elements of the transition matrix may be evaluated as in the previous problem.

$$\phi_{11} = \phi_{33} = 1$$

$$\phi_{23} = \mathscr{L}^{-1}\left(\frac{1}{s(s+1)}\right) = 1 - e^{-t}$$

$$\phi_{22} = \mathscr{L}^{-1}\left(\frac{1}{s+1}\right) = e^{-t}$$

$$\phi_{12} = \mathscr{L}^{-1}\left(\frac{1}{s(s+1)}\right) = 1 - e^{-t}$$

$$\phi_{13} = \mathscr{L}^{-1}\left(\frac{1}{s^2(s+1)}\right) = t - 1 - e^{-t}$$

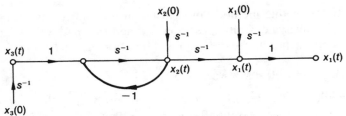

Fig. 5-3   State variable diagram for $1/s(s+1)$.

The entire transition matrix becomes

$$\phi(t) = \begin{bmatrix} 1 & (1-e^{-t}) & t-1-e^{-t} \\ 0 & e^{-t} & 1-e^{-t} \\ 0 & 0 & 1 \end{bmatrix}$$

As an exercise (in convincing yourself) you should form $[sI-A]^{-1}$ and take its inverse Laplace transform and see that it is equivalent to the transition matrix shown in the previous example.

Before continuing further several observations are in order. First, the i-jth element of the transition matrix is zero if there is no signal flow from the jth node to the ith node. Second, the term $\phi_{ij}(t)$ is the inverse Laplace transform of the overall gain from the jth node to the ith node. Finally, if the signal flow diagram becomes very complicated it may be desirable to use Mason's gain formula discussed in Chapter 3. Although the above method appears difficult initially, its clarity and overall simplicity cannot be overstated. This method is particularly suited for hand computation.

It is not necessary to obtain $\phi(t)$ by the above method. As a matter of fact there are two additional techniques for obtaining the transition matrix that we shall consider here. The first method deals directly with the matrix A and operates on the eigenvalues of A. The second, called the power series method, is an approximation method. The transition matrix is expanded in a power series and the terms retained are dictated by the speed of convergence.

The transition matrix in the s-domain expressed in terms of an adjoint matrix and determinant is

$$\phi(s) = \frac{\text{adj}\,[sI-A]}{\det\,[sI-A]} \qquad (5\text{-}25)$$

But this is identical to the $\Phi(s)$ matrix defined previously in Eq. (5-11). Therefore the Heaviside expansion may be used to evaluate the transition matrix. In using this method you will recall we had to invert a matrix, which is not always desirable, especially when the matrix $\mathbf{A}$ is large. An alternate approach is to use the Cayley–Hamilton method.†

The Cayley–Hamilton Method

This method provides a simple means of producing the inverse of a nonsingular matrix. It essentially postulates that if there existed a polynomial $P(\mathbf{A})$, where $\mathbf{A}$ is an $n \times n$ matrix, then it is possible to form another polynomial $N(\mathbf{A})$ where

★
$$P(\mathbf{A}) = N(\mathbf{A}) = h_{n-1}\mathbf{A}^{n-1} + \cdots + h_0\mathbf{I} \qquad (5\text{-}26)$$

where, $h_0, h_1, \ldots, h_{n-1}$ are treated as constants. If $\mathbf{A}$ has distinct eigenvalues, then this polynomial is related to $P(\mathbf{A})$ such that

★
$$P(s_i) = N(s_i) \qquad (5\text{-}27)$$

If there are n eigenvalues of $\mathbf{A}$, then we shall have n linear equations which when solved would yield the values of the h_i constants. This when substituted into Eq. (5-26) would yield $P(\mathbf{A})$. For the problem at hand we let $P(\mathbf{A})$ be

★
$$P(\mathbf{A}) = e^{\mathbf{A}t} = \phi(t) = \mathbf{I} + \mathbf{A}t + \frac{\mathbf{A}^2 t^2}{2!} + \cdots \qquad (5\text{-}28)$$

so that when the constants in Eq. (5-26) are obtained we get the transition matrix which is defined by Eq. (5-28).

If the coefficient matrix $\mathbf{A}$ has repeated eigenvalues, with multiplicity m_i, then

★
$$\left[\frac{d^j P(s)}{ds^j}\right]_{s=-s_i} = \left[\frac{d^j R(s)}{ds^j}\right]_{s=-s_i} \qquad (5\text{-}29)$$

and each i,j take values $0, 1, 2, \ldots, m_{i-1}$.

The use of this method is illustrated as follows. Consider a matrix of a system

$$\mathbf{A} = \begin{bmatrix} 0 & 1 \\ 0 & -2 \end{bmatrix}$$

The characteristic equation $s(s+2) = 0$ yields two eigenvalues at 0 and -2. Since these are distinct, we use Eq. (5-27). Also from Eq. (5-26) we have

$$P(\mathbf{A}) = N(\mathbf{A}) = h_0\mathbf{I} + h_1\mathbf{A}$$

†This is discussed in Appendix C.

For the two eigenvalues we have,

$$P(s_1) = N(s_1) = h_0 + h_1 s_1 = e^{s_1 t}$$

$$P(s_2) = N(s_2) = h_0 + h_1 s_2 = e^{s_2 t}$$

Inserting values of $s_1 = 0$ and $s_2 = -2$,

$$h_0 = 1; \qquad h_1 = \tfrac{1}{2}(1 - e^{-2t})$$

Substituting these values in Eq. (5-28) we obtain the transition matrix,

$$P(\mathbf{A}) = e^{\mathbf{A}t} = \phi(t) = h_0 \mathbf{I} + h_1 \mathbf{A} = \begin{bmatrix} 1 & \tfrac{1}{2}(1 - e^{-2t}) \\ 0 & e^{-2t} \end{bmatrix}$$

which is identical to the answer which was obtained by inverting a matrix.

Power Series Approach

The transition matrix may be approximated by the power series approach. As was done previously the transition matrix is expanded in a power series,

$$\phi(t) = \mathbf{I} + \mathbf{A}t + \frac{\mathbf{A}^2 t^2}{2!} + \cdots$$

for $\mathbf{M} = \mathbf{A}t$ the series becomes

★
$$\phi(t) = \mathbf{I} + \mathbf{M} + \frac{\mathbf{M}}{2!}(\mathbf{M}) + \frac{\mathbf{M}}{3}\left(\frac{\mathbf{M}^2}{2!}\right) + \cdots \tag{5-30}$$

and it is noted that each term in parentheses is equal to the entire preceding term. This property becomes useful in making computations recursively on a computer. The number of terms used in approximating the transition matrix is a function of the accuracy desired and the speed of convergence. If the transition matrix consists of exponential elements with real exponents, convergence may occur quite rapidly.

Consider the system previously considered whose coefficient matrix $\mathbf{A}$ is given by

$$\mathbf{A} = \begin{bmatrix} 0 & 1 \\ 0 & -2 \end{bmatrix}$$

then

$$\frac{\mathbf{A}^2}{2!} = \begin{bmatrix} 0 & -1 \\ 0 & 2 \end{bmatrix}$$

$$\frac{\mathbf{A}^3}{3!} = \begin{bmatrix} 0 & \tfrac{2}{3} \\ 0 & -\tfrac{4}{3} \end{bmatrix}$$

$$\frac{\mathbf{A}^4}{4!} = \begin{bmatrix} 0 & -\frac{1}{3} \\ 0 & \frac{2}{3} \end{bmatrix}$$

$$\frac{\mathbf{A}^5}{5!} = \begin{bmatrix} 0 & \frac{2}{15} \\ 0 & -\frac{4}{15} \end{bmatrix}$$

$$\frac{\mathbf{A}^6}{6!} = \begin{bmatrix} 0 & -\frac{2}{45} \\ 0 & \frac{4}{45} \end{bmatrix}$$

and so on. Substituting these values, the transition matrix becomes

$$\phi(t) = \begin{bmatrix} 1 & 0 \\ 0 & 1 \end{bmatrix} + \begin{bmatrix} 0 & 1 \\ 0 & -2 \end{bmatrix} t + \begin{bmatrix} 0 & -1 \\ 0 & 2 \end{bmatrix} t^2$$

$$+ \begin{bmatrix} 0 & \frac{2}{3} \\ 0 & -\frac{4}{3} \end{bmatrix} t^3 + \begin{bmatrix} 0 & -\frac{1}{3} \\ 0 & \frac{2}{3} \end{bmatrix} t^4$$

$$+ \begin{bmatrix} 0 & \frac{2}{15} \\ 0 & -\frac{4}{15} \end{bmatrix} t^5 + \begin{bmatrix} 0 & -\frac{2}{45} \\ 0 & \frac{4}{45} \end{bmatrix} t^6 + \cdots$$

Collecting terms,

$$\phi(t) = \begin{bmatrix} 1 & t - t^2 + \frac{2t^3}{3} - \frac{t^4}{3} + \frac{2t^5}{15} - \frac{2t^6}{45} + \cdots \\ 0 & 1 - 2t + 2t^2 - \frac{4t^3}{3} + \frac{2t^4}{3} - \frac{4t^5}{15} + \cdots \end{bmatrix}$$

Substituting some values of t we have

$$\phi(1) = \begin{bmatrix} 1 & 0.443 \\ 0 & 0.1555 \end{bmatrix} \qquad \phi(0) = \begin{bmatrix} 1 & 0 \\ 0 & 1 \end{bmatrix}$$

This may be compared to the exact solution obtained previously. For $t = 0$ and $t = 1$ the exact solution yields,

$$\phi(1) = \begin{bmatrix} 1 & 0.4322 \\ 0 & 0.1355 \end{bmatrix} \qquad \phi(0) = \begin{bmatrix} 1 & 0 \\ 0 & 1 \end{bmatrix}$$

The comparison is fair although if additional accuracy of the transition matrix is needed more terms of the series expansion are necessary.

5-3   STABILITY—EIGENVALUES OF A MATRIX

In the state space method it was seen that the system response was a function of the roots of the characteristic equation,

$$\det [s\mathbf{I} - \mathbf{A}] = 0$$

where **A** is the coefficient matrix of the system. *For the system to be* *stable we require that the roots of this equation, called the eigenvalues of the* **A** *matrix, have no positive real parts nor repeat on the imaginary axis.* Since the Routh–Hurwitz criterion is a general method for ascertaining this, we may employ it without modification to the characteristic polynomial defined above.

Consider a system characterized by the following coefficient matrix,

$$\mathbf{A} = \begin{bmatrix} 0 & 1 & 0 \\ 0 & -2 & 1 \\ -2 & -3 & -1 \end{bmatrix}$$

The characteristic equation becomes

$$\det \ [s\mathbf{I} - \mathbf{A}] = \begin{bmatrix} s & -1 & 0 \\ 0 & s+2 & -1 \\ 2 & 3 & s+1 \end{bmatrix} = 0$$

or

$$s^3 + 3s^2 + 5s + 2 = 0$$

The Routh array shows no sign reversal in the first column and therefore the system is stable.

The characteristic equation is not only useful for establishing stability but for obtaining bounds, upon system parameters, that insure stability. For example,

$$\mathbf{A} = \begin{bmatrix} -2 & 1 & 0 & 0 \\ 0 & 0 & K & 1 \\ 0 & -2 & -1 & 1 \\ 0 & 0 & \alpha & -1 \end{bmatrix}$$

then the characteristic equation becomes

$$\det \ [s\mathbf{I} - \mathbf{A}] = \begin{vmatrix} s+2 & -1 & 0 & 0 \\ 0 & s & -K & -1 \\ 0 & 2 & s+1 & -1 \\ 0 & 0 & -\alpha & s+1 \end{vmatrix} = 0$$

or

$$(s+2)[s^3 + 2s^2 + s(1 - \alpha + 2K) + 2(K + \alpha)] = 0$$

Since $s = -2$ is a stable root we need only consider the cubic polynomial of the above polynomial for ascertaining system stability. Using the Routh–Hurwitz criterion we can show that system stability requires that

$$(1 + K - 2\alpha) \geqslant 0$$
$$(K + \alpha) \geqslant 0$$

When a system is represented in state space, the stability is also studied either graphically or using more advanced analytical methods. We shall consider some of these ideas in more detail in a later chapter.

5-4 TWO EXAMPLES

The governing equations of satellite attitude motion possess the properties that make them attractive candidates for examples. This is true because the equations are simply derived using familiar concepts and can be linearized in some applications to constant coefficient linear differential equations. Also, the dynamics of the motion is such that the three rotational modes are uncoupled from the three translational motions. Finally, the three rotational motions generally appear in such a way that at least one degree is uncoupled from the other two. Such a fortunate circumstance is rare!

As our first example we will solve for the motion of two satellites connected by a tether.† The arrangement consists of two satellites connected by a massless and inelastic tether so that the center of mass of the system moves on a given circular orbit. Furthermore, the motion of the satellites is planar, i.e. restricted to the plane of the orbit.

Treating the two satellites as identical point masses the equations of motion of one of the masses are derived via Newtonian mechanics and are

$$\frac{d^2z(t)}{dt^2} = 2\omega \frac{dy(t)}{dt} + \omega^2 f_z(t) \qquad (5\text{-}31\text{a})$$

$$\frac{d^2y(t)}{dt^2} = -2\omega \frac{dz(t)}{dt} + 3\omega^2 y(t) + \omega^2 f_y(t) \qquad (5\text{-}31\text{b})$$

where ω is the mean motion of the orbit, $\omega^2 f_z(t)$ and $\omega^2 f_y(t)$ are control forces. The motion of the other mass is obtained by symmetry. If we consider the independent variable as $\tau = \omega t$, then the equations become

$$\ddot{z}(\tau) = 2\dot{y}(\tau) + f_z(\tau)$$

$$\ddot{y}(\tau) = -2\dot{z}(\tau) + 3y(\tau) + f_y(\tau)$$

where (¨) is a second derivative with respect to ωt.

---

†The problem was analyzed by J. M. Whisnant. A more complete description appears in *The Journal of the Astronautical Sciences*, Vol. XVII, No. 1, pp. 44–59, July 1969.

We now define the state vector

$$\mathbf{x}(\tau) = \begin{bmatrix} x_1(\tau) \\ x_2(\tau) \\ x_3(\tau) \\ x_4(\tau) \end{bmatrix} = \begin{bmatrix} z(\tau) \\ \dot{z}(\tau) \\ y(\tau) \\ \dot{y}(\tau) \end{bmatrix}$$

so that the state equation becomes

$$\dot{\mathbf{x}}(\tau) = \mathbf{A}\mathbf{x}(\tau) + \mathbf{b}r(\tau)$$

where

$$\mathbf{A} = \begin{bmatrix} 0 & 1 & 0 & 0 \\ 0 & 0 & 0 & 2 \\ 0 & 0 & 0 & 1 \\ 0 & -2 & 3 & 0 \end{bmatrix} \qquad \mathbf{b}r(\tau) = \begin{bmatrix} 0 \\ f_z(\tau) \\ 0 \\ f_y(\tau) \end{bmatrix}$$

The characteristic equation yields the following roots,

$$s_1 = 0; \qquad s_2 = 0; \qquad s_3 = j; \qquad s_4 = -j$$

Using the Cayley–Hamilton method we form the following equation

$$P(\mathbf{A}) = e^{\mathbf{A}\tau} = h_0 \mathbf{I} + h_1 \mathbf{A} + h_2 \mathbf{A}^2 + h_3 \mathbf{A}^3$$

Since there are four eigenvalues, this leads to the following four equations,

$$\left[\frac{dP(s)}{ds} \right]_{s=0} = h_1$$

$$[P(s)]_{s=0} = h_0$$

$$[P(s)]_{s=j} = h_0 + h_1 j + h_2 j^2 + h_3 j^3$$

$$[P(s)]_{s=-j} = h_0 - h_1 j + h_2 j^2 - h_3 j^3$$

Solving these for h_0, h_1, h_2, h_3 and substituting we obtain

$$P(\mathbf{A}) = e^{\mathbf{A}\tau} = \Phi(\tau) = \begin{bmatrix} 1 & 4\sin\tau - 3\tau & 6(\tau - \sin\tau) & 2(1 - \cos\tau) \\ 0 & 4\cos\tau - 3 & 6(1 - \cos\tau) & 2\sin\tau \\ 0 & -2(1 - \cos\tau) & (4 - 3\cos\tau) & \sin\tau \\ 0 & -2\sin\tau & 3\sin\tau & \cos\tau \end{bmatrix}$$

$$(5\text{-}32)$$

where $\tau = \omega t$. We could ascertain system stability by observing the eigenvalues of $\mathbf{A}$. Since there are two eigenvalues at the origin, the system is unstable. This is also obvious from the solution given by Eq. (5-32). This means that the satellite will continue to move away as long as there is tether. In practice, the control forces $f_z(\tau)$ and $f_y(\tau)$ are used to control the motion of the tethered satellites.

Our next example involves a spacecraft whose attitude motion is to be controlled by jets mounted orthogonally on the vehicle. We would like to obtain the response and stability of this satellite. Although this problem can get quite complex, we shall make several assumptions in order to simplify it without detracting from the salient points. If we define ϕ, θ, and ψ as the pitch, roll, and yaw motion, the linearized dynamical equations can be derived from Newtonian mechanics. We simply write down the equations† as

$$I_y\ddot{\phi}(t) + 3\omega^2(I_x - I_z)\phi(t) = M_y(t) \tag{5-33a}$$

$$I_x\ddot{\theta}(t) + 4\omega^2(I_y - I_z)\theta(t) - \omega(I_y - I_x - I_z)\dot{\psi}(t) = M_x(t) \tag{5-33b}$$

$$I_z\ddot{\psi}(t) + \omega^2(I_y - I_x)\psi(t) + \omega(I_y - I_x - I_z)\dot{\theta}(t) = M_z(t) \tag{5-33c}$$

where I_x, I_y, I_z are the principle moments of inertia, ω is the orbital velocity, and $M_x(t)$, $M_y(t)$, $M_z(t)$ are applied torques. We note that the first equation is a second-order undamped differential equation and is uncoupled from the other two. Since we have analyzed such equations previously, we shall investigate only the coupled equations. We would like to investigate the transient behavior of this satellite.

Let us first establish the physical characteristics of the satellite as follows:

$$I_x = 100 \text{ kg-m}^2$$
$$I_y = 200 \text{ kg-m}^2$$
$$I_z = 50 \text{ kg-m}^2$$

Also, if we set $\tau = \omega t$ and then substitute

$$\ddot{\theta}(\tau) + 6\theta(\tau) - 0.5\dot{\psi}(\tau) = 0$$
$$\ddot{\psi}(\tau) + 2\psi(\tau) + \dot{\theta}(\tau) = (M_z(\tau)/I_z)$$

where we have assumed only one input. Now if we define the state variables as

$$x_1(\tau) = \theta(t); \qquad x_2(\tau) = \dot{\theta}(\tau); \qquad x_3(\tau) = \psi(\tau); \qquad x_4(\tau) = \dot{\psi}(\tau)$$

then we obtain

$$\dot{\mathbf{x}}(\tau) = \mathbf{A}\mathbf{x}(\tau) + \mathbf{b}r(\tau)$$

†Any text on dynamics may be consulted. For example *see* Reference 7.

where

$$A = \begin{bmatrix} 0 & 1 & 0 & 0 \\ -6 & 0 & 0 & \frac{1}{2} \\ 0 & 0 & 0 & 1 \\ 0 & -1 & -2 & 0 \end{bmatrix} \qquad b = \begin{bmatrix} 0 \\ 0 \\ 0 \\ 1 \end{bmatrix} \qquad r(\tau) = (M_z(\tau)/I_z)$$

The output is given by

$$\theta(\tau) = c_1 x(\tau)$$
$$\psi(\tau) = c_2 x(\tau)$$

where

$$c_1 = [1 \quad 0 \quad 0 \quad 0]$$
$$c_2 = [0 \quad 0 \quad 1 \quad 0]$$

We shall investigate $\theta(\tau)$ only since the results for $\psi(\tau)$ are similar. The characteristic equation becomes

$$s^4 + 8.5s^2 + 12 = 0$$

having the following roots,

$$s = j2.59, \ -j2.59, \ j1.33, \ -j1.33$$

Since all the roots are imaginary and simple, the system is stable. The response of the homogeneous equation is

$$x(\tau) = \mathcal{L}^{-1} \left[\frac{\text{adj} \ (sI - A)}{\det \ (sI - A)} \right] x(0)$$

where

$$\text{adj} \ [sI - A] = \begin{bmatrix} s(s^2+2)+0.5s & s^2+2 & -1 & 0.5s \\ -6(s^2+2) & s(s^2+2) & -s & 0.5s^2 \\ 6 & -s & s(s^2+0.5)+6s & (s^2+6) \\ 6s & -s^2 & -2(s^2+6) & s(s^2+6) \end{bmatrix}$$

The response of θ is

$$\theta(\tau) = x_1(\tau)$$

$$= \mathcal{L}^{-1} \left\{ \frac{[s(s^2+2)+0.5s]x_1(0) + (s^2+2)x_2(0) - x_3(0) + 0.5sx_4(0)}{(s-j2.59)(s+j2.59)(s-j1.33)(s+j1.33)} \right\}$$

$$(5\text{-}34)$$

Let us assume that the only initial condition is $x_4(0)$ and the others are zero, then

$$\theta(\tau) = 0.5x_4(0)[K_1 \cos 2.59\tau + K_2 \sin 1.33\tau]$$

where K_1 and K_2 are constants.

SUMMARY

A control system is represented in state space form by the vector-matrix differential equations,

$$\dot{\mathbf{x}}(t) = \mathbf{Ax}(t) + \mathbf{b}r(t)$$
$$y(t) = \mathbf{cx}(t)$$

The solution of these equations given in terms of the transition matrix $\phi(t)$ is

$$\mathbf{x}(t) = \phi(t)\mathbf{x}(0) + \mathscr{L}^{-1}\Big[[s\mathbf{I} - \mathbf{A}]^{-1}\mathbf{b}R(s)\Big]$$
$$y(t) = \mathbf{c}\phi(t)\mathbf{x}(0) + \mathscr{L}^{-1}\Big[\mathbf{c}[s\mathbf{I} - \mathbf{A}]^{-1}\mathbf{b}R(s)\Big]$$

where the first term is the homogeneous part.

We investigated several methods for obtaining the transition matrix. Although all the methods gave similar results, their relative attraction lay on the computational aid available. The method employing the unit step response coupled with Mason's formula for obtaining the overall gain is attractive for hand computation, whereas other techniques were superior for machine computation.

The stability of the system is dependent upon the eigenvalues of the $\mathbf{A}$ matrix obtained by solving

$$\det[s\mathbf{I} - \mathbf{A}] = 0$$

As you progress further, it is important that you realize that the techniques developed in the present chapter are not to be considered as just another way of obtaining a solution to problems outlined in earlier chapters. Instead, these techniques are to be interpreted as new tools useful for not only observing variables inside a control system, but handling a very large number of input-output combinations. As systems get more complex (and interesting), we shall be more dependent upon the computer as a computational aid and consequently rely more heavily on state space techniques.

PROBLEMS

5-1. Beginning from the state representation of Problem 3-8 obtain $c(t)$.

5-2. The coefficient matrix of a physical system is given by

$$\mathbf{A} = \begin{bmatrix} -1 & +3 & -2 \\ 0 & -1 & -1 \\ 0 & -2 & -4 \end{bmatrix}$$

Derive the transition matrix using an approximation technique.

5-3. Solve Problem 5-2 using the Cayley–Hamilton method and compare $\phi(t)$ at $t = 0, 1, 5$, and 10 seconds.

5-4. Obtain the solution to $\dot{x}(t) = Ax(t) + br(t)$ using the state variable diagram for evaluating the transition matrix.

$$A = \begin{bmatrix} -1 & 3 & -2 \\ 0 & -3 & 0 \\ 0 & 2 & -3 \end{bmatrix} \quad b = \begin{bmatrix} 1 \\ 0 \\ 0 \end{bmatrix} \quad r(t) \rightarrow \text{step}$$

5-5. Obtain $x(t)$ for Example 5-2 by solving ϕ and the constant matrices.

5-6. A system has a coefficient matrix given by

$$A = \begin{bmatrix} -1 & -1 & 0 \\ 2 & 1 & -1 \\ 3 & 0 & 1 \end{bmatrix}$$

Is it stable?

5-7. For what values of α, β, γ is the system with the following coefficient matrix A stable?

$$A = \begin{bmatrix} 0 & 1 & 0 & 0 \\ 4(\beta - \gamma) & 0 & 0 & -\dfrac{\beta - \alpha - \gamma}{\alpha} \\ 0 & 0 & 0 & 1 \\ 0 & \dfrac{\beta - \alpha}{\gamma} & \dfrac{\beta - \alpha - \gamma}{\gamma} & 0 \end{bmatrix}$$

5-8. In Chapter 4 we discussed the single degree of freedom gyro. In problems where we require three axis stabilization, three gyros are used as shown in Fig. P5-8a.

The three axis platform as shown in Fig. P5-8a, is more complex owing to coupling between the three rotations as well as the resolution of the platform pickoff signals and because of nonalignment of the gimbal and platform axis.

If $\Theta_x(s)$, $\Theta_y(s)$, $\Theta_z(s)$ are the outputs of x, y, z gyros due to $\Phi_x(s)$, $\Phi_y(s)$, $\Phi_z(s)$ inputs then the pickoffs $E_x(s), E_y(s), E_z(s)$ are

$$E_x(s) = \Theta_x(s) - \Phi_x(s), \quad E_y(s) = \Theta_y(s) - \Phi_y(s), \quad E_z(s) = \Theta_z(s) - \Phi_z(s)$$

If the gimbal axes are lined up with the platform axes, the counteracting torques called for by the pickoff signals are

$$T_y(s) = A_y E_y(s)$$

This leads to a block diagram as shown in Fig. P5-8b, where Gp_x, Gg_x, etc., are defined as in Eq. (3-12). The platform torques $T_x(s)$, $T_y(s)$, $T_z(s)$ must be re-solved along the displaced gimbal axes where servomotors act. Since the counter-torques are proportional to the platform pickoff signals, the proper torques about the new gimbal axes are found by resolving the platform pickoff signals along the gimbal axes. For the moment we shall neglect this complication and study

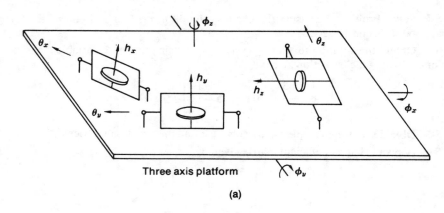

Three axis platform

(a)

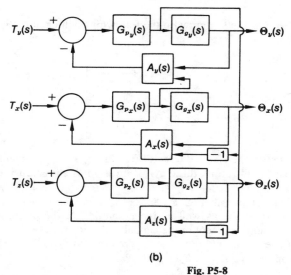

(b)

Fig. P5-8

the system as is. Let us also, assume that $A_y(s)$, $A_x(s)$, $A_z(s)$, have the form $(1+\tau_1 s)^3/(1+\tau_2 s)^3$. Obtain the state space representation for this problem.

5-9. Solve for h_0, h_1, h_2, h_3 and verify $\Phi(\tau)$ shown in Eq. (5-32).

5-10. Obtain the solution in Example 3-7 for the case where $f_x = f_y = f_z = 0$ (i.e. torque free environment), $\alpha = \beta = 1$ and initial conditions

$$\dot{\mathbf{x}}(0) = \begin{bmatrix} 1 \\ 2 \\ 0 \end{bmatrix}$$

5-11. It is desired that mass m_1 shown in Fig. P5-11 be stabilized by moving the base. If we assume that $\theta(t)$ and x are small and also that $m_2 \gg m_1$, the resulting equations are seen to be linear but the system itself is unstable. The system can be stabilized if we apply a force $f(t)$ on the cart such that

$$f(t) = k_1\theta(t) + k_2\dot{\theta}(t)$$

Write the system equations in state space form and find the values of k_1 and k_2 such that the system is stable.

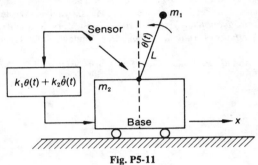

Fig. P5-11

5-12. In studying the flow of automobile traffic it was noticed that the acceleration of a car was determined by the distance between two cars, the velocity of the lead car, and natural constants that described the car and driver. If we consider the first (lead) car's position as $x_1(t)$, that of the second car as $x_2(t)$, and so on, the control system that models the automobile traffic is shown in Fig. P5-12. k_i is the natural frequency of the car and driver and τ_i a combined time constant. We wish to use this model to study the start up and stopping of traffic involving four cars. We assume that the length of the cars is neglected. For the start up we assume (1) the spacing between cars is 5 ft, (2) cars initially at rest, and (3) the lead car takes off at 25 mph. For stopping we assume that (1) the spacing between cars is 40 ft, (2) cars moving at 30 mph, and (3) the lead car decelerates in 40 ft taking 3 seconds. Using state space techniques, find various combinations of k_i, τ_i that can cause accidents. (Note that low value of k and high τ indicates a sluggish driver.) [This problem was part of a senior project at the University of Maryland.]

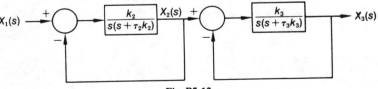

Fig. P5-12

REFERENCES

1. DeRusso, P. M., R. J. Roy, and C. M. Close, *State Variables for Engineers*, New York, Wiley, 1965.
2. Lewis, L. J., D. K. Reynolds, F. R. Bergseth, and F. J. Alexander, *Linear Systems Analysis*, New York, McGraw-Hill, 1969.
3. Kuo, B. C., *Automatic Control Systems*, 2nd Edition, Englewood Cliffs, N.J., Prentice-Hall, 1968.
4. Chen, C. F., and I. J. Haas, *Elements of Control Systems Analysis: Classical and Modern Approaches*, Englewood Cliffs, N.J., Prentice-Hall, 1968.
5. Dorf, R. C., *Modern Control Systems*, Reading, Mass., Addison-Wesley, 1967.
6. Watkins, B. O., *Introduction to Control Systems*, New York, Macmillan, 1969.
7. Meirovitch, L., *Methods of Analytical Dynamics*, Englewood Cliffs, N.J., Prentice-Hall, 1970.
8. Timothy, L. K., and B. E. Bona, *State Space Analysis: an introduction*, New York, McGraw-Hill, 1968.

6

Performance Criterion

6-1 INTRODUCTION

When a specific system is proposed for a given application, it must satisfy certain requirements. This may involve the system response or optimization of the system in a specified way. The requirements that a control system must meet are generally called performance specifications. The analysis of the system, by methods presented in the previous chapters, yields results that must be compared to the desired performance specifications. If they do not compare favorably, the response can be altered by either introducing a controller into the control system or other compensating elements.

The first part of this chapter is concerned with control system performance specifications in the time domain. We will then introduce the concept of the performance index. Also, the effects of parameter variation on system error shall be investigated. This is important since the ability of a control system to suppress the system error below a certain level is sometimes important. The chapter ends with the consideration of various types of controllers suitable for altering system performance.

6-2 CONTROL SYSTEM SPECIFICATION

The performance of a control system can be considered in three parts. The first part pertains to the specifications as they directly relate to system response. The second has to do with a performance index that is a function of the error or output. The last part is concerned with system error caused by parameter variations.

143

Control system specifications can be directly related to system response as shown in Fig. 6-1. The commonly used terms are given below.

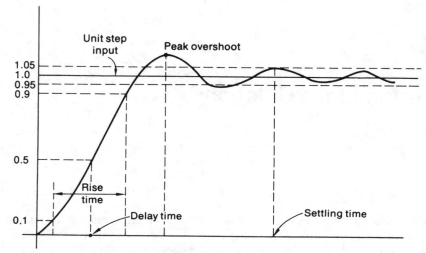

Fig. 6-1   Time domain specification of control systems.

Peak Overshoot

This is measured when the response has maximum value. It is an indication of the largest error between input and output during the transient state. For the systems considered we observed that the peak overshoot increased as the damping ratio decreased. The concept of peak overshoot is not limited to only second-order systems. It is often used for higher-order systems that have a dominant pair of complex poles. These poles are those located nearest the imaginary axis. In most well-designed systems, peak overshoots are lower than 30%.

Rise Time

The rise time is a measure of the speed of response. It is defined as the time necessary for the response to rise from 10% to 90% of its final steady state error. Sometimes an equivalent measure is to represent the rise time as the reciprocal of the slope of the response at the instant the response is 50% of its final steady state value.

For second-order underdamped systems, the time to reach the peak overshoot is also a good measure of the speed of response.

Delay Time

The time necessary for the response to reach some value (usually 50%) of its steady state value is called a delay time.

Settling Time

The settling time is defined as the time necessary for the response to decrease to and stay within a specified range of its final value. Two or five percent is often stated as the tolerable range. The number of oscillations necessary to reach this condition is also a useful index.

Bandwidth

The bandwidth is defined as the frequency at which the output magnitude is 0.707 as compared to the output magnitude at low (or zero) frequency when the system is subjected to sinusoidal inputs. We shall consider this in more detail in the next chapter.

Damping Ratio

This is a ratio of the system damping to the critical damping for a second-order system. It measures the damping of a complex pole pair. Higher-order systems may have more than one damping ratio although the damping measured by the most dominant complex pole pair is of most importance. The damping ratio is an important parameter in determining the transient performance and stability of a system.

Undamped Natural Frequency

This is directly related to the "springyness" of a system. Like the damping ratio it may be applied to second-order systems or higher-order systems possessing dominant poles.

System specifications are also given in terms of the error constants (or coefficients) as well as the system type. The error constants are used to relate the system gain and time constants to the system errors of a unity feedback system. They measure directly the minimum ideal steady state error of a system for a step, ramp, and parabolic input. The error coefficients are identical, in concept, to the error constants although generalized for any type of input. In addition to this, system performance is also given in the frequency domain. This is considered in Chapter 7.

EXAMPLE 6-1

Consider a control system whose output is given by

$$C(s) = \frac{K\omega_n^2}{s(s^2 + 2\delta\omega_n s + \omega_n^2)}$$

where $\omega_n = 8$ rad/sec and $\delta = 0.5$. Determine ω_d, $c(t)$, M_p, t_p, t_s and the number of oscillations to reach t_s.

The damped frequency becomes

$$\omega_d = \omega_n\sqrt{1 - \delta^2}$$
$$= 6.93 \text{ rad/sec}$$

The response is

$$c(t) = k[1 - 1.16e^{-4t}\sin(6.92 + \phi)]$$

where

$$\cos\phi = 0.5$$

The overshoot M_p is given by

$$M_p = \exp\left(-\frac{\delta\pi}{\sqrt{1 - \delta^2}}\right)$$
$$= 0.163$$

This 16% overshoot occurs at

$$t_p = \frac{\pi}{\omega_n\sqrt{1 - \delta^2}}$$
$$= 0.452 \text{ sec}$$

The settling time t_s is generally estimated as approximately three time constants of the envelope of the damped sinusoidal oscillation and is given by,

$$t_s = \frac{3}{\delta\omega_n}$$
$$= 0.75 \text{ sec}$$

The number of oscillations necessary to reach this are similarly obtained from

$$N = \frac{3\sqrt{1 - \delta^2}}{2\pi\delta}$$
$$= 0.827 \text{ oscillations}$$

These parameters can be computed or directly read from plots. The formulas and plots are given in Chapter 4.

___

Although the above specifications are quite popular, an increasing amount of stress is being laid on the mathematical representation of the performance of a control system. This is given in terms of the performance index to be considered next.

6-3   PERFORMANCE INDICES

A performance index is a quantitative measure of system performance. We must of course be clear as to what we mean by system performance. For example, do we mean that the error must be a minimum or constant? Or would we prefer to measure system performance by the square of the error? Clearly, the performance index will depend upon the specific criterion that we wish to invoke. It is therefore important that the design engineer must know a priori what he would like to optimize.

In general the performance index J is represented as

★
$$J = \int_0^T f(p)\,dt \tag{6-1}$$

where p may be the system error, output, input, or some combination. For many control systems, the performance index based upon the system error is quite useful. Four different indices that are in common usage are

★
$$J_1 = \int_0^T e^2(t)\,dt \tag{6-2}$$

★
$$J_2 = \int_0^T |e(t)|\,dt \tag{6-3}$$

★
$$J_3 = \int_0^T t|e(t)|\,dt \tag{6-4}$$

★
$$J_4 = \int_0^T t\,e^2(t)\,dt \tag{6-5}$$

The upper time limit is arbitrary. Quite often the settling time is used. Other times it is replaced by infinity. J_1 is the performance index based on the integral of the square error and designated by ISE. The integral of the absolute error, IAE, is given by J_2. The integral of the time multiplied by the absolute error is J_3 and designated ITAE. Finally, J_4 is designated

ITSE. If it is desired to have a minimum performance index, the indices most useful are ITAE and ITSE, in that order.

EXAMPLE 6-2

The output of a second-order control system subjected to a unit input is given by

$$c(t) = 1 - \frac{e^{-\delta\omega_n t}}{\sqrt{1-\delta^2}} \sin(\omega_d t + \phi)$$

where

$$\omega_d = \omega_n \sqrt{1-\delta^2}; \qquad \phi = \tan^{-1}\frac{\sqrt{1-\delta^2}}{\delta}$$

Obtain δ that minimizes J_1 for a fixed value of ω_n. The departure from unity may be considered as the error,

$$e(t) = -\frac{e^{-2\delta\omega_n t}}{\sqrt{1-\delta^2}} \sin(\omega_d t + \phi)$$

from which we compute ISE,

$$J_1 = \int_0^\infty \frac{e^{-2\omega_n t}}{1-\delta^2} \sin^2(\omega_d t + \phi] \, dt$$

where the upper limit has been selected as infinity. Carrying out the integration,

$$J_1 = \frac{1+4\delta^2}{4\omega_n \delta}$$

For minimizing J_1 we set $dJ_1/d\delta = 0$ and obtain

$$\delta = 0.5$$

In general, it is necessary to plot J_1 versus δ to obtain the optimum value. Various performance indices are available in the form of tables for aiding the design of control systems.

When the system is represented in state form, the performance index is written as

★
$$J = \int_0^T f(\mathbf{x}) \, dt \tag{6-6}$$

where $\mathbf{x}$ is the state vector and a function of time. In general, $f(\mathbf{x})$ will be a combination of several state variables. A performance based on the sum of the square of the state variables is obtained if

$$f(\mathbf{x}) = \mathbf{x}^T\mathbf{x}$$
$$= [x_1, x_2, \cdots, x_n] \begin{bmatrix} x_1 \\ x_2 \\ \vdots \\ x_n \end{bmatrix}$$
$$= x_1{}^2 + x_1{}^2 + \cdots + x_n{}^2$$

so that J becomes

★
$$J = \int_0^T (\mathbf{x}^T\mathbf{x})\, dt \qquad (6\text{-}7)$$

All of the indices given by Eq. (6-2) through Eq. (6-5) may be written in a more general form involving state variables. A more general form of Eq. (6-7) is considered in a later chapter.

EXAMPLE 6-3

The state vector of a control system is given by

$$\mathbf{x}(t) = \begin{bmatrix} x_1(t) \\ x_2(t) \end{bmatrix} = \begin{bmatrix} \sigma e^{-\sigma t} \\ 2e^{-\sigma t} \end{bmatrix}$$

Determine the optimum value of σ for minimizing J based on Eq. (6-7).
The performance index is

$$J = \int_0^\infty (\mathbf{x}^T\mathbf{x})\, dt$$
$$= \int_0^\infty (\sigma^2 e^{-2\sigma t} + 4e^{-2\sigma t})\, dt$$
$$= \frac{\sigma^2 + 4}{2\sigma}$$

For minimizing J we set $dJ/d\sigma = 0$, which yields

$$\sigma = 2.0$$

EXAMPLE 6-4

The state vector of a control system is given by

$$\mathbf{x}(t) = \begin{bmatrix} x_1 \\ x_2 \end{bmatrix} = \begin{bmatrix} \dfrac{\delta}{\sqrt{1-\delta^2}} e^{-\delta t} \sin \sqrt{1-\delta^2}\, t \\ 0.5 e^{-\delta t} \end{bmatrix}$$

Determine the optimum value of δ for minimizing J based on Eq. (6-7).

$$J = \int_0^\infty (\mathbf{x}^T\mathbf{x})\, dt$$

$$J = \int_0^\infty \left(\frac{\delta^2 e^{-2\delta t}}{(1-\delta^2)} \sin^2 \sqrt{1-\delta^2}t + 0.25e^{-2\delta t} \right) dt$$

$$J = \frac{0.5 + \delta^2}{4\delta}$$

For minimizing J we set $dJ/d\delta = 0$, which yields

$$\delta = 0.707$$

6-4 SENSITIVITY FUNCTIONS

The behavior of a control system changes as its system parameters change, as the reference input varies, or due to loading effects. These parameters change due to environmental conditions, manufacturing defects, aging, etc. Since mostly these changes go uncorrected, they effect the response of a system. If however, there is feedback, the change in system parameters alters the output which causes a change in the error, due to feedback, thereby reducing the overall effect of system parameter changes. Since the quality of a control system depends upon its error reducing capability, we shall investigate its sensitivity to these disturbance functions.

If a parameter K changes causing a change in M, then the percentage change in M, due to K, divided by the percentage change in K is defined as the *sensitivity* function $S_K{}^M$,

★
$$S_K{}^M = \frac{dM/M}{dK/K} = \frac{K}{M}\frac{dM}{dK} \qquad (6\text{-}8)$$

If M and K are defined for an open loop system as

$$M = \frac{C(s)}{R(s)} = G(s); \qquad K = G(s)$$

then

★
$$S_G{}^M = \frac{G}{M}\frac{dM}{dG} = 1 \qquad (6\text{-}9)$$

which states that a change in $G(s)$ and the open loop system output have a one to one ratio provided the input is fixed. It follows that there is also a one to one ratio in output changes caused by input changes.

The sensitivity for a closed loop system with unity feedback is obtained by defining

$$M = \frac{G(s)}{1+G(s)} = \frac{C(s)}{R(s)}; \qquad K = G(s)$$

Now since

$$\frac{dM}{dG} = \frac{1}{(1+G(s))^2}$$

the sensitivity function becomes

$$S_G{}^M = \frac{G}{M}\frac{dM}{dG} = G\left(\frac{1+G}{G}\right)\frac{1}{(1+G)^2}$$

★
$$S_G{}^M = \frac{1}{1+G(s)} \qquad\qquad (6\text{-}10)$$

Therefore the output is not affected as much due to feedback. If the closed loop system has a feedback element $H(s)$, then the sensitivity function becomes

★
$$S_G{}^M = \frac{1}{1+G(s)H(s)} \qquad\qquad (6\text{-}11)$$

The effect on the closed loop system output due to parameter changes in the feedback element can be obtained by defining the sensitivity function

$$S_H{}^M = \frac{H}{M}\frac{dM}{dH}$$

where

$$M = \frac{GH}{1+GH}$$

Taking the derivative and substituting yields

$$S_H{}^M = \frac{1}{1+G(s)H(s)}$$

Not only does feedback decrease the effects of parameter changes on the system output but it also reduces the effect of unwanted disturbances such as noise on the system output. Consider the system shown in Fig. 6-2 where the output without feedback is

$$C(s) = G(s)R(s) + U(s)$$

Thus any changes in $U(s)$ are directly felt in the output $C(s)$. If however

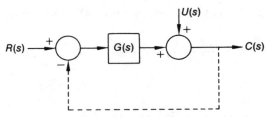

Fig. 6-2 A control system with a disturbance function.

there is feedback then

$$C(s) = \frac{G(s)}{1+G(s)} R(s) + \frac{1}{1+G(s)} U(s)$$

and the effect of $U(s)$ is reduced by $(1/1+G(s))$. We can conclude here that feedback reduces the effect of system parameter changes as well as noise in system output.

EXAMPLE 6-5

The output of a control system is given by

$$C(s) = \frac{K}{s((A+s)(B+s)+K)} = G$$

where it is known that K varies slowly. Obtain the effect of this change on system output. The change in output is

$$\Delta C(s) = G(s)(1-sG(s))\frac{\Delta K}{K}$$

The steady state value can be obtained from the final value theorem,

$$\Delta c(t) = \lim_{s \to 0} sG(s)(1-sG(s))\frac{\Delta K}{K}$$

$$= \frac{AB}{(AB+K)^2}\Delta K$$

Therefore if K changes by 1, the output varies by $AB/(AB+K)^2$ and this is the benefit of feedback.

6-5 CONTROL TYPES

We stated earlier that in many cases the transient and steady state response may not satisfy the system requirements. We may wish to modify the transient or steady state characteristics, or both, by introducing a *controller* in the control system. We shall show that an appropriate controller does indeed alter the response of the system although it also brings about additional changes that may be undesirable. It is not always possible to optimize everything and the particular price that is to be paid must be weighed against the advantages to be gained.

A general feedback control system is shown in Fig. 6-3. The output signal $M(s)$ of the controller is the actuating signal that is employed for making necessary corrections so that the output corresponds to the input in some manner. The relationship of the actuating signal $M(s)$ to the error signal is directly dependent upon $G_c(s)$,

$$\frac{M(s)}{E(s)} = G_c(s)$$

$$\frac{C(s)}{E(s)} = G_c(s)G_L(s)$$

$$\frac{C(s)}{R(s)} = \frac{G_c(s)G_L(s)}{1 + G_c(s)G_L(s)H(s)}$$

We note that the response $c(t)$ will depend upon the nature of $G_c(s)$. Since we can select $G_c(s)$ we have some control upon $C(s)$ for a given input. There are, in general, three basic types of controls that we may select,

(1) Proportional control
(2) Derivative control
(3) Integral control.

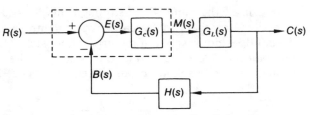

Fig. 6-3 General feedback control system.

We may, of course, select any combination of the three basic types. In the remaining section the effect of different controllers on system response is investigated.

Proportional Control

With this control the actuating signal is proportional to the error signal,

$$M(s) = K_p[R(s) - B(s)]$$
$$= K_p E(s) \tag{6-12}$$

A feedback control system with proportional control is shown in Fig. 6-4. In such a system a compromise is often necessary in selecting a proper gain so that the steady state error and maximum overshoot are within acceptable limits. Practically, however, a compromise cannot always be reached since an optimum value of K may satisfy the steady state error but may cause excessive overshoot or even instability. This problem can be overcome if we employ proportional control in conjunction with some other type of control.

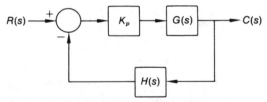

Fig. 6-4 Proportional control.

Derivative Control

When it is necessary to have an actuating signal which is proportional to the time derivative of the error signal, then we employ derivative control,

★
$$M(s) = K_d s E(s) \tag{6-13}$$

where K_d is the gain of the controller. Although this form of control is very useful when it is necessary to increase system damping, it cannot be used alone since it does not respond if the error is constant. Therefore, it is used in combination with other controls. Let us consider here derivative and proportional control of a second-order system shown in Fig. 6-5. The output becomes

★
$$\frac{C(s)}{R(s)} = \frac{K_d s + 1}{A s^2 + (B + K_d)s + 1} \tag{6-14}$$

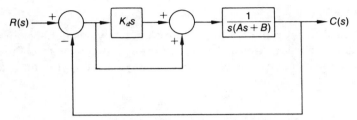

Fig. 6-5   Control system with derivative and proportional control.

We immediately note that the effective damping of the system has increased. Since the overshoot is directly dependent upon the damping ratio, derivative control enables us to control system overshoot.

The use of derivative control for improving system damping may be extended to the output signal as well. Inclusion of derivative control in the feedback† of a second-order control system is shown in Fig. 6-6. The

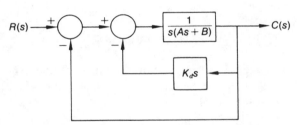

Fig. 6-6   Derivative control in feedback loop.

output becomes

$$\frac{C(s)}{R(s)} = \frac{1}{As^2 + (B + K_d)s + 1} \tag{6-15}$$

and the characteristic equation is identical to that of Eq. (6-14) and therefore we obtain the same control of the output overshoot. What then is the difference between these two types of derivative control? The difference is in the rise time of the response. Since Eq. (6-14) has an open loop zero, whereas Eq. (6-15) does not, the rise time of the derivative control is faster.

†This is often referred to as Rate-Feedback or Tachometric Control since a tachometer generator in the feedback yields the necessary derivative action.

Integral Control

Sometimes it is desirable to eliminate completely positional error as in a servomotor. In such cases a signal proportional to the integral of the error is used. Consider the control system employing integral control in Fig. 6-7. The output becomes

★
$$\frac{C(s)}{R(s)} = \frac{s + K_1}{As^3 + Bs^2 + s + K_I} \tag{6-16}$$

and the error becomes

$$E(s) = \frac{s^2(As + B)}{As^3 + Bs^2 + s + K_I} R(s)$$

We notice immediately that in employing integral control to a second-order system we have converted it to a third-order system. Whenever this is done, the system is no longer stable over all ranges of gain, i.e. if the gain is sufficiently raised, the system shall become unstable. Although this is undesirable it is the price we pay for eliminating steady state error, under load, which is

$$e_{ss}(t) = \lim_{s \to 0} sE(s)$$

and is zero for a step and ramp input. For a parabolic input it is B/K_I. Without integral control the steady state error was a constant for a ramp but infinite for a parabolic input.

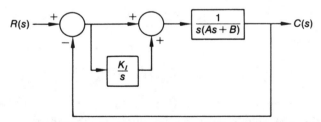

Fig. 6-7   Feedback control system with integral control.

Proportional, Derivative, and Integral Control

Knowing the advantages of individual types of control action, let us consider an example employing all three control actions. The second-order system shown in Fig. 6-8 has proportional derivative and integral

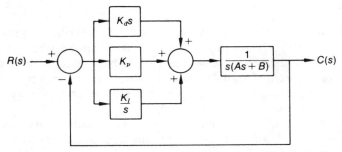

Fig. 6-8   Control system with proportional, derivative, and integral control.

control. The output and error become

★
$$C(s) = \frac{K_d s^2 + K_p s + K_I}{A s^3 + s^2(B + K_d) + K_p s + K_I} R(s) \qquad (6\text{-}17a)$$

★
$$E(s) = \frac{s^2(As + B)}{A s^3 + s^2(B + K_d) + K_p s + K_I} R(s) \qquad (6\text{-}17b)$$

With a proper choice of K_d and K_I we can get an oscillatory system with acceptable damping ratio. The error is zero for step or ramp input. In selecting the parameters K_d and K_I we need to be careful about system stability. Applying the Routh–Hurwitz criterion we have

$$
\begin{array}{c|cc}
s^3 & A & K_p \\
s^2 & B + K_d & K_I \\
\hline
s^1 & b_1 & b_2 \\
s^0 & c_1 &
\end{array}
\qquad
\begin{aligned}
b_1 &= \frac{K_p(B + K_d) - AK_I}{(B + K_d)} \\[2mm]
b_2 &= 0 \\
c_1 &= K_I
\end{aligned}
$$

This means that $K_I > 0$ and also $K_p > AK_I/(B + K_d)$. If $K_p = AK_I/(B + K_d)$, then $b_1 = 0$ and the auxiliary equation becomes

$$(B + K_d)s^2 + K_I = 0$$

This indicates pure oscillatory response whose frequency is

$$s = \pm j \sqrt{K_p/A}$$

In conclusion, we observe that whereas the effect of derivative control is to enhance system damping, the effect of integral control is to eliminate steady state error but decrease the margin of stability.

SUMMARY

We defined some commonly used terms to describe control system specifications and directly related them to the system response in the time domain. The performance index was seen to be a qualitative measure of the error of a system. This index can be mathematically represented and is useful for optimizing the system performance, which generally means a minimization of some form of the error.

The sensitivity of the system to variations in input as well as system parameters was obtained. It was seen that feedback tends to reduce the influence of parameter fluctuations.

The last section illustrated the effect of different control actions upon the transient and steady state response. We noted how control actions may be employed to enhance system damping and eliminate steady state error.

PROBLEMS

6-1. An airplane is idealized as shown in Fig. P6-1. Derive the equation for the vertical motion of the plane as it lands assuming that as it touches the ground it experiences a step input. Obtain $x(t)$ and determine the natural and damped frequency, damping ratio, peak overshoot and the time at which it occurs, settling time and the number of oscillations to reach it. Neglect the weight of the wheels and assume

$$m = 10,000 \text{ kg}; \qquad B = 10^5 \text{ n/m/sec}; \qquad k = 10^6 \text{ n/m}$$

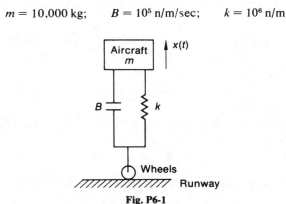

Fig. P6-1

6-2. For the system shown in Fig. P4-3, calculate the maximum overshoot and rise time for a step input.

6-3. For the system investigated in Example 6-1, if the natural frequency is 20 rad/sec, then what damping ratio is necessary for the settling time to be 0.5 sec? How much overshoot results?

6-4. Compute J_1 and J_2 for Example 6-1. Obtain the value of δ that minimizes the performance index.

6-5. For the system shown in Example 6-1, plot J_3 and J_4 as a function of δ. Obtain the value of δ that minimizes each of the performance indices.

6-6. Show that for a second-order system, the minimization of J_3 yields $\delta = 0.7$.

6-7. A third-order system is characterized by

$$\frac{C(s)}{R(s)} = \frac{\omega_n{}^3}{s^3 + b_2\omega_n s^2 + b_1\omega_n{}^2 s + \omega_n{}^3}$$

Show that if the ITAE index is minimized, then $b_1 = 2.15$ and $b_2 = 1.75$.

6-8. If B, k were to gradually change, due to aging of the shock absorbers and springs of the landing gear, what effect does this have on the output of Problem 6-1?

6-9. (a) What is the effect on the error and the output due to a change in $G_1(s)$ in Problems 3-3a, 3b, and 3f?
(b) What is the effect on the output due to a change in $H_3(s)$ in Problems 3-3f and 3g?

6-10. A control system employing proportional and derivative feedback control for stability is shown in Fig. P6-10. What must K be if the overshoot to a step input must not exceed the steady state value by more than 20%?

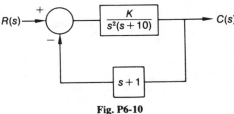

Fig. P6-10

6-11. A second-order system is given by Fig. P6-11a. For the same system derivative plus proportional control is shown in Fig. P6-11b, integral plus proportional control is shown in Fig. P6-11c, and all three in Fig. P6-11d. For each case obtain $c(t)$ for a step input. Compare the results and discuss the merits of derivative and proportional control.

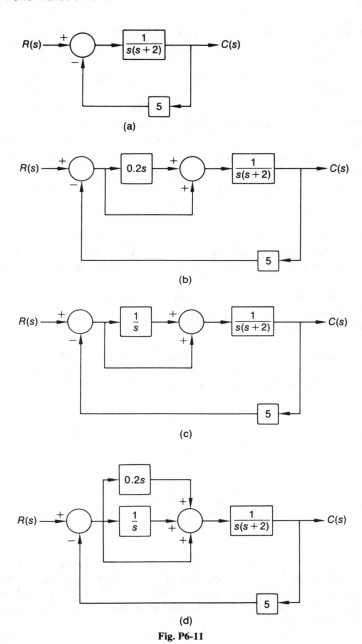

(a)

(b)

(c)

(d)

Fig. P6-11

6-12. Derivative control is shown in the forward loop in Fig. P6-11b and in the feedback loop in Fig. P6-12. What is the essential difference? Obtain $c(t)$ for each and compare the results.

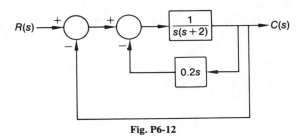

Fig. P6-12

REFERENCES

1. Elgerd, O. I., *Control Systems Theory*, New York, McGraw-Hill, 1967.
2. Schultz, W. C., and V. C. Rideout, "Control System Performance Measures: Past, Present, and Future," *IRE Trans. on Automatic Control*, February 1961.
3. Saucedo, R., and E. E. Schiring, *Introduction to Continuous and Digital Control Systems*, New York, Macmillan, 1968.
4. Graham, D., and R. C. Lathrop, "The Synthesis of Optimum Response: Criteria and Standard Forms, Part 2," *Trans AIEE*, **72**, November 1953.
5. Kuo, B. C., *Automatic Control Systems*, Englewood Cliffs, N.J., Prentice-Hall, 1962.

7

Graphical Methods

7-1 INTRODUCTION

So far, the analysis of control systems has relied exclusively on several analytical techniques. System response and stability obtained, via classical or state space methods, was dependent upon the closed loop poles. It was evident that even for relatively simple systems, the amount of algebra can be quite formidable. This is further aggravated when the characteristic polynomial is large. But that is not all. Assume that a control system has a characteristic polynomial of the form

$$s^3 + 4s^2 + (5 + K)s + 5K = 0$$

and we would like to obtain system performance for six values of K so that we can select a value that best suits our requirements. This requires that we obtain six sets of three closed loop poles! Additionally, we may not only want to know whether the system is absolutely stable but also about its relative stability as well as ways of improving system stability. Although techniques developed so far can answer some of these questions, the amount of trial and error work as well as hand computation that must necessarily accompany becomes discouraging. Clearly, the motivation for looking for quicker ways becomes strong.

We can get around the difficulties posed in the previous paragraph by either using a computer for faster computation or turning to graphical methods for investigating control systems or both. Since the information obtained from the graphical methods complements that obtained from the time domain analysis, it is important that we understand the fundamentals of graphical methods. Generally, a complete analysis of a control system includes the time domain type of analysis discussed before as well as the graphical approach to be discussed now. The power of the time domain as well as the graphical approach is greatly enhanced by relatively simple interactive (time shared) computer programs.

Although analysis based on a step input provides a uniform basis of comparison, the analysis of a system subjected to a sinusoidal input is quite common. The system response to such an input will also be sinusoidal but, in general, with different magnitude and phase angle. The frequency response technique is a graphical technique which considers the input to be a sinusoidally varying function. It is an easy, quick and powerful technique for obtaining the steady state response at specified frequencies. Furthermore, when the transfer function of a system is not known, it can be approximated using an experimentally determined frequency response of the system. This technique can also be extended to include a certain class of nonlinear problems as we shall show in a later chapter. We will also investigate the system stability in the real frequency domain, i.e. in terms of the frequency response of a system. We shall see that the frequency method of analysis enables us not only to study the relative stability of a system but is a useful tool for altering the system in order to vary this relative stability.

While the frequency response method dwells on the frequency of the system, another very useful graphical technique deals directly with the roots of the characteristic equation. This second method is called the root locus method. It shows graphically how the poles of the closed loop system migrate on the s-plane as the overall gain of the system is varied. Here it is possible to see directly what the dynamic performance of the system will be, and how it may be modified. Since we follow the closed loop poles we can obtain the transient behavior of the system as well. Before we consider details of these graphical approaches it is perhaps useful to reiterate the following important points:

(1) The response of a system is dependent upon the input, initial conditions, and the closed loop eigenvalues.
(2) The absolute stability of a system is determined by the location of the closed loop eigenvalues.
(3) The closed loop eigenvalues equal the closed loop poles, if there are no pole-zero cancellations.
(4) The relative stability is very important and is dependent upon the closeness of the closed loop poles to the $j\omega$-axis.

(5) Obtaining closed loop poles is generally difficult and often they depend upon design parameters.

(6) The graphical methods, to be considered here, allow us to quickly determine the relative stability as well as response. Although a function of the hard to find closed loop poles, we shall determine response and relative stability from open loop poles which are known.

7-2   THE FREQUENCY RESPONSE METHOD

The overall transfer function of a system can be expressed as the ratio of two polynomials,

$$F(s) = \frac{C(s)}{R(s)} = \frac{a_m s^m + a_{m-1} s^{m-1} + \cdots + a_0}{b_n s^n + b_{n-1} s^{n-1} + \cdots + b_0} = \frac{P_1(s)}{P_2(s)}$$

which corresponds to the differential equation

$$b_n \frac{d^n c(t)}{dt^n} + b_{n-1} \frac{d^{n-1} c(t)}{dt^{n-1}} + \cdots + b_0 c(t) = a_m \frac{d^m r(t)}{dt^m} + \cdots + a_0 r(t)$$

The form of the solution of $c(t)$ depends not only upon the nature of $r(t)$ but also on the roots of the characteristic equation $P_2(s) = 0$. For a stable system, i.e. the roots of $P_2(s)$ are in the left half s-plane, $c(t)$ will have a transient that goes to zero while the solution asymptotically approaches the form of the input. Since the input is sinusoidal, the output is also sinusoidal. If we represent the input by

$$r(t) = D e^{j\omega t}$$

then the output $c(t)$ will be

$$c(t) = E e^{j(\omega t + \phi)}$$

where $E = E(\omega)$ and $\phi = \phi(\omega)$. Substituting and simplifying we obtain

$$\frac{E e^{j\phi}}{D} = \frac{a_m (j\omega)^m + a_{m-1} (j\omega)^{m-1} + \cdots + a_0}{b_n (j\omega)^n + b_{n-1} (j\omega)^{n-1} + \cdots + b_0}$$

Comparing this with the transfer function suggests the substitution $s = j\omega$,

$$\frac{C(j\omega)}{R(j\omega)} = F(j\omega) = \frac{E e^{j\phi}}{D} \tag{7-1}$$

In general, $F(j\omega)$ is a complex number having magnitude, or gain, and phase angle, or shift,

$$|F(j\omega)| = \frac{E(\omega)}{D} \qquad (7\text{-}2a)$$

$$\underline{/F(j\omega)} = \phi(\omega) \qquad (7\text{-}2b)$$

The expression $F(j\omega)$ is referred to as a frequency function. The variation of the gain and phase shift as the frequency changes is the basis of the frequency response method.

Several types of frequency response plots can be constructed for variations of gain and phase shift as a function of frequency. The two most widely used methods are known as the Bode plot and the Nyquist plot.

The Bode Plot

The Bode plot is also referred to as the corner plot or the logarithmic plot. This method employs logarithms of functions and therefore multiplication and division is reduced to addition and subtraction and the work of obtaining the response is largely graphical instead of analytical. The ease of plotting makes the addition of poles and zeros to the transfer function very simple. Varying the system gain on the Bode plot simply involves the raising or lowering of the entire magnitude versus frequency plot, with respect to a reference, while the phase shift versus frequency remains unchanged.

The Bode plot consists of two plots, viz. phase shift and the logarithm of the magnitude plotted as functions of frequency. The logarithm of the magnitude of a transfer function is expressed in decibels where

$$\text{Magnitude of } F(j\omega) \text{ in decibels} = 20 \log F(j\omega)$$
$$= \text{Lm } F(j\omega) \qquad (7\text{-}3)$$

and Lm is an abbreviation for log magnitude.

Since the log magnitude is also a function of frequency, a convenient way to express frequency bands is necessary. When frequency varies† from ω_1 to ω_2 where $\omega_2 = 10\omega_1$, then the frequency band is referred to as a *decade*. The band from 1 Hz to 10 Hz or from 3.14 to 31.4 Hz is one decade. The number of decades in a given frequency band is given by

$$\frac{\log \omega_2/\omega_1}{\log 10} = \log \frac{\omega_2}{\omega_1} \text{ decades}$$

---

†The octave band is one where $\omega_2 = 2\omega_1$. This is not as widely used.

We observe that if $F(j\omega)$ increases by tenfold, or one decade, then the log magnitude increases by 20.

In general, the transfer function of a system consists of four basic types of terms in the numerator and denominator. These are

$$K$$
$$(j\omega)^{\pm n}$$
$$(1+j\omega T)^{\pm m}$$
$$(1+j2\omega\delta T + (j\omega T)^2)^{\pm p}$$

If we construct the curves of the log magnitude and angle versus frequency for each individual factor, then the Bode plot of the entire transfer function can be obtained by adding the contribution of each term.

Constant or K Factor

The constant K is independent of frequency,

$$\text{Lm } K = 20 \log K \text{ decibels} \qquad (7\text{-}4)$$

and appears as a horizontal line that raises or lowers the log magnitude curve of the complete transfer function by a fixed amount. There is no contribution on the phase shift since K is real and positive.

$(j\omega)^{\pm n}$ Factor

The log magnitude and phase shift of $(j\omega)^{\pm n}$ is

$$\text{Lm}|(j\omega)^{\pm n}| = \pm 20n \log \omega \qquad (7\text{-}5a)$$

$$\underline{/(j\omega)^{\pm n}} = \pm\frac{n\pi}{2} \qquad (7\text{-}5b)$$

The magnitude plot consists of a straight line whose slope is $\pm 20n$ db/decade and goes through 0 db at $\omega = 1$. The phase shift is a constant $\pm n\pi/2$.

$(1+j\omega T)^{\pm m}$ Factor

As a first case let us assume that $m = 1$ and consider the negative exponent. Then

$$\text{Lm}|(1+j\omega T)^{-1}| = -20 \log \sqrt{1+\omega^2 T^2} \qquad (7\text{-}6a)$$

$$\underline{/(1+j\omega T)^{-1}} = -\arctan \omega T \qquad (7\text{-}6b)$$

For very small values of ωT the log magnitude becomes

$$\text{Lm } (1+\omega T)^{-1} = -20 \log 1 = 0$$

i.e. for small frequencies the log magnitude is represented by the 0 db line. As $\omega T \gg 1$,

$$\text{Lm}(1+j\omega T)^{-1} \approx \text{Lm}(j\omega T)^{-1} \approx -20 \log \omega T$$

which is zero for $\omega = 1/T$ and a straight line with -20 db/decade slope for $\omega T > 1$. The point defined by the intersection of the line obtained for $\omega T > 1$ and $\omega T < 1$ is $\omega = 1/T$. This point is called the *corner frequency* and is shown in Fig. 7-1. The exact curve is shown by a dotted line. The

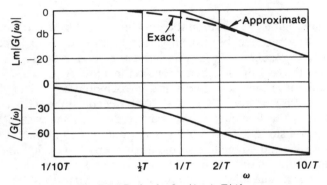

Fig. 7-1   Bode plot for $(1+j\omega T)^{\pm 1}$.

error between the exact curve and the straight lines (or the asymptotes) is greatest at the corner frequency. In practice, the actual curve is drawn freehand with corrections inserted at $\omega = 1/T$, $\omega = 1/2T$, and $\omega = 2/T$. The log magnitude correction is shown in Fig. 7-2.

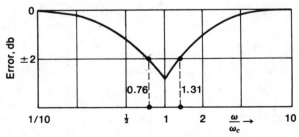

Fig. 7-2   Log magnitude correction for $(1+j\omega T)^{\pm 1}$.

Before considering the next type of factor, we return to the case where $(1+j\omega T)^{+m}$ occurs. The corner frequency is still at $\omega = 1/T$ except that the asymptote defined for $\omega T > 1$ has a slope of $\pm 20m$ db/decade. This is the only difference. When two or more factors of this form appear, we simply add the contribution of each. Consider, for example, the transfer function

$$G(s) = (1 + sT_1)^{-1}(1 + sT_2)^{-1}$$

The magnitude and phase are

$$\text{Lm}|G(j\omega)| = -20 \log \sqrt{1 + \omega^2 T_1^2} - 20 \log \sqrt{1 + \omega^2 T_2^2}$$

$$\underline{/G(j\omega)} = -\arctan \omega T_1 - \arctan \omega T_2$$

If we assume that $T_2 < T_1$, then the contribution of both the terms is 0 db until $\omega = 1/T_1$ is reached. Now the first term contributes -20 db/decade until $\omega = 1/T_2$ is reached. Up to this point the second factor has no contribution to the asymptotic behavior of the plot. At $\omega = 1/T_2$ (another corner frequency) the second term is approximated by $-20 \log |\omega T_2|$ and is represented by a straight line of -20 db/decade slope. However, since this reinforces the first factor, the magnitude becomes a straight line of -40 db/decade slope. Clearly, if the exponent of the first factor of $G(j\omega)$ had been positive, then the line would have been a horizontal line, or 0 db/decade, after the second corner frequency. The Lm plot and phase shift plot for corner frequencies at $1/T_1$ and $1/T_2$ is shown in Fig. 7-3.

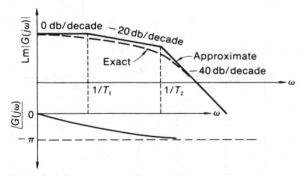

Fig. 7-3 Bode plot for $G(j\omega) = \dfrac{1}{(j\omega T_1 + 1)(j\omega T_2 + 1)}$.

$(1+j2\omega\delta T+(j\omega T)^2)^{\pm p}$ **Factor**

As before, the case of $p = -1$ is considered without loss of generality. If the quadratic term can be factored yielding real roots, then we may use the technique developed in the previous section. However, if the roots are complex conjugates, then the entire factor should be plotted without factoring. If the roots are complex conjugates, we have

$$\text{Lm}|G(j\omega)| = -20\log\left[(1-\omega^2 T^2)^2 + (2\delta\omega T)^2\right]^{\frac{1}{2}} \tag{7-7a}$$

$$\underline{/G(j\omega)} = -\arctan\frac{2\delta\omega T}{\sqrt{1-\omega^2 T^2}} \tag{7-7b}$$

Now if ω is very small, the log magnitude is zero. As ω increased the log magnitude asymptote has a slope of -40 db/decade. The point of intersection of the 0 db line and the -40 db/decade line occurs at $\omega = \omega_n$ and this is the corner frequency. The phase shift is 0 at $\omega = 0$, increases to $-\pi/2$ at the corner frequency and finally goes to $-\pi$ as ω approaches infinity. This is shown in Fig. 7-4.

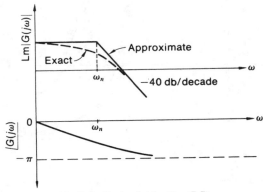

Fig. 7-4   Bode plot for Eq. (7-7).

In the above case, when $\omega = \omega_n$, resonant conditions tend to be set up. This is why ω_n is often referred to as the *resonant frequency*. Depending upon the value of the damping ratio δ, considerable error may be introduced when comparing the actual Bode plot to the straight line asymptote. The exact plot with δ as parameter is shown in Fig. 7-5. The maximum value of the magnitude seen on Fig. 7-5 is often referred to as the *resonant peak* or gain and denoted by M_p. When the exponent for this type of a factor becomes positive, the log magnitude and phase shift simply change sign.

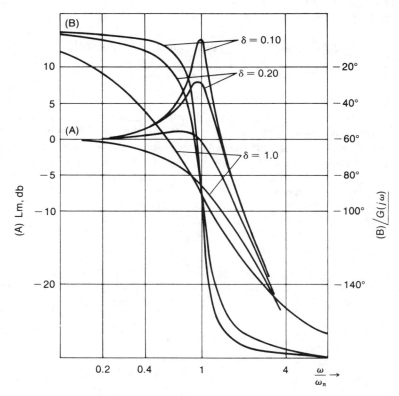

Fig. 7-5 Bode plot for a second-order system with damping ratio as parameter.

EXAMPLE 7-1

Construct the Bode plot for the following transfer function

$$G(s) = \frac{0.25(1+0.5s)}{s(1+2s)(1+4s)}$$

The log magnitude and phase shift are

$$\text{Lm}|G(j\omega)| = 20\log 0.25 + 20\log\sqrt{1+0.25\omega^2} - 20\log\omega$$
$$- 20\log\sqrt{1+4\omega^2} - 20\log\sqrt{1+16\omega^2}$$

$$\underline{/G(j\omega)} = \arctan 0.5\omega - \frac{\pi}{2} - \arctan 2\omega - \arctan 4\omega$$

There are three corner frequencies at $\omega_1 = \frac{1}{4}$, $\omega_2 = \frac{1}{2}$ and $\omega_3 = 2$. The magnitude and phase plots are seen to vary as follows.

For $0 \le \omega \le \omega_1$
$$\text{Lm}|G(j\omega)| = -20\log\omega + 20\log 0.25 = \text{Lm}_1$$
$$\underline{/G(j\omega)} = -\frac{\pi}{2} = \underline{/G_1}$$

For $\omega_1 \le \omega \le \omega_2$
$$\text{Lm}|G(j\omega)| = \text{Lm}_1 - 20\log 4\omega = \text{Lm}_2$$
$$\underline{/G(j\omega)} = \underline{/G_1} - \arctan 4\omega = \underline{/G_2}$$

For $\omega_2 \le \omega \le \omega_3$
$$\text{Lm}|G(j\omega)| = \text{Lm}_2 - 20\log 2\omega = \text{Lm}_3$$
$$\underline{/G(j\omega)} = \underline{/G_2} - \arctan 2\omega = \underline{/G_3}$$

For $\omega_3 \le \omega \le \infty$
$$\text{Lm}|G(j\omega)| = \text{Lm}_3 + 20\log 0.5\omega$$
$$\underline{/G(j\omega)} = \underline{/G_3} + \arctan 0.5\omega$$

The Bode plot is shown in Fig. 7-6.

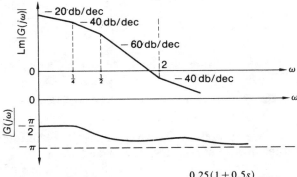

Fig. 7-6 Bode plot for $G(s) = \dfrac{0.25(1+0.5s)}{s(1+2s)(1+4s)}$.

The transfer function analyzed in the previous example is called a minimum phase transfer function. Such transfer functions have no poles and zeros in the right half s-plane. When the transfer function is nonminimum phase, a zero or pole may be in the right half s-plane.

Study of the minimum phase transfer functions show that the amplitude and phase shift characteristics are interdependent. This means that for a specified amplitude in the frequency range of interest, the phase shift cannot be independently selected in the same frequency range although it may be specified in some other range.

We mentioned that if a transfer function of a system is not known, it may be approximated using an experimentally determined frequency response of the system. This is achieved by replacing the experimental frequency response plot by appropriate asymptotes. The intersection of these asymptotes correspond to corner frequencies from which the transfer function is synthesized as shown in the next example.

EXAMPLE 7-2

Obtain the transfer function for the experimentally derived frequency response shown in Fig. 7-7. Assume that the system is minimum phase.

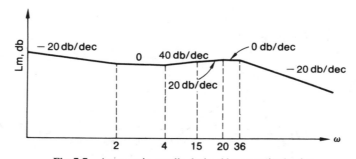

Fig. 7-7 An experimentally derived log magnitude plot.

We construct asymptotes as shown in the figure. The intersections of these asymptotes occur† at $\omega = 2, 4, 15, 20,$ and 36. A positive slope indicates a zero and a negative slope indicates the existence of a pole. The factor that would yield -20 db/decade between $\omega = 0$ and 2 is s^{-1}. Between $\omega = 2$ and 4, $(s+2)$ would give a -20 db/decade but this when added to the contribution of s^{-1} would yield a line having a slope of 0 db/decade. Carrying through this argument, the overall transfer function

---

†These are corner frequencies.

becomes

$$G(s) = \frac{(s+2)(s+4)^2}{s(s+15)(s+20)(s+36)}$$

The stability of a system can also be ascertained via the conventional Bode plot if the system is one of minimum phase. Since the characteristic equation is

$$1 + G(s)H(s) = 0$$

we can write this as

$$\text{Lm}|G(s)H(s)| = 0; \quad \underline{/G(s)H(s)} = -\pi$$

Therefore the 0 db crossover determines system stability.

Consider the third-order system with the following transfer function,

$$G(s)H(s) = \frac{K}{s(1+T_1 s)(1+T_2 s)}$$

The three possible Bode plots are shown in Fig. 7-23. These plots indicate that the system is stable for $K < K_c$, marginally stable (i.e. oscillatory) for $K = K_c$, and unstable for $K > K_c$. Notice that when $K > K_c$, the magnitude is larger than 0 db when the phase is $-\pi$. When this happens the zeros of the characteristic equation have assumed positive real parts. A stronger and more preferable criterion for ascertaining system stability is used on the Nyquist plot to be considered in the next section.

Although the Bode plot refers to the open loop transfer function we can also obtain the closed loop response. For a specific frequency ω_c, we may relate the closed loop response to $G(j\omega_c)$ as follows,

$$F(j\omega_c) = \frac{C(j\omega_c)}{R(j\omega_c)} = \frac{G(j\omega_c)}{1 + G(j\omega_c)} \qquad (7\text{-}8)$$

Since $G(j\omega_c) = u + jv$, where

$$u = |G(j\omega_c)| \cos \phi$$
$$v = |G(j\omega_c)| \sin \phi$$

we have

$$F(j\omega_c) = \frac{u+jv}{(1+u)+jv} = \frac{u(1+u)+v^2+jv}{(1+u)^2+v^2}$$

If the output is represented as a magnitude M and phase θ,

$$F(j\omega_c) = Me^{-j\theta}$$

then

$$M = \left[\frac{(u(1+u) + v^2)^2 + v^2}{((1+u)^2 + v^2)^2} \right]^{\frac{1}{2}} \qquad \theta = \arctan \frac{v}{u(1+u) + v^2}$$

We shall consider a more generalized form of this in a later section. It suffices to note here that we are able to obtain the steady state performance of the closed loop system from the Bode plot.

The Nyquist Plot

The plot of $G(j\omega)$ on the complex plane for values of frequency from zero to infinity is referred to as the polar or Nyquist plot. This kind of a plot is extremely useful in stability analysis as well as design of control systems. These plots may be generated either by obtaining the magnitude and phase shift from the Bode plot or computing directly from the transfer function. If the Nyquist plot is obtained from the Bode plot, care must be exercised in the conversion of decibels to the magnitude.

Plots of $G(j\omega)$ on the complex plane are referred to as direct plots, whereas those of $G(j\omega)^{-1}$ are referred to as inverse plots. The technique of generating either the direct or the inverse plot is identical, therefore we shall only consider direct plots.

In general, the magnitude and phase shift of $G(j\omega)$ is

$$|G(j\omega)| = \frac{K \prod_z (1 + \omega^2 T_z^2)^{\frac{1}{2}}}{\omega^m \prod_p (1 + \omega^2 T_p^2)^{\frac{1}{2}}} \tag{7-9a}$$

$$\underline{/G(j\omega)} = \sum_z \arctan \omega T_z - \frac{m\pi}{2} - \sum_p \arctan \omega T_p \tag{7-9b}$$

The magnitude and phase are computed for specific frequencies and plotted as shown in Fig. 7-8. A line joining all the permissible values of

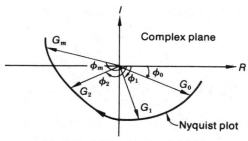

Fig. 7-8   A Nyquist plot of $G(j\omega)$.

$|G(j\omega)|$ is the required plot. In general, the frequency is varied from $-\infty$ to $+\infty$ as will be seen later. However, since the Nyquist plot is symmetrical about the real axis, the limit $0 \leqslant \omega \leqslant \infty$ suffices.

EXAMPLE 7-3

Construct the Nyquist plot for

$$G(s) = \frac{K}{1 + sT}$$

The magnitude and phase shift become

$$|G(j\omega)| = \frac{K}{\sqrt{1 + \omega^2 T^2}}$$

$$\underline{/G(j\omega)} = -\arctan \omega T$$

For specific values of ω the following table is constructed,

ω	$|G(j\omega)|$	$\underline{/G(j\omega)}$
0	K	0
$\frac{1}{T}$	$K/\sqrt{2}$	$-\frac{\pi}{4}$
$\frac{2}{T}$	$K/\sqrt{5}$	
$\vdots$	$\vdots$	$\vdots$
∞	0	$-\frac{\pi}{2}$

The Nyquist plot is shown in Fig. 7-9.

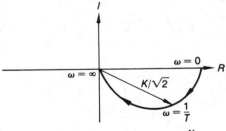

Fig. 7-9   Nyquist plot for $G(s) = \dfrac{K}{1 + sT}$.

Consider next, what happens when a pole at $s = 0$ is introduced.

$$G(s) = \frac{K}{s(1+sT)}$$

$$|G(j\omega)| = \frac{K}{\omega\sqrt{1+\omega^2 T^2}}$$

$$\underline{/G(j\omega)} = -\frac{\pi}{2} - \arctan \omega T$$

We note that at $\omega = 0$ the magnitude goes to infinity and the phase shift is $-\pi/2$. The Nyquist plot is shown in Fig. 7-10. If we were to have n poles at the origin, then the initial phase shift will be $-n\pi/2$ and the final phase shift will be $-(n+1)\pi/2$ for this type of a transfer function. In each of the

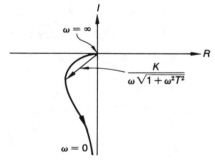

Fig. 7-10   Nyquist plot for $G(s) = \dfrac{K}{s(1+sT)}$.

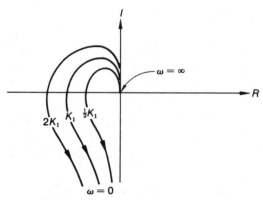

Fig. 7-11   Effect of varying system gain.

previous examples we saw that the gain K had no effect on the overall shape of the polar plot since it is a common factor to all the points. As K is varied the plot simply contracts (decreasing K) or dilates (increasing K) as shown in Fig. 7-11. Examination of the plots obtained so far show that they often cross the real and/or the imaginary axis. The point where the crossover occurs is a function of the frequency. Consider the open loop transfer function

$$G(s) = \frac{K}{s(1+sT_1)(1+sT_2)(1+sT_3)}$$

Substitution of $s = j\omega$ and writing $G(j\omega)$ as a complex number,

$$G(j\omega) = \frac{K}{j\omega(1+j\omega T_1)(1+j\omega T_2)(1+j\omega T_3)}$$

$$= \frac{1}{P(\omega)}[R(\omega) + jI(\omega)]$$

where

$$R(\omega) = \omega^2 K[T_1 T_2 T_3 \omega^2 - (T_1 + T_2 + T_3)]$$

$$I(\omega) = \omega K[\omega^2(T_1 T_2 + T_1 T_3 + T_2 T_3) - 1]$$

The solution of the equations $R(\omega) = 0$ and $I(\omega) = 0$ will yield the frequencies at which the imaginary and real axis is crossed. In this problem the imaginary axis intercept is

$$R(\omega) = 0; \qquad \omega = \omega_R = \pm\left[\frac{T_1 + T_2 + T_3}{T_1 T_2 T_3}\right]^{\frac{1}{2}}$$

and the real intercept occurs at

$$I(\omega) = 0; \qquad \omega = \omega_I = \pm\left[\frac{1}{T_1 T_2 + T_1 T_3 + T_2 T_3}\right]^{\frac{1}{2}}$$

Since the limit under investigation is $0 \leq \omega \leq \infty$ we select the positive roots. Note that the points of real and imaginary axis intercepts are independent of K but are functions of the system time constants as shown in Fig. 7-12. In all the examples so far there have been no zeros in $G(s)$. An interesting Nyquist plot occurs for a third-order system having $G(s)$ with a zero at the origin,

$$G(s) = \frac{Ks}{(1+sT_1)(1+sT_2)(1+sT_3)}$$

The magnitude of $G(j\omega)$ is zero at $\omega = 0$ and $\omega = \infty$. The phase shift is $\pi/2$ at $\omega = 0$ but $-\pi$ at $\omega = \infty$. If the zero is at $-A$, then the magnitude is

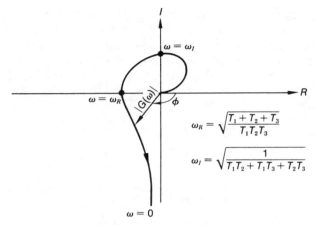

Fig. 7-12   Plot of $G(s) = \dfrac{K}{s(1+sT_1)(1+sT_2)(1+sT_3)}$.

KA at $\omega = 0$ and 0 at $\omega = \infty$. The phase varies from 0 to $-\pi$. This is shown in Fig. 7-13. The real and imaginary axis intercepts may be computed by setting the imaginary and real part of $G(s)$ equal to zero as before.

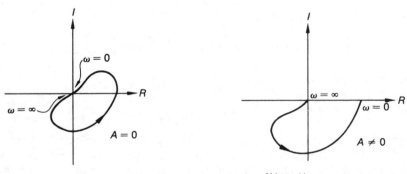

Fig. 7-13   Nyquist plot for $G(s) = \dfrac{K(s+A)}{(1+sT_1)(1+sT_2)(1+sT_3)}$.

The closed loop response can be obtained from the Nyquist plot as we did for the Bode plot. This is discussed in a later section when we speak of relative stability and performance in the frequency domain. But first we will consider the system stability via a criterion applied on the Nyquist plot.

The Nyquist Criterion

A stability criterion for application in the real frequency domain was developed by H. Nyquist and is based upon a theorem in the theory of complex variables. This theorem is Cauchy's theorem and it is concerned with the mapping of contours in the s-plane. We shall present the criterion but without any formal proof.

The stability of a system may be studied by investigating the characteristic equation,

$$F(s) = 1 + P(s) = 0 \qquad (7\text{-}10)$$

where $P(s)$ is a rational function of s. The stable response of a system requires that the zeros of $F(s)$ not be in the right half s-plane. This may be ascertained if the right half s-plane is mapped on the $F(s)$-plane and by invoking the Nyquist criterion.

The Nyquist criterion was derived from Cauchy's theorem commonly called the principle of the argument in complex variable theory. Fortunately, the consequences of the theorem may be understood without reviewing the formal proofs.

We begin defining the words *encircled* and *enclosed* with reference to the context they shall be used in the following discussion. The point P shown in Fig. 7-14a is said to be encircled by the closed path Γ. The direction of encirclement is counterclockwise. If we follow the convention that the region to the left of a path is enclosed, then the region inside the closed path Γ in Fig. 7-14a is enclosed. The point P in Fig. 7-14b is encircled in the clockwise direction, however the area outside the closed path is enclosed. The area inside the closed path is not enclosed. Finally, in Fig. 7-14c the point P is not encircled although it is enclosed.

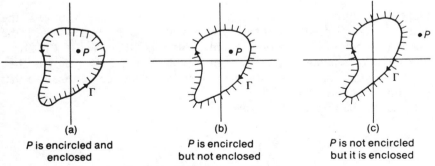

(a)	(b)	(c)
P is encircled and enclosed	P is encircled but not enclosed	P is not encircled but it is enclosed

Fig. 7-14 Encirclement and enclosure.

Let us now assume that $F(s)$ is a single valued and rational function. It must also be analytic in the s-plane except at some finite number of points. You will recall that these points are the poles of $F(s)$. Now suppose that we select a closed path Γ_s on the s-plane such that $F(s)$ is analytic everywhere on this enclosed path. We can now generate a corresponding locus on the $F(s)$-plane, i.e. for every value s_i on the closed path Γ_s we compute and plot a corresponding point $F(s_i)$ on the $F(s)$-plane. The resulting contour on the $F(s)$-plane is also a closed path and is labeled Γ_F as shown in Fig. 7-15. The generation of Γ_F is referred to as conformal mapping.

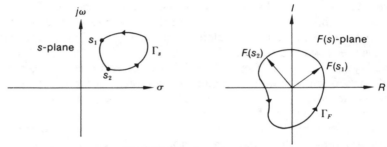

Fig. 7-15   Conformal mapping.

Now we use Cauchy's theorem, which states that,

If the contour Γ_s encircles Z zeros and P poles of $F(s)$ on the s-plane, then the $F(s)$ locus Γ_F encircles the origin on the $F(s)$-plane N times, where $N = Z - P$, in the same direction as the Γ_s direction on the s-plane.

Depending upon Z and P, N may be zero, negative, or positive. If the contour on the s-plane encircles more zeros than poles, then $N > 0$. If the number of poles is equal to the number of zeros, then $N = 0$. Finally, if the number of poles is greater, then $N < 0$. When N is negative, then $F(s)$ contour encircles the origin N times in a direction opposite to that of Γ_s on the s-plane.

Consider the function $F(s)$ given by

$$F(s) = \frac{(s+z_1)(s+z_2)}{(s+p_1)(s+p_2)}$$

Writing this as magnitude and phase,

$$|F(s)| = \frac{|s+z_1| \cdot |s+z_2|}{|s+p_1| \cdot |s+p_2|}$$

$$\underline{/F(s)} = \phi_{z_1} + \phi_{z_2} - \phi_{p_1} - \phi_{p_2}$$

where ϕ_{z_1} is the angle due to zero at z_1 and so on. Now let us select the path shown on the s-plane. For $s = s_1$, the vector $F(s_1)$ is shown in Fig. 7-16b. As we move around the contour on the s-plane along the indicated path, beginning from s_1 and returning to s_1, the net angle change is zero.

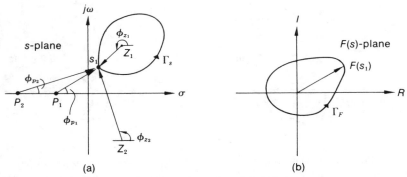

(a)   (b)

Fig. 7-16 $F(s)$ encloses the origin Z-P times.

However, as Γ_s traverses 2π on the s-plane, ϕ_{z_1} also traverses 2π in the same direction. If the path is enlarged to include Z_2, then ϕ_{z_2} also traverses 2π radians. The two zeros together traverse $2(2\pi)$ radians. In general if all the zeros are enclosed, then for Z zeros we have $Z(2\pi)$ traversals. Following the same argument, if the poles are enclosed we may say that the poles contribute $P(2\pi)$ traversals but in the opposite direction. The net traversals that the $F(s)$ contour experiences becomes

$$N(2\pi) = Z(2\pi) - P(2\pi)$$

or

$$N = Z - P \tag{7-11}$$

i.e. the number of enclosures is equal to the difference of the number of zeros and poles in the right half s-plane.

As an example consider a function $F(s)$ having the pole zero configuration shown in Fig. 7-17a. Since there is 1 pole and 2 zeros inside Γ_s, the origin on the $F(s)$-plane is encircled once by Γ_F. The pole-zero configuration of $F(s)$ in Fig. 7-17b indicates one zero and three poles inside Γ_s, therefore, Γ_F encircles the origin twice but in the opposite direction.

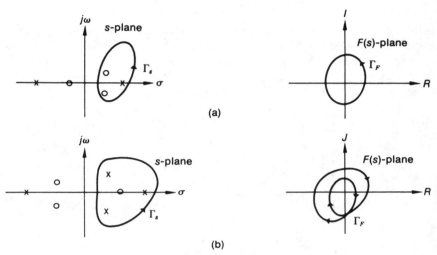

Fig. 7-17 $F(s)$ enclosing the origin for different pole-zero configurations.

We investigate the stability of a control system by considering the characteristic equation

$$F(s) = 1 + G(s)H(s) = 0$$

and requiring that the roots of this characteristic equation may not exist in the right half s-plane, i.e. to the right of the imaginary axis. Therefore, if we select Γ_s to include the entire right half s-plane, then we may employ Cauchy's theorem to determine whether any poles or zeros of $F(s)$ exist in this region. Let us define Γ_s, referred to as the Nyquist path, to consist of four paths shown in Fig. 7-18. These paths are

(1) From $+j\infty$ to $+j0$ along $j\omega$ axis
(2) From $+j0$ to $-j0$ along the semicircle with infinitesimal radius
(3) From $-j0$ to $-j\infty$ along $-j\omega$ axis
(4) From $-j\infty$ to $+j\infty$ along the semicircle with infinite radius.

We note that since the Nyquist path may not pass through any poles of $F(s)$ we must avoid them on the path.

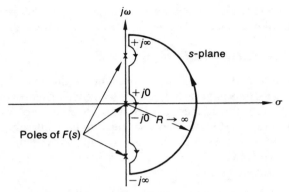

Fig. 7-18   The Nyquist path.

The Nyquist method is concerned with the mapping of $F(s)$

$$F(s) = 1 + G(s)H(s) = 1 + \frac{K \prod\limits_z (s + z_z)}{\prod\limits_p (s + p_p)} \qquad (7\text{-}12a)$$

and the consequent encirclement of the origin on the $F(s)$-plane. $G(s)H(s)$ is the open loop transfer function and a rational function in s. We define $f(s)$ such that

$$f(s) = F(s) - 1 = G(s)H(s) \qquad (7\text{-}12b)$$

and instead map on the $f(s)$-plane which is similar to the $G(s)H(s)$-plane. Clearly, since we are concerned with the encirclement of the origin on the $F(s)$-plane, this point is identical to the $(-1, 0)$ point on the $G(s)H(s)$-plane. (From now on this will be referred to as the GH-plane.) With this in mind, we state the Nyquist criterion for stability:

A control system is stable if the number of encirclements of the $(-1, 0)$ point by the GH plot is equal to the number of poles of GH with positive real parts. The direction of encirclement must be in a direction opposite to Γ_s.

If the number of poles of GH in the right half s-plane is zero, then $N = 0$, i.e. the GH plot may not encircle the $(-1, 0)$ point. If the number of poles with positive real parts is 1, then

$$N = Z - 1$$

and for stability we require that $Z = 0$, therefore

$$N = -1$$

For a stable system, the Nyquist criterion requires that $N = -P$ where N is the number of encirclement of the $(-1, 0)$ point by the GH plot.

Application of the Nyquist Criterion

The application of the Nyquist criterion to the stability analysis of linear control systems is best understood by considering several examples. The Nyquist plots introduced earlier were constructed for frequencies ranging from 0 to ∞. However, now we need to take into account negative frequencies. This is very straightforward especially if we note that the plot for negative frequencies will be a mirror image about the real axis of the positive frequency plot.

EXAMPLE 7-4

Determine the stability of the unity feedback control system with the forward loop transfer function given by

$$G(s) = \frac{K}{s+a}$$

The magnitude and phase are given as

s	$|G(s)|$	$\underline{/G(s)}$
0	K/a	0
js_1	$K/\sqrt{s_1^2 + a^2}$	$-\arctan\dfrac{s_1}{a}$
$j\infty$	0	$-\dfrac{\pi}{2}$

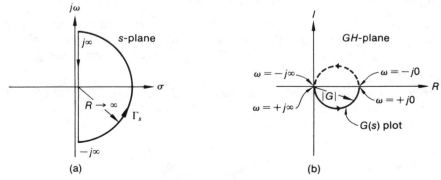

Fig. 7-19 Nyquist plot of $G(s) = K/(s+a)$.

The Nyquist plot is shown in Fig. 7-19. Note that the plot for negative frequencies is simply the image about the real axis. Since $G(s)$ does not have poles with positive real parts, the $G(s)$ plot should not enclose the $(-1, 0)$ point for stability. This in fact is the case and the system is stable for all gain.

Next we consider the transfer function with a pole at $s = 0$,

$$G(s) = \frac{K}{s(s+a)}$$

The origin on the s-plane must now be avoided by the Γ_s contour. The magnitude and phase are computed,

s	$|G(s)|$	$\angle G(s)$
0	∞	$-\dfrac{\pi}{2}$
js_1	$K/s_1\sqrt{s_1{}^2 + a^2}$	$-\dfrac{\pi}{2} - \arctan\dfrac{s_1}{a}$
$j\infty$	-0	$-\pi$

We may use this information to construct the Nyquist plot as s varies from $+j\infty$ to $+0$ and -0 to $-j\infty$. In order to complete the Nyquist plot we need two additional paths, viz. one as s varies from $+j0$ to $-j0$ and the second as s varies from $-j\infty$ to $+j\infty$.

In order to construct the Nyquist path corresponding to the Γ_s semi-circle around the origin, we represent s as

$$s = re^{-j\theta}$$

as shown in Fig. 7-20a. Substituting this in $G(s)$,

$$G(s) = \frac{K}{re^{-j\theta}(re^{-j\theta} + a)}$$

For small r,

$$G(s) \cong \frac{K}{are^{-j\theta}}$$

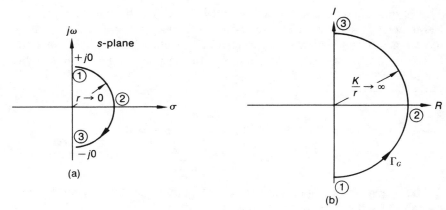

Fig. 7-20 Γ_s semicircle around origin and the corresponding Nyquist plot Γ_G.

The last approximation is valid since $r \ll a$. As r becomes vanishingly small we have

$$G(s) \rightarrow (\infty)e^{j\theta}$$

and as we go around the Γ_s semicircle, θ varies from $+\pi/2$ to $-\pi/2$ going through zero. Meanwhile $G(s)$ varies from $-\pi/2$ to $+\pi/2$ also going through zero and with a magnitude of infinity as shown on Fig. 7-20b.

We now consider the semicircle having ∞ radius on the s-plane. Again representing this as a vector

$$s = Re^{-j\phi}$$

Substituting this in $G(s)$,

$$G(s) = \frac{K}{Re^{-j\phi}(Re^{-j\phi} + a)}$$

$$G(s) \cong \frac{K}{R^2 e^{-j2\phi}}$$

The last approximation is valid since $R \gg a$. As $R \rightarrow \infty$ we have

$$G(s) \rightarrow (0)e^{j2\phi}$$

Now as we follow Γ_s along the semicircle with ∞ radius, ϕ varies from $-\pi/2$ to $+\pi/2$ through zero. Meanwhile $G(s)$ varies from π to $-\pi$ through zero and having zero magnitude. Notice that the angle variation is twice that of s on the s-plane. This is shown in Fig. 7-21. Combining the two paths just considered we obtain the complete Nyquist plot shown in

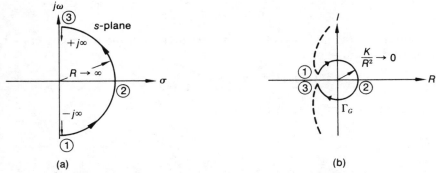

Fig. 7-21 Γ_s semicircle at ∞ and corresponding Nyquist plot Γ_G.

Fig. 7-22. We notice that the $(-1, 0)$ point is not encircled. Since $P = 0$ and $N = 0$, the system is stable. Although it is interesting to observe the behavior of the GH plot around the origin, we can generally ascertain system stability without completing this part of the plot.

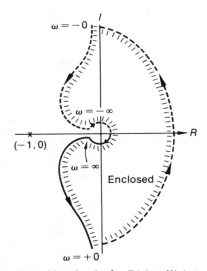

Fig. 7-22   Nyquist plot for $G(s) = K/s(s + a)$.

The Nyquist plots of the previous examples never crossed the negative real axis since the phase was always greater than $-\pi$ except at $\omega = \infty$. This was one reason that the $(-1, 0)$ point never got encircled.

EXAMPLE 7-5

Determine the stability of a control system with the following closed loop transfer function

$$G(s)H(s) = \frac{K}{s(sT_1+1)(sT_2+1)}$$

The magnitude and phase are given by

s	$\left|G(s)H(s)\right|$	$\underline{/G(s)H(s)}$
0	∞	$-\dfrac{\pi}{2}$
js_1	$K/s_1\sqrt{(s_1{}^2T_1{}^2+1)(s_2{}^2T_2{}^2+1)}$	$\left(-\dfrac{\pi}{2}-\arctan s_1T_1-\arctan s_2T_2\right)$
$j\infty$	0	$-\dfrac{3\pi}{2}$

and the Nyquist plot appears in Fig. 7-23. Note that as Γ_s goes around the origin in the s-plane, GH goes from $-\pi/2$ to $+\pi/2$ with infinite radius. Since $P = 0$, the system is stable if $(-1, 0)$ is not enclosed as shown in Fig. 7-23a. However, when K is sufficiently increased then $(-1, 0)$ is

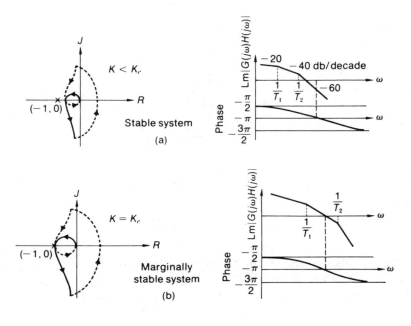

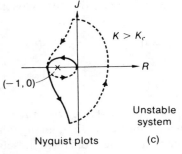
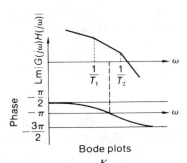

Nyquist plots   (c)   Bode plots

Fig. 7-23   Stability of minimum phase function $G(s)H(s) = \dfrac{K}{s(1+sT_1)(1+sT_2)}$ on Nyquist plot and Bode plot.

enclosed and the system becomes unstable as seen in Fig. 7-23c. When $K = K_c$ the system is marginally stable and oscillates.

The effect of K on the system stability may be investigated using the Routh–Hurwitz criterion. The characteristic equation is

$$1 + \frac{K}{s(sT_1+1)(sT_2+1)} = 0$$

or

$$\frac{[s(sT_1+1)(sT_2+1)+K]}{s(sT_1+1)(sT_2+1)} = 0$$

The zeros of the characteristic equation are determined by

$$s(sT_1+1)(sT_2+1)+K = 0$$

or

$$s^3 T_1 T_2 + s^2(T_1 + T_2) + s + K = 0$$

Forming the Routh array

s^3	$T_1 T_2$	1
s^2	$(T_1 + T_2)$	K
s^1	b_1	b_2
s^0	c_1	

$$b_1 = \frac{(T_1+T_2)-KT_1T_2}{T_1+T_2}$$

$$b_2 = 0$$

$$c_1 = K$$

For system stability $b_1 \geq 0$, therefore

$$K \leq K_c; \qquad K_c = (T_1 + T_2)/T_1 T_2$$

If $b_1 = 0$, we form the auxiliary equation to investigate the purely oscillatory behavior of the system,

$$s^2(T_1 + T_2) + K = 0$$

$$s = j\omega_\phi = \pm j \sqrt{\frac{K}{T_1 T_2}}$$

We conclude then that when $K < K_c$ the system is stable, when $K = K_c$ the system exhibits pure oscillations with a frequency ω_ϕ, and finally when $K > K_c$ the system gets unstable. We note that all the plots have the same shape and when the plot goes through $(-1, 0)$ the system exhibits pure oscillations. When this happens, the system is called a marginally stable system.

Let us for a moment review the results obtained so far. We began with the forward loop transfer function, $G(s) = K/s(s + a)$, and saw that the system was stable for all K. Then we added a pole to the transfer function and the system was no longer stable for all K. If the gain is increased without limit, the system gets unstable. We may conclude therefore that the addition of poles to the open loop transfer function tends to have a destabilizing influence on the system response.

When the number of poles of a control system become large the system exhibits many stable and unstable responses depending upon system gain. Consider the transfer function of such a control system,

$$G(s)H(s) = \frac{N_1(s)}{N_2(s)} = \frac{K(s\tau_5 + 1)(s\tau_6 + 1)}{s(s\tau_1 + 1)(s\tau_2 + 1)(s\tau_3 + 1)(s\tau_4 + 1)}$$

The Nyquist plot is shown in Fig. 7-24. Since $P = 0$, we want no enclosures of $(-1, 0)$ to assure system stability. The Nyquist plot indicates that the system is stable. However, as the gain varies it may become stable or unstable. As a matter of fact there are four possible locations of the $(-1, 0)$ point depending upon K. For low gain the system is stable. As the gain is raised it becomes unstable. If the gain is raised some more it again becomes stable and finally gets unstable for very high gain.

We have been concerned with Nyquist plots of systems having rational polynomials up to this point. However, many control systems have a time delay in the loop and this affects the system stability. Examples of systems having time delay are motors, valve delay, transmission delays and so on. In the next example we consider a control system with delay and show how the Nyquist criterion may be used to investigate its stability.

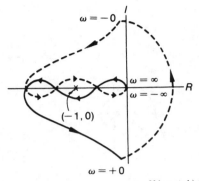

$\omega = -0$

$\omega = \infty$

$\omega = -\infty$

R

$(-1, 0)$

$\omega = +0$

Fig. 7-24 Nyquist plot of $G(s)H(s) = \dfrac{K(s\tau_5 + 1)(s\tau_6 + 1)}{s(s\tau_1 + 1)(s\tau_2 + 1)(s\tau_3 + 1)(s\tau_4 + 1)}$.

Consider the control system shown in Fig. 7-25, where $e^{-2\pi\tau s}$ characterizes the time delay. The open loop transfer function becomes

$$G(s) = \frac{K}{s(s+a)} e^{-2\pi\tau s} \qquad (7\text{-}13)$$

This is rewritten as

$$G(j\omega) = M(\omega)e^{-j\phi}$$

where

$$M(\omega) = \frac{K}{\omega\sqrt{\omega^2 + a^2}}; \qquad \phi = (2\pi\tau)\omega - \tan^{-1}\frac{\omega}{a} - \frac{\pi}{2}$$

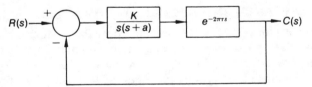

$R(s)$ + $\dfrac{K}{s(s+a)}$ $e^{-2\pi\tau s}$ $C(s)$ −

Fig. 7-25 System with time delay.

and note that the delay contributes only to the phase shift but nothing to the magnitude. As ω varies from 0 to $1/\tau$, the time delay contributes 2π to the phase. As ω varies further from $1/\tau$ to $2/\tau$, the time delay contributes another 2π to the phase as shown in Fig. 7-26. If the $(-1, 0)$ point is not enclosed the first time the negative real axis is crossed, it will never be enclosed since as ω increases the magnitude decreases. The acceptable value of τ is one which prevents $(-1, 0)$ from being enclosed the first time as seen in Fig. 7-26. We note that since $G(s) = K/s(s+a)$ was stable for

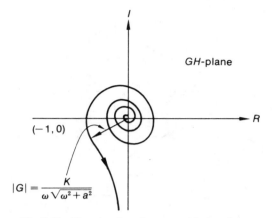

$$|G| = \frac{K}{\omega \sqrt{\omega^2 + a^2}}$$

Fig. 7-26 Nyquist plot of system with time delay.

all gain, the addition of time delay has had a destabilizing influence on system responses.

We conclude this section by observing that for a stable system the number of times the Nyquist plot of $G(s)H(s)$ must encircle $(-1, 0)$ must be equal to the number of poles of $G(s)H(s)$ in the right half s-plane. The direction of this encirclement must be negative. Several typical Nyquist plots for various transfer functions are shown in Table 7-1.

7-3 PERFORMANCE IN FREQUENCY DOMAIN

The Nyquist plot of Fig. 7-23 indicated how the system was stable for low gain, oscillatory for some critical gain, and finally unstable as the gain is increased even further. Clearly, as K varies the degree of stability varies, i.e. how close the Nyquist plot is to the $(-1, 0)$ point. If the closest point of the Nyquist plot is far away from the critical point $(-1, 0)$, then the system transient is sluggish. As the plot moves closer to $(-1, 0)$ the transient response becomes less sluggish, more oscillatory, and less damped. Eventually the response becomes unstable for values of gain that force the enclosure of $(-1, 0)$. The idea of performance and relative stability, or the proximity of the GH plot to $(-1, 0)$, is often correlated to an effective damping ratio of the closed loop poles.

We mentioned earlier that the Nyquist criterion was not only useful for establishing absolute stability of a control system but also its relative stability. In this section we propose to show how this can be done.

Table 7-1   Nyquist plots for various loop transfer functions.

$G(s)H(s)$	Nyquist Plot (Polar plots)	Stability
$\dfrac{K}{s+a}$		Stable for all gain.
$\dfrac{K}{s(s+a)}$		Stable for all gain.
$\dfrac{K}{(s+a)(s+b)}$		Stable for all gain.
$\dfrac{K}{s(s+a)(s+b)}$		Unstable as shown. May become stable if gain is decreased.
$\dfrac{K(s+c)}{s^2(s+a)(s+b)}$		Stable as shown. Becomes unstable as K is increased.
$\dfrac{K(s+a)(s+b)}{s^3}$		Conditionally stable. Becomes unstable as K is decreased.

Generally the *gain* and *phase* margins are used to define the performance or relative stability of a system in the frequency domain. Consider
the Nyquist plot of a third-order control system shown in Fig. 7-27. The
magnitude of $G(s)H(s)$ when it crosses the real axis is $|G(j\omega_\phi)H(j\omega_\phi)|$
where ω_ϕ is the frequency at which this crossing occurs. This frequency is

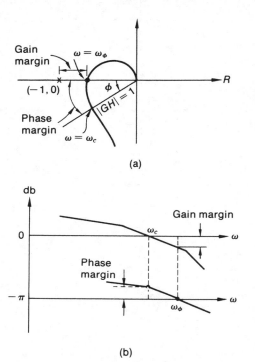

(a)

(b)

Fig. 7-27   Gain and phase margin on Nyquist and Bode plots.

called the *phase crossover frequency*. The gain margin GM is measured at
this frequency and is

GM = Additional gain needed to make the system
marginally stable

This is usually measured in decibels and is

$$GM = 20 \log \left[\frac{1}{|G(s)H(s)|} \right]_{s=j\omega_\phi} \tag{7-14}$$

The gain margin is shown on the Nyquist plot and the Bode plot of Fig. 7-27. Note how easy it is to obtain this from the Bode plot. Gain margin has little meaning for first- or second-order systems since $G(s)H(s)$ never crosses the negative real axis.

The phase margin (PM) is a measure of relative stability in terms of the angle of $G(s)H(s)$. It is defined as

PM = Additional phase lag needed to make system
      marginally stable

This phase is measured from the point where $|G(s)H(s)| = 1$. The frequency where this happens is called the *gain crossover frequency* and denoted by ω_c.

$$\text{PM} = \pi + \underline{/G(j\omega_c)H(j\omega_c)} \tag{7-15}$$

EXAMPLE 7-6

Obtain the gain and phase margins and crossover frequencies for the third-order system described by

$$G(s)H(s) = \frac{K}{(s+1)(s+2)(s+3)}$$

It is known that $K = 22.8$.

To obtain the phase crossover frequency we separate $G(s)H(s)$ into real and imaginary parts and equate the imaginary part to zero,

$$G(j\omega)H(j\omega) = \frac{22.8}{(j\omega)^3 + 6(j\omega)^2 + (j\omega)11 + 6}$$

$$= \frac{22.8}{(6 - 6\omega^2) + j(11\omega - \omega^3)}$$

Equating the imaginary part to zero yields

$$j\omega = j\omega_\phi = \pm j\sqrt{11}$$

The magnitude at $\omega = \omega_\phi$ becomes

$$|G(j\omega_\phi)H(j\omega_\phi)| = \frac{22.8}{60}$$

$$\left[\frac{1}{|GH|}\right]_{\omega=\omega_\phi} = 2.63$$

and the gain margin becomes

$$\text{GM} = 20 \log 2.63 = 8.4 \text{ db}$$

which indicates that the system gain may be increased by 8.4 db (factor of 2.63) before becoming marginally stable. The gain crossover frequency ω_c occurs when $|G(s)H(s)| = 1$. The frequency is 2.0 and the phase margin PM becomes

$$PM = \pi - [\arctan 2 + \arctan 1.0 + \arctan 0.67]$$
$$= 39°$$

which indicates that the phase can increase by 39° before the system becomes marginally stable. This implies that the magnitude shall be constant. As a general rule PM should not be less than 30° and GM about 6 db for good transient response.

It is instructive to correlate the phase margin to system damping. An exact relationship may be derived if we consider a second-order system. For higher-order systems there must be a pair of dominant poles and the ensuing discussion applies only in an approximate way.

Consider a second-order system,

$$G(s) = \frac{\omega_n^2}{(s + 2\delta\omega_n)s}; \qquad H(s) = 1$$

The open loop frequency response is

$$G(j\omega) = \frac{\omega_n^2}{j\omega(j\omega + 2\delta\omega_n)}$$

Defining $\nu = \omega_n/\omega$ we have

$$G(j\omega) = \frac{\nu^2}{j(2\delta\nu + j)}$$

The phase margin occurs at the gain crossover frequency where

$$|G(j\omega)| = 1 = \frac{\nu_c^2}{(4\delta^2\nu_c^2 + 1)^{1/2}}$$

Rewriting the above equation,

$$\nu_c^4 - 4\delta^2\nu_c^2 - 1 = 0 \qquad\qquad (7\text{-}16a)$$

which defines the necessary equation relating effecting damping δ to the gain crossover frequency. The phase margin becomes

$$PM = \pi + \underline{/G(j\nu_c)}$$

$$PM = \pi + \left(-\frac{\pi}{2} - \arctan\frac{1}{2\delta\nu_c}\right)$$

$$PM = \frac{\pi}{2} - \arctan\frac{1}{2\delta\nu_c} \tag{7-16b}$$

This equation together with Eq. (7-16a) is used to generate the plot shown in Fig. 7-28. For low damping ratio the phase margin versus δ may be approximated by a straight line given by

$$\delta = 0.01 \, PM$$

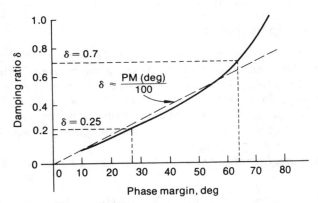

Fig. 7-28   Phase margin versus damping ratio for second-order systems.

We can go a step further and observe that the damping ratio of a second-order system is related to the peak overshoot M_p. Therefore the peak overshoot is given by

$$M_p = e^{-\pi\delta/\sqrt{1-\delta^2}} \tag{7-17}$$

and since δ is related to PM we may obtain a relationship of PM versus M_p. This is best approached graphically. The plot of PM versus M_p is shown in Fig. 7-29. For PM $\geqslant 30°$, this relationship may be approximated by a straight line

$$PM \, (\text{degrees}) = 75 \, (\text{percent}) - M_p \, (\text{percent})$$

We note that as the value of PM increases, M_p decreases and the damping increases.

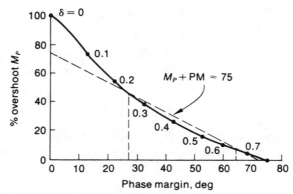

Fig. 7-29   Phase margin versus percentage overshoot for second-order systems.

The Closed Loop Response

The Nyquist criterion and phase margin index are defined for the open loop transfer function $G(s)H(s)$. However, another useful index of performance is the magnitude $|M(\omega)|$ of the closed loop frequency response which may also be related to damping ratio. The relationship between the closed loop frequency response and the open loop frequency response was established earlier. We return to that formulation, change it slightly and relate it to the damping ratio.

Consider a unity feedback control system whose frequency response is written as

$$\frac{C(j\omega)}{R(j\omega)} = \frac{G(j\omega)}{1 + G(j\omega)} = M(\omega)e^{-j\phi}$$

If $G(j\omega)$ is written as

$$G(j\omega) = u + jv$$

then the magnitude $M(\omega)$ becomes

$$M(\omega) = \left|\frac{G(j\omega)}{1 + G(j\omega)}\right| = \frac{(u^2 + v^2)^{1/2}}{((1 + u)^2 + v^2)^{1/2}}$$

Squaring and rearranging we obtain

$$u^2 + v^2 - \frac{2M^2 u}{1 - M^2} = \frac{M^2}{1 - M^2}$$

where $M = M(\omega)$. Now completing the squares, i.e. adding $(M^2/1 - M^2)^2$

to both sides, we obtain

$$\left(u - \frac{M^2}{1-M^2}\right)^2 + v^2 = \frac{M^2}{(1-M^2)^2} \tag{7-18}$$

which is an equation of a circle with center at (U_m, V_m) and radius r_m where

$$U_m = \frac{M^2}{1-M^2}$$

$$V_m = 0$$

$$r_m = \left|\frac{M}{1-M^2}\right|$$

These circles are plotted in Fig. 7-30. Note that as M increases, the radius of the circle decreases until, in the limit, the $(-1, 0)$ point is obtained. If

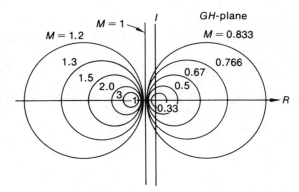

Fig. 7-30   Constant M circles on GH-plane.

enough M circles are drawn and if $G(j\omega)$ is superimposed on the plot, then at each intersection of $G(j\omega)$ plot with an M circle we obtain the closed loop response at a given frequency as shown in Fig. 7-31. The smallest circle that $G(j\omega)$ is tangent to corresponds to the highest value of M. The frequency at which this occurs is the resonant frequency.

The phase angle of the closed loop may now be written by substituting for $G(j\omega)$ in the overall transfer function,

$$\phi = \tan^{-1}\frac{v}{u} - \tan^{-1}\frac{v}{1+u}$$

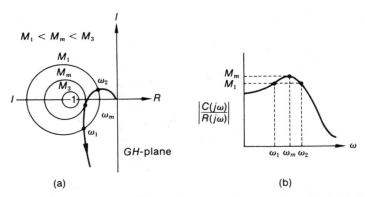

Fig. 7-31 Determination of M by plotting $G(s)$ on the same plot as the M circles.

Taking the tangent of both sides,

$$N = \tan \phi = \frac{v}{u^2 + u + v^2}$$

Rewriting and completing the squares, we obtain

$$\left(u + \frac{1}{2}\right)^2 + \left(v - \frac{1}{2N}\right)^2 = \frac{N^2 + 1}{4N^2} \qquad (7\text{-}19)$$

which represents the equation of a circle with center at (U_N, V_N) and radius r_N,

$$U_N = -\frac{1}{2}$$

$$V_N = \frac{1}{2N}$$

$$r_N = \left| \frac{1}{2} \sqrt{1 + 1/N^2} \right|$$

These circles are plotted in Fig. 7-32 for various values of N. If the open loop frequency response $G(j\omega)$ were plotted on this paper, the intersections of $G(j\omega)$ with the ϕ circles indicate the value of the closed loop phase angle.

Clearly, if M and ϕ circles were plotted on the same paper and if $G(j\omega)$ is superimposed on this paper, then we may obtain the magnitude and phase of the closed loop response.

When the M and ϕ circles are plotted on the same paper, the resulting charts are called *Nichols charts*. The plots are given in decibels versus

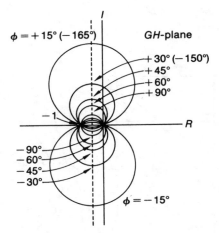

Fig. 7-32 Constant N circles on GH-plane.

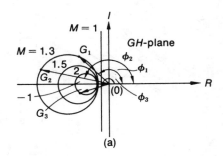

(a)

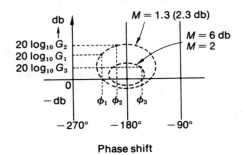

Phase shift

(b)

Fig. 7-33 Construction of Nichols charts.

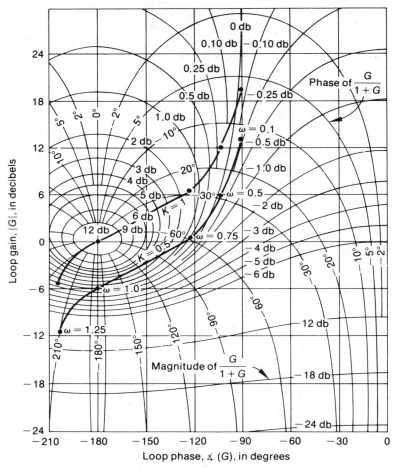

Fig. 7-34 Nichols diagram for $G(s) = \dfrac{K}{s(s^2 + s + 1)}$.

phase shift. They are obtained in the following manner. A point on a constant M locus may be obtained by drawing a vector from the origin to a particular point on the M circle. The vector length measured in decibels and its phase determine a point on the Nichols chart as shown in Fig. 7-33. The actual value of M is shown in parenthesis. The point $(-1, 0)$ corresponds to 0 db and $-\pi$ phase in the Nichols chart. The above procedure is repeated for the N circles. We therefore obtain values of M and N plotted as functions of the magnitude.

EXAMPLE 7-7

The open loop transfer function of a unity feedback system is given by

$$G(s) = \frac{K}{s(s^2 + s + 1)}$$

Construct the Nichols chart for $K = 1$ and 0.5. For $K = 0.5$, obtain the maximum magnitude of the closed loop response. What is the phase margin?

The Nichols chart is shown in Fig. 7-34 for two values of K. For $K = 0.5$, $|G(j\omega)| = 1$ occurs at a point where the phase is $-126°$. The phase margin is therefore $\pi - 126°$ or $54°$. The maximum magnitude of the closed loop response is 3 db at a phase of $-120°$.

7-4   ROOT LOCUS

The previous methods have dwelt on the analysis of the transfer function $G(s)H(s)$ when the system was excited with a sinusoidally varying input. The various methods yielded the magnitude and phase of the transfer function as the frequency was varied. It was seen that although the shape of the Bode and polar plot was unchanged as the gain K is varied, the stability was greatly affected. Actually the variation of K changes the roots of the characteristic equation and thereby the response of the control system. Assume that $G(s)H(s) = KP_1(s)/P_2(s)$, then

$$1 + G(s)H(s) = \frac{P_2(s) + KP_1(s)}{P_2(s)} = 0$$

The zeros of the characteristic equation are given by

$$P_2(s) + KP_1(s) = 0$$

and the role of K is clearly evident. The root locus, conceived by W. R.

Evans in 1948, is a graphical method that studies the roots of the characteristic equation as K varies from zero to infinity. Since the roots of the characteristic equation determine the behavior of the closed loop system, the root locus is a technique whereby we may study the behavior of the closed loop itself.

We consider $G(s)$ in factored form and write the characteristic equation as

$$1 + G(s)H(s) = 1 + \frac{K \prod\limits_{z} (s + z_z)}{s^n \prod\limits_{p} (s + p_p)} = 0$$

Here K is referred to as the static loop sensitivity, z_z is a zero, and p_p is a pole of the open loop transfer function. There are also n poles at the origin. Unlike the factored form in the frequency plots it is not necessary to have a separate quadratic form since zeros and poles may be complex.

As mentioned previously, instead of studying the zeros of the characteristic equation, it is equivalent to studying the -1 value of $G(s)H(s)$. This means that as K varies from zero to infinity, $G(s)H(s)$ must always be -1 or

$$|G(s)H(s)| = 1 \tag{7-20a}$$

$$\underline{/G(s)H(s)} = (2k + 1)\pi; \qquad k = 0, \pm 1, \pm 2, \cdots \tag{7-20b}$$

The first expression is referred to as the *magnitude condition* and the second as the *angle condition*. Substituting for $G(s)H(s)$ these conditions become

$$\frac{K|s + z_1| \cdot |s + z_2| \cdot |s + z_3| \cdots |s + z_z|}{|s^n| \cdot |s + p_1| \cdot |s + p_2| \cdots |s + p_p|} = 1$$

$$\underline{/s + z_1} + \underline{/s + z_2} + \cdots + \underline{/s + z_z} - \underline{/s + p_1} \cdots \underline{/s + p_p} - \frac{n\pi}{2} = (2k + 1)\pi$$

The first of these equations may be written as

$$K = \frac{|s^n| \cdot |s + p_1| \cdots |s + p_p|}{|s + z_1| \cdot |s + z_2| \cdots |s + z_z|}$$

The rest of the section will dwell extensively on satisfying the angle and magnitude condition as the static loop sensitivity K is varied.

In theory, the entire s-plane should be searched in order to find points satisfying the magnitude and angle condition. This however is unnecessary since the proper interpretation of the magnitude and angle condition yields several rules that facilitate the rapid construction of the root loci plot. Although this plot is approximate, it suffices for purposes of a preliminary study. The following rules are therefore to be considered as aids for an approximate root loci:

1. The root loci begin at the open loop poles. From the magnitude condition

$$\frac{|s+z_1||s+z_2| \cdots |s+z_z|}{|s^n||s+p_1| \cdots |s+p_p|} = \frac{1}{K}$$

and since the root loci begin at $K = 0$, $G(s)H(s) \to \infty$ which occurs at a pole of $G(s)H(s)$.

2. The root loci end at the open loop zeros. Since the root loci end at $K = \infty$, the magnitude of $G(s)H(s)$ goes to zero which occurs at a zero of $G(s)H(s)$.

3. The number of separate loci is equal to the open loop poles. In accordance with the first rule, each branch of the loci begins at $K = 0$ or the open loop pole. Therefore, the number of branches is equal to the number of poles. Now each branch must end at a zero and if the number of zeros Z and the number of poles P are not equal, then it is assumed that $P - Z$ zeros exist at infinity. This implies that Z loci begin at the poles and end at zeros, whereas $P - Z$ loci beginning at the poles end at infinity on the s-plane.

4. The loci are symmetrical about the real axis. The root locus is symmetrical about the real axis since the roots of $1 + G(s)H(s) = 0$ must either be real or appear as complex conjugates.

5. Asymptotes of the root locus. The open loop transfer function may be expressed as

$$G(s)H(s) = \frac{K(s^z + a_1 s^{z-1} + \cdots)}{s^p + b_1 s^{p-1} + \cdots}$$

$$= \frac{K}{s^n + (b_1 - a_1)s^{n-1} + \cdots} = -1$$

where $n = P - Z$. Assuming s to be large so that terms lower than s^{n-1} may be neglected

$$-K \cong s^n + (b_1 - a_1)s^{n-1} = \left(1 + \frac{b_1 - a_1}{s}\right)s^n$$

Taking the nth root and expanding in a binomial

$$(-K)^{1/n} = \left(1 + \frac{b_1 - a_1}{ns} + \cdots\right)s$$

Substituting $s = \sigma + j\omega$, again neglecting higher-order terms, and writing

$(-K)^{1/n}$ as a complex number

$$\left[\sigma+\frac{b_1-a_1}{n}\right]+j\omega = |K^{1/n}|\left[\cos\frac{(2k+1)\pi}{n}+j\sin\frac{(2k+1)\pi}{n}\right]$$

This leads to two equations when the real and imaginary parts are equated,

$$\sigma+\frac{b_1-a_1}{n} = |K^{1/n}|\cos\frac{(2k+1)\pi}{n}$$

$$\omega = |K^{1/n}|\sin\frac{(2k+1)\pi}{n}$$

Each of the above equations may be solved for $K^{1/n}$ and equated to each other yielding an equation for ω,

$$\omega = \tan\frac{(2k+1)\pi}{n}\left[\sigma+\frac{b_1-a_1}{n}\right]$$

which has the form of $\omega = m(\sigma-\sigma_0)$ where m is the slope of the asymptote and σ_0 the real axis intercept. Since $n = P-Z$, we write the slope of the asymptote as

$$m = \frac{(2k+1)\pi}{P-Z}; \qquad k = 0,\pm1,\cdots \tag{7-21a}$$

and the real axis intercept as

$$\sigma_0 = -\frac{b_1-a_1}{P-Z}; \qquad \begin{array}{l} b_1 = \text{sum of the poles} \\ a_1 = \text{sum of the zeros} \end{array} \tag{7-21b}$$

6. Root loci on the real axis. The angle condition established that

$$\left[\sum \text{angles from zeros}\right] - \left[\sum \text{angles from poles}\right] = (2k+1)\pi$$

Consider first the case of real poles and zeros to the left of a search point on the real axis. The angular contribution of each is zero. Also if these poles and zeros are complex, the angle contribution will be zero since the zeros and poles appear as conjugates. This leaves real poles and zeros to the right of a search point on the real axis. If the number of poles plus zeros is even, then the total angular condition is 0 or 2π. However, if the number is odd, then the angular contribution will be $(2k+1)\pi$. We conclude therefore that the root loci exist on the real axis if the total number of poles and zeros to right is odd.

EXAMPLE 7-8

Construct a root locus plot for the open loop transfer function given by

$$G(s) = \frac{K(s+1)}{(s+2)(s+3)(s+4)}$$

The poles and zeros are shown in Fig. 7-35a. From the six rules established so far, we may conclude

(1) the root loci begin at $-2, -3,$ and $-4,$
(2) one branch ends at $-1,$
(3) there are three different loci, one ending at -1 and two at infinity,
(4) the loci are symmetrical about the real axis,

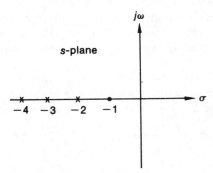

(a) Pole-zero configuration

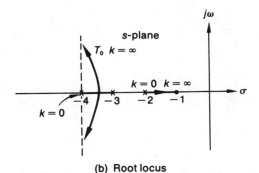

(b) Root locus

Fig. 7-35   Root locus of $G(s) = \dfrac{K(s+1)}{(s+2)(s+3)(s+4)}$.

(5) the asymptotes intersect the real axis at

$$\sigma_0 = \frac{(-2) + (-3) + (-4) - (-1)}{3 - 1} = -4$$

and the angle is

$$\frac{(2k+1)\pi}{P - Z} = \frac{(2k+1)\pi}{2} = \pm\frac{\pi}{2}$$

(6) the region on the real axis between -1 and -2 as well as between -3 and -4 exists on the root loci.

The root locus is shown in Fig. 7-35b.

In Fig. 7-35 we did not address ourselves to the question as to what the exact point, between -3 and -4,.is where the root locus departs from the real axis. Also we are not sure about the angles associated with the loci as it leaves the real axis. These and other questions are considered in the next five rules.

7. The angles of arrival and departure. The angles of arrival and departure of the root locus may be obtained from the angle condition. Consider a search point s_0 near the pole at $-2+j$, then the angle condition yields, *see* Fig. 7-36,

$$\theta_5 - (\theta_1 + \theta_2 + \theta_3 + \theta_4) = (2k+1)\pi$$

$$\theta_1 = \theta_5 - (\theta_2 + \theta_3 + \theta_4) - (2k+1)\pi \tag{7-22}$$

and since $\theta_2, \theta_3, \theta_4, \theta_5$ are known, θ_1 may be computed.

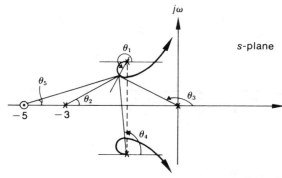

Fig. 7-36   Departure and arrival angles for $G(s) = \dfrac{K(s+5)}{s(s+3)(s^2+4s+5)}$.

8. Breakaway point on real axis. A breakaway point on the real axis is a point where the root locus leaves the real axis. Since the root loci are symmetrical, the number of branches leaving to go toward the positive frequencies is equal to those going toward the negative frequencies. The angles at which these loci depart may be shown to be π/N, where N is the number of loci departing. The breakaway point itself is also interpreted as the point where the characteristic equation has double roots.

The calculation of breakaway points depends on the pole-zero configuration.

(a) Poles and zeros on the real axis. Let the breakaway point be at $-\alpha$. Then the angle condition yields

$$\theta_5 + (\pi - \theta_2) - (\theta_4 + \pi - \theta_3 + \pi - \theta_1) = (2k+1)\pi$$

$$\theta_5 - \theta_2 - \theta_4 + \theta_3 + \theta_1 = 0$$

From Fig. 7-37 it is seen that the angles are small, therefore they may be approximated by their tangents

$$\frac{\epsilon}{z_2 - \alpha} - \frac{\epsilon}{\alpha - z_1} - \frac{\epsilon}{p_3 - \alpha} + \frac{\epsilon}{\alpha - p_2} + \frac{\epsilon}{\alpha} = 0$$

$$\frac{1}{z_1 - \alpha} + \frac{1}{z_2 - \alpha} - \frac{1}{p_2 - \alpha} - \frac{1}{p_3 - \alpha} - \frac{1}{0 - \alpha} = 0$$

The breakaway point may now be computed by trial and error. This can be generalized as follows: the breakaway point α can be computed by solving

$$\sum \frac{1}{z_i - \alpha} - \sum \frac{1}{p_j - \alpha} = 0 \qquad (7\text{-}23)$$

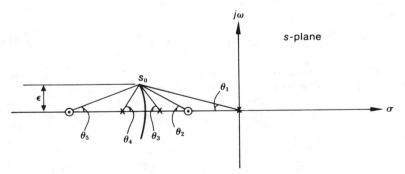

Fig. 7-37   Breakaway points for poles and zeros on real axis.

If there are Z zeros and N poles, this equation is equivalent to solving a polynomial of order $N + Z$.

(b) Complex poles and zeros. Consider a conjugate set of poles as shown in Fig. 7-38. If a search point exists at s_0, then

$$\theta_1 = \arctan \frac{\omega_1}{\alpha - \sigma_1}; \qquad \theta_2 = \arctan \frac{\omega_1 - \epsilon}{\alpha - \sigma_1}$$

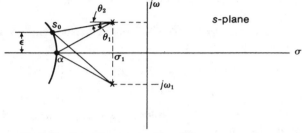

Fig. 7-38 Breakaway point for complex roots and zeros.

The angle $(\theta_1 - \theta_2)$ can be approximated by $\tan(\theta_1 - \theta_2)$ if s_0 is very close to the breakaway point. Then we have

$$(\theta_1 - \theta_2) \approx \tan(\theta_1 - \theta_2) = \frac{\tan \theta_1 - \tan \theta_2}{1 + \tan \theta_1 \tan \theta_2}$$

$$= \frac{\epsilon(\alpha - \sigma_1)}{(\alpha - \sigma_1)^2 + (\omega_1)^2}$$

Since the poles are conjugates, the total angle contribution is $2(\theta_1 - \theta_2)$. This contribution is positive for zeros and negative for poles. Also if the conjugate pair (pole or zero) were to the left, the sign changes. In general we can write

$$\Delta\theta = (\theta_1 - \theta_2) = \frac{\epsilon|\sigma_1 - \alpha|}{(\sigma_1 - \alpha)^2 + (\omega_1)^2} \qquad (7\text{-}24)$$

This can be generalized by computing terms like Eq. (7-24) for all the zeros and poles. The breakaway point is then obtained by solving,

$$\Delta\theta\Big]_{\text{zeros}} - \Delta\theta\Big]_{\text{poles}} = 0$$

(c) Breakaway point not on the real axis. In some situations the breakaway point is not situated on the real axis as shown in Fig. 7-39. The original poles are located at $0, -3, -2+j$, and $-2-j$. In order to obtain

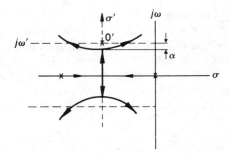

Fig. 7-39   Breakaway point not on the real axis.

the breakaway point we rotate the coordinate system with the new origin at $0'$ as shown in Fig. 7-39. The location of the new poles in the σ', $j\omega'$ system are at 0, -4, $-1-j1.5$, and $-1+j1.5$. In the new system the breakaway point α is on the real axis and the previous equations are applicable.

(d) **Breakaway points computed analytically.** The final case considered here is the analytical method. Consider the open loop transfer function in the following form,

$$G(s)H(s) = K\frac{Q(s)}{P(s)}$$

The characteristic polynomial becomes $P(s) + KQ(s) = F(s)$. If K is varied by ΔK, then

$$P(s) + (K + \Delta K)Q(s) = 0$$

$$1 + \frac{\Delta K Q(s)}{F(s)} = 0$$

Since multiple roots, say L, occur at the breakaway point, the characteristic equation may be written as $F(s) = (s - s_0)^L M(s)$ which when substituted into the previous expression yields

$$\frac{\Delta K}{(s - s_0)} = -(s - s_0)^{L-1}\frac{M(s)}{Q(s)}$$

Recalling that $M(s)$ and $Q(s)$ do not contain factors such as $(s - s_0)$, then the limit of this equation as $\Delta K \to 0$ and $s \to s_0$ yields

$$\frac{dK}{ds} = 0 \tag{7-25}$$

This requirement is independent of whether the roots are real or complex.

9. Intersection of the root loci with the imaginary axis. In several of the previous examples, as K was varied the root locus intersected the imaginary axis and entered the other side of the complex plane. The point where the imaginary axis is intersected represents the frequency where pure oscillations occur. Had we used the Routh–Hurwitz criterion to study the characteristic equation, this condition becomes evident when one of the constants in the Routh–Hurwitz array goes to zero as was seen in Chapter 4.

EXAMPLE 7-9

Obtain the root locus plot and the frequency at which it crosses the imaginary axis for the following,

$$G(s)H(s) = \frac{K(s+5)}{s(s^2+4s+5)}$$

The characteristic equation becomes

$$s^3 + 4s^2 + (5+K)s + 5K = 0$$

The Routhian array may be now formed,

$$
\begin{array}{c|cc}
s^3 & 1 & (5+K) \\
s^2 & 4 & 5K \\
\hline
s^1 & b_1 & b_2 \\
s^0 & c_1 &
\end{array}
\qquad
\begin{aligned}
b_1 &= \frac{20-K}{4} \\[4pt]
b_2 &= 0 \\
c_1 &= 5K
\end{aligned}
$$

For stability, the constraint of $b_1 \geqslant 0$ yields that $K \leqslant 20$. If K reaches the

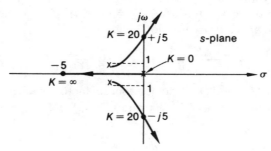

Fig. 7-40   Root locus of $G(s) = \dfrac{K(s+5)}{s(s^2+4s+5)}$.

critical value of 20, then $b_1 = 0$ and the auxiliary equation is formed,

$$4s^2 + 5K = 0$$
$$s^2 = -25$$
$$s = \pm j5$$

The root loci cross the imaginary axis at $\pm j5$ and the static loop sensitivity at this point is 20. Beyond this point, K increases and the system becomes unstable. In the Routh array if $b_1 < 0$, then two complex roots appear in the right half s-plane as shown in Fig. 7-40.

Once the root loci are constructed with the aid of the previous nine rules, the gain K at any specific point may be found by using the magnitude condition.

10. The value of K on the root loci. If $s = s_0$, then from the magnitude condition

$$K = K_0 = \left[\frac{1}{|G(s)H(s)|} \right]_{s=s_0} \tag{7-26}$$

From the Example 7-9 when $s = j5$,

$$K = (A)(B)(C)/D$$
$$= \frac{|(-2-j)-j5| \cdot |(-2+j)-j5| \cdot |j5|}{|-5-j5|}$$
$$K = 20$$

11. The sum of closed loop poles is a constant. If the order of the denominator of the open loop transfer function is greater than the numerator by at least 2, then the coefficient of s^{n-1} is independent of K. The coefficient is then the negative of the closed loop poles.

The above fact may be used to follow the migration of the closed loop poles as the gain K is varied. In Example 7-9, for the open loop transfer function, the coefficient of s^{n-1} is 4, therefore the sum of the closed loop poles is -4 for the characteristic equation. At $K = 20$ we know that $s = j5$ and $-j5$. The third pole may be located by

$$s_1 + s_2 + s_3 = -4, \ s_1 = -s_2 = j5, \ s_3 = -4$$

For $K = 20$, the three poles of the closed loop system are $j5, -j5$, and -4.

By the application of the above eleven rules the root locus may be very simply constructed. We have said previously that the root locus is very useful for studying the zeros of the characteristic equation as the gain is varied from zero to infinity. This method should be used in conjunction with other methods, previously discussed, to study the overall performance of a control system.

Once the root locus of the system is obtained, we may then obtain the transient behavior of the closed loop system. In order to show this we shall first show the relationship between the closed loop poles and the root locus plot. Consider the third-order closed loop transfer function,

$$\frac{C(s)}{R(s)} = \frac{G(s)}{1 + G(s)}$$

If the forward loop transfer function is

$$G(s) = \frac{K}{(s+A)(s^2+bs+c)}$$

then

$$\frac{C(s)}{R(s)} = \frac{K}{K + (s+A)(s^2+bs+c)}$$

Now let us set the gain at $K = K_s$, then

$$\frac{C(s)}{R(s)} = \frac{K_s}{(s+p_1)(s+p_2)(s+p_3)}$$

where p_1, p_2, and p_3 are poles of the closed loop system which is equivalent to the zeros of the characteristic equation. We stated earlier that for a given value of K, the zeros of the characteristic equation are obtained whenever

$$G(s)H(s) = -1$$

is satisfied. Therefore, for a specific value of $K = K_s$, the poles p_1, p_2, and p_3 of the closed loop are the zeros of the characteristic equation as shown in Fig. 7-41. The response may now be obtained by techniques discussed in Chapter 4.

Having established the previous relationship we can go a step further and say something about system damping. If we designate the poles p_1, p_2, p_3, as

$$p_1 = \frac{1}{\tau_1}$$

$$p_2 = \delta\omega_n + j(1-\delta^2)^{1/2}\omega_n = \delta\omega_n + j\omega_d$$

$$p_3 = \delta\omega_n - j(1-\delta^2)^{1/2}\omega_n = \delta\omega_n - j\omega_d$$

then we observe that $\delta\omega_n$ or $1/\tau_1$ represents a line parallel to the imaginary

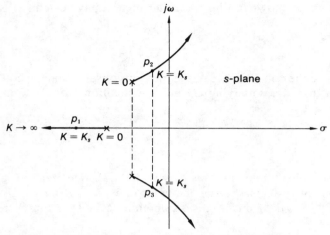

Fig. 7-41   Relationship of the closed loop poles and the root locus plot.

axis, whereas $(1 - \delta^2)^{1/2}\omega_n$ or ω_d represents a line parallel to the real axis. For a given ω_d and $\delta\omega_n$, the radial line has a magnitude

$$\sqrt{\omega_d{}^2 + \delta^2\omega_n{}^2} = \omega_n$$

Therefore, lines of constant ω_n are circles. Along the radius of the circle,

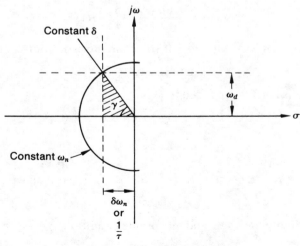

Fig. 7-42   Constant δ and ω_n lines.

δ is constant as shown in Fig. 7-42. The angle γ may be defined as

$$\cos \gamma = \delta \omega_n / \omega_n$$

or

$$\gamma = \cos^{-1} \delta$$

We can use the consequence of the previous observations to constrain the variation in K for satisfying certain specifications. For example, if it is required that

$$\delta < \delta_m$$

$$\omega_d < \omega_{d_m}$$

$$1/\tau < 1/\tau_m$$

then the root loci must always stay within the shaded area of Fig. 7-42. In many control systems, the specific value of δ, ω_d, and $1/\tau$ are given which essentially fixes the gain K. This is sometimes called "setting system gain."

7-5   USING STATE EQUATIONS

When a system is represented in state form, then it was shown in Chapter 3 that the output $Y(s)$ is given by

$$Y(s) = c[sI - A]^{-1}bR(s)$$

where A is the coefficient matrix, whereas c and b are the output and input vectors. Substituting for the inverse,

$$Y(s) = \frac{c \, \text{adj} \, [sI - A]b}{\det [sI - A]} R(s) \qquad (7\text{-}27)$$

so that the output is a function of the characteristic roots obtained from

$$\det [sI - A] = 0$$

In general this can be expanded to yield

$$s^n + a_{n-1}s^{n-1} + \cdots a_1 s + a_0 = 0$$

or

$$1 + \frac{a_0}{s^n + a_{n-1}s^{n-1} + \cdots} = 0$$

If we set $a_0 = K$ and $G(s) = K/(s^n + a_{n-1}s^{n-1} + \cdots)$, then we obtain

$$1 + G(s) = 0$$

and we can apply the angle and magnitude condition to $G(s)$.†

†We can actually apply all the previous graphical methods. Since the extension is so obvious, we will not pursue it except in this one example.

EXAMPLE 7-10

The coefficient matrix of a system is given by

$$\mathbf{A} = \begin{bmatrix} 0 & 1 & 0 \\ 0 & 0 & 1 \\ -K & -20 & -9 \end{bmatrix}$$

Construct the root locus and set the system gain K so that the damping ratio is 0.5.

The characteristic equation is

$$\det [s\mathbf{I} - \mathbf{A}] = s^3 + 9s^2 + 20s + K = 0$$

which can be written as

$$1 + G(s) = 0$$

where

$$G(s) = \frac{K}{s^3 + 9s^2 + 20s}$$

$$G(s) = \frac{K}{s(s+4)(s+5)}$$

which is the function whose locus must be obtained.

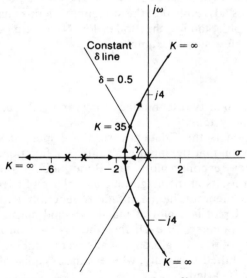

Fig. 7-43   Root locus of $\dfrac{K}{s(s+4)(s+5)}$.

The root locus plot is obtained by following the previous rules and is shown in Fig. 7-43. Since $\delta = 0.5$,

$$\gamma = \cos^{-1} 0.5 = 60°$$

and this is represented by a radial line in Fig. 7-43. Along this line $\delta = 0.5$. This line intersects the root locus at $K = K_s$ and $s = s_s$. The gain may be obtained by using rule 10.

$$K = \left| \frac{1}{G(s)} \right|_{s=s_s}$$
$$\cong 35$$

For the closed loop response to have a damping ratio of 0.5, the gain must be set around $K = 35$.

As we conclude this chapter it is important to stress a point made earlier. This pertained to the use of a computer. Much of what we have discussed is amenable to a computer analysis. The time domain as well as graphical analysis may be compiled as a package of interactive programs using a time sharing computer. It is often necessary to resort to this when real systems of sufficient complexity arise. Reference 12 describes one such package. Although it is beyond the scope of this book to consider it in much detail, it is advisable that the student finish this chapter by writing some programs for obtaining the Bode plot, Nyquist plot, and the Root locus for at least a few simple examples.

SUMMARY

We have developed two techniques for graphically analyzing the behavior of a control system.

The first method is the frequency response method which is based upon the assumption that the input is a sinusoidal function. There are two types of frequency response plots, viz. Bode plot and the Nyquist plot. The Bode plot consists of the magnitude and phase of a transfer function plotted versus frequency. The magnitude is generally expressed in decibels. The Nyquist plot is a plot of magnitude and phase on polar paper where ω is the parameter. In each case the overall gain K has no effect on the basic shape of the plot although it affects the stability of the system. The Bode plot is shifted vertically, whereas the Nyquist plot contracts or dilates as the gain is varied.

The stability of linear systems has been investigated using the Nyquist stability criterion. This criterion, derived from the theory of complex variables and involving the conformal mapping of the right half s-plane into the $G(s)H(s)$ complex plane, states that for a system to be stable the $GH(s)$ contour must encircle the $(-1, 0)$ counterclockwise as many times as the number of poles of $GH(s)$ with real parts. The corresponding path on the s-plane must be the right half plane encircled clockwise.

From Nyquist plots of the open loop transfer functions, we obtained measures of system performance and relative stability by defining gain and phase margin. It was seen that the phase margin is related to system damping and overshoot. The closed loop response was obtained from the Nyquist plots in the form of constant gain and phase plots. Open loop gain and phase to the closed loop gain and phase were related using Nichols charts.

The second graphical technique is the root locus method. It investigates the migration of the closed loop poles of a control system on the complex s-plane as the gain K is varied. This technique yields information on the transient response of a system.

It should be noted that both the techniques are applicable to systems whether represented in state or classical form.

PROBLEMS

7-1. What are the restrictions on the frequency response method of analysis?

7-2. Obtain the Bode plot and closed loop response for the following transfer functions:

(a) $G(s) = K(s+1)$

(b) $G(s) = \dfrac{K(s+1)}{s+2}$

(c) $G(s) = \dfrac{K}{s}$

(d) $G(s) = \dfrac{K}{s(s+1)}$

(e) $G(s) = \dfrac{K(s+2)}{s(s+1)}$

(f) $G(s) = \dfrac{K(s+0.02)}{s(s+0.01)}$

(g) $G(s) = \dfrac{K}{s(s+4)(s+5)}$

(h) $G(s) = \dfrac{K}{s^3}$

(i) $G(s) = \dfrac{K(s+100)}{s^3}$

(j) $G(s) = \dfrac{K(s+1)}{s^2+2s+10}$

7-3. Construct the Nyquist plots for the transfer functions shown in Problem 7-2.

7-4. Obtain the frequency at which the Nyquist plot intersects the real and imaginary axis, for Problem 7-2g, and verify your results via the Routh–Hurwitz.

7-5. Determine the stability via the Nyquist criterion for the following systems:

(a) $G(s)H(s) = K/s(s+1)(s+2)$

(b) $G(s)H(s) = K/s^2(s+1)(s+2)$

(c) $G(s)H(s) = 2.5(s+1)/(s^2+s+1)$

(d) $G(s)H(s) = 10(2-s)/s(s+10)(s-5)$

(e) $G(s)H(s) = K(s+1)/s^2(s+2)$

(f) $G(s)H(s) = 100/(s-0.5)(s+10)$

7-6. Verify the comments given for the Nyquist plots in Table 7-1.

7-7. For the following transfer function study the system stability for

(a) T_3, T_4 are very small, and (b) T_3, T_4 are very large.

$$G(s)H(s) = \frac{K(1+sT_3)(1+sT_4)}{s^3(1+sT_1)(1+sT_2)}$$

7-8. A closed loop system with a controller is shown in Fig. P7-8. The controller $G_c(s)$ is necessary to stabilize the system. If $G_c(s) = (10s + K)$, then what is the maximum value of K for which the system is stable? Obtain the phase and gain margin if $K = 5$.

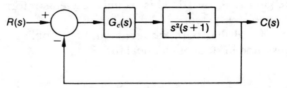

Fig. P7-8

7-9. The open loop transfer function of system with delay is

$$G(s)H(s) = \frac{Ke^{-sT}}{s(s+1)}$$

If $K = 5$, what is the maximum value of T for which the system is stable?

7-10. Using Nichols charts, find the maximum overshoot and the corresponding frequency of the closed loop response if

$$G(s)H(s) = \frac{1}{s(s^2+s+2)}$$

7-11. Determine the stability for the following systems using the Bode plot. Compare results to those obtained by using the Nyquist plot. Explain any differences.

(a) $G(s)H(s) = K/s(1+T_s)$

(b) $G(s)H(s) = K(1-T_1s)/(1+T_2s)$

(c) $G(s)H(s) = K(1-T_1s)/s(1+T_2s)$

7-12. Obtain the gain necessary to achieve a damping ratio of 0.2 for

$$G = \frac{K}{s(s+1)(s+5)}$$

What is the value of M_p? Obtain the gain and phase margin for this gain setting.

7-13. An idealized nuclear power plant is shown in Fig. P7-13. The controller comprises of proportional plus integral control. The actuator and reactor have a time delay. It is required that the system overshoot be less than 20%. What values of K_P and K_I satisfy these criteria? How can this system become unstable?

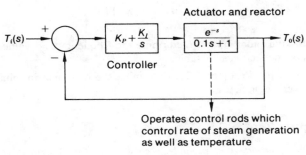

Fig. P7-13

7-14. Construct the root loci for the following transfer functions:
(a) $G(s) = K/s^2 + s + 1$
(b) $G(s) = K(s+9)/s(s+1)(s+2)$
(c) $G(s) = K/s^2$
(d) $G(s) = K/s(s+1)(s+2)$
(e) $G(s) = K/s(s+1)$
If any of the loci cross the imaginary axis, obtain the frequency at which this happens.

7-15. Obtain the root locus plot for the transfer function given in Problem 7-2h and i. What has happened to the system with the addition of an open loop zero at $s = -100$?

7-16. We would like to make sure that the closed loop response has a damping ratio of 0.5 for a unity feedback system whose forward loop $G(s)$ is given by Problem 7-14d. What must the gain be set at? Also, what values must K be constrained to if $\delta < 0.707$ and $\omega_d < 0.8$.

7-17. Write a computer program for drawing a root locus for an nth-order system. Assume that all the open loop poles are available.

7-18. Write a computer program for drawing the Nyquist plot.

7-19. For the system having the following coefficient matrix:

$$A = \begin{bmatrix} 0 & 1 & 0 \\ 0 & 0 & 1 \\ 0 & -8 & K \end{bmatrix}$$

show how the eigenvalues vary as K is varied.

7-20. If a damping ratio of 0.707 is required for Problem 7-19, what value of K satisfies this?

7-21. A system whose coefficient matrix is

$$A = \begin{bmatrix} 0 & 1 & 0 \\ 0 & 0 & 1 \\ K & -12 & -7 \end{bmatrix}$$

is subjected to sinusoidal inputs. Determine the frequency and value of $K = K_c$ at which the system becomes unstable.

7-22. If $K = K_c/2$ for Problem 7-21, determine the gain margin, phase margin, and the crossover frequencies.

REFERENCES

1. Bode, H. W., *Network Analysis and Feedback Amplifier Design*, Princeton, N.J., D. Van Nostrand, 1945.
2. Thaler, G. J., and R. G. Brown, *Analysis and Design of Feedback Control Systems*, 2nd Edition, New York, McGraw-Hill, 1960.
3. D'Azzo, J. J., and C. H. Houpis, *Feedback Control System Analysis and Synthesis*, 2nd Edition, New York, McGraw-Hill, 1966.
4. Evans, W. R., *Graphical Analysis of Control Systems*, Trans. AIEE, Vol. 67, pp. 547–551, 1948.
5. Truxal, J. G., *Automatic Feedback Control System Synthesis*, New York, McGraw-Hill, 1955.
6. Kuo, B. C., *Analysis and Synthesis of Sampled-Data Control Systems*, Englewood Cliffs, N.J., Prentice Hall, 1963.
7. Horowitz, I. M., *Synthesis of Feedback Systems*, New York, Academic Press, 1963.
8. Evans, W. R., *Control System Dynamics*, New York, McGraw-Hill, 1954.
9. Nyquist, H., "Regeneration Theory," *Bell System Tech. J.*, 1932.
10. James, H. M., N. B. Nichols, and R. S. Phillips, *Theory of Servomechanisms*, New York, McGraw-Hill, 1947.
11. Chestnut, H., and R. W. Mayer, *Servomechanisms and Regulatory Systems Design*, Vol. I., New York, Wiley, 1951.
12. Wallace, F. E., A. F. Starr, and M. B. Newman, "The use of a time-shared computer for control synthesis and design," *JACC*, June 1970.

8

System Compensation

8-1 INTRODUCTION

It was mentioned earlier that the performance of a control system is measured by its stability, accuracy, and speed of response. In general these items are specified when a system is being designed to satisfy a specific task. Quite often the simultaneous satisfaction of all these requirements cannot be achieved by using the basic elements in the control system. Even after introducing controllers and feedback as shown in Chapter 6, we are limited as to the choice we may exercise in selecting a certain transient response while requiring a small steady state error. We will show how the desired transient as well as the steady state behavior of a system may be obtained by introducing compensatory elements (also called equalizer networks) into the control system loop. These compensation elements are designed so that they help achieve system performance, i.e. bandwidth, phase margin, peak overshoot, steady state error, etc. without modifying the entire system in a major way.

From our experience so far we recognize that any changes in system performance can be achieved only through varying the forward loop gain. Consider the third-order unity feedback system with the following forward loop transfer function,

$$G(s) = \frac{K}{s(s+a)(s+b)}$$

From the Routh–Hurwitz criterion we know that stability requires

$$K \leqslant ab(a+b)$$

We also know that the steady state error to a ramp input is

$$e_{ss} = \lim_{s \to 0} s \left[\frac{1}{s^2} \cdot \frac{1}{1 + G(s)} \right] = \frac{ab}{K}$$

Obviously if it is necessary to minimize the steady state error, the gain K should be increased. Since K is constrained to a maximum value of $ab(a+b)$, the minimum steady state error becomes

$$[e_{ss}]_{min} = \frac{1}{a+b}$$

A further decrease in the error requires an increase in K which in turn has a destabilizing effect on the system. It is therefore clear that the forward "gain game" is rather limited.

8-2 THE STABILIZATION OF UNSTABLE SYSTEMS

Since the increasing of the forward loop gain K tends to destabilize a system, we must find ways to compensate it in such a way as to stabilize it again. It was established in Chapter 7 that the addition of a pole in $G(s)H(s)$ tends to have a destabilizing influence on system response. Can we then reverse the argument and say that the addition of a zero tends to have a stabilizing influence on system response? Let us answer this by considering an example. Consider the control system with its transfer function given in Example 7-5. This system is unstable if $K > K_c$.

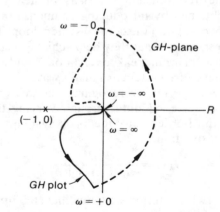

Fig. 8-1   Nyquist plot for $G(s)H(s) = \dfrac{K(s\tau_3 + 1)}{s(s\tau_1 + 1)(s\tau_2 + 1)}$.

Now consider the same system but with the addition of a zero,

$$G(s)H(s) = \frac{K(s\tau_3+1)}{s(s\tau_1+1)(s\tau_2+1)}$$

This is the type of function we obtain if we were to add derivative and proportional control to a third-order servomechanism. The characteristic equation becomes

$$\frac{s^3\tau_1\tau_2 + s^2(\tau_1+\tau_2) + (K\tau_3+1)s + K}{s(s\tau_1+1)(s\tau_2+1)} = 0$$

and the zeros of the characteristic equation are determined by

$$s^3\tau_1\tau_2 + s^2(\tau_1+\tau_2) + (K\tau_3+1)s + K = 0$$

The Routh array becomes

s^3	$\tau_1\tau_2$	$(K\tau_3+1)$	$b_1 = \dfrac{(K\tau_3+1)(\tau_1+\tau_2) - K\tau_1\tau_2}{\tau_1+\tau_2}$
s^2	$\tau_1+\tau_2$	K	
s^1	b_1	b_2	$b_2 = 0$
s^0	c_1		$c_1 = K$

For stability $b_1 \geqslant 0$, and therefore

$$K(\tau_1\tau_3 + \tau_2\tau_3 - \tau_1\tau_2) + (\tau_1+\tau_2) > 0$$

Clearly, with a proper selection of the time constants, this may be satisfied. The Nyquist plot for this is shown in Fig. 8-1.

As another example, let us begin with an unstable system whose transfer function is given by

$$G(s)H(s) = \frac{K}{s^2(s\tau_1+1)}$$

and the Nyquist plot is shown in Fig. 8-2a. We now add a zero to the transfer function so that

$$G(s)H(s) = \frac{K(s\tau_2+1)}{s^2(s\tau_1+1)}$$

and the new Nyquist plot is shown in Fig. 8-2b. We again note that the addition of a zero has stabilized the system for all gain.

Since the addition of the poles and zeros, called compensating, not only affects the system stability but also its performance characteristics, the location of these poles and zeros must be carefully determined. There are various ways this compensation can be achieved. The different methods are discussed next.

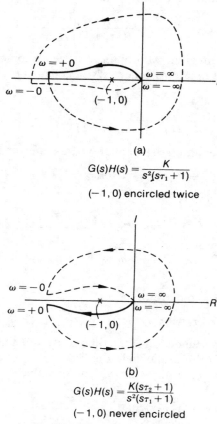

(a)

$$G(s)H(s) = \frac{K}{s^2(s\tau_1 + 1)}$$

$(-1, 0)$ encircled twice

(b)

$$G(s)H(s) = \frac{K(s\tau_2 + 1)}{s^2(s\tau_1 + 1)}$$

$(-1, 0)$ never encircled

Fig. 8-2   Effect of adding a zero.

8-3   TYPES OF COMPENSATION

The performance of a control system may be modified by adding compensation elements in the control loop. The types of compensation we shall discuss fall into the following categories:

(a) Cascade or series compensation
(b) Feedback compensation
(c) Feedforward compensation.

These schemes are illustrated in Fig. 8-3.

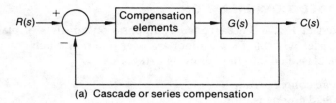

(a) Cascade or series compensation

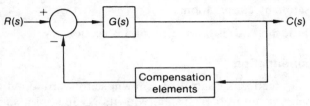

(b) Feedback compensation

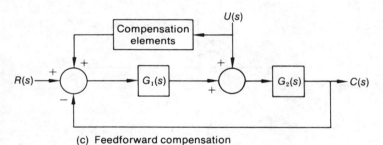

(c) Feedforward compensation

Fig. 8-3   Types of compensation.

The study and design of compensated control systems can be most readily carried out in the frequency or complex domain or via the root locus. The use of the frequency domain is straightforward and quite simple. When the characteristics of the closed loop response are desired, use is made of Nichols charts. The root locus is generally used to study the poles and zeros directly.

The consideration of compensation elements in this chapter shall be restricted to passive elements consisting of resistors and capacitors. We shall assume that they are physically realizable. This generally implies that the transfer function of compensation networks must be rational algebraic functions and all coefficients must be real.

8-4 CASCADED COMPENSATION

As indicated in Fig. 8-3a, cascaded compensation consists of placing elements in series with the forward loop transfer function. Such compensation may be classified into the following categories:

(a) Phase-lag compensation
(b) Phase-lead compensation
(c) Lag-lead compensation
(d) Compensation by cancellation.

The details of these methods is the subject of this section.

Phase-lag Compensation

Consider a unity feedback control system whose forward loop transfer function represents a third-order system with its Nyquist plot shown in Fig. 8-4. It is required that the gain be K_1 for satisfying the margin of

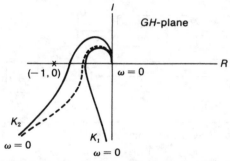

Fig. 8-4   Nyquist plot of a third-order system for different gains.

stability but K_2 for satisfying the steady state performance. This seemingly contradictory requirement may be satisfied if we were to reshape the plot to the one indicated by the dotted lines. The reshaped plot may be obtained if the low-frequency part of K_1 is rotated clockwise while the high-frequency part be unaltered. Since the phase of the low-frequency part of K_1 must lag, the type of compensation used to achieve this is phase-lag compensation. Such compensation is obtained by a phase-lag element.

When the output of an element lags the input in phase and the magnitude decreases as a function of frequency, the element is called a phase-lag element. Consider the lag network of Fig. 8-5. The transfer function for

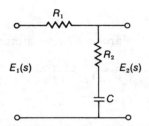

Fig. 8-5   A phase-lag network.

this is

★

$$\frac{E_2(s)}{E_1(s)} = G_c(s) = \frac{1 + aTs}{1 + Ts} \qquad (8\text{-}1)$$

where

$$aT = R_2C; \qquad a = \frac{R_2}{R_1 + R_2}; \qquad a < 1$$

The Bode, Nyquist, and root locus plots for Eq. (8-1) are shown in Fig. 8-6. We observe that the magnitude decreases with increasing frequency and lagging phase angle. The value of a determines the separation on the root locus plot. The minimum phase ϕ_m occurs at ω_m which is the geometric average of the corner frequencies

$$\log \omega_m = \frac{1}{2} \left(\log \frac{1}{T} + \log \frac{1}{aT} \right)$$

★

$$\omega_m = \frac{1}{T\sqrt{a}} \qquad (8\text{-}2a)$$

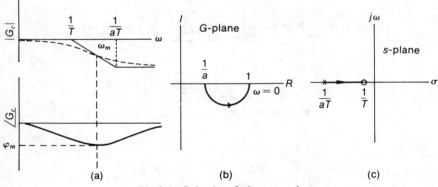

Fig. 8-6   Behavior of a lag network.

The phase angle becomes

$$\phi_m = + \arctan aT\omega_m - \arctan \omega_m T$$

$$\tan \phi_m = \frac{(-T + aT)\omega_m}{1 + (aT\omega_m)(T\omega_m)}$$

$$\tan \phi_m = (1-a)/2\sqrt{a}$$

or

★
$$\sin \phi_m = (1-a)/(a+1) \tag{8-2b}$$

The maximum phase lag is strictly a function of a. Let us investigate how such a network alters the performance of a feedback control system.

EXAMPLE 8-1

For the system shown in Fig. 8-7a, it is desired that the velocity error constant be at least 5 sec^{-1} and that the phase margin be 40° or more. Design an appropriate lag compensator for this system. Construct the Bode and root locus plots with and without compensation. Compute the maximum gain and minimum steady state error with and without compensation.

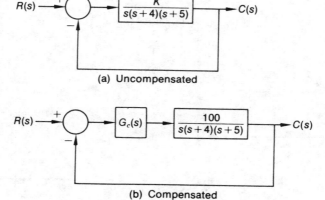

(a) Uncompensated

(b) Compensated

Fig. 8-7   Phase-lag compensation.

Since

$$K_1 = \lim_{s \to 0} sG(s) = \frac{K}{20} = 5$$

the gain becomes

$$K = 20K_1 = 100$$

We therefore construct the Bode plot for

$$G(s) = \frac{100}{s(s+4)(s+5)}$$

as shown in Fig. 8-8. We note that the gain crossover frequency is $\omega_c = 3.25$ rad/sec and the phase margin is 18° which is not satisfactory. Since a

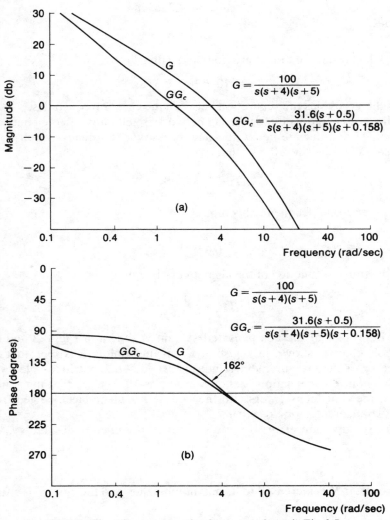

$$G = \frac{100}{s(s+4)(s+5)}$$

$$GG_c = \frac{31.6(s+0.5)}{s(s+4)(s+5)(s+0.158)}$$

Fig. 8-8 Phase-lag compensation for system shown in Fig. 8-7.

lag network will contribute to phase (generally between 5° and 15°) we select the phase at the new crossover frequency to be the required 40° plus 12° or 52°. This occurs at $\omega_c = 1.5$ rad/sec. At this point $G(j\omega)$ needs an additional 10 db gain so that the magnitude curve comes to 0 db. To achieve this we employ a phase-lag network which provides the additional magnitude. The magnitude is approximated by

$$|G(j\omega)| = -20 \log a$$

so that

$$a = 10^{-|G(j\omega)|/20}$$

Since the lag network must provide the 10 db gain,

$$a = 10^{-10/20} = 0.316$$

This then provides the separation between the corner frequencies.

The corner frequency for the lag network is generally selected between an octave and decade below the new crossover frequency which is 1.5 rad/sec. We select $\omega = 0.5$ so that

$$aT = \frac{1}{\omega} = \frac{1}{0.5} = 2$$

The other corner frequency becomes

$$T = \frac{2}{0.316} = 6.42$$

and the transfer function of the lag network becomes

$$G_c(s) = \frac{1 + 2s}{1 + 6.42s}$$

The Bode plot of the compensated system is shown in Fig. 8-8 and the Nichols chart is shown in Fig. 8-9. From these plots it is seen that the phase crossover requirement is now satisfied. The root locus plot with and without compensation is shown in Fig. 8-10. We see that the gain at which the root locus enters into the right half s-plane has changed from 180 to 620, or a factor close to a^{-1}.

The steady state error to a ramp input of the uncompensated system was

$$e_{ss} = \frac{1}{K_v} = 0.2$$

However, if K is increased to its maximum value, and the system is still to

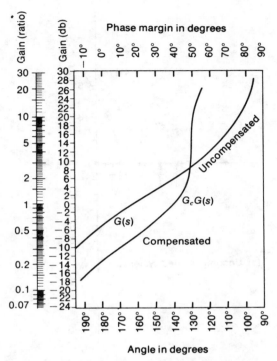

Fig. 8-9 Nichols chart for uncompensated (U) system and compensated (C) system using phase-lag compensation.

be stable, then

$$(e_{ss})_{min} = \frac{1}{(K_1)_{max}}$$

$$(K_1)_{max} = \lim_{s \to 0} s \frac{K_{max}}{s(s+4)(s+5)} = \frac{K_{max}}{20}$$

Since $K_{max} = 180$,

$$[K_1]_{max} = 9$$

and

$$[e_{ss}]_{min} = \frac{1}{9} = 0.11$$

When the system is compensated however, $K_{max} = 620$, therefore the

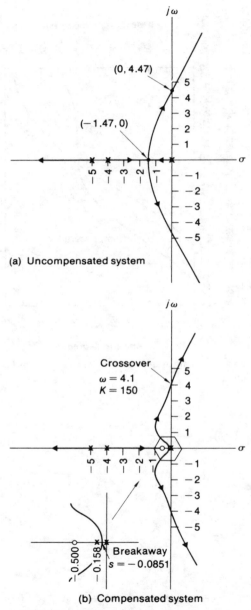

(a) Uncompensated system

(b) Compensated system

Fig. 8-10 Root locus for lag compensation.

maximum error constant is

$$[K_1]_{max} = \frac{620}{20} = 31$$

and

$$[e_{ss}]_{min} = \frac{1}{31} = 0.0323$$

The effect of the lag compensation, then, is to increase the velocity error constant which decreases the steady state error.

From the previous example we may conclude that the phase-lag method of compensation achieves the following:

(1) Reduces high-frequency gain and improves the phase margin;
(2) Increases the velocity error constant for a fixed relative stability;
(3) The gain crossover frequency is decreased. This also reduces the bandwidth of the system;
(4) The time response usually gets slower.

Phase-lead Compensation

Let us return to the Nyquist plot shown in Fig. 8-4. We could have reshaped the plot by beginning with the Nyquist plot for K_2 and rotating the high-frequency part in the counterclockwise direction but without altering the low-frequency part. Since the phase of the high-frequency part must now lead, the type of compensation used to achieve this is phase-lead compensation. Such compensation is achieved by a phase-lead element.

When the output of an element leads the input in phase and the magnitude increases as a function of frequency, the element is called a phase-lead element. Consider the lead element shown in Fig. 8-11. The transfer function is

$$\frac{E_2(s)}{E_1(s)} = \frac{1}{\alpha} \frac{1 + \alpha s T}{1 + s T}$$

where

$$T = \frac{R_1 R_2 C}{R_1 + R_2}; \qquad \alpha = \frac{R_1 + R_2}{R_2}; \qquad \alpha > 1$$

The phase-lead transfer function is

$$\frac{E_2(s)}{E_1(s)} = G_c(s) = \frac{1}{\alpha} \frac{1 + \alpha s T}{1 + s T} \qquad (8\text{-}3)$$

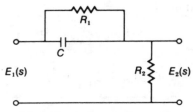

Fig. 8-11 A phase-lead network.

where the gain of the forward loop transfer function is increased to offset the effect of α. The Bode plot, polar plot, and root locus plot are shown in Fig. 8-12. We note that the magnitude increases with increasing frequency. The value of α determines the separation on the root locus. The

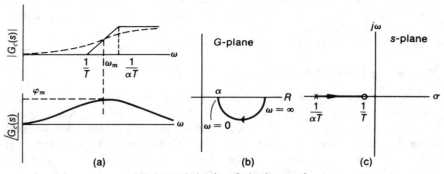

Fig. 8-12 Behavior of a lead network.

maximum phase lead ϕ_m occurs at ω_m. Using the previous method, it may be shown that

$$\omega_m = \frac{1}{\sqrt{\alpha T}}; \qquad \sin \phi_m = \frac{\alpha - 1}{\alpha + 1}$$

EXAMPLE 8-2

Obtain a lead compensation network for the servo system shown in Fig. 8-13a. It is required that the phase margin be 45° while the velocity error must be less than 2%.

Since the steady state error to a ramp input is

$$e_{ss} = \frac{2000}{K} = 0.02$$

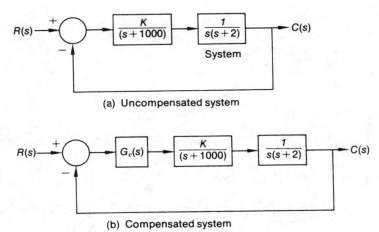

(a) Uncompensated system

(b) Compensated system

Fig. 8-13 System compensated by lead network.

the necessary gain becomes $K = 100,000$ and the forward loop transfer
function becomes

$$G(s) = \frac{100,000}{s(s+1000)(s+2)}$$

The Bode plot of $G(s)$ is plotted in Fig. 8-14. The gain crossover frequency is close to 10 rad/sec and the phase margin is about 18° which is
27° less than desired. The phase-lead network must provide this phase.
We select a phase margin addition of 38° in order to offset any shift in gain
crossover frequency caused by the addition of the compensating network.
Since $\phi_m = 38°$,

$$\sin \phi_m = \frac{\alpha - 1}{\alpha + 1} = 0.616$$

$$\alpha = 4.21$$

This establishes the separation of the lead network corner frequencies.
Recall that the maximum phase-lead occurs at the geometric mean of
$1/\alpha T$ and $1/T$. This maximum phase lead should occur at the new crossover frequency. This may be achieved by setting the gain crossover
frequency at the point where

$$|G(j\omega)| = -20 \log \sqrt{\alpha}$$

or

$$|G(j\omega)| = -6.25 \text{ db}$$

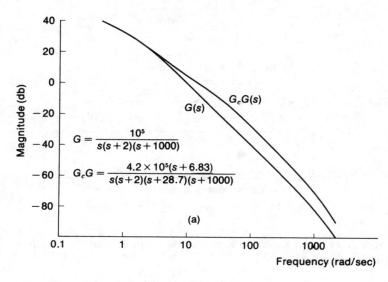

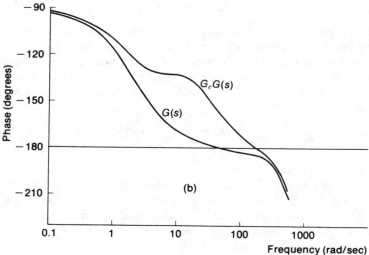

Fig. 8-14 Lead compensation of system shown in Fig. 8-13.

This is shown in Fig. 8-14 and the frequency corresponding to this is 14 rad/sec where the maximum phase shift occurs. We now compute the corner frequencies of the lead network,

$$\frac{1}{T} = \sqrt{\alpha}\,\omega_m = \sqrt{4.21}\,(14) = 28.7$$

$$\frac{1}{\alpha T} = 6.83 \text{ rad/sec}$$

The transfer function of the lead network becomes

$$G_c(s) = \frac{1}{4.2}\left(\frac{s+6.83}{s+28.7}\right)$$

If the gain of the amplifier is increased by a factor of 4.2, then the com-

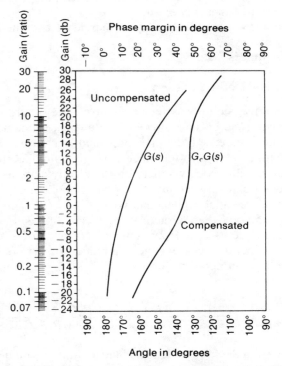

Fig. 8-15   Nichols chart for uncompensated (U) system and compensated (C) system using phase-lead compensation.

pensated open loop transfer function becomes,

$$G_cG(s) = \frac{(s+6.83)100,000}{s(s+28.7)(s+2)(s+1000)}$$

The Bode plot for this is shown in Fig. 8-14 and it is seen that the phase margin is in the satisfactory range. The magnitude versus phase shift is shown on the Nichols chart in Fig. 8-15.

For systems compensated by phase-lead networks the following is concluded.

(1) The velocity constant is increased and therefore the steady state error to a ramp input is decreased for a given relative stability.
(2) The damping ratio is increased and the overshoot is reduced while the phase margin is increased.
(3) The gain crossover frequency is increased and the bandwidth is usually increased.
(4) The rise time is faster.

Phase Lag-Lead Compensation

Phase-lag compensation was seen to improve the steady state response although the rise time became slower. The phase-lead compensation, on the other hand, decreased the rise time and decreases the overshoot rather substantially. It is often necessary to combine these different properties for simultaneously satisfying the steady state as well as transient behavior of control systems. Compensation elements that combine these properties are called lag-lead networks.

In order to embody the characteristics of lag and lead networks, it is possible to cascade two independent networks. However, there are individual networks that possess the combined property of lead and lag. Consider the lag-lead network shown in Fig. 8-16. The transfer function for this network is

$$\frac{E_2(s)}{E_1(s)} = \frac{(1+R_1C_1s)(1+R_2C_2s)}{1+(R_1C_1+R_1C_2+R_2C_2)s+R_1R_2C_1C_2s^2}$$

This may be cast in the familiar lead and lag notation by defining,

$$T_1a^{-1} = R_1C_1; \qquad T_2a = R_2C_2; \qquad T_1T_2 = R_1R_2C_1C_2$$

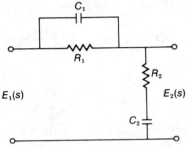

Fig. 8-16   A lag-lead network.

Substituting

$$\frac{E_2(s)}{E_1(s)} = \overbrace{\left[\frac{1+sT_1a^{-1}}{1+sT_1}\right]}^{\text{lead}}\overbrace{\left[\frac{1+sT_2a}{1+sT_2}\right]}^{\text{lag}} \qquad (8\text{-}4)$$

The computational procedure of obtaining a, T_1, and T_2 is as before. It is appropriate to offer a word of caution here. The previous examples seemed to yield the necessary results in a straightforward manner. In practice this does not occur. Instead the application of compensation elements requires, in general, an iterative procedure.

Compensation by Cancellation

Although we have tried to categorize and generalize the compensation and design of control systems, it is important to realize that the real way to design a system is to have some "feel" for the problem. It is possible that none of the techniques we have considered really help, or possibly a very simple method exists. One such simple technique is the method of direct cancellation.

Consider a second-order system whose forward loop transfer function is given by

$$G(s) = \frac{K_0}{s(s+a)}$$

Let us assume that the system performance is not satisfactory. We therefore introduce a compensation network,

$$G_c(s) = \frac{s+T_1}{s+T_2}$$

so that the new forward loop transfer function becomes

$$G_c(s)\,G(s) = \frac{K_0(s+T_1)}{s(s+a)(s+T_2)}$$

If we now select $T_1 = a$, then

$$G_c(s)\,G(s) = \frac{K_0}{s(s+T_2)}$$

Clearly, the appropriate selection of T_2 allows us to obtain whatever response we desire.

The technique of cancellation is particularly attractive when the open loop poles are complex conjugates. If the location of the complex conjugates is not satisfactory, then new zeros may be introduced to cancel their effect. A compensation network that achieves this is shown in Fig. 8-17. This network is known as a Bridged-T network. The transfer function is

★
$$\frac{E_2(s)}{E_1(s)} = \frac{R^2C_1C_2s^2+2RC_2s+1}{R^2C_1C_2s^2+R(C_1+2C_2)s+1} \qquad (8\text{-}5)$$

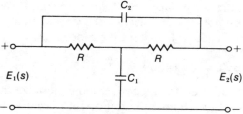

Fig. 8-17   A Bridged-T network.

Consider the system shown in Fig. 8-18a. The location of poles is not satisfactory. We therefore introduce, in cascade, the Bridged-T network as shown in Fig. 8-18b. The new open loop transfer function becomes

$$G_cG(s) = \frac{[s^2+2(1/RC_1)s+1/R^2C_1C_2]K}{[s^2+(1/RC_2+2/RC_1)s+1/R^2C_1C_2]s(s^2+bs+c)}$$

If we now select $b = 2/RC_1$, $c = 1/R^2C_1C_2$, then

$$G_cG(s) = \frac{K}{s(s^2+(b'+b)s+c)}$$

where $b' = 1/RC_2$. The value of b' is selected on the basis of the desired

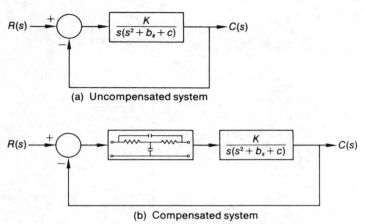

(a) Uncompensated system

(b) Compensated system

Fig. 8-18   Compensation by a Bridged-T network.

response. The introduction of such a cancellation compensator is shown on the root locus in Fig. 8-19. This method is very useful when the open loop poles are close to the imaginary axis.

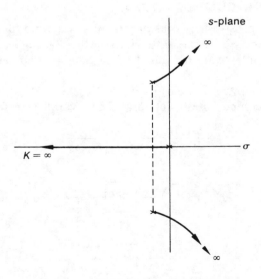

(a) Uncompensated

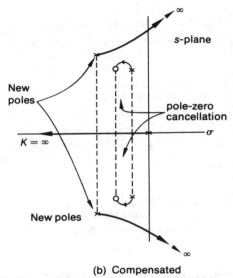

(b) Compensated

Fig. 8-19   Root locus showing effect of compensation using a Bridged-T network as shown in Fig. 8-18.

8-5 FEEDBACK COMPENSATION

Although the passive networks discussed so far were for cascade compensation, they may be incorporated into the feedback of a control system. Here we shall investigate the effect of introducing compensation in the feedback loop.

Consider the control system of Fig. 8-20 where $H_c(s)$ is the transfer function of a compensation network. The overall transfer function is

$$\frac{C(s)}{R(s)} = \frac{G(s)}{1 + G(s)H_c(s)}$$

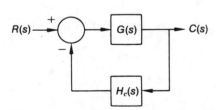

Fig. 8-20   Compensation in the feedback loop.

The characteristic equation becomes

$$1 + G(s)H_c(s) = 0$$

and is identical to that obtained if the compensation elements are added in cascade. The difference is in the addition of zeros in the closed loop function. Let $H_c(s) = P_1(s)/P_2(s)$, then the closed loop transfer function becomes

Feedback compensation: $\dfrac{C(s)}{R(s)} = \dfrac{G(s)P_2(s)}{P_2(s) + G(s)P_1(s)}$

Cascade compensation: $\dfrac{C(s)}{R(s)} = \dfrac{G(s)P_1(s)}{P_2(s) + G(s)P_1(s)}$

Although the denominator is the same, the numerator is different.
    Rewriting this equation, we have

$$\frac{C(s)}{R(s)} = \left[\frac{G(s)H_c(s)}{1 + G(s)H_c(s)} \right] \frac{1}{H_c(s)}$$

Since $|GH| \gg 1$ in the low-frequency range, we have

★

$$\frac{C(s)}{R(s)} \approx \frac{1}{H_c(s)} \qquad \omega \to \text{small} \tag{8-6}$$

In the high-frequency range, $|GH| \ll 1$ and

★

$$\frac{C(s)}{R(s)} \approx G(s) \qquad \omega \to \text{high} \tag{8-7}$$

We conclude, then, that the feedback compensated control system behaves as the inverse of the feedback characteristics for low frequency and as the system itself at high frequencies.
    Besides the passive networks in feedback controls, the use of tachometric control is very common. Here a tachometer is used to feedback a signal proportional to the derivative of the output variables. Consider a second-order system with tachometric control as shown in Fig. 8-21. The overall transfer function becomes

★

$$\frac{C(s)}{R(s)} = \frac{K_0}{s^2 + (a + K_0 K_f)s + K_0} \tag{8-8}$$

We observe that the addition of tachometric compensation has increased system damping.

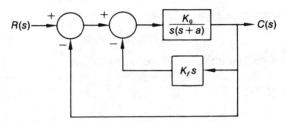

Fig. 8-21 Tachometric feedback.

Consider tachometric feedback with proportional control as shown in Fig. 8-22. The overall transfer function becomes

$$\frac{C(s)}{R(s)} = \frac{K_0}{s^2 + (a + K_f K_0)s + (1 + K_p)K_0}$$

Here we are able to effect the natural frequency as well as the damping ratio of the system.

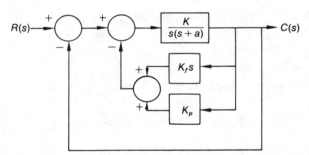

Fig. 8-22 Tachometric feedback with proportional control.

8-6 FEEDFORWARD COMPENSATION

The concept of the feedforward method of compensation is useful for reducing the effect of disturbances on system response. Consider the system shown in Fig. 8-23 with and without feedforward control. The overall transfer functions for the two cases become

No feedforward: $\quad C(s) = \dfrac{R(s)G_1(s)G_2(s)}{1 + G_1(s)G_2(s)} + \dfrac{U(s)G_2(s)}{1 + G_1(s)G_2(s)}$

Feedforward: $\quad C(s) = \dfrac{R(s)G_1(s)G_2(s)}{1 + G_1(s)G_2(s)} + \dfrac{U(s)G_2(s)[1 - G_0(s)G_1(s)]}{1 + G_1(s)G_2(s)}$

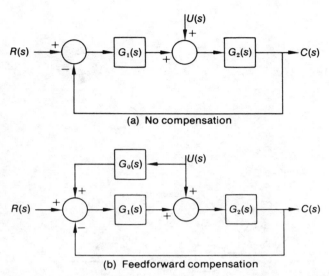

(a) No compensation

(b) Feedforward compensation

Fig. 8-23 Use of feedforward compensation for decreasing disturbance effects.

We notice that the inclusions of feedforward control has reduced the effect of the disturbance $U(s)$ on system response by a factor $(1 - G_0(s) G_1(s))$.

8-7 A PRACTICAL EXAMPLE

In this section we employ a practical example, discussed in Chapter 1, to illustrate the procedure of design, analysis, and compensation of a control system.

Let us assume that we wish to design a platform for use as a calibration test stand for a digital sun sensor. This requires the platform to remain in a fixed orientation with respect to the sun, i.e. the platform should automatically† track the sun. Since the precision of this sun tracker would limit the precision of the calibration of the digital sun sensor, it is necessary to limit the tracking error to no more than 0.0004°.

The postulated system, that we thought could do the necessary job, is pictorially illustrated in Fig. 8-24. Briefly, it consists of an astronomical telescope mount, two silicon solar cells, an amplifier, a motor, and gears.

---

†Manual tracking using a rheostat is ruled out since the precision desired would require tremendous continuous concentration.

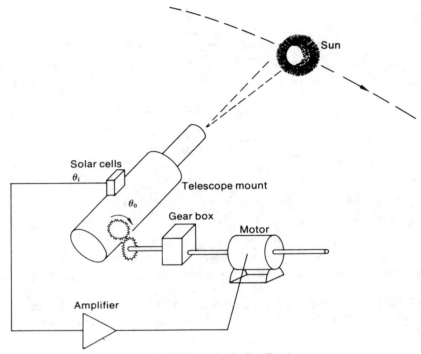

Fig. 8-24 Schematic of a Sun Tracker.

The solar cells are attached to the polar axis of the telescope so that if the pointing direction is in error, more of the sun's image falls on one cell than the other. This pair of cells, when connected in parallel opposition, appear as a current source and act as a positional error sensing device. A simple differential input transistor amplifier can provide sufficient gain so that the small error signal produces an amplifier output sufficient for running the

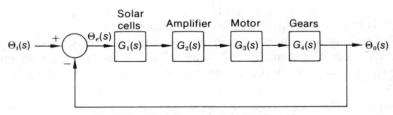

Fig. 8-25 Block diagram of the Sun Tracker.

motor. This motor sets the rotation rate of the polar axis of the telescope mount to match the apparent motion of the sun.

Having postulated one possible system, we now draw a block diagram of the sun tracker as shown in Fig. 8-25. We idealize the system and assume that it shall behave in a linear way. The various transfer functions can be obtained as outlined in Chapter 2. These transfer functions are

$$G_1(s) = K_1 \qquad \text{Solar cells}$$

$$G_2(s) = K_2 \qquad \text{Amplifier}$$

$$G_3(s) = K_3/s(As+B) \quad \text{Motor}$$

$$G_4(s) = K_4 \qquad \text{Gear ratio}$$

The output and error of the postulated system become

$$\frac{\Theta_0(s)}{\Theta_i(s)} = \frac{K}{s(As+B)+K}$$

$$\frac{\Theta_e(s)}{\Theta_i(s)} = \frac{s(As+B)}{s(As+B)+K}$$

where

$$K = K_1 K_2 K_3 K_4$$

In obtaining these relationships we have assumed that the time constant of the amplifier is small and therefore neglected; there is no friction or backlash, etc., in the gears; the gear ratio is so high that the reflected inertia of the telescope mount is small and therefore neglected; and finally the system is performing in a linear way.

The sun is assumed to move at a constant rate over the region of interest so that

$$\theta_i(t) = mt$$

where m is 2π radians per day or about 4.14×10^{-3} deg/sec. The output becomes

$$\Theta_0(s) = \frac{4.14 \times 10^{-3}K}{s^2[s(As+B)+K]}$$

Assuming that the system is underdamped, the error and output can be obtained in the time domain from the techniques developed in Chapter 4,

$$\theta_0(t) = C_0 + C_1 t + C_2 e^{-\sigma t} \sin(\omega t + \phi)$$

where C_0 is the constant error and $C_1 = 4.14 \times 10^{-3}$. The last term goes to zero in the steady state. The error is

$$C_0 = \frac{B(4.14 \times 10^{-3})}{K}$$

If this is constrained to 0.0004, then the overall gain must be set a

$$K = 10.35B$$

The predicted output and error of the linear system are shown in Fig. 8-26.

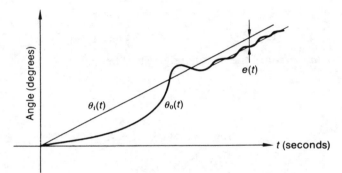

Fig. 8-26   The input and output of the Sun Tracker.

Satisfied that the idealized linear system meets the specifications, the actual hardware was built and tested.† The hardware used were off-the-shelf items with the following characteristics,

$$A = 20 \text{ g cm}^2$$

$$B = 0.45 \text{ g-cm}^2/\text{sec}$$

$$K_1 = 80 \text{ m amp/deg}$$

Using the previous analysis of the idealized system, the overall gain was set at

$$K = (10.35)(0.45) = 4.65$$

Initial tests showed that the performance was erratic with suddenly changing error that was not well damped. After a careful analysis, it was concluded that the erratic behavior was due to noise and varying friction

†This was built and tested by George Bush at The Applied Physics Laboratory of The Johns Hopkins University.

in the gear train which had frequency components commensurate with the system itself. Since the amplifier gain was set very high, the Nyquist plot of the open loop system looks like that shown in Fig. 8-27. We therefore concluded that the system was being excited at and operating near the resonant peak. It was apparent that a compensation network would be necessary to increase the damping and thereby suppress the resonant peak.

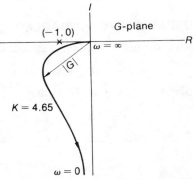

Fig. 8-27   Nyquist plot of the Sun Tracker.

A tachometric generator,† as shown in Fig. 8-28, was employed for compensation.

$$H(s) = K_5 s$$

The effect of this compensator is to add system damping and therefore move the Nyquist plot away from the resonant area. The output now becomes

$$\frac{\Theta_0(s)}{\Theta_i(s)} = \frac{K}{s(As + B_e) + K}$$

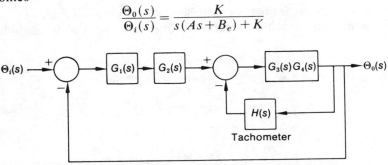

Fig. 8-28   Sun Tracker compensated by tachometric feedback.

†This was readily available.

where

$$B_e = K_3 K_4 K_5 + B$$

This allows us some control over the system damping. The above scheme was found adequate to correct the problem and meet the needs of the calibration facility. Notice that the amplifier gain must now be increased if the same steady state positional error is desired.

8-8 FEEDBACK USING STATE VARIABLES

Consider a system represented by its state equation

$$\dot{\mathbf{x}}(t) = \mathbf{A}\mathbf{x}(t) + \mathbf{b}r(t)$$

For brevity we use the notation $\dot{\mathbf{x}}$, $\mathbf{x}$, and r so that

$$\dot{\mathbf{x}} = \mathbf{A}\mathbf{x} + \mathbf{b}r \tag{8-9}$$

We select a feedback controller which is some linear combination of the state variables.

$$r = \mathbf{h}\mathbf{x} \tag{8-10}$$

Here the selection of $\mathbf{h}$ depends upon which state variables are available for feedback since not all variables can be observed and monitored, as shown in Fig. 8-29. Substituting this into Eq. (8-9),

★

$$\dot{\mathbf{x}} = [\mathbf{A} + \mathbf{b}\mathbf{h}]\mathbf{x}$$
$$= \mathbf{N}\mathbf{x} \tag{8-11}$$

where

$$\mathbf{N} = \mathbf{A} + \mathbf{b}\mathbf{h}$$

The purpose of the feedback controller is to satisfy some design criterion. We assume here that this criterion is to minimize a performance index

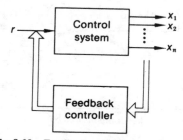

Fig. 8-29   Feedback using state variables.

given by

$$J = \int_0^\infty (\mathbf{x}^T\mathbf{x})\, dt \tag{8-12}$$

In order to minimize this function, we assume the existence of a differential of the form

$$\frac{d}{dt}(\mathbf{x}^T\mathbf{Q}\mathbf{x}) = -\mathbf{x}^T\mathbf{x} \tag{8-13}$$

where the constant symmetric matrix $\mathbf{Q}$ must be determined. Substituting this into Eq. (8-12),

$$J = \int_0^\infty -\frac{d}{dt}(\mathbf{x}^T\mathbf{Q}\mathbf{x})\, dt$$

$$= \mathbf{x}^T(0)\mathbf{Q}\mathbf{x}(0) - [\mathbf{x}^T\mathbf{Q}\mathbf{x}]_{t=\infty}$$

The last term of the above equation is assumed to be zero, thereby insuring system stability. We have therefore

★
$$J = \mathbf{x}^T(0)\mathbf{Q}\mathbf{x}(0) \tag{8-14}$$

The minimization of this satisfies the objective of our design. The matrix $\mathbf{Q}$ can be related to the system by carrying out the differentiation of Eq. (8-13), and substituting Eq. (8-11),

$$\frac{d}{dt}(\mathbf{x}^T\mathbf{Q}\mathbf{x}) = \frac{d\mathbf{x}^T}{dt}\mathbf{Q}\mathbf{x} + \mathbf{x}^T\mathbf{Q}\frac{d\mathbf{x}}{dt}$$

$$= \mathbf{x}^T\mathbf{N}^T\mathbf{Q}\mathbf{x} + \mathbf{x}^T\mathbf{Q}\mathbf{N}\mathbf{x}$$

$$= \mathbf{x}^T[\mathbf{N}^T\mathbf{Q} + \mathbf{Q}\mathbf{N}]\mathbf{x}$$

We can satisfy Eq. (8-13) only if

★
$$\mathbf{N}^T\mathbf{Q} + \mathbf{Q}\mathbf{N} = -\mathbf{I} \tag{8-15}$$

The use of Eqs. (8-14) and (8-15) together satisfy our design requirements. When the size of the matrices is large, which is often the case in modern systems, the use of a digital computer is necessary.

EXAMPLE 8-3

A system is characterized by $\dot{\mathbf{x}} = \mathbf{A}\mathbf{x} + \mathbf{b}r$ where

$$\mathbf{A} = \begin{bmatrix} 0 & 1 \\ -\alpha & -\beta \end{bmatrix}; \qquad \mathbf{b} = \begin{bmatrix} 0 \\ 1 \end{bmatrix}$$

It is desired to minimize the performance index of Eq. (8-12) and use feedback so that $r = (-x_1 - ax_2)$. Obtain a in order to minimize the value of J. Let $x^T(0) = [1 \quad 0]$.

From $r = -x_1 - ax_2$, we have

$$h = [-1 \quad -a]$$

The N matrix becomes

$$N = \begin{bmatrix} 0 & 1 \\ -\alpha & -\beta \end{bmatrix} + \begin{bmatrix} 0 \\ 1 \end{bmatrix} [-1 \quad -a]$$

$$= \begin{bmatrix} 0 & 1 \\ -\alpha - 1 & -\beta - a \end{bmatrix}$$

We now satisfy Eq. (8-15)

$$\begin{bmatrix} 0 & -\alpha - 1 \\ 1 & -\beta - a \end{bmatrix} \begin{bmatrix} q_{11} & q_{12} \\ q_{12} & q_{22} \end{bmatrix} + \begin{bmatrix} q_{11} & q_{12} \\ q_{12} & q_{22} \end{bmatrix} \begin{bmatrix} 0 & 1 \\ -\alpha - 1 & -\beta - a \end{bmatrix} = \begin{bmatrix} -1 & 0 \\ 0 & -1 \end{bmatrix}$$

which leads to the following equations:

$$-q_{12}(1+\alpha) - q_{12}(1+\alpha) = -1$$

$$-q_{22}(1+\alpha) + q_{11} - q_{12}(a+\beta) = 0$$

$$2q_{12} - 2q_{22}(a+\beta) = -1$$

Solving these equations,

$$q_{11} = \frac{(2+\alpha)(1+\alpha) + (a+\beta)^2}{2(a+\beta)(1+\alpha)}; \quad q_{12} = \frac{1}{2(1+\alpha)}; \quad q_{22} = \frac{2+\alpha}{2(1+\alpha)(a+\beta)}$$

The performance index is

$$J = x^T(0)Qx(0)$$

$$= [1 \quad 0] \begin{bmatrix} q_{11} & q_{12} \\ q_{12} & q_{22} \end{bmatrix} \begin{bmatrix} 1 \\ 0 \end{bmatrix}$$

$$= q_{11}$$

Minimizing J with respect to a,

$$\frac{dJ}{da} = \frac{4(a+\beta)(1+\alpha)(a+\beta) - 2(1+\alpha)[(2+\alpha)(1+\alpha) + (a+\beta)^2]}{4(a+\beta)^2(1+\alpha)^2}$$

$$= 0$$

Solving this, we obtain

$$a = \sqrt{(2+\alpha)(1+\alpha)} - \beta$$

SUMMARY

We have been concerned with different compensating techniques useful for changing system performance in order to meet specifications. The compensating elements considered here were passive elements.

Compensation of control systems may be achieved by cascading, feedback, feedforward, or cancellation techniques.

The method of compensation was most easily understood using frequency plots. The effect of compensation on closed loop performance was obtained using Nichols charts.

It was shown how feedback compensation using state variables is achieved. The feedback gain was selected for the case where a quadratic performance index was minimized.

PROBLEMS

8-1. A second-order control system has an open loop transfer function given by

$$G(s) = \frac{K}{s(s+2)}$$

It is required that the phase margin be 50° and the velocity error constant 20 sec⁻¹. Design compensating networks using
(a) A phase-lead network.
(b) Cancellation techniques.
Discuss the relative advantages of each method.

8-2. The unstable transfer function

$$G(s) = \frac{2}{s^2(1+0.1s)}$$

is to be stabilized using a lead circuit whose transfer function is

$$G_c(s) = \frac{1+1.585s}{1+0.158s}$$

Show the compensated and uncompensated circuits on the Bode plot. Indicate all the changes brought about by the compensator.

8-3. A third-order servomechanism is shown in Fig. P8-3. It is required that the steady state error be 0.1 of the final output velocity and the phase margin be 50°. What suitable values of R_1, R_2, and C would satisfy the above conditions?

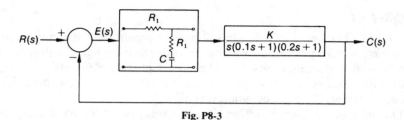

Fig. P8-3

8-4. The block diagram of a servomechanism with feedback compensation is shown in Fig. P8-4. Study the effect of varying T on system response.

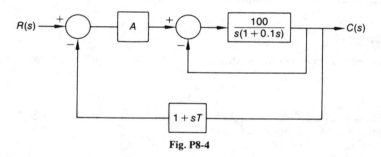

Fig. P8-4

8-5. It is known that tachometric feedback affects the relative damping of a system. What value of K_f is necessary for a damping ratio of 0.707, of the system shown in Fig. P8-5?

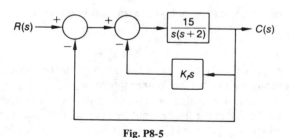

Fig. P8-5

8-6. A feedforward compensation scheme is shown in Fig. P8-6. Assume that $U(s)$ is a step disturbance whose magnitude is 0.5. Let $R(s)$ also be a step input of magnitude 1. Study the response as a function of K.

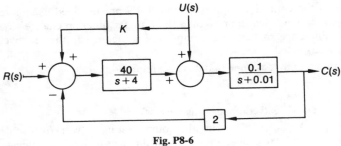

Fig. P8-6

8-7. The block diagram of two compensating systems is shown in Fig. P8-7. Where

$$G_1 = 4K/s(s+1000)(s+20)$$

$$G_2 = \frac{\tau_1\tau_2 s + \tau_2}{\tau_1\tau_2 s + \tau_1} \qquad \tau_1 = \frac{1}{120}, \qquad \tau_2 = \frac{1}{1200}$$

K is to be selected so that the velocity constant is 10 sec^{-1}. Compare the two schemes of compensating and discuss the behavior of each in the high-frequency and low-frequency range.

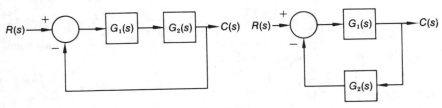

Fig. P8-7

8-8. Using Nichols charts and Bode's diagram, select a cascaded compensator for a unity feedback system with

$$G(s) = K/(s+10)(s+30)$$

It is required that the velocity error constant be greater than 90 sec^{-1}, and maximum overshoot < 40%.

8-9. A unity feedback control system has an open loop transfer function

$$G(s) = \frac{K}{s^2(s+1)}$$

We would like to use a cascaded phase-lead or phase-lag network to stabilize it, have $K_v = 10$ sec^{-1}, and a phase margin of 45°. Which network would you suggest? Obtain the transfer function for the one you select.

8-10. Could the control system of Problem 8-9 be stabilized using a lead or lag network in the feedback loop? Would the transfer function change? What is the principle difference of having a compensation element in the feedback loop as opposed to cascaded elements?

8-11. In Problem 8-1, assume that it is also required that

$$|G(j\omega)|_{\omega=0.1} = 200$$

Design a phase lag-lead compensating network.

8-12. What is the effect of placing the compensating network of Problem 8-2 in the feedback path? How does the behavior differ at the high-frequency from the low-frequency region?

8-13. The mass m was shown to be unstable in Problem 4-13. We wish to stabilize this by employing a feedback system, i.e. driving the base by a signal that is proportional to θ and $\dot{\theta}$. Suggest a compensation network and show that m can be stabilized in this manner.

8-14. If the initial state vector in Example 8-4 is $x^T(0) = [1\ 1]$ and $r = -ax_1 - ax_2$, obtain the value of a necessary to minimize the performance index shown in Eq. (8-12).

8-15. A system is characterized by $\dot{x} = Ax + br$ where

$$A = \begin{bmatrix} 0 & 1 \\ 1 & 1 \end{bmatrix} \qquad b = \begin{bmatrix} 0 \\ 1 \end{bmatrix}$$

and $r = -x_1 - ax_2$. If the initial condition is $x^T(0) = [1\ 1]$, obtain a that minimizes the performance index of Eq. (8-12).

REFERENCES

1. Truxal, J. G., *Control System Synthesis*, New York, McGraw-Hill, 1955.
2. Shinners, S. M., *Control System Design*, New York, Wiley, 1964.
3. Savant, C. J., *Control System Design*, New York, McGraw-Hill, 1964.
4. Cannon, R. H., *Dynamics of Physical Systems*, New York, McGraw-Hill, 1967.
5. Edwin, G., and T. Roddam, *Principles of Feedback Design*, New York, Hayden Book, 1964.
6. Dorf, R. C., *Modern Control Systems*, Reading, Mass., Addison-Wesley, 1967.
7. Melsa, J. L., and D. G. Schultz, *Linear Control Systems*, New York, McGraw-Hill, 1969.
8. Huggins, W. H., and D. R. Entwisle, *Introductory Systems and Design*, Waltham, Mass., Blaisdell, 1968.

9

Discrete Systems – Classical Method

9-1 INTRODUCTION

The study of linear systems has been restricted to the consideration of signals that are continuous with respect to time. Since digital computers have become such valuable aids to modern control systems, instances of systems operating with intermittent data are many. For example, a computer enables us to solve, in real time, navigation and guidance problems. As another example, the increased plant efficiency and product quality in chemical processes is the direct result of computer control. Additionally, in many instances the existence of telemetry links, time sharing due to the multiplicity of signals, or high precision computations, leads to the use of digitized information. It is therefore necessary that we modify our previous approach to allow for the inclusion of discrete signals in control systems. The method that we develop in this chapter is the classical approach. If the system is represented in state form, then it is desirable to use the state approach of the next chapter.

This chapter is concerned with control systems receiving data at intermittent intervals. Such systems are known as "sampled data systems" or "digital control systems" although the former implies a more general system. We shall assume that although the signals are intermittent, they are received at regular intervals, i.e. they are periodic. A fairly general sampled-data system is shown in Fig. 9-1. Let us take a close look at it. The signals $r(t)$, $c(t)$, $b(t)$, and $m(t)$ are continuous, whereas $e^*(t)$ and $m^*(t)$ are intermittent. The signal $e(t)$, after it passes through the sampling device (called a sampler), becomes intermittent in nature. As a matter of fact, the amplitude of $e(t)$ is equal to $e^*(t)$ when the sampler closes

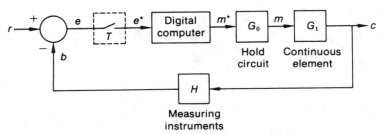

Fig. 9-1 Representation of a general sampled-data control system.

every T seconds. The discrete signal $m^*(t)$ is the input to G_0 which reconstructs† it to a continuous signal $m(t)$. (G_0 is called a hold circuit.)

The simultaneous existence of continuous and discrete signals requires a unified theory that may be applied to both type of signals. The operational technique best suited for this is the z-transform. We shall first introduce the mathematics of the sampler and then develop the techniques to obtain the response of sampled systems. It is not intended here to introduce mathematics for sampled systems in rigor or include all its subtle nuances. We take several liberties in order to introduce the subject matter in as straightforward a way as possible.

9-2 THE SAMPLER

A sampler, or sampling switch, is a device that converts a continuous signal to a discrete signal. A schematic representation of a sampler is shown in Fig. 9-2. The input signal is a continuous signal, whereas the output signal is in the form of pulses. In a real sampler these pulses have a nonzero width. In an ideal sampler the pulses are assumed to have no width. This assumption greatly simplifies the analysis. The pulse amplitude of the output of the ideal sampler, then, is equal to the input at $t = 0$, $T, 2T, \ldots$. We assume that the output of the ideal sampler is defined and finite at the sampled instants, i.e. there are no jump discontinuities in the system. If we define a unit impulse train $I(t)$ so that

★
$$I(t) = \sum_{n=0}^{\infty} \delta(t - nT) \qquad (9\text{-}1)$$

where $\delta(t - nT)$ is an impulse of unit area at $t = nT$, then the output of the

---

†It will be seen, in a later section, that sampling introduces higher harmonics into the signal which must be suppressed before input to a continuous element. Data reconstruction by a hold circuit minimizes the effect of these harmonics.

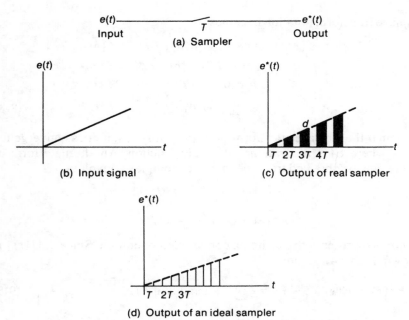

(a) Sampler

(b) Input signal

(c) Output of real sampler

(d) Output of an ideal sampler

Fig. 9-2 Schematic representation of the sampling process.

ideal sampler may be related to the input by

★
$$e^*(t) = \sum_{n=0}^{\infty} e(nT)\delta(t - nT) \tag{9-2}$$

The last equation states that the output of an ideal sampler consists of a sequence of pulses whose strength is equal to the amplitude of the input at $t = 0, T, 2T, \dots$. The sampling frequency ω_s is related to T by $\omega_s = 2\pi/T$. This is schematically shown in Fig. 9-3. The output of an ideal sampler in

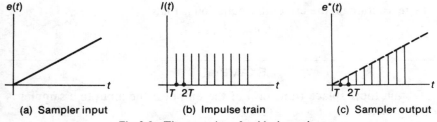

(a) Sampler input

(b) Impulse train

(c) Sampler output

Fig. 9-3 The operation of an ideal sampler.

Laplace transform notation becomes

$$E^*(s) = \mathcal{L}[e^*(t)] = e(0)\mathcal{L}[\delta(0)] + e(T)\mathcal{L}[\delta(t-T)]$$
$$+ e(2T)\mathcal{L}[\delta(t-2T)] + \cdots$$
$$= e(0) + e(T)e^{-Ts} + e(2T)e^{-2Ts} + \cdots$$
$$= \sum_{n=0}^{\infty} e(nT)e^{-nTs} \qquad (9\text{-}3)$$

Although the Laplace transform of $e^*(t)$ is a series, it does converge for cases where $E(s)$ is a rational algebraic function. An alternate form of $E^*(s)$ may be obtained from the theory of complex convolution

$$\mathcal{L}[e^*(t)] = \mathcal{L}[e(t) \cdot I(t)]$$

or

$$E^*(s) = \mathcal{L}[e(t)] * \mathcal{L}[I(t)] \qquad (9\text{-}4)$$

where * represents the complex convolution operation. Since $\mathcal{L}[I(t)]$ is known, Eq. (9-4) becomes

$$E^*(s) = E(s) * \frac{1}{1 - e^{sT}} = \sum_{\substack{\text{poles of} \\ E(p)}} \text{Residues of } E(p)\left[\frac{1}{1 - e^{-T(s-p)}}\right] \qquad (9\text{-}5)$$

where

$$E(p) = \frac{N(p)}{D(p)}$$

Applying the residue theorem and assuming k simple poles,

$$E^*(s) = \sum_{n=1}^{k} \frac{N(s_n)}{D'(s_n)} \frac{1}{1 - e^{-T(s-s_n)}} \qquad (9\text{-}6)$$

where

$$D'(s_n) = \left[\frac{dD(p)}{dp}\right]_{p=s_n}$$

The restriction on the use of this equation is that

$$\lim_{s \to \infty} sE(s) = 0$$

EXAMPLE 9-1

Obtain the Laplace transform of the output if the input to a sampler is $e(t) = \sin \omega t$.

From Eq. (9-3)

$$e(nT) = \sin n\omega T$$

$$E^*(s) = \sum_{n=0}^{\infty} \sin n\omega T\, e^{-nTs}$$

Since

$$\sin n\omega T = \frac{e^{jn\omega T} - e^{-jn\omega T}}{2j}$$

then

$$E^*(s) = \sum \frac{e^{-n(sT - j\omega T)}}{2j} - \sum \frac{e^{-n(j\omega T - sT)}}{2j}$$

$$= \frac{1}{2j(1 - e^{-(sT - j\omega T)})} - \frac{1}{2j(1 - e^{-(j\omega T + sT)})}$$

which is combined to yield

$$E^*(s) = \frac{e^{-sT} \sin \omega T}{1 + e^{-2sT} - 2e^{-sT} \cos \omega T}$$

This may also be obtained via the residue theorem. Using Eq. (9-6) and noting that there are 2 poles,

$$E^*(s) = \sum_{n=1}^{2} \frac{N(s_n)}{D'(s_n)} \frac{1}{1 - e^{-T(s - s_n)}}; \qquad \begin{array}{l} N(s) = \omega \\ D'(s) = 2s \end{array}$$

Substituting this we obtain

$$E^*(s) = \frac{\omega}{2j\omega} \left[\frac{1}{1 - e^{-T(s - j\omega)}} - \frac{1}{1 - e^{-T(s + j\omega)}} \right]$$

$$= \frac{e^{-sT} \sin \omega T}{1 + e^{-2sT} - 2e^{-sT} \cos \omega T}$$

which is the same as obtained previously.

Having obtained the Laplace transform of the sample signal, let us see what are its characteristics in the frequency domain. Substituting†

---

† By doing this we are stating that $E^*(s)$ is a periodic function. The ensuing development confirms and therefore justifies this statement.

$s + jm\omega_s$ for s in Eq. (9-3),

$$E^*(s + jm\omega_s) = \sum_{n=0}^{\infty} e(nT) \, e^{-n(s + jm\omega_s)T}$$

$$= \sum_{n=0}^{\infty} e(nT) \, e^{-jnm2\pi} \, e^{-nsT}$$

Since the term $e^{-jnm2\pi}$ simply contributes 2π to the phase, the above simplifies to

★ $$E^*(s + jm\omega_s) = E^*(s) \tag{9-7}$$

This states that $E^*(s)$ is a periodic function with period ω_s which is the sampling period. In other words, sampling has introduced an infinite number of higher frequency components into the signal as shown in Fig. 9-4. If the fundamental frequency of the input signal is ω_h and $\omega_s > 2\omega_h$, then the output of the sampler exhibits no overlapping of its complemen-

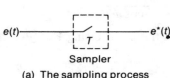

(a) The sampling process

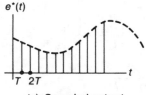

(c) Sampled output

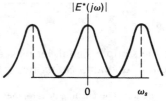

(e) Output spectrum for $\omega_s > 2\omega_h$

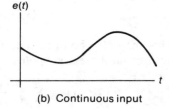

(b) Continuous input

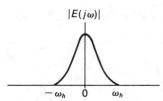

(d) Frequency spectrum of input

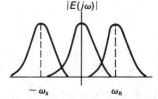

(f) Output spectrum for $\omega_s < 2\omega_h$

Fig. 9-4 Characteristics of a sampler.

tary components. However, if $\omega_s < 2\omega_h$, then overlapping does indeed occur. It is evident that if $\omega_s < 2\omega_h$, then even an ideal filter shall be unable to recover completely the input signal. If the input signal must be completely recovered, then ω_s must be *at least* equal to $2\omega_h$. These observations were first made by C. E. Shannon and form the basis of Shannon's theorem.

9-3 THE z-TRANSFORM

When the signal in a given system is represented in a discrete form, then the Laplace transform is seen to possess terms like e^{-nTs},

$$\star \qquad E^*(s) = \sum_{0}^{\infty} e(nT)\, e^{-nsT} \qquad (9\text{-}8)$$

The term renders $E^*(s)$ a nonalgebraic function of s thereby adding greatly to the complexity of analysis necessary to study discrete systems. This can be overcome however if we define a change of variables,

$$\star \qquad z = e^{sT} \qquad (9\text{-}9)$$

where s is the Laplace operator and T is the sampling period. Substituting this into Eq. (9-8) we obtain

$$E^*\left(s = \frac{1}{T}\ln z\right) = E(z) = \sum_{0}^{\infty} e(nT)z^{-n} \qquad (9\text{-}10)$$

where

$$\star \qquad z[e^*(t)] = E(z)$$

Here $E(z)$ is called the z-transform† of $e^*(t)$. Expanding Eq. (9-10) we have

$$E(z) = e(0) + e(T)z^{-1} + e(2T)z^{-2} + \cdots \qquad (9\text{-}11)$$

It is interesting to note the role z plays in this equation. Clearly, it indicates the time at which the signal is defined. For example, if we have

$$E(z) = 1 + 2z^{-1} + 2.1z^{-2} + 2.3z^{-3} + \cdots$$

then $e(t) = 1$ at $t = 0$, $e(t) = 2$ at $t = T$, $e(t) = 2.1$ at $t = 2T$, $e = 2.3$ at $t = 3T$ and so on. This is to be expected since z^{-n} replaces e^{-sTn} which represents a time translation by nT.

In general, any continuous function possessing a Laplace transform also has a z-transform. If the Laplace transform is convergent on the s-plane,

†For a more complete discussion, *see* Reference 6.

then generally the z-transform is convergent on the z-plane. It is perhaps instructive to see what is the relationship between the s-plane and the z-plane. To establish this we shall map the s-plane onto the z-plane. However, since we have established that $E^*(s)$ is a periodic function in s, we need to map only the primary strip shown in Fig. 9-5. Representing $s = \sigma + j\omega$ we have

$$z = |e^{\sigma T}| e^{j\omega T} \qquad (9\text{-}12)$$

Therefore, for any point $s = \sigma + j\omega$ on the s-plane the corresponding point on the complex z-plane has a magnitude $e^{\sigma T}$ and angle of ωT.

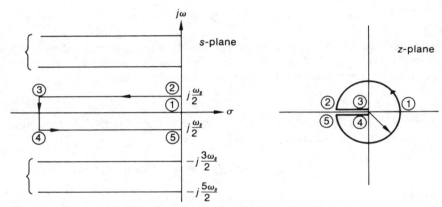

Fig. 9-5   Mapping of the s-plane onto the z-plane.

When $s = 0$, $z = 1$ with zero phase. As the imaginary part of s increases, the point z changes phase but not its magnitude. Finally, when $s = j\omega_s/2$, z has a phase of

$$\omega T = \left(\frac{\omega_s}{2}\right)\left(\frac{2\pi}{\omega_s}\right) = \pi$$

Now as the imaginary part of s stays constant while the real part goes to $-\infty$, the magnitude of z goes to zero but the phase stays at π. Note that the strips from $j\omega_s/2$ to $j3\omega_s/2$, $-j\omega_s/2$ to $-j3\omega_s/2$, etc. plot into the same region on the z-plane as did the primary strip. We conclude then that the region inside the unit circle on the z-plane corresponds to the left half of the s-plane. The right half of the s-plane corresponds to the region outside the unit circle on the z-plane. The imaginary axis in the s-plane corresponds to the circumference of the unit circle on the z-plane.

Having established the basic concepts of the z-transform, let us consider a few examples.

EXAMPLE 9-2

Obtain the z-transform of $e(t) = 1$. We have already established that

$$E^*(s) = \frac{1}{1 - e^{-sT}}$$

Substituting Eq. (9-9),

$$E(z) = \frac{1}{1 - z^{-1}} = \frac{z}{z - 1}$$

EXAMPLE 9-3

Obtain the z-transform of $e(t) = t$ using the convolution method. Since

$$E(s) = \frac{1}{s^2}$$

there is a double pole. In this case,

$$E(z) = \Sigma \text{ Residues of } \left[\frac{E(p)}{1 - e^{pT}(z^{-1})} \right]_{p = s_k}$$

$$R(p) = \frac{E(p)}{1 - e^{pT} z^{-1}} = \frac{k_1}{p} + \frac{k_2}{p^2} + \cdots$$

Evaluating k_1,

$$k_1 = \frac{d}{dp} [p^2 R(p)]_{p=0} = \frac{Tz^{-1}}{(1 - z^{-1})^2}$$

Therefore,

$$E(z) = \frac{Tz}{(z - 1)^2}$$

Some of the basic properties given without proofs of z-transforms are listed below. A table of z-transforms incorporating some of these ideas appears in Appendix A.

Linearity. If $e_1(nT)$ and $e_2(nT)$ have z-transform, $E_1(z)$ and $E_2(z)$, then

$$E(z) = z[a_1 e_1(nT) + a_2 e_2(nT)]$$
$$= a_1 E_1(z) + a_2 E_2(z) \qquad (9\text{-}13a)$$

★

where a_1 and a_2 are constants.

Real translation. When a function $e(nT)$ is delayed by nT, then the z-transform is given by

★
$$z[e(nT \pm mT)] = z^{\pm m}E(z) \qquad (9\text{-}13b)$$

Multiplication by an exponential. When $e(nT)$ is multiplied by $e^{\alpha t}$ in the time domain, then

★
$$z[e^{\alpha t}e^{nT}] = E(ze^{-\alpha T}) \qquad (9\text{-}13c)$$

Initial value theorem. If $e(nT)$ has the z-transform $E(z)$, then

★
$$\lim_{n \to 0} e(nT) = \lim_{z \to \infty} E(z) \qquad (9\text{-}13d)$$

provided the limit exists.

Final value theorem. Let the function $e(nT)$ have the z-transform $E(z)$ and further let $(1 - z^{-1})E(z)$ have no poles on or outside the unit circle centered at the origin on the z-plane,† then

★
$$\lim_{n \to \infty} e(nT) = \lim_{z \to 1} \left(\frac{z-1}{z}\right)E(z) \qquad (9\text{-}13e)$$

As an example, consider

$$E(z) = \frac{0.4z^2}{(z-1)(z^2-0.5z+0.3)}$$

The initial value of $e(nT)$ is zero while the steady state or final value is

$$\lim_{n \to \infty} e(nT) = \lim_{z \to 1} \frac{z-1}{z}E(z)$$

Substituting for $E(z)$ we have

$$\lim_{n \to \infty} e(nT) = \lim_{z \to 1} \frac{0.4z}{(z^2-0.5z+0.3)} = 0.5$$

This can be verified by expanding $E(z)$,

$$E(z) = 0.4z^{-1} + 0.6z^{-2} + 0.58z^{-3} + 0.51z^{-4} + \cdots$$

We note that $e(nT)$ is rapidly converging to 0.5.

The Inverse z-Transform

In order to obtain the response in the time domain, we need to obtain the inverse z-transform of functions expressed in the z-domain. It should

---

†This condition is identical to the requirements of the Final Value Theorem for the Laplace transform.

be emphasized that the inverse transform yields information at $t = 0$, $T, 2T, \ldots$, i.e. at discrete time steps. It gives no information about the variable in between the time steps.

The inverse z-transform can be obtained from tables only for the most elementary functions. When the systems get complex, other methods for obtaining the inverse are used. We shall consider the first three of the following four methods:

(1) The partial fraction method,
(2) The power series expansion method,
(3) The difference method,
(4) The real inversion integral method.

In each case we shall assume that the function in the z-domain appears as

$$E(z) = \frac{N(z)}{D(z)}$$

where $N(z)$ and $D(z)$ are rational polynomials in z.

The partial fraction method. Analogous to the Laplace transform we expand the z-transform function in partial fractions and take the inverse of each term. Consider the function $E(z)$ expressed as

$$E(z) = \frac{N(z)}{D(z)} = \frac{N(z)}{(z - e^{-a_1 T})(z - e^{-a_2 T}) \cdots (z - e^{-a_m T})} \qquad (9\text{-}14)$$

We expand $E(z)/z$ in partial fractions,

$$\frac{E(z)}{z} = \frac{K_1}{z - e^{-a_1 T}} + \frac{K_2}{z - e^{-a_2 T}} + \cdots \qquad (9\text{-}15)$$

★

where the coefficients are obtained as in the Laplace transform method. The inverse z-transform is taken term by term,

$$z^{-1}[E(z)] = z^{-1}\left[\frac{K_1 z}{z - e^{-a_1 T}}\right] + \cdots + z^{-1}\left[\frac{K_m z}{z - e^{-a_m T}}\right]$$

or

$$e(nT) = K_1 e^{-a_1 nT} + \cdots K_m e^{-a_m nT} \qquad (9\text{-}16)$$

As an example, consider

$$E(z) = \frac{z}{(z - 1)(z - e^{-T})}$$

Expanding this,

$$\frac{E(z)}{z} = \frac{K_1}{z-1} + \frac{K_2}{z-e^{-T}}$$

where

$$K_1 = \lim_{z \to 1} \left(\frac{z-1}{z}\right) E(z) = \frac{1}{1-e^{-T}}$$

$$K_2 = \lim_{z \to e^{-T}} \left(\frac{z-e^{-T}}{z}\right) E(z) = -\frac{1}{1-e^{-T}}$$

Substituting

$$E(z) = \frac{1}{1-e^{-T}} \left[\frac{z}{z-1} - \frac{z}{z-e^{-T}}\right]$$

and the inverse is

$$e(nT) = \frac{1}{1-e^{-T}} [\delta(t-nT) - e^{-nT}]$$

When the function $E(z)$ has double poles we form the coefficients in a way analogous to the Laplace method.

Power series. This method involves the representation of $E(z)$ in the form of a series. We represent $E(z)$ as

$$E(z) = e_0 + e_1 z^{-1} + e_2 z^{-2} + \cdots \tag{9-17}$$

Since multiplication by z^{-m} means that the function is shifted in time by mT time units, we may rewrite Eq. (9-17) in the time domain as

$$e(nT) = e_0\delta(0) + e_1\delta(t-T) + e_2\delta(t-2T) + \cdots \tag{9-18}$$

As an example, consider

$$E(z) = \frac{z^2 + 2z - 1}{z^2 + 3z - 3}$$

Using long division we obtain the following series

$$E(z) = 1 - z^{-1} + 5z^{-2} - 18z^{-3} + \cdots$$

and the inverse is

$$e(nT) = \delta(t) - \delta(t-T) + 5\delta(t-2T) - 18\delta(t-3T) + \cdots$$

The difference method. This method is iterative and can be programmed very easily on the computer. Assume that we know

$$\frac{C(z)}{R(z)} = \frac{z^2}{z^2 - \alpha z + \beta}$$

dividing through by z^2 and multiplying we obtain

$$C(z)[1 - \alpha z^{-1} + \beta z^{-2}] = R(z)$$

Recognizing z^{-1} as a time shift and letting $t = nT$, we have

$$c(nT) - \alpha c[(n-1)T] + \beta c[(n-2)T] = r(nT)$$

or

$$c(nT) = r(nT) + \alpha c[(n-1)T] + \beta c[(n-2)T]$$

An example using this method is considered in a later section.

9-4 THE HOLD CIRCUIT

From the analysis of the previous section we saw that the sampling process introduces an infinite number of higher harmonics into the output signal. When this signal is applied to a continuous control system, it is often desirable to suppress these higher harmonics It would be ideal if a device could be designed which while reconstructing the original continuous signal would completely eliminate all the higher harmonics. However this is not physically realizable. Therefore, devices that only approximately reconstruct the original signal are used. Such devices are called data reconstruction devices or hold circuits

A signal $e(t)$ between $t = nT$ and $t = (n+1)T$ may be expressed as a power series,

$$e(t) = e(nT) + \dot{e}(nT)(t - nT) + \frac{\ddot{e}(nT)}{2!}(t - nT)^2 + \cdots \qquad (9\text{-}19)$$

In order to construct $e(t)$, we must have the derivatives $\dot{e}(nT), \ddot{e}(nT)$, etc., which, in general, are unavailable. These derivatives can however be estimated from the sampled data itself. The use of sampled data for $t < nT$ requires time delays and this generally has a destabilizing effect on system stability. Most hold circuits, therefore, do not employ higher-order derivatives.

The simplest form of a data reconstruction device *holds* the amplitude of the sample from one sampling instant to the next, i.e.

★
$$e(t) = e(nT) \qquad nT \leqslant t \leqslant (n+1)T \qquad (9\text{-}20)$$

Such a device is called a zero-order hold.† The output of a zero-order hold, shown in Fig. 9-6, corresponds exactly to the sampled signal at $t = 0, T, 2T, \ldots$. The impulse response of a zero-order hold (abbreviated as zoh)

†It is also referred to as a clamper, data hold, or staircase generator.

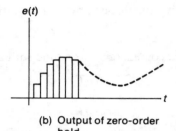

(a) Input to zero-order hold

(b) Output of zero-order hold

Fig. 9-6   A zero-order hold.

is shown in Fig. 9-7. The Laplace transform of the impulse response is

★
$$G_0(s) = \mathcal{L}[g_0(t)] = \frac{1}{s} - \frac{e^{-sT}}{s} = \frac{1-e^{-sT}}{s} \tag{9-21}$$

The frequency response is obtained by forming $G_0(j\omega)$ and is

$$G_0(j\omega) = \frac{1-e^{-j\omega T}}{j\omega} = \frac{2 \sin (\omega T/2)}{\omega} e^{-j\omega T/2}$$

or

$$G_0(j\omega) = T \frac{\sin (\pi\omega/\omega_s)}{\pi(\omega/\omega_s)} e^{-j(\pi\omega/\omega_s)}$$

The amplitude of $G_0(j\omega)$ is given by

$$|G_0(j\omega)| = T \left| \frac{\sin (\pi\omega/\omega_s)}{(\pi\omega/\omega_s)} \right|$$

and the phase is given by

$$\underline{/G_0(j\omega)} = -\frac{\pi\omega}{\omega_s} \frac{\sin (\pi\omega/\omega_s)}{|\sin (\pi\omega/\omega_s)|}$$

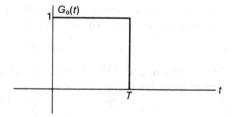

Fig. 9-7   Impulse response of a zero-order hold.

and is shown in Fig. 9-8. We note that the behavior is quite similar to that of a low pass filter. As a matter of fact it is possible to approximate a zoh by passive elements. Let us show this by expanding $G_0(s)$ in a power series of e^{sT},

$$G_0(s) = \frac{1 - e^{-sT}}{s} = \frac{1}{s}\left[1 - \frac{1}{1 + sT + \cdots}\right]$$

$$G_0(s) \approx \frac{T}{1 + sT} \qquad (9\text{-}22)$$

★

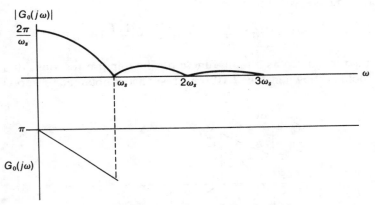

Fig. 9-8   Characteristics of a zero-order hold.

This is recognized as the transfer function of an $R\text{-}C$ network shown in Fig. 9-9. This approximation is sometimes referred to as an exponential hold device. As we seek better approximations to a zoh device we need to include additional terms of the power series expansion. This, however,

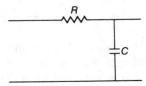

Fig. 9-9 $R\text{-}C$ low pass filter as a hold device.

gets complicated; therefore, networks employing operational amplifiers are used to implement zoh circuits more accurately. Let us now return to the power series expansion of $e(t)$ between $t = nT$ and $t = (n+1)T$. We have discussed the zoh approximation, i.e. $e(t) = e(nT)$. Now if we took one additional term in $e(t)$, then,

$$e(t) \cong e(nT) + \dot{e}(nT)(t - nT)$$

This is called a *first-order hold*. Notice that we are now using information about the derivative of $e(t)$. The first derivative may be represented using finite difference as,

$$\dot{e}(nT) = \frac{1}{T}[e(nT) - e(n-1)T]$$

Substituting this, we obtain

★
$$e(t) = e(nT) + \frac{e(nT) - e(n-1)T}{T}(t - nT) \qquad (9\text{-}23)$$

which is recognized as a ramp function. The impulse response of a first-order hold is shown in Fig. 9-10. This response is obtained by applying an

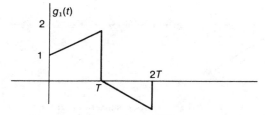

Fig. 9-10   Impulse response of first-order hold.

impulse of unit strength at $t = 0$ as input to a first-order hold device. The transfer function $G_{01}(s)$ of the first-order hold may be obtained by taking the Laplace transform of the impulse response and is

$$G_{01}(s) = \mathscr{L}[g_0(t)] = \frac{1 + sT}{T} \frac{(1 - e^{-sT})^2}{s} \qquad (9\text{-}24)$$

The analysis of $G_{01}(s)$ in the frequency domain is left as an exercise. The output of a first-order hold is shown in Fig. 9-11. Although a first-order generally is better in signal recovery it does indeed complicate the problem of system stability. Additionally, the complexity of construction makes it rather unattractive.

There are several other types of hold circuits however their representation is complex. Also the additional time delay introduced by higher-order approximations has an adverse effect on system stability. For these

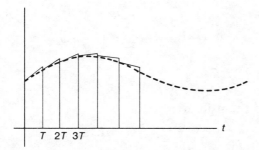

Fig. 9-11   Output of a first-order hold.

reasons the zero-order hold is widely used for signal recovery in sampled data systems.

9-5   PULSED TRANSFER FUNCTION

When a signal is not continuous but consists of periodic pulses, then the output of the transfer function shown in Fig. 9-12 becomes

$$C(s) = G(s)E^*(s) \qquad (9\text{-}25)$$

where $E^*(s)$ is the pulsed transform of $E(s)$ and can be written as

$$E^*(s) = \frac{1}{T} \sum_0^\infty E(s + jn\omega_s)$$

Similarly, the output $C(s)$ may be denoted by the pulsed transform as

$$C^*(s) = \frac{1}{T} \sum_0^\infty C(s + jn\omega_s) = \frac{1}{T} \sum_0^\infty G(s + jn\omega_s)E^*(s + jn\omega_s)$$

The pulsed function $E^*(s)$ was shown to be a periodic function with period ω_s and

$$E^*(s) = E^*(s + jn\omega_s)$$

Therefore the above may be modified to

$$C^*(s) = E^*(s) \frac{1}{T} \sum_0^\infty G(s + jn\omega_s)$$

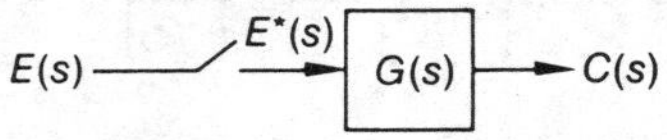

$E(s)$ ———$/$—————▸ $E^*(s)$ ▸ $\boxed{G(s)}$ ——▸ $C(s)$

Fig. 9-12   Block diagram with sampled signal.

Since

$$G^*(s) = \frac{1}{T} \sum_0^\infty G(s + jn\omega_s)$$

we obtain

★ $$C^*(s) = E^*(s)G^*(s) \tag{9-26}$$

Now taking the z-transform

$$C(z) = G(z)E(z)$$

or

$$\frac{C(z)}{E(z)} = G(z) \tag{9-27}$$

We use this consequence to develop the transfer function of systems having sampled signals. If there is more than one sampler, we shall assume that they are all synchronized.

Combinations of Pulsed Transfer Functions

Consider the cascaded elements shown in Fig. 9-13a.
Using the notion developed previously the output $C(s)$ is,

$$C(s) = G_1(s)G_2(s)E^*(s) \tag{9-28}$$

Defining $G(s) = G_1(s)G_2(s)$ we have

$$C(s) = G(s)E^*(s)$$

and using the result developed in the previous section

$$C^*(s) = G^*(s)E^*(s)$$

Taking the z-transform,

$$C(z) = G(z)E(z) \tag{9-29}$$

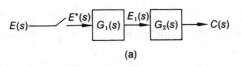

(a)

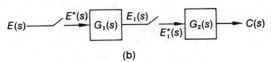

(b)

Fig. 9-13 Cascaded elements with sampler.

where $G(z) = z[G_1(s)G_2(s)]$, i.e. the z-transform is taken *after* $G_1(s)G_2(s)$ is formed. Now consider the same cascaded elements but with a sampler between each transfer function as shown in Fig. 9-13b. By inspection we write

$$E_1(s) = G_1(s)E^*(s) \qquad (9\text{-}30a)$$

$$C(s) = G_2(s)E_1^*(s) \qquad (9\text{-}30b)$$

Taking the pulsed transform we obtain

$$E_1^*(s) = G_1^*(s)E^*(s)$$

and substituting in Eq. (9-30b) and again taking the pulsed transform

$$C^*(s) = G_1^*(s)G_2^*(s)E^*(s)$$

Taking the z-transform we obtain

$$C(z) = G_1(z)G_2(z)E(z) \qquad (9\text{-}31)$$

and clearly this is different from Eq. (9-29). We conclude that in general

★
$$G_1(z)G_2(z) \neq G_1G_2(z) \qquad (9\text{-}32)$$

As an example, assume

$$G_1(s) = \frac{1}{s^2} \quad \text{and} \quad G_2(s) = \frac{a}{s+a}$$

then for Fig. 9-13a we have

$$\frac{C(z)}{E(z)} = G_1G_2(z) = z\left[\frac{a}{s^2(s+a)}\right]$$

$$= \frac{Tz}{(z-1)^2} - \frac{(1-e^{-aT})z}{a(z-1)(z-e^{-aT})}$$

whereas for Fig. 9-13b we have

$$\frac{C(z)}{E(z)} = G_1(z)G_2(z) = z\left[\frac{1}{s^2}\right]z\left[\frac{a}{s+a}\right]$$

$$= \frac{aTz^2}{(z-1)^2(z-e^{-aT})}$$

Closed Loop Pulsed Systems

The previous techniques may be extended to include closed loop systems with sample data. Consider the closed loop system of Fig. 9-14. We

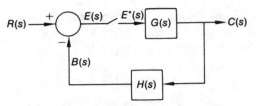

Fig. 9-14   Error sampled closed loop system.

can write the following equations by inspection,

$$E(s) = R(s) - B(s)$$
$$C(s) = G(s)E^*(s)$$
$$B(s) = H(s)C(s)$$

Substituting the second and third into the first equation,

$$E(s) = R(s) - GH(s)E^*(s) \qquad (9\text{-}33a)$$

Taking the pulsed transform of this and rearranging, we obtain

$$E^*(s) = R^*(s)/(1 + GH^*(s))$$

Now substituting for $E^*(s)$ we obtain the overall transfer function,

$$C^*(s) = G^*(s)R^*(s)/(1 + GH^*(s))$$

and taking the z-transform

★
$$\frac{C(z)}{R(z)} = \frac{G(z)}{1 + GH(z)} \qquad (9\text{-}33b)$$

The overall transfer function given by Eq. (9-33b) may be applied only to the closed loop system shown in Fig. 9-14 where the error is being sampled. If the sampler were moved to a different location, a different transfer function would result. Consider the sampled data system shown in Fig. 9-15. The following equations may be written:

$$E(s) = R(s) - B(s)$$
$$C_1(s) = G_1(s)E(s)$$
$$C(s) = G_2(s)C_1^*(s)$$
$$B(s) = H(s)C(s)$$

Substituting these equations, rearranging, taking the pulsed transform,

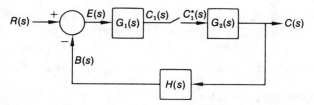

Fig. 9-15   Sampled data system with sampler between cascaded element.

and then taking the z-transform yields

$$C(z) = \frac{RG_1(z)G_2(z)}{1 + G_1G_2H(z)} \tag{9-34}$$

Since generally $R(z)G(z) \neq RG(z)$, we are unable to obtain the transfer function $C(z)/R(z)$ but can only obtain the output in terms of $RG(z)$ as shown in Eq. (9-34). This is not uncommon in sampled data control systems.

As a final example we consider the multiloop system shown in Fig. 9-16. We may write down the following equations by inspection,

$$E_2(s) = R(s) - B_2(s)$$
$$B_2(s) = H_2(s)C^*(s)$$
$$C(s) = E_2(s)[G_1(s)/(1 + G_1(s)H_1(s))]$$

We note that the last equation is the result of reducing the block diagram within the dotted lines indicated in Fig. 9-16. These equations can be

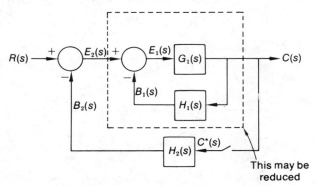

Fig. 9-16   Multi-loop sampled data system.

shown to yield

$$C^*(s) = \frac{[RG_1(s)/(1+G_1(s)H_1(s))]^*}{1+[G_1(s)H_2(s)/(1+G_1(s)H_1(s))]^*}$$

and again we obtain the output but not the "usual" transfer function.

Pulsed Signal Flow Graphs

The occurrence of a sampling switch interrupts the flow of a signal in the control system. Therefore, the conventional techniques developed may not be applied, since Mason's gain formula requires a forward path and in many cases this is not available. The only time the previous technique may be applied is if all the signals are interrupted by sampling switches. This does not often happen since most control systems contain continuous as well as sampled elements.

The previous method may be modified however as follows:

(1) We first construct the signal flow diagram from the original block diagram. All samplers are included.
(2) Equations relating the nodes (these are system variables) and branch gains are written by inspection.
(3) The equations are cast in pulsed transform notation.
(4) A signal source having the strength of the sampler output is created.
(5) A new signal flow diagram is constructed using information generated in (3) and (4).
(6) Finally, the overall gain is obtained using Mason's gain formula.

As an example, let us consider the error sampled system whose signal flow diagram is shown in Fig. 9-17. The equations are written as follows:

$$x_2 = R - HC_4$$

$$x_3 = x_2^*$$

$$C = Gx_3$$

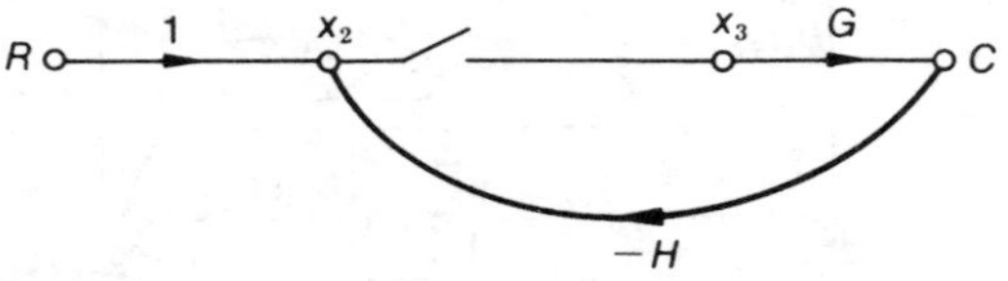

Fig. 9-17   Signal flow for error sampled system.

Substituting the previous equations and taking the pulsed transform

$$x_2^* = R^* - (HG)^* x_2^*$$
$$C^* = G^* x_2^*$$

We now redraw the signal flow diagram as shown in Fig. 9-18 where we assume that x_2^* is available. Also notice that x_3^* is not needed anymore.

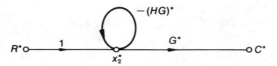

Fig. 9-18   Modified pulsed signal flow diagram.

The overall transfer function may be obtained and is

$$\frac{C^*(s)}{R^*(s)} = G^*(s)/(1 + GH^*)$$

Although this method may be used to obtain C^* it does not yield $C(s)$. If $C(s)$ is required, we employ the original diagram in conjunction with the new diagram to form a composite flow diagram as shown in Fig. 9-19. We now see that there is a forward path from R^* to C and the output C may be obtained in terms of R^* but not R.

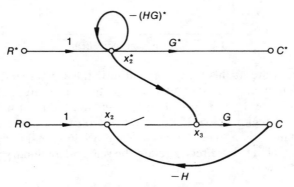

Fig. 9-19   Composite signal flow diagram.

9-6 SYSTEM RESPONSE

Consider the unity feedback error sampled system shown in Fig. 9-20 where $G_0(s)$ is a zero-order hold and $G_1(s)$ represents a continuous element. The pulsed transfer function is

$$\frac{C(z)}{R(z)} = \frac{G_0G_1(z)}{1+G_0G_1(z)}$$

For any given $R(z)$, the response may be obtained using the classical techniques developed in the previous section.

For the system shown in Fig. 9-20, let $G_0G_1(s)$ be a second-order system, then

$$\frac{C(z)}{R(z)} = \frac{Kz}{z^2+\alpha z+\beta}$$

and the response may be obtained by using partial fractions. Comparison of this characteristic equation to that of a continuous system suggests some generalization. If we write $C(z)/R(z)$ as

★
$$\frac{C(z)}{R(z)} = \frac{Kz}{z^2+2\delta_0\omega_0z+\omega_0{}^2} \qquad (9\text{-}35)$$

then, by definition, δ_0 is the discrete damping ratio and ω_0 is the discrete undamped frequency. Unlike the continuous case, $\omega_0{}^2$ can be negative in Eq. (9-35).

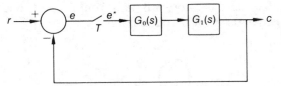

Fig. 9-20   Error sampled system.

It is appropriate at this time to recall how the s-plane and z-plane are related. As indicated in the previous section, the left half s-plane is mapped inside the region $|z| < 1$ in the z-plane, the right half s-plane is mapped in the region $|z| > 1$. Points at $-\infty$ on the s-plane are mapped into the z-plane origin, whereas the s-plane origin is mapped into the $+1$ point on the z-plane. To directly relate the real and imaginary parts on the s- and z-planes we observe that if

$$s = \sigma+j\omega; \qquad z = \alpha+j\beta$$

then

$$z = e^{sT} = e^{\sigma T}e^{j\omega T} = e^{\sigma T}[\cos \omega T +j \sin \omega T]$$

which yields

$$\alpha = e^{\sigma T} \cos \omega T$$
$$\beta = e^{\sigma T} \sin \omega T$$

Now since we have established the response of continuous systems for closed loop poles, we may take advantage of this, as well as our observa-

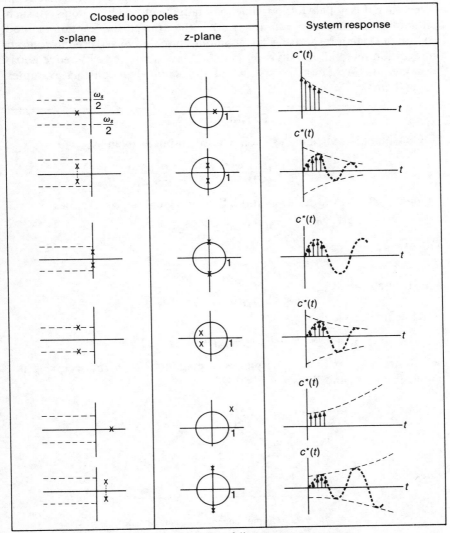

Fig. 9-21   Characteristics of discrete system response.

tions of the previous paragraph, to ascertain the discrete response as a function of closed loop poles on the z-plane. This is shown in Fig. 9-21 and you are asked to verify the various responses as an exercise.

The roots of the characteristic equation and consequently the partial fractions are easy to obtain when the order of the polynomial is small as in Eq. (9-35). However, when the order of the characteristic equation is large, then it is not always possible to obtain the closed loop poles. In such situations, we may use techniques other than the partial fraction method to obtain system response. The techniques popularly used are the contour integration method, the division method, and finally the difference equation method. We favor the last two methods and shall consider examples using them.

EXAMPLE 9-4

Consider a sampled data system whose output is given by

$$C(z) = \frac{\alpha_4 z^4 + \alpha_3 z^3 + \alpha_2 z^2 + \alpha_1 z + \alpha_0}{\beta_5 z^5 + \beta_4 z^4 + \beta_3 z^3 + \beta_2 z^2 + \beta_1 z + \beta_0}$$

Obtain $c(nT)$ by the series method. Division yields a power series

$$C(z) = b_0 z^{-1} + b_1 z^{-2} + b_2 z^{-3} + \cdots$$

where

$$b_0 = \frac{\alpha_4}{\beta_5}; \qquad b_1 = \frac{\alpha_3 \beta_5 - \beta_4 \alpha_4}{\beta_5^2}$$

Substituting $z = e^{sT}$,

$$C^*(s) = b_0 e^{-sT} + b_1 e^{-2sT} + \cdots$$

and the inverse yields

$$c(nT) = b_0 + b_1 \delta(t - T) + b_2 \delta(t - 2T) + \cdots$$

which are a series of delayed pulses of magnitude b_0, b_1, b_2 occurring at $t = 0, T, 2T, \ldots$ and shown in Fig. 9-22.

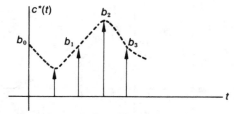

Fig. 9-22   Output sequence of Example 9-4.

EXAMPLE 9-5

Using the difference method and assuming unit impulse input at $t = 0$, obtain $c(nT)$ for the system having an overall transfer function given by

$$\frac{C(z)}{R(z)} = \frac{z^2}{z^2 - 1.5z + 0.5}$$

Dividing through by z^2 we obtain

$$C(z)[1 - 1.5z^{-1} + 0.5z^{-2}] = R(z)$$

Recognizing z^{-1} as a time shift and letting $t = nT$, we can write this as

$$c(nT) - 1.5c[(n-1)T] + 0.5c[(n-2)T] = r(nT) \qquad (9\text{-}36)$$

If we assume $r(t)$ to be a unit impulse, then we can form a table shown in Table 9-1. The output $c^*(t)$ is in the form of pulses at $t = 0, T, 2T, \ldots$ given in the last column.

Table 9-1   Difference table for Eq. (9-36).

n	$1.5c[(n-1)T]$	$-0.5c[(n-2)T]$	$r(nT)$	$c(nT)$
0	0	0	1	1
1	1.5	0	0	1.5
2	2.25	-0.5	0	1.75
3	2.63	-0.75	0	1.88
4	2.83	-0.875	0	1.945
5	2.917	-0.94	0	1.963
6	2.945	-0.972	0	1.973

In order to understand fully the behavior of sampled systems, we must not only be concerned with the transient behavior but must also know its steady state response. Analogous to continuous systems, we examine the steady state response of discrete systems by defining error constants. These error constants are defined with the assumption that the function under consideration converges to a finite value.

The error constants for a discrete system are defined as:

$$K_0 = \lim_{z \to 1} [G(z)] \qquad (9\text{-}37a)$$

$$K_1 = \frac{1}{T} \lim_{z \to 1} [(z-1)G(z)] \qquad (9\text{-}37b)$$

$$K_2 = \frac{1}{T^2} \lim_{z \to 1} [(z-1)^2 G(z)] \qquad (9\text{-}37c)$$

where K_0 is the positional error constant, K_1 is the velocity error constant, and K_2 is the acceleration error constant. For a step input to a unity feedback sampled system, the steady state error e_{ss} becomes

$$e_{ss} = \lim_{n \to \infty} e(nT) = \lim_{z \to 1} \left[\frac{1}{1+G(z)} \right]$$

$$= \frac{1}{1+K_0}$$

For a ramp input, $R(z) = Tz/(z-1)^2$, the error becomes

$$e_{ss} = \lim_{z \to 1} \left[\frac{1}{1+G(z)} \cdot \frac{T}{(z-1)} \right]$$

$$e_{ss} = T \lim_{z \to 1} \left[\frac{1}{(z-1)(1+G(z))} \right]$$

$$e_{ss} = \frac{1}{K_1}$$

Finally, for a parabolic input, $R(z) = T^2 z(z+1)/2(z-1)^3$, the error becomes

$$e_{ss} = \lim_{z \to 1} \left[\frac{1}{1+G(z)} \cdot \frac{T^2}{(z-1)^2} \right]$$

$$= \frac{1}{K_2}$$

Having defined the error constants of discrete systems, we may now classify them as to type. In discrete systems the number of open loop poles at $z = 1$ determines the system type. If $G(z)$ has 0, 1, or 2 poles at $z = 1$, then the discrete system is referred to as type 0, 1, or 2. Let us consider an example clarifying some of the points made so far.

EXAMPLE 9-6

The open loop transfer function of a system is given by

$$G(z) = \frac{0.98z + 0.66}{(z-1)(z-0.368)}$$

Compute the error constants and relate them to the steady state error.

The error constants are

$$K_0 = \lim_{z \to 1} \left[\frac{0.98z + 0.66}{(z-1)(z-0.3683)} \right] = \infty$$

$$K_1 = \frac{1}{T} \lim_{z \to 1} \left[(z-1)G(z) \right] = \frac{2.59}{T}$$

$$K_2 = \frac{1}{T^2} \lim_{z \to 1} \left[(z-1)^2 G(z) \right] = 0$$

The steady state error for a step input is

$$e_{ss} = 0$$

If the input is a ramp,

$$e_{ss} = \frac{T}{2.59}$$

and finally,

$$e_{ss} = \infty$$

The steady state error indicates that this system can follow a step input with no error and a ramp input with a finite error of $T/2.59$. However, for a parabolic input the error pulses continue to diverge from the input pulses as time becomes large.

If it was desired that the error be finite for a parabolic input in the previous example, the system type would have to be 2, i.e. another open loop pole at $z = 1$ must be introduced. A table showing the error constants and system type for discrete systems is shown in Table 9-2.

Table 9-2   Error constants and steady state error for discrete systems.

Open loop poles at $z = 1$	System type	Error constants K_0	K_1	K_2	Position	Steady state error, e_{ss} Velocity	Acceleration
0	0	F	0	0	F	∞	∞
1	1	∞	F	0	0	F	∞
2	2	∞	∞	F	0	0	F
3	3	∞	∞	∞	0	0	0

F — Nonzero and finite.

9-7 STABILITY TESTS

The previous section has shown us how we may study the transient as well as the steady state behavior of sampled data systems. No mention was made of the stability of the control systems, i.e. we had no a priori knowledge about the roots of the characteristic equation. In a practical situation, we would like to extract some information from the characteristic equation *before* going down the tortuous path of obtaining time response. In this section we shall consider two popular methods for studying the characteristic equation, viz. Jury's test and the Routh–Hurwitz test.

We begin by assuming that the pulse transfer function can be represented† by $P(z)$

$$P(z) = \frac{C(z)}{R(z)} = \frac{\sum\limits_{j=0}^{k} b_j z^j}{\sum\limits_{j=0}^{n} a_i z^i} \qquad (9\text{-}38)$$

The denominator of $P(z)$, when equated to zero, yields the characteristic roots. For stability it is desired that there be no characteristic roots outside the unit circle on the z-plane.

The stability criterion called Jury's test provides stability information for z-transforms as the Routh–Hurwitz test provides stability information for s-transforms. Let the characteristic equation of Eq. (9-38) be represented as

★
$$F(z) = \sum_{i=0}^{n} a_i z^i = 0 \qquad (9\text{-}39)$$

We assume that all a_i's are real coefficients and $F(z)$ is written so that $a_n > 0$. We now form an array as follows.

Row			Array					
1	a_0	a_1	a_2	a_3	$\cdots$		a_{n-1}	a_n
2	a_n	a_{n-1}	a_{n-2}	$\cdots$		$\cdots$	a_1	a_0
3	b_0	b_1	b_2	$\cdots$		$\cdots$	$\cdots$ b_{n-1}	
4	b_{n-1}	b_{n-2}	$\cdots$		$\cdots$	b_1	b_0	
5	c_0	c_1	c_2	$\cdots$		$\cdots$ c_{n-2}		

†The pulse transfer function can sometimes not be derived owing to the location of the sampler. In such cases the output may be written as the ratio of two polynomials in z. The denominator polynomial when equated to zero yields the characteristic zeros.

Row	Array				
6	c_{n-2}	c_{n-3}	$\cdots$	$\cdots$	c_0
$\vdots$	$\vdots$	$\vdots$			
$m-2$	x_0	x_1	x_2	x_3	
$m-1$	x_3	x_2	x_1	x_0	
m	y_0	y_1	y_2		

The first row consists of the original coefficients from a_0 to a_n while the second row consists of the same coefficients but in *reverse* order. Each row is computed using Eq. (9-40) and then reentered in *reverse* order. We notice that the number of coefficients in each row is one less than the previous row. The array is terminated when a row of three numbers is obtained. The various coefficients are evaluated as follows.

$$b_i = \begin{vmatrix} a_0 & a_{n-1} \\ a_n & a_i \end{vmatrix} \qquad c_i = \begin{vmatrix} b_0 & b_{n-1-i} \\ b_{n-1} & b_i \end{vmatrix}$$

$$d_i = \begin{vmatrix} c_0 & c_{n-2-i} \\ c_{n-2} & c_i \end{vmatrix} \qquad y_i = \begin{vmatrix} x_0 & x_{3-i} \\ x_3 & x_i \end{vmatrix} \tag{9-40}$$

Having obtained the array, we may now apply Jury's test. This test states that the roots of $F(z) = 0$ will be inside of the unit circle on the z-plane if

$$F(1) > 0$$

$$F(-1) > 0 \quad \text{for } n \text{ even}$$

$$F(-1) < 0 \quad \text{for } n \text{ odd}$$

and also if the following constraints are satisfied,

$$|a_0| < a_n$$

$$|b_0| > |b_{n-1}|$$

$$|d_0| > |d_{n-3}|$$

$$\vdots$$

$$|y_0| > |y_2|$$

If any of the previous requirements are not satisfied, then $F(z) = 0$ does have roots outside the z-plane and the system response shall be unstable. The test yields no information as to the number of roots outside the unit circle on the z-plane.

EXAMPLE 9-7

Determine the stability of a system governed by a cubic characteristic equation given by

$$F(z) = z^3 + 2z^2 + 1.9z + 0.8$$

Before the array is formed we check $F(1)$ and $F(-1)$.

$$F(1) > 0: \quad F(1) = 1 + 2 + 1.9 + 0.8 = 5.7$$

$$F(-1) < 0: \quad F(-1) = -1 + 2 - 1.9 + 0.8 = -0.1$$

Having satisfied these tests, we form the array

Row	Array			
1	0.8	1.9	2	1
2	1	2	1.9	0.8
3	−1.36	−0.48	−0.4	

We now check the constraints

$$|a_0| < a_3: \quad 0.8 < 1$$

$$|b_0| > |b_2|: \quad |-1.36| > |-0.4|$$

Since all the requirements are met, Jury's test states that the characteristic equation has no roots outside the unit circle on the z-plane.

If the characteristic equation were in the form

$$F(z) = a_3 z^3 + a_2 z^2 + a_1 z + a_0 = 0$$

then this test may be used to ascertain relationships between the coefficients such that $F(z) = 0$ has roots inside the unit circle on the z-plane.

Although Jury's test tells us whether roots exist inside or outside the unit circle on the z-plane, it gives no information as to how many roots exist outside the unit circle as mentioned previously. In this respect it is a weaker test than the Routh–Hurwitz test although it is much easier to apply.

In order to use the Routh–Hurwitz criterion we need to work on a plane similar to the s-plane. This is achieved by using the bilinear transformation into the r-plane.† This essentially maps the interior of the unit circle of the z-plane onto the left half r-plane. The Routh–Hurwitz criterion may be applied to the r-plane where stability requires that the roots of the characteristic equation be in the left half r-plane. All the notions developed about the Routh–Hurwitz criterion on the s-plane may be applied on the r-plane. Let us take an example to elucidate this further.

Consider the previous characteristic equation

$$F(z) = z^3 + 2z^2 + 1.9z + 0.8$$

Using the bilinear transformation

$$z = \frac{1+r}{1-r} \tag{9-41}$$

we obtain

$$F\left(z = \frac{1+r}{1-r}\right) = f(r) = \left(\frac{1+r}{1-r}\right)^3 + 2\left(\frac{1+r}{1-r}\right)^2 + 1.9\left(\frac{1+r}{1-r}\right) + 0.8 = 0$$

After a considerable amount of algebra we obtain the equation

$$0.1r^3 + 1.5r^2 + 0.7r + 5.7 = 0$$

which is the characteristic equation representation on the r-plane. The Routh array becomes

$$
\begin{array}{c|cc}
r^3 & 0.1 & 1.5 \\
r^2 & 0.7 & 5.7 \\
\hline
r^1 & b_0 & b_1 \\
r^0 & c_0 &
\end{array}
\qquad b_0 = 0.68, \quad b_1 = 0, \quad c_0 = 5.7
$$

which shows that there are no sign changes in the first column and therefore the system is stable as we expected. If however there had been sign reversals in the first column, then the number of reversals is equal to the number of zeros in the right half r-plane which is identical to the region exterior to the unit circle on the z-plane..

9-8 GRAPHICAL METHODS FOR DISCRETE SYSTEMS

Before we may apply the graphical techniques developed in Chapter 7 to sampled data systems, certain modifications are in order. Since the

†The relation between the frequency on the r-plane and s-plane to the sampling frequency is discussed in the next section.

pulsed transfer function is obtained in the z-transform domain where the exterior of the unit circle corresponds to the right half s-plane, the obtaining of a stable system involves the avoidance of poles outside the unit circle. However, it is not convenient to study all the graphical methods on the z-plane; therefore a bilinear transformation into the r-plane is necessary. This procedure takes the exterior of the unit circle on the z-plane and conformally maps it into the complex right half r-plane. The frequency response may now be studied as $-\infty \leqslant \omega_r \leqslant +\infty$ or $0 \leqslant \omega_r \leqslant \infty$ since the frequency plot is symmetrical about the real axis. When the s-plane was mapped on the z-plane, we saw that it is sufficient to consider the range $-\omega_s/2 \leqslant \omega \leqslant \omega_s/2$ where ω_s is the sampling frequency. This is true since other regions when divided into parallel bands having widths of ω_s conformally mapped into the same region obtained when the region $-\omega_s/2 \leqslant \omega \leqslant \omega_s/2$ was considered. Indeed ω_r on the r-plane may now be written as

$$r = \frac{z-1}{z+1}; \qquad j\omega_r = \frac{e^{j\omega T} - 1}{e^{j\omega T} + 1} = j \tan\left(\frac{\omega T}{2}\right)$$

and since $T = 2\pi/\omega_s$ we obtain $\omega_r = \tan \pi\omega/\omega_s$. This yields the following limiting values

$$\omega = 0 \qquad \omega_r = 0$$
$$\omega = \frac{\omega_s}{2} \qquad \omega_r = \infty$$
$$\omega = -\frac{\omega_s}{2} \qquad \omega_r = -\infty$$

The mapping of the unit circle on the r-plane is shown in Fig. 9-23 and

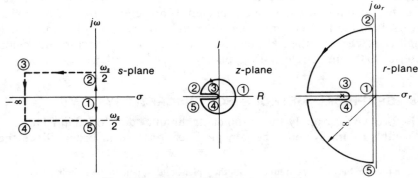

Fig. 9-23   Relationships of s-, z-, and r-planes.

so is the relationship with the s-plane. When ω varies from $\omega_s/2$ to $-\omega_s/2$ on the s-plane, the corresponding frequency on the r-plane varies from $-\infty$ to $+\infty$. It may be easily deduced that the entire left half s-plane, while mapping into the unit circle on the z-plane, also maps into the left half r-plane.

The Bode and Nyquist plots, discussed previously for continuous systems, may now be modified for sampled systems by focusing attention on the r-plane. The root locus technique can, however, be studied on the z-plane without any difficulty.

The Bode Plot

In making frequency plots we assumed that the output frequency was the same as the input frequency, although the output had a different magnitude and phase shift. For sampled systems we saw earlier that the output sequence has an envelope that is also sinusoidal having the same frequency as the input. Therefore the frequency concepts developed for continuous systems may be applied to sampled systems without modification.

The Bode plot is a plot of the log magnitude and phase shift as a function of frequency. We obtain the frequency function by substituting $r = j\omega_r$ and then using the method described earlier in Chapter 7 to construct the plot.

Consider the pulsed transfer function

$$G(z) = \frac{K(z+1)}{(z-2)(z-3)}$$

Substituting the bilinear transformation

$$G(r) = \frac{K(1-r)}{(3r-1)(2r-1)}$$

Writing the frequency function as magnitude and phase shift,

$$\mathrm{Lm}\, G(j\omega_r) = 20 \log K + 20 \log \sqrt{1+\omega_r^2}$$
$$- 20 \log \sqrt{1+9\omega_r^2} - 20 \log \sqrt{1+4\omega_r^2}$$

$$\underline{/G(j\omega_r)} = \arctan \omega_r - \arctan 3\omega_r - \arctan 2\omega_r$$

The three corner frequencies are at $1, 2,$ and 3. The Bode plot is shown in Fig. 9-24. The dotted line in the figure is the exact plot. As before the maximum error occurs at the corner frequencies.

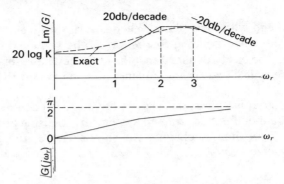

Fig. 9-24   Bode plot of $G(z) = K(z+1)/(z-2)(z-3)$ constructed on the r-plane.

The Nyquist Plot

The Nyquist plot may be directly constructed from the Bode plot or independently from the transfer function. Consider the open loop transfer function

$$G(z) = \frac{Kz}{(z-1)(z-0.5)}$$

Representing this in the r-domain,

$$G(r) = \frac{K(1-r^2)}{r(1+3r)}$$

For $\omega_r = \infty$, the above function has a magnitude of $K/3$ and a phase of π. When $K > 3$ the system will become unstable as shown in Fig. 9-25. Although a second-order system is always stable for a continuous control system having positive feedback, we note that the inclusion of sampling tends to introduce instability.

The concept of the Nyquist criterion may be readily extended to sampled data systems. The closed loop pulse transfer function is

$$\frac{C(z)}{R(z)} = \frac{G(z)}{1+GH(z)} = M(z)$$

The characteristic equation is

$$1 + GH(z) = 0$$

and the roots of the characteristic equation must be within the unit circle for stability.

Now we have seen that a bilinear transformation plots the exterior of

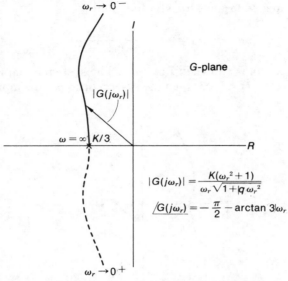

Fig. 9-25   Nyquist plot of $G(z) = Kz/(z-1)(z-0.5)$ constructed on the r-plane.

the unit circle onto the right half r-plane. Therefore, if the function $GH(z)$ is transformed using a bilinear transformation, then the Nyquist path shown in Fig. 9-26 may be employed. We now look for the encirclement of the $(-1, 0)$ point on the $GH(r)$-plane. All the techniques developed before may be applied without modification.

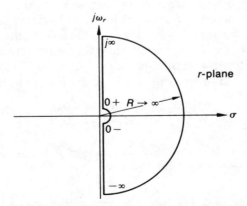

Fig. 9-26   The Nyquist path on the r-plane.

For the open loop pulse transfer function,

$$G(z) = \frac{Kz}{(z-1)(z-0.5)}$$

the Nyquist plot is shown in Fig. 9-27. The system is stable since $(-1, 0)$ is not encircled. If $K > 3$, then the system becomes unstable.

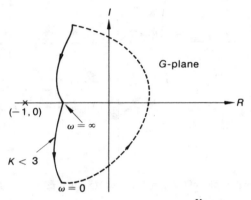

Fig. 9-27   Nyquist plot of $G(z) = \dfrac{Kz}{(z-1)(z-0.5)}$.

The Root Locus

The root locus technique may be directly adapted to the analysis of sampled data systems on the z-plane. The principle difference between the continuous and sampled case is that whereas in the former system the loci is on the s-plane and crossover of the imaginary axis is important, the loci is on the z-plane for sampled systems and the unit circle is significant for investigating stability. All the other rules for constructing the root locus on the s-plane still apply on the z-plane.

Consider a second-order system having an open loop transfer function,

$$G_0G(z) = \frac{Ke^{-T}(1-e^{-T})z}{(z-e^{-T})(z-e^{-2T})}$$

The transfer function is not only a function of K but also the sampling period T. For a sampling period $T = 1$ sec,

$$G_0G(z) = \frac{0.233Kz}{(z-0.368)(z-0.135)}$$

Applying the previously enunciated rules for root loci construction, we obtain:

(1) The root loci begin at $z = 0.368$ and $z = 0.135$.
(2) The root loci end at $z = 0$ and $z = \infty$.
(3) There are two branches of root loci.
(4) The loci are symmetrical about the real axis.
(5) Asymptotes have an angle π. [The real axis intercept is not applicable. Why?]
(6) The region between $z = 0.368$ and $z = 0.135$ on the real axis is part of the root loci and so is the region between $z = 0$ and $z = -\infty$.
(7) Not applicable. [Why?]
(8) Breakaway points occur due to real poles and zeros.

$$-\frac{1}{\alpha} + \frac{1}{(0.368 + \alpha)} + \frac{1}{(0.135 + \alpha)} = 0$$

Solving the quadratic, $\alpha = \pm 0.229$. [The same result may be obtained by setting the derivative of the function with respect to z equal to zero.]

(9) Intersection with the unit circle is obtained by first forming the characteristic equation $1 + G_0 G(r) = 0$,

$$(0.542 + 0.233K)r^2 + 1.897r + (1.562 - 0.233K) = 0$$

and from Routh–Hurwitz, $K \leqslant 6.67$. [We could have used the Jury's test and worked on the z-plane also and obtained the same result.]

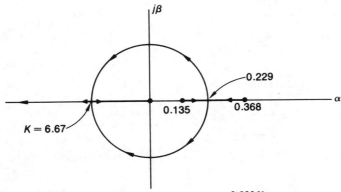

Fig. 9-28 Root locus for $G(z) = \dfrac{0.233Kz}{(z - 0.368)(z - 0.135)}$.

The root locus may now be constructed and is shown in Fig. 9-28. Since $G(z)$ is a function of the sampling time constant T, let us see the effect of varying T. The transfer function for two different values of T is

$$T = 0.1 \text{ sec:} \quad G_0 G(z) = \frac{0.08 K z}{(z - 0.905)(z - 0.819)}$$

$$T = 10 \text{ sec:} \quad G_0 G(z) = \frac{0.454 \times 10^{-4} K z}{(z - 0.208 \times 10^{-4})(z - 0.452 \times 10^{-4})}$$

The root locus plot is shown in Fig. 9-29a and Fig. 9-29b. The characteristic equations for these two cases are

$$T = 0.1 \text{ sec:} \quad (0.017 + 0.086 K) r^2 + 0.518 r + (3.465 - 0.086 K) = 0$$

$$T = 10 \text{ secs:} \quad (1 + 0.454 \times 10^{-4} K) r^2 + 2r + (1 - 0.454 \times 10^{-4} K) = 0$$

and the unit circle is crossed at $K = 40$ and 22,000.

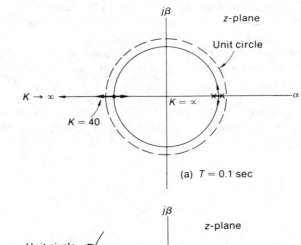

(a) $T = 0.1$ sec

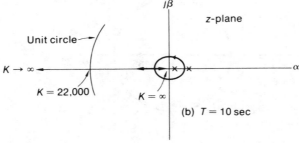

(b) $T = 10$ sec

Fig. 9-29   Root loci plots for $G_0 G(z) = \dfrac{K e^{-T}(1 - e^{-T}) z}{(z - e^{-T})(z - e^{-2T})}$.

SUMMARY

In this chapter we have been concerned with control systems receiving data at intermittent intervals. A sampler was employed to convert continuous signals to intermittent data. It was assumed that the sampler was periodic, i.e. data was received at regular intervals. Also the width of the periodic pulse was neglected. We observed that sampling introduces higher frequency components in the sampled signal and before applying the signals to a continuous element these undesirable components must be removed. This was why it was necessary to employ data reconstruction devices. The simplest one was the zero-order hold.

The existence of sampling also necessitated that we shift our analysis from the s-plane to the z-plane. Given a transfer function in the z-domain, we showed how transient response may be obtained using partial fractions, division, and the difference method. For better understanding the steady state performance, we defined error coefficients and steady state error in a manner analogous to continuous systems.

The stability of sampled systems was investigated using Jury's test and the Routh–Hurwitz criterion. The former could be applied on the z-plane, whereas the latter required a bilinear transformation to the r-plane.

Finally, we modified our graphical techniques for application to sampled systems. The Bode and Nyquist plots required a bilinear transformation, whereas the root locus was constructed on the z-plane. The last example indicated how the stability of a sampled data control system was a function of the sampling period.

PROBLEMS

9-1. Derive the z-transform of the following time functions: (a) e^{-at}; (b) $\cos \omega t$; (c) At; and (d) At^2.

9-2. Obtain $C(s)$ by generating the composite signal flow graph for the control system shown in Fig. P9-2.

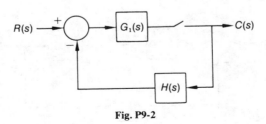

Fig. P9-2

9-3. Obtain the modified signal flow diagram and then the pulsed output for Fig. P9-3. Was it necessary to generate the modified signal flow diagram? How is this control system fundamentally different from all the others discussed so far?

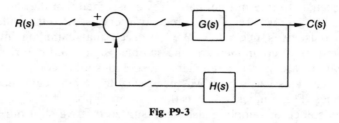

Fig. P9-3

9-4. Obtain the pulsed output for the sampled systems shown in Fig. P9-4.

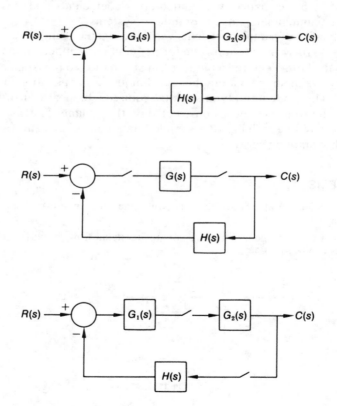

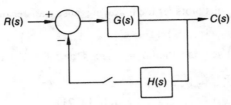

Fig. P9-4

9-5. Verify Eq. (9-24) describing the first-order hold device.

9-6. Starting with Eq. (9-35), show that the output response for different closed loop poles is given by Fig. 9-21.

9-7. A closed loop sampled data system is given in Fig. P9-7 where G_0 is a zero-order hold. It is desired to have a response such that the envelope of the output pulses is an exponentially decaying oscillation. What constraint does this impose on K? Assume that

$$G_0G_1(z) = \frac{K(z+0.71)}{(z-1)(z-0.37)}; \qquad T = 1 \text{ sec}$$

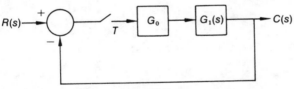

Fig. P9-7

9-8. Obtain the output for the system shown in Fig. P9-8.

$$G_0G_1(z) = \frac{Kz(z^2-0.736z+0.276)}{(z-1)(z-0.368)(z-0.146)}$$

Assume $r(t) =$ step ramp.

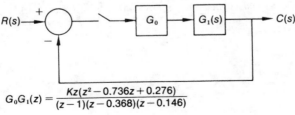

$$G_0G_1(z) = \frac{Kz(z^2-0.736z+0.276)}{(z-1)(z-0.368)(z-0.146)}$$

Fig. P9-8

9-9. Obtain the Nyquist plots for the following pulse transfer function,

$$G(z) = z^2(1 - e^{-T})/(z - 1)^2(2 - e^{-T})$$

Assume that $T = 1$ sec and then $T = 5$ sec. Does T effect the stability of the system?

9-10. Repeat the above problem for

$$G_0 G_1(z) = \frac{K(z + 0.71)}{(z - 1)(z - 0.37)}$$

9-11. A control system is given in Fig. P9-11. What is the steady state response if $T = 1$ sec. Replace the zoh by a low pass R-C filter and let the forward loop transfer function be

$$G_1 = \frac{1}{s(s + 5)}$$

Assume a unit step input.

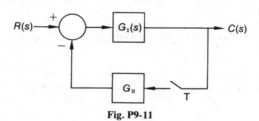

Fig. P9-11

REFERENCES

1. Jury, E. I., *Sampled Data Control Systems*, New York, McGraw-Hill, 1958.
2. Ragazzini, J. R., and G. F. Franklin, *Sampled-Data Control Systems*, New York, McGraw-Hill, 1958.
3. Lindorf, D. P., *Theory of Sample-Data Control Systems*, New York, Wiley, 1965.
4. Kuo, B. C., *Analysis and Synthesis of Sampled Data Control Systems*, Englewood Cliffs, N.J., Prentice-Hall, 1963.
5. Tsypkin, Ya. Z., *Sampling Systems Theory and Its Application*, Vol. 1, New York, Macmillan, 1964.
6. Jury, E. I., *Theory and Application of z-Transform Method*, New York, Wiley, 1964.

10

Discrete Systems – State Space Method

Discrete systems in the previous section were represented using transfer functions and analyzed via classical techniques. For reasons discussed in earlier chapters, it is often desirable to represent discrete systems in state space form. When this is done, the governing equations of the system become a vector-matrix difference equation that must be solved using state space methods. The basic concepts of state variables introduced earlier still apply and are therefore not repeated here. The special form of the state variables and equations becomes evident in the ensuing discussion.

10-2 STATE REPRESENTATION

Consider a discrete system characterized by the following transfer function,

$$\frac{C(z)}{R(z)} = \frac{z^2 + a_1 z + a_0}{z^4 + b_3 z^3 + b_2 z^2 + b_1 z + b_0} \tag{10-1}$$

Notice that the leading coefficient of both the numerator and denominator polynomial is unity. Dividing the numerator and denominator by z^4 and then multiplying by an arbitrary variable $A(z)$ we have

$$C(z) = A(z)[z^{-2} + a_1 z^{-3} + a_0 z^{-4}]$$

$$R(z) = A(z)[1 + b_3 z^{-1} + b_2 z^{-2} + b_1 z^{-3} + b_0 z^{-4}]$$

We now generate a state variable diagram for a discrete system as shown

303

in Fig. 10-1. In place of an integrator we use a unit delay element z^{-1}. If we consider the output of each unit delay as a state variable, then

$$X_1 = z^{-1}X_2$$
$$X_2 = z^{-1}X_3$$
$$X_3 = z^{-1}X_4$$
$$X_4 = z^{-1}[-b_0X_1 - b_1X_2 - b_2X_3 - b_3X_4 + R(z)]$$

and the output $C(z)$ is a linear combination of the state variables. We now recall that each z^{-1} in the z-domain corresponds to a shift back in time in the time domain, i.e. if

$$X_1 = z^{-1}X_2$$

in the z-domain, then in the time domain we have

$$x_1[(n+1)T] = x_2(nT)$$

Substituting this in the previous equation we obtain

$$x_1[(n+1)T] = x_2(nT)$$
$$x_2[(n+1)T] = x_3(nT)$$
$$x_3[(n+1)T] = x_4(nT)$$
$$x_4[(n+1)T] = -b_0x_1(nT) - b_1x_2(nT) - b_2x_3(nT)$$
$$- b_3x_4(nT) + r(nT)$$

Representing this in state space form,

$$\mathbf{x}[(n+1)T] = \mathbf{A}\mathbf{x}(nT) + \mathbf{b}r(nT)$$

and the output is

$$y[nT] = \mathbf{c}\mathbf{x}[nT]$$

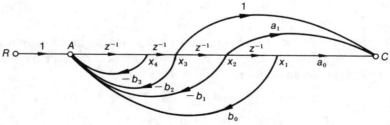

Fig. 10-1   State variable diagram for $\dfrac{C(z)}{R(z)} = \dfrac{z^2 + a_1z + a_0}{z^4 + b_3z^3 + b_2z^2 + b_1z + b_0}$.

where

$$\mathbf{x}[(n+1)T] = \begin{bmatrix} x_1[(n+1)T] \\ x_2[(n+1)T] \\ x_3[(n+1)T] \\ x_4[(n+1)T] \end{bmatrix}; \qquad \mathbf{A} = \begin{bmatrix} 0 & 1 & 0 & 0 \\ 0 & 0 & 1 & 0 \\ 0 & 0 & 0 & 1 \\ -b_0 & -b_1 & -b_2 & -b_3 \end{bmatrix};$$

$$\mathbf{b} = \begin{bmatrix} 0 \\ 0 \\ 0 \\ 1 \end{bmatrix}$$

and $\mathbf{c}$ is the output vector. If we denote $x[(n+1)T]$ as simply† $x(n+1)$, then the previous equations become

★.

$$\mathbf{x}(n+1) = \mathbf{A}\mathbf{x}(n) + \mathbf{b}r(n) \tag{10-2}$$

★

$$y(n) = \mathbf{c}\mathbf{x}(n) \tag{10-3}$$

which is the state space representation of the system defined by Eq. (10-1). The equation given by Eq. (10-2) is quite similar to that given for the continuous case. The only difference being that Eq. (10-2) is a *difference equation*.

It is perhaps instructive to begin with Eqs. (10-2) and (10-3) and directly relate them to the transfer function as we did for the continuous case. Taking the z-transform of Eqs. (10-2) and (10-3)

$$z\mathbf{X}(z) - z\mathbf{x}(0) = A\mathbf{X}(z) + \mathbf{b}R(z)$$

$$Y(z_j = \mathbf{c}\mathbf{X}(z)$$

or

$$\mathbf{X}(z) = z[z\mathbf{I} - \mathbf{A}]^{-1}\mathbf{x}(0) + [z\mathbf{I} - \mathbf{A}]^{-1}\mathbf{b}R(z)$$

$$Y(z) = \mathbf{c}\mathbf{X}(z)$$

If $\mathbf{x}(0) = 0$, then

$$Y(z) = \mathbf{c}[z\mathbf{I} - \mathbf{A}]^{-1}\mathbf{b}R(z)$$

and the transfer function of the system governed by the difference equations such as in Eqs. (10-2) and (10-3) is

★

$$\frac{Y(z)}{R(z)} = \mathbf{c}[z\mathbf{I} - \mathbf{A}]^{-1}\mathbf{b} \tag{10-4}$$

†We shall use this notation in the balance of this chapter.

If we are given a pulsed transfer function, then it is clear that the three methods, viz. parallel, iterative, and series methods, of obtaining the state space equations for continuous systems may be directly applied to obtaining the state equations for discrete systems. Instead of using s^{-1} to denote an integrator in the state variable diagram, we use z^{-1} to signify a shifter or unit delay operator.

Consider the difference equation

$$y(n+2) + \alpha y(n+1) + \beta y(n) = f(n)$$

We can again draw the state variable diagram and use the method described for linear differential equations. If we assume that

$$x_1(n) = y(n)$$
$$x_2(n) = y(n+1)$$

then the difference equation can be represented by

$$x_1(n+1) = x_2(n)$$
$$x_2(n+1) = -\beta x_1(n) - \alpha x_2(n) + f(n)$$

The state equation becomes

$$\mathbf{x}(n+1) = \mathbf{A}\mathbf{x}(n) + \mathbf{b}r(n)$$

where

$$\mathbf{x}(n+1) = \begin{bmatrix} x_1(n+1) \\ x_2(n+1) \end{bmatrix}; \quad \mathbf{A} = \begin{bmatrix} 0 & 1 \\ -\beta & -\alpha \end{bmatrix}; \quad \mathbf{b} = \begin{bmatrix} 0 \\ 1 \end{bmatrix}; \quad r(n) = f(n)$$

The state variable diagram corresponding to this equation is given by Fig. 10-2. The output is given by

$$y(n) = \mathbf{c}\mathbf{x}(n)$$

where

$$\mathbf{c} = \begin{bmatrix} 1 & 0 \end{bmatrix}$$

The generalization to higher-order difference equations is identical to the continuous case discussed previously and therefore not considered here any further.

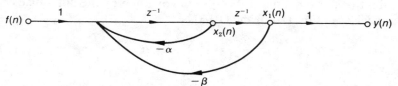

Fig. 10-2   State variable diagram for a second-order difference equation.

From the previous discussion we conclude that when a discrete system is characterized by a pulsed transfer function or a difference equation, the state and output equations are given by

$$\mathbf{x}(n+1) = \mathbf{A}\mathbf{x}(n) + \mathbf{b}r(n)$$
$$y(n) = \mathbf{c}\mathbf{x}(n)$$

where $x(n)$ is a state vector consisting of state variables $x_1(n), x_2(n) \ldots$, $x_k(n)$; $\mathbf{A}$ is a constant $k \times k$ matrix; $\mathbf{b}$ is the input vector, $\mathbf{c}$ is the output vector, $y(n)$ is the output while $r(n)$ is the system input.

10-3 SOLUTION OF THE DISCRETE STATE EQUATIONS

When the dynamical equations of a continuous system were obtained, we knew that they possessed a solution of the exponential form. For a differential equation given by

$$\ddot{y} + B\dot{y} + ky = F(t)$$

the solution is given by

$$y(t) = B_1 e^{s_1 t} + B_2 e^{s_2 t} + g(t)$$

where the first two terms represent the homogeneous solution, whereas the last term is the particular solution. When the governing dynamical equations are difference equations however, we seek a solution in a somewhat different form. Consider a linear time invariant second-order difference equation given by

$$y(n+2) + \alpha y(n+1) + \beta y(n) = F(n)$$

Here we expect to obtain a solution in the form

★ $$y(n) = D_1 A_1{}^n + D_2 A_2{}^n + g(n)$$

where the first two terms represent the homogeneous solution while the third term is the particular solution.

As an example consider the following difference equation,

$$y(n+2) + 2y(n+1) + 3y(n) = 0 \tag{10-5}$$

where

$$y(0) = 0; \qquad y(1) = N$$

We assume that $y(n) = A^n$ represents a solution of the above equation. Substituting this into the difference equation we have

$$A^{n+2} + 2A^{n+1} + 3A^n = 0$$

or

$$A^2 + 2A + 3 = 0$$

The last equation is recognized as the characteristic equation having the following roots,

$$A = -1 \pm j\sqrt{2} = \sigma \pm j\omega$$

The solution becomes

$$y(n) = D_1 A_1{}^n + D_2 A_2{}^n$$

where

$$A_1 = \sigma + j\omega; \qquad A_2 = \sigma - j\omega$$

Representing this in complex notation form we obtain

$$y(n) = D_1 (me^{j\phi})^n + D_2 (me^{-j\phi})^n$$

where

$$m = \sqrt{\sigma^2 + \omega^2}; \qquad \tan \phi = \frac{\omega}{\sigma}$$

This may be rewritten using trigonometric functions,

$$y(n) = [K_1 \cos \phi n + K_2 \sin \phi n] m^n$$

Now using the initial conditions,

$$K_1 = 0; \qquad K_2 = \frac{N}{\omega}$$

the solution becomes

★
$$y(n) = \frac{N}{\omega} m^n \sin \phi n \qquad (10\text{-}6)$$

Notice that the solution is oscillatory and is damped only if m is less than unity. If the characteristic equation is given by

$$A^2 + 3A + 2 = 0 \qquad (10\text{-}7)$$

then

$$A_1 = -2; \qquad A_2 = -1$$

and

$$y(n) = D_1 (-2)^n + D_2 (-1)^n$$

From the initial conditions

$$y(0) = 0; \qquad y(1) = N$$

we obtain

$$D_1 + D_2 = 0$$

$$2D_1 + D_2 = -N$$

solving these

$$D_1 = -N; \qquad D_2 = N$$

so that the solution becomes

★
$$y(n) = -N(-2)^n + N(-1)^n \tag{10-8}$$

When solving the state equations for discrete systems we shall seek solutions having the form of Eq. (10-6) or Eq. (10-8). The particular form shall naturally depend upon the governing characteristic equation.

z-Transform Method

We shall obtain the solution to the discrete equations several different ways. As the first method we employ the z-transform technique. Consider the state equation given by

★
$$\mathbf{x}(n+1) = \mathbf{A}\mathbf{x}(n) + \mathbf{b}r(n)$$

where you will recall $\mathbf{x}(n+1) = x[(n+1)T]$. Representing this equation in the z-domain we have

★
$$\mathbf{X}(z) = z[z\mathbf{I} - \mathbf{A}]^{-1}\mathbf{x}(0) + [z\mathbf{I} - \mathbf{A}]^{-1}\mathbf{b}R(z) \tag{10-9}$$

where we suppose the inverse of $(z\mathbf{I} - \mathbf{A})$ exists. This inverse can be represented as

$$[z\mathbf{I} - \mathbf{A}]^{-1} = \frac{\text{adj } [z\mathbf{I} - \mathbf{A}]}{\det (z\mathbf{I} - \mathbf{A})} \tag{10-10}$$

The zeros of $\det (z\mathbf{I} - \mathbf{A})$ represent the poles of $\mathbf{X}(z)$. Notice that the form of Eq. (10-9) is similar to the continuous case except that instead of having $(s\mathbf{I} - \mathbf{A})^{-1}$ we now have $z(z\mathbf{I} - \mathbf{A})^{-1}$. Once $\mathbf{X}(z)$ is obtained, the inverse z-transform yields $x(n)$.

The output for the system is given

★
$$y(n) = \mathbf{c}\mathbf{x}(n)$$

Taking the z-transform and substituting for $\mathbf{X}(z)$,

$$Y(z) = \mathbf{c}z[z\mathbf{I} - \mathbf{A}]^{-1}\mathbf{x}(0) + \mathbf{c}[z\mathbf{I} - \mathbf{A}]^{-1}\mathbf{b}R(z) \tag{10-11}$$

EXAMPLE 10-1

Consider the control system governed by the state equation $x(n+1) = Ax(n)$ and the output vector $c = [1 \ 1]$ where

$$A = \begin{bmatrix} 0 & 1 \\ -8 & 6 \end{bmatrix}; \qquad x_1(0) = 0; \qquad x_2(0) = 10$$

obtain the output $y(n)$.

Taking the z-transform and casting it in a form similar to Eq. (10-9) we have

$$X(z) = z \begin{bmatrix} z & -1 \\ 8 & z-6 \end{bmatrix}^{-1} x(0)$$

$$X(z) = \frac{z \begin{bmatrix} z-6 & 1 \\ -8 & z \end{bmatrix} x(0)}{z^2 - 6z + 8}$$

Taking the inverse z-transform

$$x(n) = \frac{1}{2} \begin{bmatrix} 4(2^n) - 2(4^n) & 4^n - 2^n \\ 8(2^n - 4^n) & 4^{n+1} - 2^{n+1} \end{bmatrix} x(0)$$

Substituting for the initial condition we obtain

$$\begin{bmatrix} x_1(n) \\ x_2(n) \end{bmatrix} = \begin{bmatrix} 5(4^n - 2^n) \\ 5(4^{n+1} - 2^{n+1}) \end{bmatrix}$$

$$y(n) = cx(n) = 25(4)^n - 15(2)^n$$

Recursive Method

Next we consider the recursive method for obtaining the solution of the discrete state equation. We begin by expanding the state equation for $t = 0, T, 2T, \ldots, nT$, (i.e. $n = 0, 1, 2, \ldots$). The state equation is

$$x(n+1) = Ax(n) + br(n)$$

which when expanded becomes

$$\begin{aligned} n = 0: \quad & x(1) = Ax(0) + br(0) \\ n = 1: \quad & x(2) = Ax(1) + br(1) \\ n = 2: \quad & x(3) = Ax(2) + br(2) \\ & \vdots \qquad \vdots \qquad \vdots \qquad \vdots \end{aligned}$$

Now substituting the third equation into the second and then into the first,

$$\mathbf{x}(3) = \mathbf{A}^2\mathbf{x}(1) + \mathbf{A}\mathbf{b}r(1) + \mathbf{b}r(2)$$
$$= \mathbf{A}^3\mathbf{x}(0) + \mathbf{A}^2\mathbf{b}r(0) + \mathbf{A}^1\mathbf{b}r(1) + \mathbf{A}^0\mathbf{b}r(2)$$

which can be compactly written as

★
$$\mathbf{x}(n) = \mathbf{A}^n\mathbf{x}(0) + \sum_{m=0}^{n-1} \mathbf{A}^{n-1-m}\mathbf{b}r(m) \tag{10-12}$$

This form is very useful for computer application. The output may be computed directly for any time and is given by

★
$$y(n) = \mathbf{c}\mathbf{A}^n\mathbf{x}(0) + \mathbf{c} \sum_{m=0}^{n-1} \mathbf{A}^{n-1-m}\mathbf{b}r(m) \tag{10-13}$$

EXAMPLE 10-2

Using the recursive method obtain $\mathbf{x}(n)$ for $n = 2$ for the state equation given in Example 10-1.

We obtain the solution to $t = 2T$, i.e. $n = 2$

$$\mathbf{x}(2) = \mathbf{A}^2\mathbf{x}(0)$$

$$= \begin{bmatrix} 0 & 1 \\ -8 & 6 \end{bmatrix} \begin{bmatrix} 0 & 1 \\ -8 & 6 \end{bmatrix} \mathbf{x}(0)$$

$$= \begin{bmatrix} -8 & 6 \\ -48 & 28 \end{bmatrix} \mathbf{x}(0)$$

We can compare this to the solution obtained by directly using the z-transform solution,

$$\mathbf{x}(2) = \frac{1}{2} \begin{bmatrix} 4(2^2) - 2(4^2) & 4^2 - 2^2 \\ 8(2^2 - 4^2) & 4^3 - 2^3 \end{bmatrix} \mathbf{x}(0)$$

which becomes

$$\mathbf{x}(n) = \frac{1}{2} \begin{bmatrix} -16 & 12 \\ -96 & 56 \end{bmatrix} \mathbf{x}(0)$$

and is seen to be identical to the solution obtained by the recursive method.

An interesting example where the recursive technique finds an application concerns the modeling of the national income. Let us define the following terms,

$$y(n) \quad \text{National Income at time } t = t_n$$

$$c(n) \quad \text{Consumer Spending at time } t = t_n$$

$$g(n) \quad \text{Governmental Spending at time } t = t_n$$

$$i(n) \quad \text{Industrial Spending at time } t = t_n$$

An elementary mathematical model may be formed if we assume that

$$y(n) = c(n) + g(n) + i(n) \qquad (10\text{-}14)$$

and

$$c(n) = \alpha y(n-1)$$
$$i(n) = \beta[c(n) - c(n-1)]$$

where α and β vary between 0 and 1.† A signal flow graph of this is shown in Fig. 10-3. Clearly if we consider $t = 1, 2, \ldots$ years, then the national income in any given year can be obtained if the income of the past two

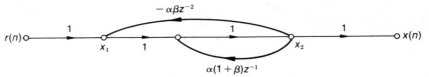

Fig. 10-3   A simple control system of the economy.

years as well as the governmental expenditure of the present year is known. We are also assuming that the habits (α) of the consumer and (β) of the private sector are known. If we substitute for $c(n)$ and $i(n)$ in Eq. (10-14), we obtain

$$y(n) - \alpha(1+\beta)y(n-1) + \alpha\beta y(n-2) = g(n),$$

which can be rewritten as

$$y(n+2) - \alpha(1+\beta)y(n+1) + \alpha\beta y(n) = g(n+2)$$

The state equation is obtained by defining

$$x_1(n) = y(n) \qquad r(n) = g(n+2)$$
$$x_2(n) = y(n+1)$$

so that

$$x_1(n+1) = x_2(n)$$
$$x_2(n+1) = \alpha(1+\beta)x_2(n) - \alpha\beta x_1(n) + r(n)$$

†In our elementary model we avoid deficit spending. (*See* Reference 6.)

This can be written more compactly as

$$x(n+1) = Ax(n) + br(n)$$

where

$$A = \begin{bmatrix} 0 & 1 \\ -\alpha\beta & \alpha(1+\beta) \end{bmatrix}; \qquad b = \begin{bmatrix} 0 \\ 1 \end{bmatrix}$$

The solution to this depends upon α and β and is left as an exercise. It suffices to note that the solution contains a damped oscillatory term and a constant term.

The Transition Matrix

Examination of Eq. (10-12) indicates that A^n defines the transition of the discrete element states at $t = 0$ to the state at $t = nT$. The matrix A^n, therefore, satisfies the definition of a *state transition matrix* or a *fundamental matrix*. Employing the previous nomenclature we define

$$\phi(n) = A^n \tag{10-15}$$

where $\phi(n)$ is the *transition* matrix of the discrete system. The properties of this state transition matrix are similar to those of the continuous system and the evaluation of $\phi(n)$ may be carried out much the same way. Here we shall consider two methods.

The first method exploits the property of the transition matrix itself, viz. that the transition matrix satisfies its own state equation,

$$\phi(n+1) = A\phi(n) \tag{10-16}$$

This may be used to evaluate the elements of $\phi(n)$. Consider an example where

$$A = \begin{bmatrix} 0 & 1 \\ -8 & 6 \end{bmatrix}$$

Substituting this in Eq. (10-16) we obtain

$$\begin{bmatrix} \phi_{11}(n+1) & \phi_{12}(n+1) \\ \phi_{21}(n+1) & \phi_{22}(n+1) \end{bmatrix} = \begin{bmatrix} 0 & 1 \\ -8 & 6 \end{bmatrix} \begin{bmatrix} \phi_{11}(n) & \phi_{12}(n) \\ \phi_{21}(n) & \phi_{22}(n) \end{bmatrix}$$

This leads to four equations,

$$\phi_{11}(n+1) = \phi_{21}(n)$$
$$\phi_{12}(n+1) = \phi_{22}(n)$$
$$\phi_{21}(n+1) = -8\phi_{11}(n) + 6\phi_{21}(n)$$
$$\phi_{22}(n+1) = -8\phi_{12}(n) + 6\phi_{22}(n)$$

Taking the z-transform, we obtain

$$z\phi_{11}(z) = \phi_{21}(z) + z\phi_{11}(0)$$
$$z\phi_{12}(z) = \phi_{22}(z) + z\phi_{12}(0)$$
$$z\phi_{21}(z) = -8\phi_{11}(z) + 6\phi_{21}(z) + z\phi_{21}(0)$$
$$z\phi_{22}(z) = -8\phi_{12}(z) + 6\phi_{22}(z) + z\phi_{22}(0)$$

Since the initial conditions are dictated by

$$\phi(0) = \begin{bmatrix} 1 & 0 \\ 0 & 1 \end{bmatrix}$$

the above equations can be reduced and solved simultaneously to yield the elements of the transition matrix. It is left as an exercise for you to show that the elements obtained by solving this equation are identical to the result shown previously.

The transition matrix can also be obtained by the use of the state variable diagram. Consider the state equation represented as

$$\mathbf{x}(n+1) = \phi(n)\mathbf{x}(0)$$

Expanding this we obtain

$$x_1(n+1) = \phi_{11}(n)x_1(0) + \cdots + \phi_{1k}(n)x_k(0)$$
$$x_2(n+1) = \phi_{21}(n)x_1(0) + \cdots + \phi_{2k}(n)x_k(0)$$
$$\vdots$$
$$x_k(n+1) = \phi_{k1}(n)x_1(0) + \cdots + \phi_{kk}(n)x_k(0)$$

We now interpret $\phi_{11}(n)$ as the response at the first unit delay for a unit input at node 1. Generalizing this, we observe that $\phi_{ij}(n)$ is the response at the ith unit delay for a unit input at the jth node. The development here is identical to the continuous case.

The Cayley–Hamilton Method

The last method for solving the dynamical equations of a discrete system to be considered here is the Cayley–Hamilton method. Let us assume that the roots of $\det(z\mathbf{I} - \mathbf{A})$ are given by $\lambda_1, \lambda_2, \ldots, \lambda_k$ distinct roots. Then we form the polynomials,

$$R(\lambda_1) = \alpha_0 + \alpha_1\lambda_1 + \alpha_2\lambda_1^2 + \cdots + \alpha_{k-1}\lambda_1^{k-1}$$
$$\vdots$$
$$R(\lambda_k) = \alpha_0 + \alpha_1\lambda_k + \alpha_2\lambda_k^2 + \cdots + \alpha_{k-1}\lambda_k^{k-1}$$

where A is a $k \times k$ matrix. The Cayley–Hamilton theorem states that

$$F(\lambda_1) = \lambda_1{}^n = R(\lambda_1)$$
$$\vdots \qquad \qquad \vdots$$
$$F(\lambda_k) = \lambda_k{}^n = R(\lambda_k) \qquad (10\text{-}17)$$

We solve these equations to obtain $\alpha_0, \alpha_1, \ldots, \alpha_{k-1}$ and form the solution as

★ $$\phi(n) = \alpha_0 I + \alpha_1 A + \alpha_2 A^2 + \cdots + \alpha_{k-1} A^{k-1} \qquad (10\text{-}18)$$

If the roots of $\det(\lambda I - A)$ are not distinct, then we must modify our procedure somewhat. Let us assume that we have three roots $\lambda_1, \lambda_2, \lambda_3$ where $\lambda_2 = \lambda_3$. Then we form the solution as

$$\phi(n) = \alpha_0 I + \alpha_1 A + \alpha_2 A^2 \qquad (10\text{-}19)$$

where $\alpha_0, \alpha_1, \alpha_2$ are obtained by solving

$$R(\lambda_1) = \lambda_1{}^n$$
$$R(\lambda_2) = \lambda_2{}^n$$
$$R'(\lambda_2) = n\lambda_2{}^{n-1}$$

and

$$R(\lambda_1) = \alpha_0 + \alpha_1\lambda_1 + \alpha_2\lambda_1{}^2$$
$$R(\lambda_2) = \alpha_0 + \alpha_1\lambda_2 + \alpha_2\lambda_2{}^2$$
$$R'(\lambda_2) = \alpha_1 + 2\alpha_2\lambda_2$$

EXAMPLE 10-3

The state equation of a control system is given by

$$x(n+1) = Ax(n)$$

where

$$A = \begin{bmatrix} 0 & 1 & 0 \\ 0 & 0 & 1 \\ 6 & -11 & 6 \end{bmatrix}$$

Obtain $x(n)$ using the Cayley–Hamilton method.

First we obtain the roots of the characteristic polynomial,

$$\det(\lambda I - A) = 0; \qquad \lambda = 1, 2, 3$$

Next we form the three equations,

$$\alpha_0 + \alpha_1 + \alpha_2 = 1$$
$$\alpha_0 + 2\alpha_1 + 4\alpha_2 = 2^n$$
$$\alpha_0 + 3\alpha_1 + 9\alpha_2 = 3^n$$

Solving these equations, we obtain

$$\alpha_0 = 3 - 3(2^n) + 3^n$$
$$\alpha_1 = -\tfrac{5}{2} + 4(2^n) - \tfrac{3}{2}(3^n)$$
$$\alpha_2 = \tfrac{1}{2} - 2^n + \tfrac{1}{2}(3^n)$$

The transition matrix becomes

$$\phi(n) = \alpha_0 \mathbf{I} + \alpha_1 \mathbf{A} + \alpha_2 \mathbf{A}^2$$

Substituting for $\mathbf{A}$ and $\alpha_1, \alpha_2, \alpha_3$ we obtain $\phi(n)$. The solution to the state equation is

$$\mathbf{x}(n) = \phi(n)\mathbf{x}(0) \tag{10-20}$$

where

$$\phi(n) = \begin{bmatrix} 3-3(2^n)+3^n & -\tfrac{5}{2}+4(2^n)-\tfrac{3}{2}(3^n) & \tfrac{1}{2}-2^n+\tfrac{1}{2}(3^n) \\ 3-6(2^n)+3(3^n) & -\tfrac{5}{2}+8(2^n)-\tfrac{9}{2}(3^n) & \tfrac{1}{2}-2(2^n)+\tfrac{3}{2}(3^n) \\ 3-12(2^n)+9(3^n) & -\tfrac{5}{2}+16(2^n)-\tfrac{27}{2}(3^n) & \tfrac{1}{2}-4(2^n)+\tfrac{9}{2}(3^n) \end{bmatrix}$$

The output $y(n)$ is given by

$$y(n) = \mathbf{c}\,\mathbf{x}(n)$$

where the output vector $\mathbf{c}$ is

$$\mathbf{c} = \begin{bmatrix} 1 & 0 \end{bmatrix}$$

and $y(n)$ is the output at $t = nT$.

A review of the methods considered so far, for solving the state equations of discrete systems, indicates that the z-transform method as well as the method employing the property of the transition matrix to satisfy its own state equation are inefficient and cumbersome. The method employing the state variable diagram although direct is applicable only to relatively simple systems amenable to hand computations. The recursive method is direct as well as useful for computer application. The Cayley–Hamilton method is also a very powerful method since it yields the transition matrix without matrix inversion.

Having developed techniques for obtaining the state equations as well as solutions for discrete systems, we shall now apply these techniques to the analysis of open loop and closed loop systems with sampling.

10-4 OPEN LOOP SYSTEM

In the investigation of open loop and closed loop systems we shall assume that we have an ideal sampler as discussed in Chapter 9. Consider the open loop system shown in Fig. 10-4 where G_0 is the transfer

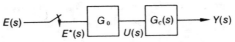

Fig. 10-4   Open loop system with sampling.

function of a zero-order hold. Now we can obtain the output as a function of the input and the transfer function by expressing everything in the z-domain and employing the method of Chapter 9. As an alternate method we develop the state space technique to obtain the output.

Let us begin by representing

$$\frac{Y(s)}{U(s)} = G_c(s)$$

in state space notation. Let $x(t)$ be the applicable state vector and the state equation be represented by

$$\dot{\mathbf{x}}(t) = \mathbf{A}\mathbf{x}(t) + \mathbf{b}u(t) \tag{10-21}$$

From our discussions of Chapter 5 we know that the solution to this equation is given by

$$\mathbf{x}(t) = \phi(t)\mathbf{x}(0) + \int_0^t \phi(t-\alpha)\mathbf{b}u(\alpha)\,d\alpha$$

where $\phi(t)$ describes the fundamental characteristics of $G_c(s)$. Now at $t = (n+1)T$ we have

$$\mathbf{x}(n+1) = \phi(n+1)\mathbf{x}(0) + \int_0^{n+1} \phi(n+1-\alpha)\mathbf{b}u(\alpha)\,d\alpha$$

where we are using our usual notation to express $x(n+1)T$. Since the transition matrix satisfies its own state equation,

$$\phi(n+1) = \phi(T)\phi(n)$$

where $\phi(T)$ is the continuous transition matrix evaluated at $t = T$. Substitution in the above equation yields,

$$\mathbf{x}(n+1) = \phi(T)\{\phi(n)\mathbf{x}(0) + \int_0^n \phi(n-\alpha)\mathbf{b}u(\alpha)d\alpha\}$$
$$+ \int_n^{n+1} \phi(n+1-\alpha)\mathbf{b}u(\alpha)d\alpha$$

The term in the first bracket is equal to $\mathbf{x}(n)$, therefore,

$$\mathbf{x}(n+1) = \phi(T)\mathbf{x}(n) + \int_n^{n+1} \phi(n+1-\alpha)\mathbf{b}u(\alpha)d\alpha$$

The input $u(t)$ is equal to $e(t)$ when the sampling switch is closed and stays at this level, due to the zero-order hold circuit, for one time interval,

$$u(t) = e(nT) = e(n); \qquad nT \leq t \leq (n+1)T$$

Substituting this fact into the previous equation we have

$$\mathbf{x}(n+1) = \phi(T)\mathbf{x}(n) + e(n) \int_n^{n+1} \phi(n+1-\alpha)\mathbf{b}d\alpha$$

If we set

$$\beta = (n+1-\alpha)T$$

then we obtain

$$\mathbf{x}(n+1) = \phi(T)\mathbf{x}(n) + e(n) \int_0^T \phi(\beta)\mathbf{b}d\beta$$

Finally, we define

$$\mathbf{h}(T) = \int_0^T \phi(\beta)\mathbf{b}d\beta$$

We obtain

★
$$\mathbf{x}(n+1) = \phi(T)\mathbf{x}(n) + \mathbf{h}(T)e(n) \qquad (10\text{-}22)$$

and the output $y(n)$ is a linear combination of the state variables as before. We note that although a zero-order hold is used, the sampling rate need not be uniform. We can simply replace T in the above equation by a variable T_V which must be taken into account when performing the integration to determine $\mathbf{h}(T)$.

EXAMPLE 10-4

If the continuous element of the open loop system of Fig. 10-4 is characterized by

$$\mathbf{A} = \begin{bmatrix} 0 & 1 \\ 0 & -10 \end{bmatrix}; \qquad \mathbf{b} = \begin{bmatrix} 0 \\ 1 \end{bmatrix}$$

then obtain the state equation corresponding to Eq. (10-22).

To obtain the solution as in Eq. (10-22) we need to obtain $\phi(T)$ and $\mathbf{h}(T)$. The transition matrix can be shown to be

$$\phi(t) = \begin{bmatrix} 1 & 0.1(1-e^{-10t}) \\ 0 & e^{-10t} \end{bmatrix}$$

Evaluating $\mathbf{h}(T)$,

$$\mathbf{h}(T) = \int_0^T \phi(\beta)\mathbf{b}\,d\beta = \int_0^T \begin{bmatrix} 0.1(1-e^{-10\beta}) \\ e^{-10\beta} \end{bmatrix} d\beta$$

$$= 0.1\begin{bmatrix} T + 0.1e^{-10T} - 0.1 \\ 1 - e^{-10T} \end{bmatrix}$$

10-5 CLOSED LOOP SYSTEM

Let us now extend the previous work to include feedback and analyze the closed loop system shown in Fig. 10-5. We observe that

$$e(n) = r(n) - c(n) \tag{10-23}$$

and also that

$$c(n) = \mathbf{c}\mathbf{x}(n)$$

where $\mathbf{c}$ is the output vector and $\mathbf{x}(n)$ is the state variable vector characterizing $G_c(s)$. Substituting into Eq. (10-23) we have

$$e(n) = r(n) - \mathbf{c}\mathbf{x}(n)$$

From our investigation of the open loop system we already know that

$$\mathbf{x}(n+1) = \phi(T)\mathbf{x}(n) + \mathbf{h}(T)e(n)$$

Substituting for $e(n)$ into the above we obtain

★ $$\mathbf{x}(n+1) = [\phi(T) - \mathbf{h}(T)\mathbf{c}]x(n) + \mathbf{h}(T)r(n) \tag{10-24}$$

and the output $c(n)$ is given by

$$c(n+1) = \mathbf{c}\mathbf{x}(n+1)$$

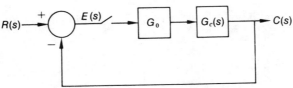

Fig. 10-5 A closed loop error sampled system.

Consider a closed loop system whose open loop characteristics are those discussed in the last example. Then

$$\mathbf{h}(T)\mathbf{c} = 0.1\begin{bmatrix} T + 0.1e^{-10T} - 0.1 \\ 1 - e^{-10T} \end{bmatrix}[1 \quad 0]$$

$$\mathbf{h}(T)\mathbf{c} = 0.1\begin{bmatrix} T + 0.1e^{-10T} - 0.1 & 0 \\ 1 - e^{-10T} & 0 \end{bmatrix}$$

We now form $\phi(T) - \mathbf{h}(T)\mathbf{c}$,

$$\phi(T) - \mathbf{h}(T)\mathbf{c} = \begin{bmatrix} 1 - 0.1(T + 0.1e^{-10T} - 0.1) & 0.1(1 - e^{-10T}) \\ e^{-10T} - 1 & e^{-10T} \end{bmatrix}$$

which when combined with the previous results yields the necessary solution. This method may be extended to include discrete as well as continuous elements in the forward path. Generally the state vector is composed of continuous as well as discrete state variables. When this is so it is referred to as a hybrid state vector.

10-6 HYBRID SYSTEMS

We first consider an open loop system consisting of a discrete as well as continuous element as shown in Fig. 10-6. For the continuous element we denote the state vector by $\mathbf{x}_c(n)$, then from Eq. (10-22) we have

$$\mathbf{x}_c(n+1) = \phi(T)\mathbf{x}_c(n) + \mathbf{h}(T)a(n) \tag{10-25}$$

where $\phi(T)$ is the continuous transition matrix evaluated at $t = T$ and $a(n)$ is the input. The discrete element may be written in state space form as

$$\mathbf{x}_D(n+1) = \mathbf{A}_D\mathbf{x}_D(n) + \mathbf{b}_D e(n) \tag{10-26}$$

where $\mathbf{x}_D(n)$ is the state vector for the discrete system. Now we recall that the output of the discrete element is a function of a linear combination of state vectors, therefore

$$a(n) = \mathbf{c}_D\mathbf{x}_D(n) + D_D e(n) \tag{10-27}$$

Note that D_D and $e(n)$ are scalars. Substituting Eq. (10-27) into Eq.

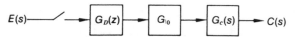

Fig. 10-6 Open loop system with discrete and continuous element.

(10-25) yields

$$\mathbf{x}_c(n+1) = \phi(T)\mathbf{x}_c(n) + \mathbf{h}(T)\mathbf{c}_D\mathbf{x}_D(n) + \mathbf{h}(T)D_De(n)$$

Let us assume that the continuous element is kth order and the discrete element is pth order, then if a new state vector is defined as

$$\mathbf{x}(n) = \begin{bmatrix} \mathbf{x}_c(n) \\ \\ \mathbf{x}_D(n) \end{bmatrix} = \begin{bmatrix} x_1(n) \\ x_2(n) \\ \vdots \\ x_k(n) \\ x_{k+1}(n) \\ \vdots \\ x_{k+p}(n) \end{bmatrix} \qquad (10\text{-}28)$$

the state equation defined for the entire system becomes

$$\mathbf{x}(n+1) = \mathbf{A}_H\mathbf{x}(n) + \mathbf{b}_H e(n) \qquad (10\text{-}29)$$

where

$$\mathbf{A}_H = \begin{bmatrix} \phi(T) & \mathbf{h}(T)\mathbf{c}_D \\ 0 & \mathbf{A}_D \end{bmatrix}; \qquad \mathbf{b}_H = \begin{bmatrix} \mathbf{h}(T)D_D \\ \mathbf{b}_D \end{bmatrix}$$

In defining a system like this there should be no ambiguity. We do not have a mixture of continuous and discrete elements. Instead we have a mixture of discrete elements and continuous elements *defined* at discrete times only.

Consider an example where

$$G_D = \frac{0.5 + z^{-1}}{1 - z^{-1}}$$

The state diagram is shown in Fig. 10-7. The state equation is

$$\mathbf{x}(n+1) = \mathbf{x}(n) + e(n)$$

The output $a(n)$ is

$$a(n) = \mathbf{x}(n) + \tfrac{1}{2}e(n)$$

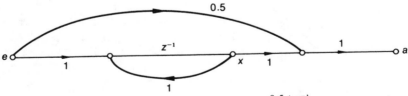

Fig. 10-7 State variable diagram for $\dfrac{0.5 + z^{-1}}{1 - z^{-1}}$.

therefore

$$A_D = b_D = c_D = 1; \qquad D_D = \tfrac{1}{2}$$

The elements of the hybrid state equations may now be computed once the continuous element is known. Let us assume the continuous element transition matrix is as that in Example 10-4,

$$\phi(T) = \begin{bmatrix} 1 & 0.1(1-e^{-10T}) \\ 0 & e^{-10T} \end{bmatrix}$$

$$h(T)c_D = 0.1 \begin{bmatrix} T+0.1e^{-10T}-0.1 \\ 1-e^{-10T} \end{bmatrix}[1]$$

$$b_H = \begin{bmatrix} 0.05(T+0.1e^{-10T}-0.1) \\ 0.05(1-e^{-10T}) \\ 1 \end{bmatrix}$$

To obtain the solution for the hybrid system we need to finally obtain A_H,

$$A_H = \begin{bmatrix} 1 & 0.1(1-e^{-10T}) & 0.1(T+0.1e^{-10T}-0.1) \\ 0 & e^{-10T} & 0.1(1-e^{-10T}) \\ 0 & 0 & 1 \end{bmatrix}$$

Let us extend this and consider the closed loop system with discrete as well as continuous elements as shown in Fig. 10-8. In addition to Eqs. (10-25), (10-26), and (10-27) we need the following equations,

$$c(n) = c_c x_c(n) \tag{10-30}$$

$$e(n) = r(n) - c(n) \tag{10-31}$$

The first is the output equation of the continuous system, whereas the second is the error equation. The output equation is often stated in a more general form but this adds considerably to the complexity. Substituting Eq. (10-30) into Eq. (10-31),

$$e(n) = r(n) - c_c x_c(n) \tag{10-32}$$

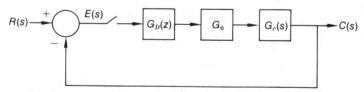

Fig. 10-8   Closed loop system with discrete and continuous elements.

Substituting this into Eq. (10-27),

$$a(n) = \mathbf{c}_D\mathbf{x}_D(n) + D_D r(n) - D_D\mathbf{c}_c\mathbf{x}_c(n)$$

We finally substitute this into Eqs. (10-25), (10-32), and (10-26),

$$\mathbf{x}_c(n+1) = [\phi(T) - \mathbf{h}(T)D_D\mathbf{c}_c]\mathbf{x}_c(n) + \mathbf{h}(T)\mathbf{c}_D\mathbf{x}_D(n)$$
$$+ \mathbf{h}(T)D_D r(n) \tag{10-33}$$

$$\mathbf{x}_D(n+1) = A_D\mathbf{x}_D - \mathbf{b}_D\mathbf{c}_c\mathbf{x}_c(n) + \mathbf{b}_D r(n) \tag{10-34}$$

Now we define a new state vector $\mathbf{x}(n)$ as in Eq. (10-28) and the two above equations are combined into a hybrid state equation of the closed system,

★
$$\mathbf{x}(n+1) = A_{HC}\mathbf{x}(n) + \mathbf{b}_{HC} r(n) \tag{10-35}$$

where

$$A_{HC} = \begin{bmatrix} \phi(T) - \mathbf{h}(T)D_D\mathbf{c}_D & \mathbf{h}(T)\mathbf{c}_D \\ -\mathbf{b}_D\mathbf{c}_c & A_D \end{bmatrix}; \qquad \mathbf{b}_{HC} = \begin{bmatrix} \mathbf{h}(T)D_D \\ \mathbf{b}_D \end{bmatrix}$$

To illustrate the use of this, let us consider a closed loop system whose discrete element is described by

$$G_D(z) = \frac{0.5 + z^{-1}}{1 - z^{-1}}$$

and the continuous characteristics of Example 10-4. The state representation of the open loop system was also derived previously. We also know the output vector,

$$\mathbf{c}_c = [1 \quad 0]$$

We compute the elements of A_{HC} and $\mathbf{b}_{HC}$

$$\mathbf{h}(T)D_D\mathbf{c}_c = 0.1\begin{bmatrix} T + 0.1e^{-10T} - 0.1 \\ 1 - e^{-10T} \end{bmatrix}\tfrac{1}{2}[1 \quad 0]$$

$$= \begin{bmatrix} 0.05(T + 0.1e^{-10T} - 0.1) & 0 \\ 0.05(1 - e^{-10T}) & 0 \end{bmatrix}$$

$$\mathbf{b}_D\mathbf{c}_c = [1 \quad 0]$$

$$A_D = 1$$

which when substituted in A_{HC} and $\mathbf{b}_{HC}$ yields

$$A_{HC} = \begin{bmatrix} 1 - 0.05(T + 0.1e^{-10T} - 0.1) & 0.1(1 - e^{-10T}) & 0.1(T + 0.1e^{-10T} - 0.1) \\ -0.05(1 - e^{-10T}) & e^{-10T} & 0.1(1 - e^{-10T}) \\ -1 & 0 & 1 \end{bmatrix}$$

$$\mathbf{b}_{HC} = \begin{bmatrix} 0.05(T + 0.1e^{-10T} - 0.1) \\ 0.05(1 - e^{-10T}) \\ 1 \end{bmatrix}$$

Notice that the input vector is unchanged. The effect of feedback is felt in the matrix $\mathbf{A}_{HC}$.

10-7 STABILITY

When the dynamical equation is in discrete form, then the characteristic equation is given by

$$\det(z\mathbf{I} - \mathbf{A}) = 0 \qquad (10\text{-}36)$$

For the system to be stable it is necessary that the roots of Eq. (10-36) be contained within the unit circle on the complex z-plane. We can insure this most conveniently via Jury's test established in Chapter 9.

Consider the coefficient matrix for a discrete system given by

$$\mathbf{A} = \begin{bmatrix} 0 & 0.2 \\ -1 & -1 \end{bmatrix}$$

we form the characteristic equation

$$F(z) = z^2 + z + 0.2 = 0$$

Applying Jury's test,

$$F(1) = 2.2 > 0$$
$$F(-1) = 0.2 > 0 \quad (\text{even } n)$$
$$|a_0| = 0.2 < 1$$

Therefore the system is stable. We now recall that Jury's test determines whether the zeros of $F(z)$ are inside the unit circle or not. It however provides no information as to the number of zeros, if any, outside the unit circle. For this purpose we apply the Routh–Hurwitz test. Since this test is applicable on a complex plane like the s-plane, we must transform from the z-plane to a different plane. This transformation is achieved via the bilinear transformation to the r-plane.

$$z = \frac{1 + r}{1 - r}$$

The details of this were developed in Chapter 9 and since it is applicable without modification, we shall not repeat it here.

We still need to consider the hybrid system defined in the previous chapter. Do we apply the test of the continuous system or the discrete system? We can answer this question by recalling that although the co-efficient matrix **A** includes continuous as well as discrete elements, these elements are *defined only* at discrete time steps. This is obviously necessary in order to make all the system elements compatible. We therefore, treat the entire matrix as a discrete matrix and the characteristic equation is of the form of Eq. (10-36).

Before leaving the topic of stability of systems represented in state variable form, we need to mention the phase space representation of these systems. The phase space will be introduced in the next chapter and is applicable primarily to second-order systems. These systems are represented by a plot of x versus $\dot{x}$ with time as parameter. Indeed, since the state variables of a second-order system are x and $\dot{x}$, the phase space is not only a natural choice for graphical representation but for observing the response and stability as well. The particular portraits generated by a system shall depend upon the roots of the characteristic equation as shown in the next chapter.

SUMMARY

The state space techniques developed for continuous control systems in Chapter 5 were extended and modified in this chapter to include discrete systems. Whereas we dealt with differential equations in the continuous system, we considered difference equations in this chapter. In order to use state variable diagrams for discrete systems we defined a unit delay or shifter. Otherwise the general techniques developed for representing continuous systems in state space form were seen to be applicable to the discrete case.

The solution to discrete state equations was obtained employing the inverse z-transform method, the state variable diagram method, a recursive method, and the Cayley–Hamilton method. The last two were generally superior.

Having investigated the state space representation and solution of discrete systems, open loop and closed loop systems in the state space domain were considered. Such an approach greatly simplifies the investigation of sampled data systems where it may be necessary to investigate multi-inputs and outputs or several variables inside the system.

The stability of the discrete system was ascertained via Jury's test or the Routh–Hurwitz criterion. For the latter, it is necessary to perform a bilinear transformation on the r-plane. Finally, it was stated that the stability as well as response could be checked on the phase plane for second-order systems to be discussed in the next chapter.

PROBLEMS

10-1. Obtain the state space representation for the following transfer functions,

(a) $G(z) = z/z - 1$
(b) $G(z) = Az/(z^2 - Bz + c)$
(c) $G(z) = Az/(z - 1)^2$
(d) $G(z) = z(z - A)/(z^2 - Bz + c)$
(e) $G(z) = Az(z + 1)/(z - 1)^2$

10-2. Show that the homogeneous solution of

$$x(n) - x(n - 1) + 0.5x(n - 2) = 1; \qquad x(0) = 2; \qquad x(1) = 3$$

is given by

$$x(n) = 2\left(\frac{1}{\sqrt{2}}\right)^n \sin \frac{\pi n}{4}$$

10-3. Using the inverse z-transform, obtain the solution to the autonomous equation,

$$\mathbf{x}[(n + 1)T] = \mathbf{A}\mathbf{x}[nT]$$

where

$$\mathbf{A} = \begin{bmatrix} 0 & 1 & 0 \\ 0 & 0 & 1 \\ 6 & -11 & 6 \end{bmatrix}$$

Show that this is identical to the result obtained by using the Cayley–Hamilton method.

10-4. The coefficient matrix for a discrete system is given by

$$\mathbf{A} = \begin{bmatrix} 5 & 1 \\ 0 & 5 \end{bmatrix}$$

Obtain $\phi(T)$ using the Cayley–Hamilton method.

10-5. Using the recursive method, solve Problem 10-4 and compute the solution for $T = 0, 1, 5, 10$.

10-6. Obtain $c(nT)$ for the open loop system shown in Fig. P10-6

$$G_1(s) = \frac{1}{s}; \qquad G_2(s) = \frac{1}{s + 1}$$

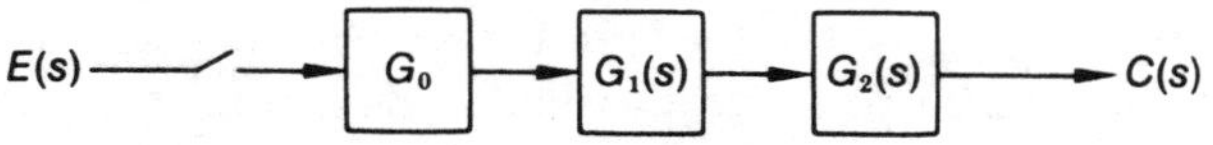

$E(s) \longrightarrow \boxed{G_0} \longrightarrow \boxed{G_1(s)} \longrightarrow \boxed{G_2(s)} \longrightarrow C(s)$

Fig. P10-6

10-7. Obtain $c(nT)$ for the open loop system shown in Fig. P10-7, where $G_1(s)$ and $G_2(s)$ are the same as in Problem 10-6.

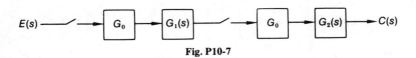

Fig. P10-7

10-8. Obtain $c(nT)$ for the closed loop systems shown in Fig. P10-8a and P10-8b. Assume $r(nT)$ to be a unit step input.

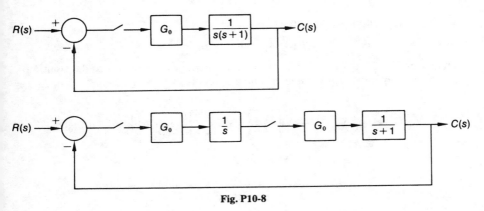

Fig. P10-8

10-9. Obtain the dynamical equations of the system shown in Fig. P10-9. Assume $r(nT)$ to be a unit step.

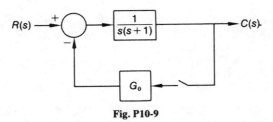

Fig. P10-9

10-10. Obtain the state space form representation of the open loop system shown in Fig. P10-10 where

$$G_D(z) = \frac{1+z}{1-z}$$

$$G(s) = \frac{1}{s^2+3s+2}$$

Express $c(nT)$ as a function of state variables.

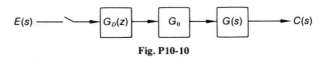

Fig. P10-10

10-11. The output $c(nT)$ for the closed loop system shown in Fig. P10-11 is

$$c(nT) = \mathbf{cx}(nT)$$

where $\mathbf{c}$ is the output vector and

$$\mathbf{x}(nT) = \mathbf{A}_{HC}\mathbf{x}(nT) + \mathbf{b}_{HC}r(nT)$$

Obtain $c(nT)$ for the closed loop system and compare the results to the solution given by Problem 10-10. What is the effect of feedback?

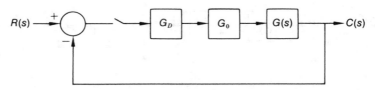

Fig. P10-11

REFERENCES

1. Freeman, H., *Discrete-Time Systems, An Introduction to the Theory*, New York, Wiley, 1965.
2. Tou, J. T., *Digital and Sampled-Data Systems*, New York, McGraw-Hill, 1959.
3. Saucedo, R., and E. E. Schiring, *Introduction to Continuous and Digital Control Systems*, New York, Macmillan, 1968.
4. Cuenod, M., and A. Durling, *A Discrete Time Approach for System Analysis*, New York, Academic Press, 1969.
5. Peschon, J., *Disciplines and Techniques of Systems Control*, New York, Blaisdell, 1965.
6. Goldberg, S., *Introduction to Difference Equations*, New York, Science Editions, 1965.
7. Ogata, K., *State Space Analysis of Control Systems*, Englewood Cliffs, N.J., Prentice-Hall, 1967.
8. Tou, J. T., *Modern Control Theory*, New York, McGraw-Hill, 1964.
9. Athans, M., and P. L. Falb, *Optimal Control*, New York, McGraw-Hill, 1966.
10. Elgerd, O. I., *Control Systems Theory*, New York, McGraw-Hill, 1967.

11

System Nonlinearities

11-1 INTRODUCTION

The analysis of linear control systems has been our primary goal so far. We assumed that the springs, motors, dampers, etc., all possessed linear characteristics in the range of operation of the control system as shown in Fig. 11-1. These systems were represented by linear differential equations with constant coefficients. The transient response, steady state response and stability was readily obtained by classical as well as state space techniques.

In practice all control systems have some degree of nonlinearity. This may be caused by hysteresis, backlash, saturation, etc. Sometimes nonlinearities such as relays and deadband may be intentionally introduced for obtaining some desired feature. In cases where these nonlinearities

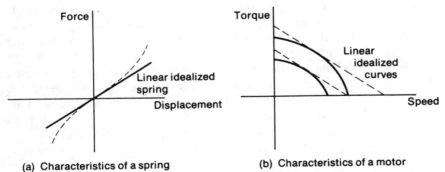

(a) Characteristics of a spring   (b) Characteristics of a motor

Fig. 11-1   Examples of nonlinearities.

affect the system performance in a significant way, they must be included in system analysis.

When nonlinearities have to be included in the system, then the principle of superposition is invalid and the methods developed so far may not be used. We must therefore develop different ways of investigating such systems. It must be stressed, however, that no general ways for analyzing nonlinear systems have been developed. Methods exist only for specific types of nonlinearities.

When the nonlinearities are large, generally numerical techniques are employed or the analog computer with nonlinear function generation is used. When the nonlinearities are small, methods are employed to linearize the equations as a first step. These linearized equations are then solved to obtain the approximate behavior. The exact behavior of the system is considered as a deviation from this result.

The type of nonlinearities we shall consider in this chapter are small nonlinearities. They will be analyzed by one of the following methods:

(1) The describing function technique;
(2) The phase-plane technique.

The first method is attractive since the classical techniques developed for linear control systems are used after the quasi-linear replacement of a nonlinear element. The second method is mostly useful for second-order systems and involves the investigation of the output variable as a function of its derivative, i.e. the familiar state space variables.

11-2   THE DESCRIBING FUNCTION TECHNIQUE

If a linear system is excited with a sinusoidal function, the output is also a sinusoid with the same frequency but with a different amplitude and phase angle. However if a nonlinear element is excited with a sinusoidal function, then the output is nonsinusoidal, although periodic with the same period as the input. Let us assume that we represent the output in Fourier components. In the describing function technique it is assumed that the fundamental component of the output of the nonlinear element is the most significant and the higher harmonics may be neglected. This means that the behavior of the control system resembles that of a low pass filter. Indeed, many control systems tend to operate in this manner. The transfer function of the nonlinear element as shown in Fig. 11-2 is defined as

★ $$G_N = \frac{\text{Amplitude of the fundamental component of the output}}{\text{Amplitude of input sinusoid}}$$

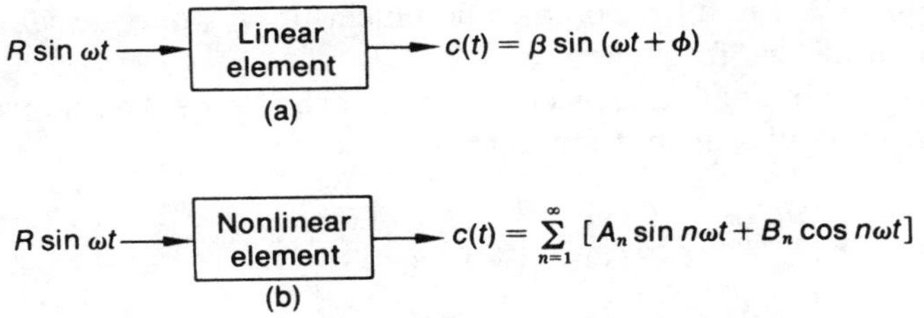

R sin ωt → | Linear element | → $c(t) = \beta \sin(\omega t + \phi)$

(a)

R sin ωt → | Nonlinear element | → $c(t) = \sum_{n=1}^{\infty} [A_n \sin n\omega t + B_n \cos n\omega t]$

(b)

Fig. 11-2   Linear and nonlinear response to a sinusoidal input.

Since the fundamental component is

$$A_1 \sin \omega t + B_1 \cos \omega t = \sqrt{A_1^2 + B_1^2} \sin(\omega t + \phi)$$

the transfer function G_N becomes

★
$$G_N = \frac{\sqrt{A_1^2 + B_1^2}}{R} e^{j\phi} \tag{11-1}$$

where

$$A_n = \frac{1}{\pi} \int_{-\pi}^{\pi} c(t) \sin n\omega t \, d(\omega t)$$

$$B_n = \frac{1}{\pi} \int_{-\pi}^{\pi} c(t) \cos n\omega t \, d(\omega t); \qquad \phi = \arctan \frac{A_1}{B_1}$$

and R is the amplitude of the sinusoidal input. The transfer function G_N is also referred to as the describing function and it may be real or complex. If the nonlinear element is single valued, G_N is generally a function of the

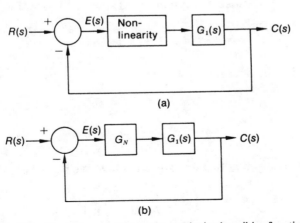

(a)

(b)

Fig. 11-3   Replacing a nonlinear element by its describing function.

input amplitude. For more complex nonlinearities G_N may be a function of input amplitude and frequency.

Once G_N is obtained, it replaces the nonlinear element as shown in Fig. 11-3b. The overall transfer function becomes

★
$$\frac{C(s)}{R(s)} = \frac{G_N G_1(s)}{1 + G_N(s) G_1(s)} \qquad (11\text{-}2)$$

We may now obtain system response by employing the classical methods developed for linear systems. However, before we consider closed loop systems let us derive G_N for some nonlinearities.

EXAMPLE 11-1

Obtain the describing function for the saturation (sometimes called limiting) shown in Fig. 11-4.

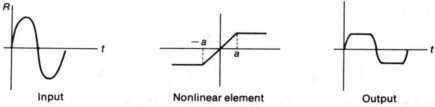

Fig. 11-4   Characteristics of saturation or limiting.

Since the output is nonsymmetrical about the origin, the cosine terms do not appear. Also since it is symmetrical about $\pi/2$, we may write

$$A_1 = \frac{4}{\pi} \int_0^{\pi/2} c(t) \sin \omega t \, d(\omega t)$$

From Fig. 11-4 the output is

$$c(t) = R \sin \omega t; \qquad 0 < \omega t < \omega t_1$$

$$= a; \qquad \omega t_1 < \omega t < \frac{\pi}{2}$$

Substituting in A_1 and noting that $\sin \omega t_1 = a/R$, we have

$$A_1 = \frac{2R}{\pi} \left(\sin^{-1} \frac{a}{R} + \frac{a}{R} \sqrt{1 - \left(\frac{a}{R}\right)^2} \right)$$

and the describing function becomes

$$G_N = \frac{A_1}{R} = \frac{2}{\pi}\left(\sin^{-1}\frac{a}{R} + \frac{a}{R}\sqrt{1-\left(\frac{a}{R}\right)^2}\right)$$

which is a function of the input amplitude and the nonlinear element characteristics. The phase contribution is zero. Since only the fundamental component is used to define the transfer function, it has been assumed that the higher harmonic terms are small. That this indeed is the case is shown in Fig. 11-5. Here the relative magnitude of the fundamental is compared to the third harmonic which is seen to be considerably smaller.

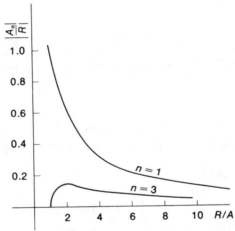

Fig. 11-5 Comparison of the third harmonic with the fundamental for a limiter.

EXAMPLE 11-2

The appearance of a relay or contactor is quite common in control systems. Obtain the describing function for (a) the ideal relay shown in Fig. 11-6, and (b) relay with deadband shown in Fig. 11-7.

(a) Since the output is odd, we compute A_1

$$A_1 = \frac{4}{\pi}\int_0^{\pi/2} c(t)\,\sin \omega t\, d(\omega t)$$

where

$$c(t) = a; \qquad 0 < \omega t < \frac{\pi}{2}$$

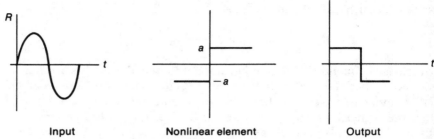

Input   Nonlinear element   Output

Fig. 11-6   Characteristics of an ideal relay.

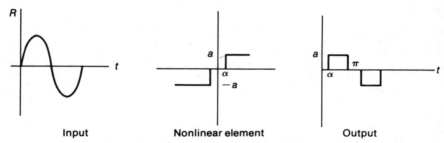

Input   Nonlinear element   Output

Fig. 11-7   Characteristics of a relay with deadband.

Substituting in A_1 we have

$$A_1 = \frac{4}{\pi} \int_0^{\pi/2} a \sin \omega t \; d(\omega t)$$

$$A_1 = \frac{4a}{\pi}$$

and the transfer function becomes

$$G_N = \frac{A_1}{R} = \frac{4a}{\pi R}$$

Again this transfer function is a function of the input amplitude. There is however no phase.

(b) Now consider the relay with deadband shown in Fig. 11-7. The output is

$$c(t) = 0; \qquad 0 < \omega t < \alpha$$

$$= a; \qquad \alpha < \omega t < \frac{\pi}{2}$$

The fundamental amplitude becomes

$$A_1 = \frac{4a}{\pi} \cos \alpha$$

From Fig. 11-7 we have

$$\sin \alpha = \frac{a}{R}; \qquad \cos \alpha = \sqrt{1 - \left(\frac{a}{R}\right)^2}$$

Substituting this, the transfer function becomes

$$G_N = \frac{A_1}{R} = \frac{4a}{\pi R} \sqrt{1 - \left(\frac{a}{R}\right)^2}$$

EXAMPLE 11-3

Obtain the describing function for the quadratic function (this could be the behavior of a spring) shown in Fig. 11-8.

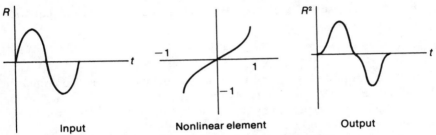

Input   Nonlinear element   Output

Fig. 11-8   Characteristics of a quadratic function.

The output $c(t)$ is

$$c(t) = [R \sin \omega t]^2; \qquad 0 < \omega < \frac{\pi}{2}$$

The fundamental coefficient becomes

$$A_1 = \frac{4R^2}{\pi} \int_0^{\pi/2} \sin^3 \omega t \, d(\omega t)$$

$$A_1 = \frac{8}{3} \frac{R^2}{\pi}$$

The describing function becomes

$$G_N = \frac{A_1}{R} = \frac{8}{3} \frac{R}{\pi}$$

The describing function of several common nonlinear elements is shown in Table 11-1.

Since the transfer function of the nonlinear element is input amplitude dependent, the gain of G_N will constantly change with changing magnitude of the input signal. This will in turn produce a change in the gain of the closed loop system. For the closed loop system shown in Fig. 11-3b, the overall transfer is

$$\frac{C(s)}{R(s)} = \frac{G_N(E)G_1(s)}{1 + G_N(E)G_1(s)} \tag{11-3}$$

The transfer function of the nonlinear element is a function of E, since the amplitude of the input to the nonlinear element is E. The characteristic equation for this system is

★
$$1 + G_N(E)G_1(s) = 0 \tag{11-4}$$

and the roots of this equation determine the system stability. We shall investigate this stability using the Nyquist and Bode plots.

For the purposes of the Nyquist analysis, the characteristic equation may be rewritten as

★
$$G_1(s) = -\frac{1}{G_N(E)} \tag{11-5}$$

The critical point $(-1, 0)$ used for linear system analysis has been replaced by $-1/G_N(E)$ which is a locus obtained as E varies. The stability on the Nyquist plot is investigated by observing the position of $G_2(s)$ relative to the locus of $-1/G_N(E)$.

For the Bode plot we write the characteristic equation

$$G_1(s)G_N(E) = -1 \tag{11-6}$$

and observe that $G_N(E)$ contributes magnitude but no phase. Therefore as E varies, the 0 db line on the Bode plot moves up or down. The amount this line moves is equal to $G_N(E)$ measured in decibels.

EXAMPLE 11-4

Consider the third-order control system shown in Fig. 11-9 where the nonlinear element is a simple relay. Study system stability using the Nyquist and Bode plots.

Note that the amplitude of the input to the nonlinear element is E, therefore

$$G_N = \frac{4a}{\pi E}$$

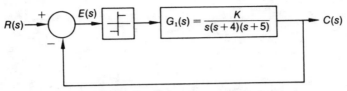

Fig. 11-9   Closed loop system with an ideal relay.

The Nyquist plot of $G_1(s)$ for three values of gain is shown in Fig. 11-10. Superimposed on this plot also is the locus of $-1/G_N(E)$ where

$$-\frac{1}{G_N(E)} = -\frac{\pi E}{4a}$$

As the error E gets large, $-1/G_N(E)$ moves away from the origin and as the error E gets small, $-1/G_N(E)$ approaches the origin.

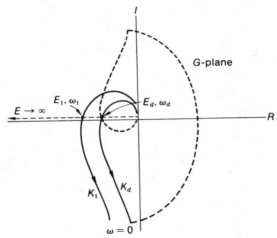

Fig. 11-10   Nyquist plot of $G_1(s) = K/s(s+4)(s+5)$ and the locus of $-E/4a$ for $0 \leqslant E \leqslant \infty$.

Let us assume that the error of the system at some point is E_1 and that the gain is K_1. The frequency corresponding to the point where the locus and Nyquist plot cross is ω_1 as indicated on Fig. 11-10. This point is where the system oscillates. Now let us suppose that the error signal decreases, possibly due to a sudden change in input, to E_d, then the system gets unstable since $-E_d/4a$ is now enclosed. Since the system gets unstable the error begins to increase and the locus of $-1/G_N(E)$ begins to

Table 11-1 Characteristics and describing functions of some nonlinear elements.

Type	Input	Nonlinear Element	Output	Describing Function
Saturation with dead zone				$R < \alpha$, $G_N = 0$ $R > \dfrac{\beta}{k}$, $G_N = \dfrac{2k}{\pi}\left[\beta_2 - \beta_1 - \dfrac{\sin 2\beta_2}{2} + \dfrac{\sin 2\beta_1}{2}\right]$ $A > R > \alpha$, $G_N = \dfrac{2k}{\pi}\left[\dfrac{\pi}{2} - \beta_1 - \dfrac{\sin 2\beta_1}{2}\right]$ $\beta_1 = \sin^{-1}\dfrac{\alpha}{R}$, $\beta_2 = \sin^{-1}\dfrac{A}{R}$
Dead zone				$G_N = 0$, $R < \alpha$ $G_N = \dfrac{2k}{\pi}\left[\dfrac{\pi}{2} - \beta - \dfrac{\sin 2\beta}{2}\right]$ $R > \alpha$
Dead zone and hysteresis in a relay				$G_N = Me^{j\phi}$ $M = \dfrac{4A}{\pi R}\sin\left(\dfrac{\beta_2 - \beta_1}{2}\right)$ $\phi = \dfrac{\pi}{2} + \dfrac{\beta_1 + \beta_2}{2}$ $\beta_1 = \sin^{-1}\dfrac{b}{R}$ $\beta_2 = \sin^{-1}\dfrac{a}{R}$

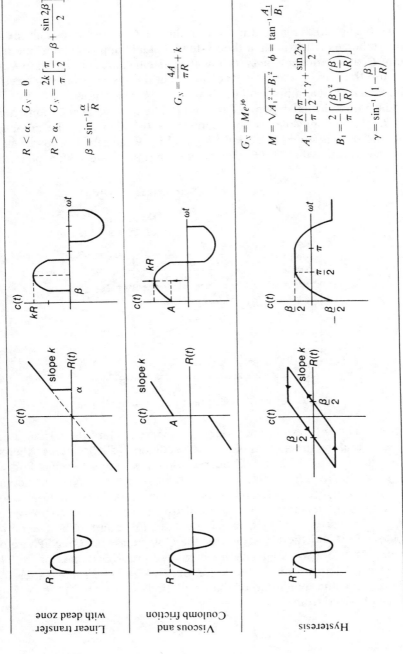

Linear transfer with dead zone

$R < \alpha, \quad G_N = 0$

$R > \alpha, \quad G_N = \dfrac{2k}{\pi}\left[\dfrac{\pi}{2} - \beta + \dfrac{\sin 2\beta}{2}\right]$

$\beta = \sin^{-1}\dfrac{\alpha}{R}$

Viscous and Coulomb friction

$G_N = \dfrac{4A}{\pi R} + k$

Hysteresis

$G_N = Me^{j\phi}$

$M = \sqrt{A_1^2 + B_1^2} \qquad \phi = \tan^{-1}\dfrac{A_1}{B_1}$

$A_1 = \dfrac{R}{\pi}\left[\dfrac{\pi}{2} + \gamma + \dfrac{\sin 2\gamma}{2}\right]$

$B_1 = \dfrac{2}{\pi}\left[\left(\dfrac{\beta}{R}\right)^2 - \left(\dfrac{\beta}{R}\right)\right]$

$\gamma = \sin^{-1}\left(1 - \dfrac{\beta}{R}\right)$

move to the left. This continues until the $-1/G_N(E)$ moves and the system stabilizes. Clearly then the system is stable and oscillates about the point E_1 at a frequency of ω_1. If now the system gain is increased to K_2, we can use the previous argument to show that the system shall still be stable although it shall exhibit oscillations with a larger amplitude.

The Bode plot is shown in Fig. 11-11. The plot of $G(s)$ is constructed for $K = 200$. The line A_2 corresponds to $4a/\pi E = 1$. If the error E is decreased, then $4a/\pi E > 1$ and $|G_N|$ will have the effect of lowering the 0 db line. Notice that $G_N(E)$ has no contribution to the system phase. Let

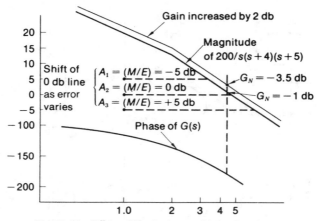

Fig. 11-11   Effect of ideal relay on third-order system.

us begin with the system operating at $G_N = 5$ db. Here the system is unstable, therefore the amplitude of the oscillations shall increase thereby increasing E. This in turn will decrease $|G_N|$ whereby the 0 db line will move up on the phase plot. This continues until the system becomes stable. As a matter of fact, the system exhibits stable oscillations about the point of intersection of $G_N = -1$ db and the phase plot for $K = 200$. Let us now increase the system gain by 2 db. The point of intersection of $|G_N| = -1$ db and the $G(s)$ plot for the new gain is unstable. Therefore the amplitude of oscillations shall increase so that E becomes larger. This decrease $|G_N|$ to a new stable value of -3.5 db. The system therefore stabilizes but the amplitude of the oscillations increase. The magnitude may be obtained from

$$\frac{4a}{\pi E} = -3.5 \text{ db} = 0.67$$

or

$$E = 1.91a$$

The exact value of E depends upon a which is dependent upon the characteristics of the nonlinear element.

It was mentioned earlier that the describing function is an attractive method since the techniques developed for linear systems may be used with slight modification as we have seen. Also this method allows us to analyze higher-order control systems. The chief drawback however is that it is limited to sinusoidal inputs.

11-3   THE PHASE-PLANE METHOD

The phase-plane method is useful for studying the transient behavior as well as the stability of second-order systems by applying the state space approach. This method essentially involves the graphical plotting of a system variable as a function of its time derivative with time as parameter, i.e. the familiar state variables. The resulting curve is called a *trajectory*. A family of trajectories depicting the behavior of the system, for different initial conditions, is called a *phase portrait*.

Consider the motion of a mass and spring,

$$m\ddot{x} + kx = 0$$

which may be rewritten as

$$m\ddot{x}\dot{x} + kx\dot{x} = 0$$

or

$$\int_0^t m\dot{x}d\dot{x} + k \int_0^t xdx = 0$$

$$\frac{m\dot{x}^2}{2} + \frac{kx^2}{2} = C \qquad (11\text{-}7)$$

If we define $\dot{x} = y$, $a^2 = 2/m$, $b^2 = 2/k$, then

$$\frac{y^2}{a^2} + \frac{x^2}{b^2} = C$$

where x, y are the state variables of the system. This equation simply states that the total energy, kinetic plus potential, of a system is conserved for an undamped system. For $k > 0$, Eq. (11-7) may be graphically interpreted as a family of ellipses as shown in Fig. 11-12a. If $k < 0$, then Eq.

(11-7) yields a family of hyperbolas as shown in Fig. 11-12b. We notice that the point $(0,0)$ is either approached or circumscribed periodically. This point is called a *singular* or *critical* point. If the motion is stable and purely periodic, the singular point is called a *vortex* or *center*. The singular point of Fig. 11-12a is a vortex. The critical point shown in the unstable motion of Fig. 11-12b is called a *saddle* point.

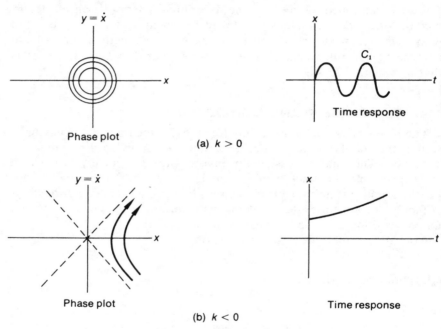

Fig. 11-12   Phase plot for $m\ddot{x} + kx = 0$.

Having introduced the concept of a phase plot we shall relate the phase-plane method to control system analysis. Consider the overall transfer function of a second-order control system,

$$\frac{C(s)}{R(s)} = \frac{K}{As^2 + K}$$

This corresponds to the differential equation

$$A\frac{d^2c(t)}{dt^2} + Kc(t) = Kr(t)$$

If $dx/dt = y, c = x$, then

$$\frac{d^2c(t)}{dt^2} = \dot{y} = \frac{dy}{dt} = y\frac{dy}{dx}$$

and the equation becomes

$$Kr = Ay\frac{dy}{dx} + Kx$$

or

$$\frac{dy}{dx} = \frac{K(r-x)}{Ay} \qquad (11\text{-}8)$$

If we plot y versus x to obtain the phase plane of a control system, then Eq. (11-8) is the slope of the trajectory on the phase plane. For any *constant* slope m,

$$m = K(r-x)/Ay$$

or

$$y = (Kr/Am) - (K/Am)x \qquad (11\text{-}9)$$

This then gives the equation of lines which cross all trajectories with the same slope. Such lines are called *isoclines*. Often phase-plane trajectories are obtained from isoclines. If r is a unit step, then Eq. (11-9) gives straight lines with slope $-K/Am$. All trajectories intersecting this line must have the same slope. The trajectories and isoclines for this example are shown in Fig. 11-13. We notice that the point $y = 0, c = 1$ is a singular point. The type of singular point is related to the roots of the characteristic equation. In this case the roots of the characteristic equation are pure imaginaries and the singular point is a vortex or center. Notice that this system does not have any damping.

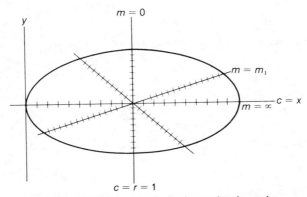

Fig. 11-13 Isoclines and trajectories on the phase plane.

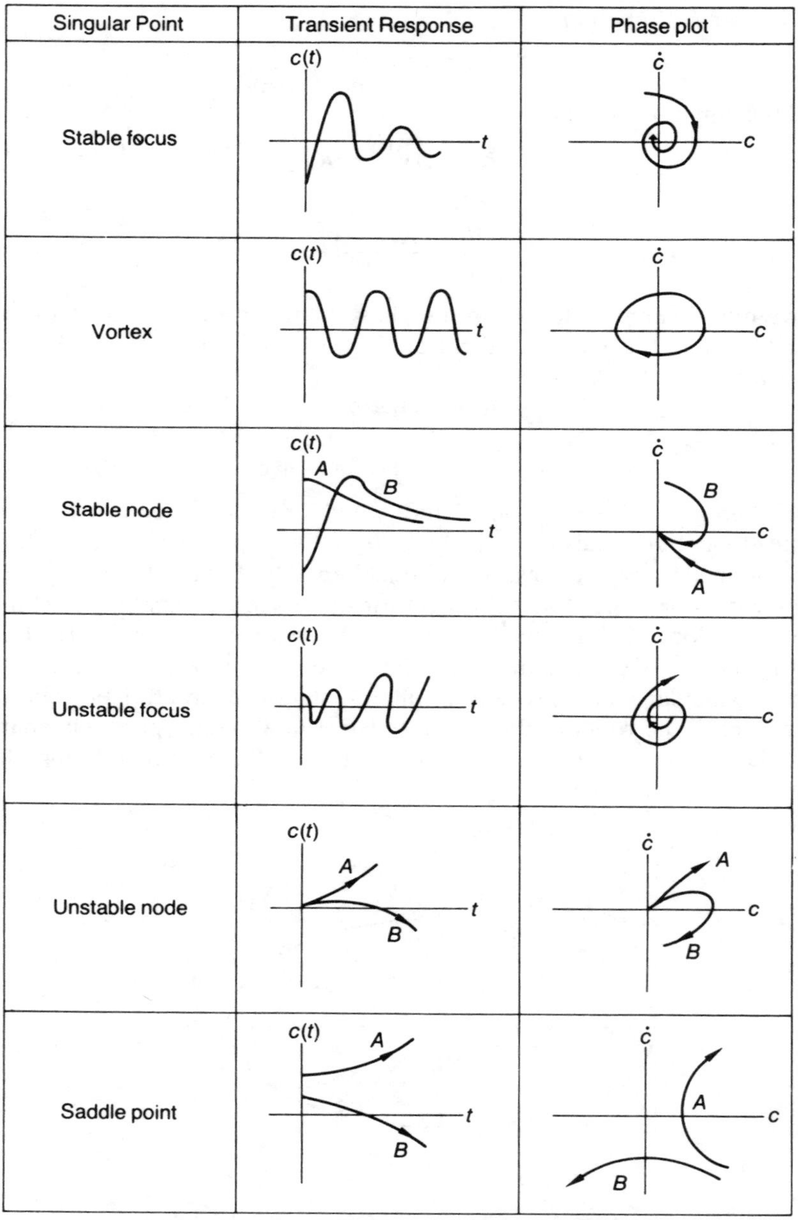
Singular Point
Transient Response
Phase plot
Stable focus
Vortex
Stable node
Unstable focus
Unstable node
Saddle point
c(t)
t
ċ
c
A
B

Fig. 11-14 Phase trajectories for second-order linear system.

The general characteristic equation of a second-order control system may be written as

$$s^2 + 2\delta\omega_n s + \omega_n{}^2 = 0 \qquad (11\text{-}10)$$

with the following singular points and roots:

Singular Points	Roots
Stable focus	$\omega_n{}^2 > 0, \quad 0 < \delta < 1$
Vortex, center	$\omega_n{}^2 > 0, \quad \delta = 0$
Stable node	$\omega_n{}^2 > 0, \quad \delta \geq 1$
Unstable focus	$\omega_n{}^2 > 0, -1 < \delta < 0$
Unstable node	$\omega_n{}^2 > 0, \quad \delta \leq -1$
Saddle point	$\omega_n{}^2 < 0, \quad \delta = 0$

The phase-plane diagrams for linear systems are shown in Fig. 11-14. The particular phase-plane plots of a nonlinear control system may now be compared to the models of linear systems shown in Fig. 11-14. The departure from these linear plots is a measure of the system nonlinearity. Before we consider examples, we would like to say that the analog computer is very useful for obtaining the phase portraits of a control system. Generally, the linear part of the system is very easily programmed. The nonlinear element may require a special function generator which may be directly tied in with the analog computer. The system output and its derivative can then be obtained for various initial conditions and plotted on an X-Y plotter.

EXAMPLE 11-5

A control system with a relay is shown in Fig. 11-15. We wish to study this system via the phase-plane method.

The transfer function $G_1(s)$ is given by

$$G_1(s) = \frac{C(s)}{E'(s)} = \frac{1}{s(Is + B)}$$

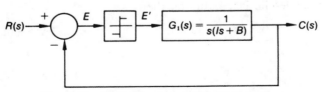

Fig. 11-15   A second-order system with ideal relay.

and the differential equation corresponding to this is

$$I\frac{d^2c(t)}{dt^2} + B\frac{dc(t)}{dt} = e'(t) \tag{11-11a}$$

where

$$\begin{aligned}e' &= \quad A; \quad\quad e > 0 \\ &= -A; \quad\quad e < 0\end{aligned}$$

when $e' = A$, the differential equation given by Eq. (11-11a) may be directly solved. For zero initial conditions we obtain

$$c(t) = \frac{A}{B}(t - \tau + \tau e^{-t/\tau}) \tag{11-11b}$$

where

$$\tau = \frac{I}{B}$$

The velocity becomes

$$v(t) = c(t) = \frac{A}{B}(1 - e^{-t/\tau})$$

Time may be eliminated by solving for t,

$$t = -\tau \ln\left(1 - \frac{vB}{A}\right)$$

and then substituting back in Eq. (11-11b), to obtain

$$c = -\frac{A}{B}\tau\left[\ln\left(1 - \frac{vB}{A}\right)\right] - \tau v \tag{11-12}$$

If $x = CB/A\tau, y = vB/A$, we have

$$x = -y - \ln(1 - y) \tag{11-13}$$

which is the equation for a phase trajectory as long as $e' = +A$. When $e < 0$, then $e' = -A$ and we may show that the phase trajectory is governed by

$$x = -y + \ln(1 + y) \tag{11-14}$$

If we had included initial conditions, then

$$e' = A; \quad\quad x = -y - \ln(1 - y) - \text{i.c.}; \quad\quad \text{i.c.} = -(x_0 + y_0) - \ln(1 - y_0) \tag{11-15a}$$

$$e' = -A; \quad\quad x = -y + \ln(1 + y) - \text{i.c.}; \quad\quad \text{i.c.} = -(x_0 + y_0) + \ln(1 + y_0) \tag{11-15b}$$

These equations simply indicate that the trajectories shift horizontally by an amount corresponding to the contribution of the initial conditions. The time on the phase plot may be obtained by substituting for t into Eq. (11-15a)

$$t = \tau[(x - x_0) + (y - y_0)]$$

For $e' = -A$ we may show that

$$t = -\tau[(x - x_0) - (y - y_0)]$$

Assuming that the control system is subjected to a step input, we have

$$e_0 = r_0 - c_0 = 1$$

Since $e > 0$, we use Eq. (11-15a) to plot the trajectory from 0 to 1 on the phase plot shown in Fig. 11-16. After point 1,

$$t = t_1: \quad e_1 = 1 - (> 1) = \; < 0$$

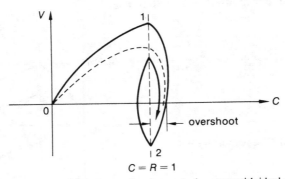

Fig. 11-16 Phase plot for second-order control system with ideal relays.

Since $e < 0$, we use Eq. (11-15b) to plot the trajectory from 1 to 2 on the phase plot. At point 2 the system switches and the above repeats. The time when $c = c_{max}$, $v = 0$ is the time required for the system to overshoot the first time. The amount of overshoot is a function of system damping.

If we include deadband in the previous problem, then

$$
\begin{aligned}
e' &= A; & e &> \alpha \\
&= 0; & -\alpha &< e < \alpha \\
&= -A; & e &< -\alpha
\end{aligned}
$$

For $e' > \alpha$ the previous equations apply. For $e' = 0$,

$$I\frac{d^2c(t)}{dt^2} + B\frac{dc(t)}{dt} = 0$$

For c_0, v_0 initial conditions, we have

$$c(t) = c_0 + v_0(1 - e^{-t/\tau})\tau \qquad (11\text{-}16a)$$

$$v(t) = v_0 e^{-t/\tau} \qquad (11\text{-}16b)$$

Eliminating t, we obtain

$$c = c_0 + (v_0 - v)\tau \qquad (11\text{-}17)$$

Again the previous definitions of x and y permit us to write

$$x = x_0 + (y_0 - y)$$

which is the equation of a straight line. The trajectory between $-\alpha < e < \alpha$ varies in a linear manner as shown in Fig. 11-17.

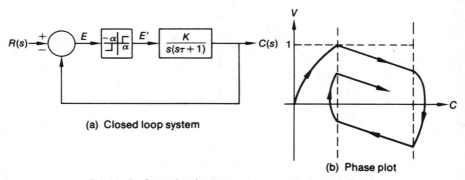

(a) Closed loop system   (b) Phase plot

Fig. 11-17   Second-order system with relay having deadband.

EXAMPLE 11-6

Using the error and its derivative construct a phase-plane plot for the second-order system with saturation shown in Fig. 11-18a.

The transfer function is

$$\frac{C(s)}{E'(s)} = \frac{K_1}{s(s\tau + 1)}$$

or

$$\frac{R(s) - E(s)}{E'(s)} = \frac{K_1}{s(s\tau + 1)}$$

The corresponding differential equation for $R(s) = 0$ is

$$\ddot{e} + \frac{1}{\tau}\dot{e} = \frac{K_1}{\tau}e'$$

where

$$
\begin{aligned}
e' &= K_2 e; & -\alpha < e < \alpha \\
&= K_2 \alpha; & e \geq \alpha \\
&= -K_2 \alpha; & e \leq -\alpha
\end{aligned}
$$

The three differential equations become

$$\ddot{e} + \frac{1}{\tau}\dot{e} + \frac{K_1 K_2}{\tau}e = 0; \qquad -\alpha < e < \alpha \tag{11-18a}$$

$$\ddot{e} + \frac{1}{\tau}\dot{e} = -\frac{K_1 K_2}{\tau}\alpha; \qquad e \geq \alpha \tag{11-18b}$$

$$\ddot{e} + \frac{1}{\tau}\dot{e} = \frac{K_1 K_2}{\tau}\alpha; \qquad e \leq -\alpha \tag{11-18c}$$

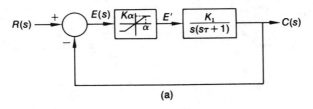

(a)

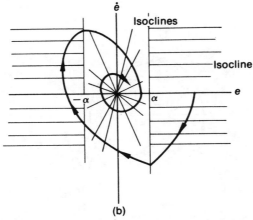

(b)

Fig. 11-18 Phase-plane diagram for second-order system with saturation.

The form of the last two equations is identical to the previous example. The isoclines for this case may be shown to be straight horizontal lines. The isoclines for Eq. (11-18a) are also straight lines but are radial. Assuming that Eq. (11-18a) is underdamped, i.e. it has a stable focus, the phase trajectories may be constructed as shown in Fig. 11-18b.

EXAMPLE 11-7

If deadband is introduced as shown in Fig. 11-19a, obtain the phase-plane plot of e versus $\dot{e}$.

The applicable differential equations become

$$\ddot{e} + \frac{1}{\tau}\dot{e} = 0; \qquad -\alpha < e < \alpha \qquad (11\text{-}19a)$$

$$\ddot{e} + \frac{1}{\tau}\dot{e} + \frac{K_1 K_2}{\tau} e = \frac{K_1 K_2}{\tau}\alpha; \qquad |e| > \alpha \qquad (11\text{-}19b)$$

The first equation is similar to the one obtained for deadband with a relay. The trajectories in this region are linear. The phase-plane diagram is shown in Fig. 11-19b.

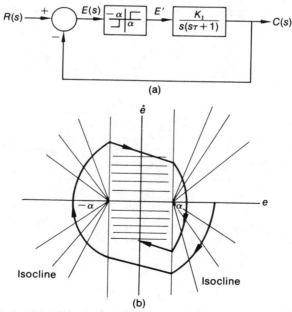

(a)

(b)

Fig. 11-19   Phase-plane diagram for second-order system with deadband.

11-4 LYAPUNOV'S STABILITY CRITERION

In recent years, considerable interest has been centered upon the stability analysis of nonlinear control systems without solving the actual governing equations. Much of the work has been based upon the work of A. M. Lyapunov who developed his theory during the turn of the century. He developed a very fundamental theory to ascertain the stability of a system via energy considerations.

Before we get involved any further, we need to clearly understand the meaning of stability. In general, the stability of a nonlinear system is dependent upon the range of the state vector as well as the perturbation. If the system is subjected to small perturbations and it stays within an infinitesimal region about the singular point, the system has *local stability*. If a system is perturbed and, thereby displaced to any point within a finite region, it returns to the singular point, then this system has *finite stability*. Finally, if the finite region encompasses the entire state space, then the system is said to have *global stability*. If a system, initially beginning from any point in the region of stability, approaches the singular point as time goes to infinity, it is said to be *asymptotically stable*. Here when we speak of stability, we speak of asymptotic stability.

Consider the second-order system of Fig. 11-20 governed by

$$m\ddot{x}(t) + B\dot{x}(t) + kx(t) = 0$$

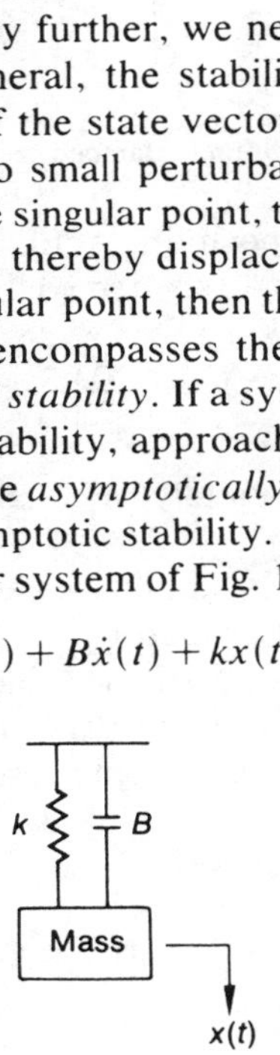

Fig. 11-20   Second-order linear system.

Assuming that the system is underdamped, the phase plot of this system is shown in Fig. 11-21. Now we form the sum of the potential and kinetic energy of the system

$$V = k_1 x_1{}^2 + k_2 x_2{}^2$$

where

$$x_1 = x; \qquad x_2 = \dot{x}$$

and k_1, k_2 are positive constants. We note that if the system whose total energy is given by V is perturbed from its rest position, it will oscillate and

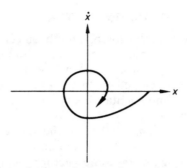

Fig. 11-21 Phase plot for underdamped second-order linear system.

eventually return to its rest position. Actually the energy increase of the system, due a perturbation, is dissipated so that

$$\dot{V} = -\frac{Bx_2^2}{2}$$

provided k_1 and k_2 are appropriately selected. Such a system is said to be asymptotically stable.

Fundamental to Lyapunov's stability criterion is the function V. Such a function has two important properties. The first is that V is positive for all nonzero values of the state variables that are used to define V. The second is that $V = 0$ if all the state variables are zero. When a scalar function, such as V, has these two properties it is said to be *positive definite*. If V is given by

$$V = x_1^2 + x_2^2$$

then $V(x_1, x_2)$ is shown in Fig. 11-22. If V is given by

$$V = x_1^2 + x_2^2 + x_3^2$$

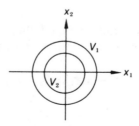

Fig. 11-22 Plot of constant $V(x_1, x_2)$ loci.

then $V(x_1, x_2, x_3)$ is shown in Fig. 11-23. If V is given by

★
$$V = \sum_{i}^{n} x_i^2 \qquad (11\text{-}20)$$

then we have an nth-order system and V cannot be geometrically illustrated for $n > 3$.

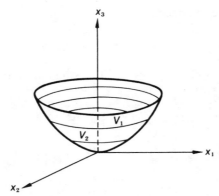

Fig. 11-23   Plot of constant $V(x_1, x_2, x_3)$ loci.

The stability criterion of Lyapunov is stated in terms of V and $\dot{V}$. Let us assume that a suitable function V of a system can be found. Then the criterion states that if

(1) V is positive definite
(2) $\dot{V}$ is negative definite

along the trajectory of the system, then the system is asymptotically stable. It is important to understand that we have not said that V *must* be defined as in Eq. (11-20). Often the function V turns out to be quite different from that shown in Eq. 11-20. Generally, it is quite difficult to obtain these V functions. Much of today's research is directed at ways of constructing or obtaining the Lyapunov functions.

EXAMPLE 11-8

Using the sum of potential and kinetic energies for V, show that the following mechanical system with a nonlinear spring is stable,

$$m\ddot{x} + a\dot{x} + k\left(x - \frac{x^3}{6}\right) = 0$$

The kinetic energy is $\frac{1}{2}m\dot{x}^2$ and the potential energy is

$$\text{Potential energy} = \int_0^x k\left(y - \frac{y^3}{6}\right) dy$$

$$= \frac{kx^2}{2}\left(1 - \frac{x^2}{12}\right)$$

The Lyapunov function becomes

$$V = \frac{1}{2}m\dot{x}^2 + \frac{kx^2}{2}\left(1 - \frac{x^2}{12}\right)$$

which is positive definite if $|x| \leq 12$. The singular point for the system is the origin. We now form $\dot{V}$,

$$\dot{V} = m\dot{x}\ddot{x} + kx\dot{x}\left(1 - \frac{x^2}{6}\right)$$

$$= -a\dot{x}^2 - kx\dot{x}\left(1 - \frac{x^2}{6}\right) + kx\dot{x}\left(1 - \frac{x^2}{6}\right)$$

$$= -a\dot{x}^2$$

so that $\dot{V} \leq 0$. Therefore the system is stable provided $|x| \leq 12$. In this example we cannot infer that the system is asymptotically stable since $\dot{V}$ is not a function of x and $\dot{x}$. Actually a different choice of V or the invoking of a different theorem shows that the system indeed is asymptotically stable.

EXAMPLE 11-9

The equations of a rotating spacecraft are given by

$$I_x\dot{\omega}_x + (I_z - I_y)\omega_y\omega_z = -B\omega_x$$

$$I_z\dot{\omega}_z + (I_y - I_x)\omega_x\omega_y = -B\omega_z$$

$$I_y\dot{\omega}_y + (I_x - I_z)\omega_x\omega_z = -B\omega_y$$

where I_x, I_y, I_z are principal inertias, B is a positive damping constant, and ω_x, ω_y, ω_z are angular rates. Show that the point $(0, 0, 0)$ is asymptotically stable.

We consider the scalar function V as

$$V = \frac{1}{2}I_x\omega_x^2 + \frac{1}{2}I_y\omega_y^2 + \frac{1}{2}I_z\omega_z^2$$

which is positive definite since V is positive for all values of ω_x, ω_y, ω_z and zero only at $(0, 0, 0)$. Forming $\dot{V}$,

$$\dot{V} = I_x\dot{\omega}_x\omega_x + I_y\dot{\omega}_y\omega_y + I_z\dot{\omega}_z\omega_z$$
$$= -(I_z - I_y)\omega_x\omega_y\omega_z - (I_x - I_z)\omega_x\omega_y\omega_z - (I_y - I_x)\omega_x\omega_y\omega_z$$
$$-B(\omega_x^2 + \omega_y^2 + \omega_z^2)$$
$$= -B(\omega_x^2 + \omega_y^2 + \omega_z^2)$$

so that $V \leq 0$ is zero only at $(0, 0, 0)$. Therefore the system is asymptotically stable.

SUMMARY

Since systems in real life are not linear, we have briefly discussed nonlinearities in this chapter. It has been assumed that the nonlinearities are small. Systems with small linearities were analyzed by two methods, via the describing function technique, and the phase-plane technique.

The describing function technique involved the representation of the nonlinear element by its quasi-linearized form. The input to the nonlinear element was assumed to be a sinusoid. The output was represented by Fourier coefficients. It was assumed that the fundamental component is the most important part of the output. The transfer function, or the describing function, of the nonlinear element was defined as G_N,

$$G_N = \frac{\text{Fundamental amplitude of output}}{\text{Amplitude of sinusoidal input}}$$

whereas this method was deemed attractive by virtue of the application of classical techniques already developed, its chief drawback was the constraint that the input must be a sinusoid.

The phase-plane method involves the plotting of the variable versus its derivative with time as a parameter. This method is useful for studying the transient behavior as well as the stability of a system. Its chief drawback is its applicability to primarily second-order systems. It should be remembered however, that the number of second-order systems describing physical phenomena is very substantial.

Finally, the stability criterion of Lyapunov was introduced. This criterion is based on energy considerations. If a suitable scalar function V can be obtained, the stability of a system can be ascertained from V and $\dot{V}$. The difficulty lies in the fact that V is not readily available.

PROBLEMS

11-1. Derive the equation of a pendulum. Linearize the equation and solve it. Under what conditions are the assumptions of linearization violated?

11-2. Verify the describing function for hysterisis given in Table 11-1.

11-3. For the quadratic spring shown in Fig. 11-8 derive the third and fifth harmonic and compare to the first harmonic. Are you justified in neglecting the third and fifth harmonic? Show that the nth harmonic has an amplitude given by

$$B_n = \frac{-8}{(n+2) \cdot n \cdot (n-2) \cdots 1} \frac{R^2}{\pi}$$

11-4. For Example 11-4, how does the Nyquist and Bode plot change if the relay has deadband?

11-5. Using the describing function technique study the behavior of the control system shown in Fig. P11-5.

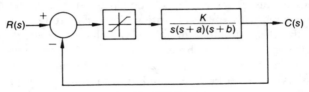

Fig. P11-5

11-6. Could you analyze Problem 11-5 using phase-plane techniques? Explain.

11-7. Verify Eq. (11-15).

11-8. For the control system shown in Fig. P11-8, obtain c versus $\dot{c}$. Assume the input to be a step.

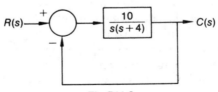

Fig. P11-8

11-9. Derive the equation of the isoclines for the system described by Eq. (11-18).

11-10. Verify Eq. (11-19).

11-11. Problem 11-8 is modified with the nonlinear element as shown in Fig. P11-11. How has the system changed as far as overshoot is concerned? Assume a step input.

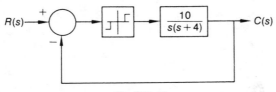

Fig. P11-11

11-12. Could Problem 11-11 be solved if the input is a ramp?

11-13. Obtain the phase-plane plot for the system shown in Fig. P11-13.

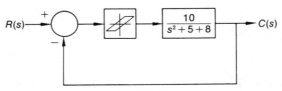

Fig. P11-13

11-14. Can we say something about steady state error about the last three problems? [Remember Problem 11-9 is a type 1 system and Problem 11-11 is a type 0 system.]

11-15. Using the sum of the kinetic and potential energies, of a simple pendulum with damping, as a V function, obtain the conditions for asymptotic stability.

REFERENCES

1. Thaler, G. J., and M. P. Pastel, *Analysis and Design of Nonlinear Feedback Control Systems*, New York, McGraw-Hill, 1962.
2. Graham, D., and D. McRuer, *Analysis of Non Linear Control Systems*, New York, Wiley, 1961.
3. Elgerd, O. I., *Control Systems Theory*, New York, McGraw-Hill, 1967.
4. Shinners, S. M., *Modern Control System Theory and Application*, Reading, Mass., Addison-Wesley, 1972.
5. Popov, E. P., *The Dynamics of Automatic Control Systems*, Reading, Mass., Addison-Wesley, 1962.
6. Cosgriff, R. L., *Non Linear Control Systems*, New York, McGraw-Hill, 1958.
7. Smith, O. J. M., *Feedback Control Systems*, New York, McGraw-Hill, 1958.
8. Takahashi, Y., M. J. Rabins, and D. M. Anslander, *Control and Dynamic Systems*, Reading, Mass., Addison-Wesley, 1970.
9. Gibson, J. E., *Non Linear Automatic Control*, New York, McGraw-Hill, 1963.
10. Lefferts, E. J., "A Guide to the Application of the Lyapunov Direct Method to Flight Control Systems," Martin Marietta Corp. Report ER-13736.

Appendix **A**

Laplace and z-Transforms

1. If a function $f(t)$ is zero for $t < 0$, then the Laplace transform of $f(t)$ written as $F(s)$ is

$$F(s) = \mathcal{L}[f(t)] = \int_0^\infty f(t)e^{-st}dt$$

Some useful properties of Laplace transforms are:

(a) Linearity

$$\mathcal{L}[f_1(t) + f_2(t)] = F_1(s) + F_2(s)$$

(b) Multiplication by a constant

$$\mathcal{L}[af(t)] = aF(s)$$

(c) Scale change (a is real and positive)

$$\mathcal{L}\left[f\left(\frac{t}{a}\right)\right] = aF(s)$$

(d) Real differentiation

$$\mathcal{L}\left[\frac{d^n f(t)}{dt^n}\right] = s^n F(s) - s^{n-1}f(+0) - \cdots - f^{(n-1)}(+0).$$

(e) Real translation

$$\mathcal{L}[f(t-t_0)] = e^{-t_0 s}F(s)$$
$$= 0 \qquad\qquad \text{for } t < t_0$$

(f) Initial and final value theorems.

$$f(0) = \lim_{s \to \infty} [sF(s)]$$

$$f(\infty) = \lim_{s \to 0} [sF(s)]$$

2. The z-transform is obtained by the substitution $z = e^{st}$,

$$z[f(t)] = F\left(s = \frac{1}{T} \ln z\right) = F(z)$$

Some useful properties of z-transforms are given in Chapter 9.

3. Table of Laplace and z-transforms.

Appendix A: *Continued*

Time Function	Laplace Transform	z-Transforms
$\delta(t)$	1	1
$\delta(t - nT)$	e^{-nTs}	z^{-n}
A	$\dfrac{A}{s}$	$\dfrac{Az}{z-1}$
t	$\dfrac{1}{s^2}$	$\dfrac{Tz}{(z-1)^2}$
t^{n-1}	$\dfrac{(n-1)!}{s^n}$	$\displaystyle\lim_{a \to 0} (-1)^{n-1} \dfrac{d^{n-1}}{da^{n-1}} \left(\dfrac{z}{z - e^{-aT}}\right)$
e^{-at}	$\dfrac{1}{s+a}$	$\dfrac{z}{z - e^{-aT}}$
$\dfrac{1}{b-a}(e^{-at} - e^{-bt})$	$\dfrac{1}{(s+a)(s+b)}$	$\dfrac{1}{b-a}\left(\dfrac{z}{z-e^{-aT}} - \dfrac{z}{z-e^{-bT}}\right)$
$\dfrac{1}{a}(1 - e^{-at})$	$\dfrac{1}{s(s+a)}$	$\dfrac{1}{a}\dfrac{(1-e^{-aT})z}{(z-1)(z-e^{-aT})}$
te^{-at}	$\dfrac{1}{(s+a)^2}$	$\dfrac{Tze^{-aT}}{(z-e^{-aT})^2}$
$\sin \omega t$	$\dfrac{\omega}{s^2 + \omega^2}$	$\dfrac{z \sin \omega T}{z^2 - 2z \cos \omega T + 1}$
$\cos \omega t$	$\dfrac{s}{s^2 + \omega^2}$	$\dfrac{z(z - \cos \omega T)}{z^2 - 2z \cos \omega T + 1}$

Appendix B

Symbols and Units

System	Quantity	Symbol	mKs Units	English Units
Mechanical translational	Force	F, f	Newton (n)	Pound (lb)
	Displacement	x	Meter (m)	Foot (ft)
	Velocity	v	m/sec	ft/sec
	Acceleration	a	m/sec²	ft/sec²
	Mass	M	Kilogram (kg)	Slugs
		M	n/m/sec²	lb/ft/sec²
	Stiffness	K	n/m	lb/ft
	Damping	B	n/m/sec	lb/ft/sec
Mechanical rotational	Torque	T	m-n	ft-lb
	Angle	θ	Radian (rad)	rad
	Angular speed	ω	rad/sec	rad/sec
	Angular acceleration	α	rad/sec²	rad/sec²
	Moment of inertia	I	kg-m²	slug-ft²
	Stiffness	K	n-m/rad	lb-ft/rad
	Damping	B	n-m-sec/rad	lb-ft-sec/rad
Hydraulic	Force	F	n	lb
	Displacement	x	m	ft
	Density	ρ	kg/m³	slugs/ft³
	Pressure	P	n/m²	lb/ft²
	Flow rate	q	kg/sec	slugs/sec

System	Quantity	Symbol	mKs Units	English Units
Thermal	Heat energy	Q	Kilogram calorie (Kcal)	British Thermal Unit (BTU)
	Temperature	T	°K or °C (Kelvin or Centigrade)	°F or °R (Fahrenheit or Rankine)
	Specific heat	c	Kcal/Kg/°K	BTU/lb/°F
	Heat flow rate	q	Kcal/min	BTU/min
	Thermal capacitance	C	Kcal/°K	BTU/°F
	Thermal resistance	R	°K/Kcal/min	°F/BTU/min
Electrical	Voltage	e, v	Volts	
	Current	i	Amperes	
	Inductance	L	Henrys	
	Capacitance	C	Farads	
	Resistance	R	Ohms	

Appendix C

Fundamentals of Matrix Theory

C-1 INTRODUCTION

The word "matrix" is used to denote an orderly array of objects called elements. These elements are mathematical symbols, constants, complex numbers, functions, etc. A matrix $\mathbf{A}$ is denoted by

$$\mathbf{A} = \begin{bmatrix} a_{11} & a_{12} & \cdots\cdots & a_{1m} \\ a_{21} & a_{22} & \cdots\cdots & a_{2m} \\ \vdots & \vdots & & \vdots \\ a_{n1} & a_{n2} & \cdots\cdots & a_{nm} \end{bmatrix} \tag{C-1}$$

where a_{ij} are the elements of $\mathbf{A}$. The entire array of elements is sometimes referred to as $[a_{ij}]$. The subscripts follow a numerical sequence such that the first subscript i refers to the effect, whereas the second refers to the cause. The term $a_{ij}x_j$ causes the effect y_i. If there are n effects and m causes, then the matrix is an $n \times m$ matrix. The number of columns is equal to m and the number of rows to n.

A matrix having one column or row can be interpreted as a vector. For example the 3×1 column matrix,

$$\mathbf{A} = \begin{bmatrix} a_1 \\ a_2 \\ a_3 \end{bmatrix}$$

can be thought of as a vector with components a_1, a_2, a_3 in the orthogonal system, or three-dimensional space. If the number of elements is larger than three, then we must think of a vector in a higher dimensional space, at least conceptually. A column matrix with n elements is a vector in n-dimensional space.

A rectangular matrix may be thought of as consisting m vectors. The matrix

$$\mathbf{A} = \begin{bmatrix} a_{11} & \cdots & a_{1m} \\ \vdots & & \vdots \\ a_{n1} & \cdots & a_{nm} \end{bmatrix}$$

can be interpreted to consist of m vectors,

$$\mathbf{A} = [\,\mathbf{B}_1 \mathbf{B}_2 \cdots \mathbf{B}_m\,]$$

where each vector has n elements,

$$\mathbf{B}_i = \begin{bmatrix} a_{1i} \\ a_{2i} \\ \vdots \\ a_{ni} \end{bmatrix}$$

Vectors, like matrices, combine linearly. A vector may be formed by adding several vectors each having the same dimension. Let $a_1, a_2, \ldots$ be vectors, then a vector c can be formed such that

$$c = \alpha_1[a_1] + \alpha_2[a_2] + \cdots$$

where $\alpha_1, \alpha_2, \ldots$ are constants. Such an equation is called a linear combination of vectors.

When the number of rows and columns of a matrix are unequal, it is a rectangular matrix; and when they are equal, it is a square matrix. Every square matrix has associated with it a scalar quantity called the determinant of the matrix. It is designated as $\det \mathbf{A}$ or simply as $|\mathbf{A}|$. For a matrix $\mathbf{A}$ the determinant is written as

$$\det \mathbf{A} = |\mathbf{A}| = \begin{vmatrix} a_{11} & a_{12} & \cdots & a_{1n} \\ a_{21} & a_{22} & \cdots & a_{2n} \\ \vdots & & & \\ a_{n1} & a_{n2} & \cdots & a_{nn} \end{vmatrix}$$

If the square matrix is $n \times n$, then the determinant is called an nth-order determinant. The value of the determinant can be defined in terms of its minors and cofactors. The determinant obtained by deleting the ith row and jth column is called the i-jth minor of $\det \mathbf{A}$ and is denoted by $|\mathbf{M}_{ij}|$. This minor is associated with, or belongs to, the element a_{ij}. As an example, consider a third-order determinant,

$$\det \mathbf{A} = a_{11}|M_{11}| - a_{12}|M_{12}| + a_{13}|M_{13}|$$

where

$$M_{11} = \begin{vmatrix} a_{22} & a_{23} \\ a_{32} & a_{33} \end{vmatrix}; \qquad M_{12} = \begin{vmatrix} a_{21} & a_{23} \\ a_{31} & a_{33} \end{vmatrix}; \qquad M_{13} = \begin{vmatrix} a_{21} & a_{22} \\ a_{31} & a_{32} \end{vmatrix}$$

If the diagonal elements of the minor are the diagonal elements of $|\mathbf{A}|$, then the minor is a principal minor. In the above expansion, only $|M_{11}|$ is a principal minor.

Associated with each minor $|M_{ij}|$ is a cofactor C_{ij} such that

$$C_{ij} = (-1)^{i+j}|M_{ij}|$$

Using this, the determinant of $\mathbf{A}$ becomes

$$\det \mathbf{A} = |\mathbf{A}| = \sum_{i}^{n} a_{ij}C_{ij}; \qquad i = 1, 2, \ldots, n$$

$$= \sum_{j}^{n} a_{ij}C_{ij}; \qquad j = 1, 2, \ldots, n \qquad \text{(C-2)}$$

C-2   MATRIX ALGEBRA

In combining matrices, the following rules must be observed:

Equality. The equality of matrices requires that all the elements in the same relative position of each matrix be equal. Obviously for matrices to be equal, the dimensions of one matrix must be equal to the dimensions of the other matrix. If an $n \times m$ matrix $\mathbf{A}$ is equal to another $n \times m$ matrix $\mathbf{B}$,

$$\mathbf{A} = \mathbf{B}$$

then

$$a_{ij} = b_{ij} \quad \text{for all } i \text{ and } j$$

Addition and subtraction. Two matrices must have the same dimensions in order to be added or subtracted. If two matrices $\mathbf{A}$ and $\mathbf{B}$ are combined,

$$\mathbf{A} \mp \mathbf{B} = \mathbf{C}$$

then

$$a_{ij} \mp b_{ij} = c_{ij} \quad \text{for all } i, j$$

In addition and subtraction the associative as well as commutative law applies.

Multiplication of matrices. Multiplication of a matrix by a scalar is achieved by multiplying each element by this scalar. If

$$C = k\mathbf{A}$$

where k is a constant, then we have

$$c_{ij} = ka_{ij} \quad \text{for all } i, j$$

For two matrices to be multiplied, the number of columns of the first matrix must be equal to the number of rows of the second matrix. If $\mathbf{A}$ is an $n \times m$, then $\mathbf{B}$ must be $m \times p$ for multiplying them together. The resulting product is a $n \times p$ matrix. Let

$$\mathbf{A} = \begin{bmatrix} a_{11} & \cdots & a_{1m} \\ \vdots & & \\ a_{n1} & \cdots & a_{nm} \end{bmatrix}; \quad \mathbf{B} = \begin{bmatrix} b_{11} & \cdots & b_{1p} \\ \vdots & & \\ b_{m1} & \cdots & b_{mp} \end{bmatrix}$$

Then if

$$C = \mathbf{AB}$$

the elements of $\mathbf{C}$ become

$$\mathbf{C} = \begin{bmatrix} (a_{11}b_{11} + a_{12}b_{21} + \cdots + a_{1m}b_{m1}) & \cdots & (a_{11}b_{1p} + \cdots + a_{1m}b_{mp}) \\ \vdots & & \vdots \\ (a_{n1}b_{11} + \cdots + a_{nm}b_{m1}) & \cdots & (a_{n1}b_{1p} + \cdots + a_{nm}b_{mp}) \end{bmatrix}$$

The operation of obtaining the i-jth term of $\mathbf{C}$ involves taking the sum of all the terms obtained by multiplying the ith row of the first matrix with the jth column of the second matrix. Note that there are no restrictions on the number of rows of the first matrix or the number of columns of the second matrix. This simply determines the dimension of the new matrix.

Matrix multiplication does not obey the law of commutation, i.e. in general,

$$\mathbf{AB} \neq \mathbf{BA}$$

Therefore when a matrix $\mathbf{A}$ is multiplied such that

$$C = \mathbf{BA}$$

we say that $\mathbf{A}$ is premultiplied by $\mathbf{B}$. If instead

$$C = \mathbf{AB}$$

then $\mathbf{A}$ is said to be postmultiplied by $\mathbf{B}$.

Division. The division by a matrix is perhaps the most difficult operation. If

$$C = \mathbf{AB}$$

and we are given $\mathbf{C}$ and $\mathbf{A}$, how do we obtain $\mathbf{B}$? We can answer this by premultiplying by $\mathbf{A}^{-1}$

$$\mathbf{A}^{-1}\mathbf{C} = \mathbf{A}^{-1}\mathbf{A}\mathbf{B}$$

where $\mathbf{A}^{-1}$ is the inverse of $\mathbf{A}$ and is analogous to division. Note that this is valid only if $\mathbf{A}$ is a square matrix and det $\mathbf{A} \neq 0$. The term $\mathbf{A}^{-1}\mathbf{A}$ is unity, i.e.

$$\mathbf{A}^{-1}\mathbf{A} = \mathbf{I} = \begin{bmatrix} 1 & 0 & 0 & \cdots \\ 0 & 1 & 0 & \cdots \\ 0 & 0 & \cdots & 1 \end{bmatrix} \tag{C-3}$$

where $\mathbf{I}$ is called the unit matrix. Substituting

$$\mathbf{IB} = \mathbf{B} = \mathbf{A}^{-1}\mathbf{C}$$

The value of $\mathbf{A}^{-1}$ is obtained by satisfying Eq. (C-3).

C-3   TYPES OF MATRICES

There are many square matrices having special properties that make them unique. Some of the ones useful to us are listed below.

Diagonal matrix. The principal diagonal of this matrix has nonzero elements. All the other elements are zero.

$$\text{Diagonal matrix } \mathbf{A} = \begin{bmatrix} a_{11} & \cdots & \vdots & \cdots & 0 \\ \vdots & & \dot{a}_{22} & & \vdots \\ 0 & \cdots & \vdots & \cdots & a_{nm} \end{bmatrix}$$

Null matrix. This matrix has all its elements equal to zero. This is sometimes called a zero matrix.

Unity matrix. Sometimes called an identity matrix, this matrix is a diagonal matrix except that all the diagonal elements are unity. The identity matrix when multiplied by another matrix leaves the matrix unchanged,

$$\mathbf{IA} = \mathbf{AI} = \mathbf{A}$$

Transpose matrix. The transpose of a matrix is obtained by interchanging the rows and columns of a matrix. The transpose matrix is denoted by $\mathbf{A}^T$. If

$$\mathbf{A} = \begin{bmatrix} a_{11} & a_{12} & \cdots & a_{1n} \\ \vdots & & & \\ a_{n1} & \cdots & & a_{nn} \end{bmatrix}$$

Then

$$\mathbf{A}^T = \begin{bmatrix} a_{11} & \cdots & a_{n1} \\ a_{12} & & \vdots \\ \vdots & & \vdots \\ a_{1n} & & a_{nn} \end{bmatrix}$$

Symmetric matrix. A matrix is symmetric if it is equal to its transpose, i.e.

$$a_{ij} = a_{ji} \quad \text{for all } i, j$$

Skew-symmetric matrix. If the transpose of the matrix is equal to the negative of the matrix, it is skew symmetric,

$$a_{ij} = -a_{ji} \quad \text{for all } i, j$$

Orthogonal matrix. An orthogonal matrix is one which when multiplied by its transpose yields the identity matrix,

$$\mathbf{A}\mathbf{A}^T = \mathbf{I}$$

which implies

$$\mathbf{A}^T = \mathbf{A}^{-1}$$

Matrices defining coordinate transformations are generally orthogonal.

Triangular matrix. When all the elements above or below the main diagonal are zero, then the matrix is a triangular matrix. If the elements above the main diagonal are zero, the matrix is a lower triangular matrix. If the elements below the main diagonal are zero, the matrix is an upper triangular matrix. An example of a lower triangular matrix is

$$\mathbf{A} = \begin{bmatrix} 1 & 0 & 0 & 0 \\ 2 & 2 & 0 & 0 \\ 3 & 0 & 4 & 0 \\ 1 & 5 & 2 & 3 \end{bmatrix}$$

Adjoint matrix. This matrix is the transpose of a matrix formed by replacing each element by its cofactor. If C_{ij} is the cofactor of the element a_{ij}, then the adjoint matrix is

$$\text{adj } \mathbf{A} = [c_{ji}] \tag{C-4}$$

It is denoted by adj $\mathbf{A}$. Consider a matrix $\mathbf{A}$,

$$\mathbf{A} = \begin{bmatrix} 0 & 0 & 1 \\ 2 & 1 & 2 \\ 3 & 1 & 1 \end{bmatrix}$$

The matrix formed by the cofactors is

$$\mathbf{C} = \begin{bmatrix} -1 & 4 & -1 \\ 1 & -3 & 0 \\ -1 & 2 & 0 \end{bmatrix}$$

The adjoint becomes

$$\text{adj } \mathbf{A} = \mathbf{C}^T = \begin{bmatrix} -1 & 1 & -1 \\ 4 & -3 & 2 \\ -1 & 0 & 0 \end{bmatrix}$$

Nonsingular matrix. If the determinant of a matrix is nonzero, then the matrix is nonsingular. If

$$\det \mathbf{A} = 0$$

then it is a singular matrix.

Inverse matrix. The inverse $\mathbf{A}^{-1}$ of a matrix $\mathbf{A}$ must satisfy the property that

$$\mathbf{A}^{-1}\mathbf{A} = \mathbf{I}$$

Not all matrices have an inverse. It can be shown that every matrix poses an inverse if it is nonsingular. The inverse of a matrix can be constructed by satisfying Eq. (C-3). Here we shall investigate an alternate way.

Consider a matrix $\mathbf{A}$ whose $|\mathbf{A}|$ is

$$|\mathbf{A}| = \sum_{i=1}^{n} a_{ij}c_{ij}; \qquad j = 1, 2, \ldots, n$$

The cofactor does not contain any elements of the ith row of $\mathbf{A}$. If instead of a_{ij} we had a_{ik}, then

$$\sum_{i=1}^{n} a_{ik}c_{ij} = 0; \qquad k \neq j$$

The two previous equations can be combined to yield

$$\sum_{i=1}^{n} a_{ik}c_{ij} = \delta_{kj}|\mathbf{A}|$$

where

$$\delta_{kj} = 0; \qquad j \neq k$$
$$= 1 \qquad j = k$$

This may be rewritten as

$$[a_{ij}][c_{ji}] = |\mathbf{A}|\mathbf{I}$$

or

$$\mathbf{A} \text{ adj } \mathbf{A} = |\mathbf{A}|\mathbf{I}$$

or

$$I = \frac{A \text{ adj } A}{|A|}$$

Since $AA^{-1} = I$, we have

$$A^{-1} = \frac{\text{adj } A}{|A|} \qquad \text{(C-5)}$$

and the inverse exists if and only if $|A| \neq 0$.

Complex matrices. When all or some of the elements of a matrix are complex numbers, then the matrix is a complex matrix. The conjugate of a complex matrix is obtained by taking the conjugate of each element.

Partitioned matrices. The elements of a matrix can not only be numbers and functions but may be other matrices. Consider the matrix

$$A = \begin{bmatrix} a_{11} & a_{12} & a_{13} & a_{14} \\ a_{21} & a_{22} & a_{23} & a_{24} \\ a_{31} & a_{32} & a_{33} & a_{34} \\ a_{41} & a_{42} & a_{43} & a_{44} \end{bmatrix}$$

This may be rewritten as

$$A = \begin{bmatrix} B_{11} & B_{12} \\ B_{21} & B_{22} \end{bmatrix}$$

where

$$B_{11} = \begin{bmatrix} a_{11} & a_{12} \\ a_{21} & a_{22} \end{bmatrix}; \qquad B_{12} = \begin{bmatrix} a_{13} & a_{14} \\ a_{23} & a_{24} \end{bmatrix}$$

$$B_{21} = \begin{bmatrix} a_{31} \\ a_{41} \end{bmatrix}; \qquad B_{22} = \begin{bmatrix} a_{32} & a_{33} & a_{34} \\ a_{42} & a_{43} & a_{44} \end{bmatrix}$$

The rules of matrix algebra apply to partitioned matrices without modifications. Extra care should be exercised to insure that the various matrices to be combined are conformable.

C-4 MATRIX CALCULUS

Having defined the algebraic operations of matrices we now consider operations involving calculus. In this section we shall be concerned with differentiation, integration, and transformation of a matrix. The transformation will be from the time domain to the complex s- and z-domains and vice versa.

Differentiation and integration. Consider a matrix $\mathbf{A}(t)$ whose elements are functions of time. Then the derivative of $\mathbf{A}(t)$ is obtained by taking the derivative of each element of $\mathbf{A}(t)$,

$$\frac{d\mathbf{A}(t)}{dt} = \left[\frac{da_{ij}}{dt}\right] \tag{C-6}$$

The derivative of a product of two matrices is

$$\frac{d}{dt}\left[\mathbf{A}(t)\mathbf{B}(t)\right] = \mathbf{A}(t)\frac{d\mathbf{B}(t)}{dt} + \frac{d\mathbf{A}(t)}{dt}\mathbf{B}(t)$$

The derivative of the sum or difference is

$$\frac{d}{dt}\left[\mathbf{A}(t) \mp \mathbf{B}(t)\right] = \frac{d\mathbf{A}(t)}{dt} \mp \frac{d\mathbf{B}(t)}{dt}$$

The integral of a matrix is obtained by taking the integral of each element of the matrix,

$$\int \mathbf{A}(t)\,dt = \left[\int a_{ij}dt\right] \tag{C-7}$$

The integral of the sum or difference is

$$\int \left[\mathbf{A}(t) \mp \mathbf{B}(t)\right]dt = \int \mathbf{A}(t)\,dt \mp \int \mathbf{B}(t)\,dt$$

The integral of a product is taken after the two matrices are multiplied.

Laplace and z-transform. We shall assume that the matrix $\mathbf{A}$ is such that its Laplace and z-transforms exist. Then the Laplace transform of $\mathbf{A}$ is simply obtained by taking the Laplace transform of each element of $\mathbf{A}$,

$$\mathscr{L}[\mathbf{A}(t)] = [\mathscr{L}a_{ij}] \tag{C-8}$$

The Laplace transform of the sum of two matrices is

$$\mathscr{L}(\mathbf{A}(t) + \mathbf{B}(t)) = \mathscr{L}[\mathbf{A}(t)] + \mathscr{L}[\mathbf{B}(t)]$$

The Laplace transform of the derivative of a matrix may be written as

$$\mathscr{L}\left[\frac{d\mathbf{A}(t)}{dt}\right] = \left[\mathscr{L}\frac{da_{ij}}{dt}\right]$$

The inverse Laplace transform of a matrix is obtained by taking the inverse of each element,

$$\mathbf{A}(t) = \mathscr{L}^{-1}[\mathbf{A}(s)] = [\mathscr{L}^{-1}a_{ij}] \tag{C-9}$$

The z-transform of a matrix requires that a matrix be defined at discrete time steps,

$$\mathbf{A}(nT) = [a_{ij}(nT)] \tag{C-10}$$

The z-transform of $\mathbf{A}(nT)$ can be obtained by taking the z-transform of each element,

$$\mathbf{A}(z) = z[\mathbf{A}(nT)] = [z(a_{ij}(nT))] \tag{C-11}$$

The z-transform of the sum or difference of two matrices is equal to the sum or difference of the z-transforms of the matrices. If the matrix $\mathbf{A}(nT)$ is defined at $\mathbf{A}[(n+1)T]$, then it can be shown that

$$z[\mathbf{A}[(n+1)T]] = z\mathbf{A}(z) - z\mathbf{A}(0)$$

The inverse z-transform is obtained by taking the inverse z-transform of each element,

$$\mathbf{A}(nT) = z^{-1}\mathbf{A}(z) = [z^{-1}(a_{ij}(z))]$$

The rules developed for the z-transform and the inverse z-transform apply to each element of the matrix without modification.

C-5 LINEAR ALGEBRAIC EQUATIONS

Consider a set of linear algebraic equations,

$$
\begin{aligned}
a_{11}x_1 + a_{12}x_2 + \;\cdots\; + a_{1n}x_n &= y_1 \\
\vdots \qquad \vdots \qquad\qquad \vdots \qquad \vdots & \\
a_{n1}x_1 + a_{n2}x_2 + \;\cdots\; + a_{nn}x_n &= y_n
\end{aligned}
\tag{C-12}
$$

where all the a's and y's are known. We wish to determine the x's that satisfy these equations. It is worth noting that the a's and y's can be constants, functions of s or functions of z. Now Eq. (C-12) can be represented in matrix form

$$\mathbf{A}\mathbf{x} = \mathbf{y} \tag{C-13}$$

where $\mathbf{A}$ is an $n \times n$ matrix, $\mathbf{x}$ is an $n \times 1$ column matrix or vector, and $\mathbf{y}$ is an $n \times 1$ column matrix or vector. The solution to Eq. (C-13) can be obtained using Cramer's rule,

$$x_k = \sum_{i=1}^{n} \frac{c_{ik} y_i}{|\mathbf{A}|} \tag{C-14}$$

where c_{ik} is the cofactor of a_{ik}. The numerator of Eq. (C-14) is the determinant of $\mathbf{A}$ with the kth column replaced by the column formed by the right side of Eq. (C-12). Note that a solution exists only if $\mathbf{A}$ is a nonsingular matrix. A slightly different formulation of Eq. (C-14) results if we premultiply Eq. (C-13) by $\mathbf{A}^{-1}$,

$$\mathbf{A}^{-1}\mathbf{A}\mathbf{x} = \mathbf{A}^{-1}\mathbf{y}$$

and since

$$\mathbf{A}^{-1} = \frac{\text{adj } \mathbf{A}}{|\mathbf{A}|}$$

we have

$$\mathbf{x} = \frac{\text{adj } \mathbf{A}}{|\mathbf{A}|}\mathbf{y} \qquad (\text{C-15})$$

It is left for you as an exercise to show that the use of Eq. (C-15) in the previous example gives the same result.

If the right-hand side of Eq. (C-13) is zero,

$$\mathbf{A}\mathbf{x} = 0 \qquad (\text{C-16})$$

then the equations are said to be homogeneous. When this happens the numerator of Eq. (C-15) vanishes and if $|\mathbf{A}|$ does not vanish, then the set of equations has a trivial solution. If the determinant does vanish, then two or more vectors, whose elements are the elements of the columns of $\mathbf{A}$, are linearly related.

C-6   CHARACTERISTIC EQUATIONS AND EIGENVECTORS

Since the behavior of a linear system is dependent upon the characteristic values (or roots) of a system, we will develop some fundamental concepts pertaining to the characteristic equation. Consider the matrix equation,

$$\mathbf{y} = \mathbf{A}\mathbf{x}$$

This equation may be thought of as one that transforms the vector $\mathbf{x}$ into the vector $\mathbf{y}$. In linear systems we wish to know if a vector $\mathbf{x}$ exists such that the vector $\mathbf{y}$ is linearly related to $\mathbf{x}$, i.e.

$$\mathbf{y} = \lambda\mathbf{x}$$

Substituting this in the matrix equation we have

$$\mathbf{y} = \mathbf{A}\mathbf{x} = \lambda\mathbf{x} \qquad (\text{C-17})$$

This becomes a characteristic value problem. The values of λ that satisfy Eq. (C-17), for $x_i \neq 0$, are the characteristic values of $\mathbf{A}$. The vector solutions $x_i \neq 0$ are called the eigenvectors of $\mathbf{A}$. Equation (C-17) can be expressed as

$$[\lambda\mathbf{I} - \mathbf{A}]\mathbf{x} = 0 \qquad (\text{C-18})$$

where

$$[\lambda\mathbf{I} - \mathbf{A}] = \begin{bmatrix} \lambda - a_{11} & -a_{12} & -a_{13} \cdots & -a_{1n} \\ -a_{21} & \lambda - a_{22} & \cdots\cdots\cdots & -a_{2n} \\ \vdots & \vdots & \vdots & \vdots \\ -a_{n1} & \cdots\cdots\cdots\cdots\cdots & \lambda - a_{nn} \end{bmatrix}$$

The system of homogeneous equations has a nontrivial solution if

$$\det (\lambda\mathbf{I} - \mathbf{A}) = 0 \qquad (\text{C-}19)$$

This is called the characteristic equation or polynomial. This polynomial is an nth degree polynomial in λ. These values of λ satisfy Eq. (C-17). Consider

$$\mathbf{A} = \begin{bmatrix} 0 & 1 \\ -2 & -3 \end{bmatrix}$$

Then

$$|\lambda\mathbf{I} - \mathbf{A}| = \begin{vmatrix} \lambda & -1 \\ 2 & \lambda + 3 \end{vmatrix} = \lambda^2 + 3\lambda + 2$$

The characteristic equation, denoted by $P(\lambda) = 0$, is

$$P(\lambda) = \lambda^2 + 3\lambda + 2 = 0$$

The roots of $P(\lambda) = 0$ are $\lambda_1 = -2, \lambda_2 = -1$ and are called the eigenvalues. Depending upon $P(\lambda)$, these eigenvalues may be real, imaginary, distinct, or repeated.

Since each root of the characteristic equation satisfies Eq. (C-18), we have

$$[\lambda_i\mathbf{I} - \mathbf{A}]\mathbf{x}(i) = 0 \qquad (\text{C-}20)$$

where $\mathbf{x}(i)$ refers to $\mathbf{x}$ evaluated for $\lambda = \lambda_i$. The vectors that are the solutions to this equation are the eigenvectors of $\mathbf{A}$.

C-7 FUNCTIONS OF A MATRIX

We shall now consider some aspects of matrix polynomials and infinite series after which we shall introduce functions of a matrix and the Cayley–Hamilton theorem. This theorem is very useful in solving matrix differential equations.

When a square matrix is raised to a power it obeys the following rules,

$$\mathbf{A}^n\mathbf{A}^m = \mathbf{A}^{n+m}$$
$$(\mathbf{A}^n)^m = \mathbf{A}^{nm}$$
$$\mathbf{A}^0 = \mathbf{I}$$

where n and m are positive integers. They may be negative only if the matrix $\mathbf{A}$ is nonsingular.

A matrix polynomial $P(\mathbf{A})$ is defined as

$$P(\mathbf{A}) = \alpha_n\mathbf{A}^n + \alpha_{n-1}\mathbf{A}^{n-1} + \cdots + \alpha_1\mathbf{A} + \alpha_0\mathbf{I} \qquad (\text{C-21})$$

where the α's are scalar quantities. The factorization of a matrix polynomial follows the rule of scalar polynomials. If

$$P(\mathbf{A}) = \mathbf{A}^2 + 3\mathbf{A} + 2\mathbf{I}$$

then factorizing yields

$$P(\mathbf{A}) = (\mathbf{A} + 2\mathbf{I})(\mathbf{A} + \mathbf{I})$$

An infinite series of matrices may be written as

$$S(\mathbf{A}) = \alpha_0\mathbf{I} + \alpha_1\mathbf{A} + \alpha_2\mathbf{A}^2 + \cdots \qquad (\text{C-22})$$

If the eigenvalues of $\mathbf{A}$ are given by $\lambda_1, \lambda_2, \ldots, \lambda_n$ and the series defined by

$$S(\lambda_i) = \alpha_0\mathbf{I} + \alpha_1\lambda_i + \alpha_2\lambda_i^2 + \cdots \qquad (\text{C-23})$$

converges, then the series defined by Eq. (C-22) is also convergent. A convergent series that appears quite often in the solution of matrix differential equations is the exponential function series,

$$e^{\mp\mathbf{A}} = \mathbf{I} \pm \mathbf{A} + \frac{\mathbf{A}^2}{2!} \pm \frac{\mathbf{A}^3}{3!} + \cdots \qquad (\text{C-24})$$

Cayley–Hamilton Theorem

We can now state the Cayley–Hamilton theorem which is useful in the definition of any matrix function. The Cayley–Hamilton theorem states *that every square matrix satisfies its own characteristic equation.* Consider $\mathbf{A}$ to be a 2×2 matrix, then we know that the characteristic equation of $\mathbf{A}$ is

$$P(\lambda) = \lambda^2 + \beta_1\lambda + \beta_2 = 0$$

The Cayley–Hamilton theorem states that

$$P(\mathbf{A}) = \mathbf{A}^2 + \beta_1\mathbf{A} + \beta_2\mathbf{I} = 0$$

We can demonstrate the theorem in a straightforward manner. Let

$$\mathbf{A} = \begin{bmatrix} 0 & 1 \\ -3 & -4 \end{bmatrix}$$

then

$$|\lambda\mathbf{I} - \mathbf{A}| = \begin{vmatrix} \lambda & -1 \\ 3 & \lambda + 4 \end{vmatrix} = \lambda^2 + 4\lambda + 3$$

and the characteristic equation is

$$P(\lambda) = \lambda^2 + 4\lambda + 3 = 0$$

The Cayley–Hamilton theorem states that

$$P(\mathbf{A}) = \mathbf{A}^2 + 4\mathbf{A} + 3\mathbf{I} = 0$$

Is this true? We can find out by direct substitution,

$$P(\mathbf{A}) = \begin{vmatrix} 0 & 1 \\ -3 & -4 \end{vmatrix} \begin{vmatrix} 0 & 1 \\ -3 & -4 \end{vmatrix} + 4 \begin{vmatrix} 0 & 1 \\ -3 & -4 \end{vmatrix} + 3 \begin{vmatrix} 1 & 0 \\ 0 & 1 \end{vmatrix}$$

$$P(\mathbf{A}) = \begin{vmatrix} -3 & -4 \\ 12 & 13 \end{vmatrix} + \begin{vmatrix} 0 & 4 \\ -12 & -16 \end{vmatrix} + \begin{vmatrix} 3 & 0 \\ 0 & 3 \end{vmatrix}$$

$$= 0$$

which illustrates the contention of the theorem.

For a given matrix polynomial, the Cayley–Hamilton theorem may be used to reduce the order of the polynomial. Consider a polynomial

$$N(\mathbf{A}) = \mathbf{A}^3 + 2\mathbf{A}^2 + \mathbf{A} + 5\mathbf{I} \tag{C-25}$$

where

$$\mathbf{A} = \begin{bmatrix} 0 & 1 \\ -1 & -2 \end{bmatrix}$$

How can we find a simpler form for $N(\mathbf{A})$? First we obtain the characteristic polynomial,

$$P(\lambda) = \lambda^2 + 2\lambda + 1$$

From the Cayley–Hamilton theorem we know that

$$P(\mathbf{A}) = \mathbf{A}^2 + 2\mathbf{A} + \mathbf{I} = 0$$

Solving for $\mathbf{A}^2$, we have

$$\mathbf{A}^2 = -(2\mathbf{A} + \mathbf{I})$$

Forming $\mathbf{A}^3$,

$$\mathbf{A}^3 = \mathbf{A} \cdot \mathbf{A}^2 = -\mathbf{A}(2\mathbf{A} + \mathbf{I}) = -2\mathbf{A}^2 - \mathbf{A}\mathbf{I}$$

Now we substitute for $\mathbf{A}^2$ once again

$$\mathbf{A}^3 = -2[-2\mathbf{A} - \mathbf{I}] - \mathbf{A}\mathbf{I}$$

$$= 3\mathbf{A} + 2\mathbf{I}$$

We can substitute these into Eq. (C-25) and

$$N(\mathbf{A}) = (3\mathbf{A} + 2\mathbf{I}) + 2(-2\mathbf{A} - \mathbf{I}) + \mathbf{A} + 5\mathbf{I}$$

or

$$N(\mathbf{A}) = 5\mathbf{I} \tag{C-26}$$

This equation is equivalent to Eq. (C-25) and is certainly much easier. This can be generalized in that any polynomial of an $n \times n$ matrix $\mathbf{A}$ can be reduced to a polynomial of order $(n-1)$. Consider a polynomial $N(\mathbf{A})$,

$$N(\mathbf{A}) = \mathbf{A}^m + \mathbf{A}^{m-1}\alpha_{m-1} + \cdots + \mathbf{I} \tag{C-27}$$

We would like to obtain a simpler expression for $N(\mathbf{A})$. This can be done by forming

$$\frac{N(\lambda)}{P(\lambda)} = Q(\lambda) + \frac{R(\lambda)}{P(\lambda)} \tag{C-28}$$

where $P(\lambda)$ is the characteristic polynomial of $\mathbf{A}$, $Q(\lambda)$ is a unique polynomial, and $R(\lambda)$ is the remainder. Rewriting this,

$$N(\lambda) = P(\lambda)Q(\lambda) + R(\lambda) \tag{C-29}$$

Now the corresponding matrix expression is

$$N(\mathbf{A}) = P(\mathbf{A})Q(\mathbf{A}) + R(\mathbf{A})$$

and since $P(\mathbf{A}) = 0$ from the Cayley–Hamilton's theorem we have

$$N(\mathbf{A}) = R(\mathbf{A}) \tag{C-30}$$

which is the required simpler form of $N(\mathbf{A})$.

As an example let

$$N(\mathbf{A}) = \mathbf{A}^3 + 5\mathbf{A}^2 + 18\mathbf{A} + 7\mathbf{I}$$

and the characteristic polynomial of a 2×2 coefficient matrix is

$$P(\lambda) = \lambda^2 + 3\lambda + 2$$

Then

$$\frac{N(\lambda)}{P(\lambda)} = \lambda + 2 + \frac{10\lambda + 3}{\lambda^2 + 3\lambda + 2}$$

The remainder is $R(\lambda) = 10\lambda + 3$. Therefore the simpler form of $N(\mathbf{A})$ is

$$N(\mathbf{A}) = 10\mathbf{A} + 3\mathbf{I}$$

We can go a step further. If $\mathbf{A}$ is an $n \times n$ matrix having discrete eigenvalues $\lambda_1, \lambda_2, \ldots, \lambda_n$ and we have a function $F(\mathbf{A})$, then we reduce this function to $R(\mathbf{A})$,

$$F(\mathbf{A}) = R(\mathbf{A}) \tag{C-31}$$

and that $R(\mathbf{A})$ is defined as

$$R(\mathbf{A}) = h_0\mathbf{I} + h_1\mathbf{A} + h_2\mathbf{A}^2 + \cdots + h_{n-1}\mathbf{A}^{n-1} \tag{C-32}$$

where $h_0, h_1, \ldots, h_{n-1}$ are obtained by satisfying the equations

$$F(\lambda_i) = R(\lambda_i); \qquad i = 1, 2, \ldots, n \qquad \text{(C-33)}$$

The proof of this closely follows our previous arguments and shall be omitted here.

If the eigenvalues of **A** are not distinct, then the previous formulation is slightly changed. Let us assume that **A** is a 3×3 matrix and the roots are

$$\lambda_1, \lambda_2, \lambda_3 = \lambda_2$$

Then

$$R(\mathbf{A}) = h_0\mathbf{I} + h_1\mathbf{A} + h_2\mathbf{A}^2 \qquad \text{(C-34)}$$

where h_0, h_1, h_2 are determined by satisfying

$$F(\lambda_1) = R(\lambda_1)$$
$$F(\lambda_2) = R(\lambda_2) \qquad \text{(C-35)}$$
$$\left[\frac{dF}{d\lambda}\right]_{\lambda = \lambda_2} = \left[\frac{dR(\lambda)}{d\lambda}\right]_{\lambda = \lambda_2}$$

The consequence of the previous discussion becomes very important when we select $F(\mathbf{A})$ such that

$$F(\mathbf{A}) = e^{\mathbf{A}t} \qquad \text{(C-36)}$$

where $e^{\mathbf{A}t}$ is the convergent exponential function series defined previously. It happens to be the solution to linear matrix differential equations. As an example, consider

$$\mathbf{A} = \begin{bmatrix} 0 & 1 \\ -3 & -4 \end{bmatrix}$$

where the function $F(\mathbf{A})$ is given by

$$F(\mathbf{A}) = e^{\mathbf{A}t}$$

We would like to reduce $F(\mathbf{A})$ to a polynomial

$$F(\mathbf{A}) = R(\mathbf{A}) = h_0\mathbf{I} + h_1\mathbf{A}$$

which is a first-order polynomial. If this is done, we have managed to replace an infinite series by a first-order polynomial for the solution of a linear matrix differential equation. The eigenvalues of **A** are

$$\lambda_1 = -3; \qquad \lambda_2 = -1$$

Since these are distinct, we form

$$F(-3) = e^{-3t} = h_0 - 3h_1$$

$$F(-1) = e^{-t} = h_0 - h_1$$

solving these

$$h_0 = \tfrac{1}{2}(3e^{-t} - e^{-3t}); \qquad h_1 = \tfrac{1}{2}(e^{-t} - e^{-3t})$$

Therefore

$$F(\mathbf{A}) = R(\mathbf{A}) = \tfrac{1}{2}(3e^{-t} - e^{-3t})\mathbf{I} + \tfrac{1}{2}(e^{-t} - e^{-3t})\mathbf{A}$$

Substitution yields

$$F(\mathbf{A}) = e^{\mathbf{A}t} = \begin{bmatrix} \tfrac{1}{2}(3e^{-t} - e^{-3t}) & \tfrac{1}{2}(e^{-t} - e^{-3t}) \\ -\tfrac{3}{2}(e^{-t} - e^{-3t}) & \tfrac{1}{2}(-e^{-t} + 3e^{-3t}) \end{bmatrix}$$

If the matrix is given by

$$\mathbf{A} = \begin{bmatrix} -1 & 1 \\ 0 & -1 \end{bmatrix}$$

then the characteristics roots are

$$\lambda_1 = -1; \qquad \lambda_2 = -1$$

which are not distinct. We therefore must satisfy Eq. (C-34) and Eq. (C-35),

$$\left[\frac{dF(\lambda)}{d\lambda}\right]_{\lambda_1} = \left[\frac{dR(\lambda)}{d\lambda}\right]_{\lambda_1}$$

$$F(\lambda_1) = R(\lambda_1)$$

The derivatives are

$$\frac{dF(\lambda)}{d\lambda} = te^{\lambda t}; \qquad \frac{dR(\lambda)}{d\lambda} = h_1$$

We form two equations,

$$e^{-t} = h_0 - h_1$$

$$te^{-t} = h_1$$

Solving this,

$$h_0 = e^{-t}(1 + t); \qquad h_1 = te^{-t}$$

Therefore

$$F(\mathbf{A}) = e^{\mathbf{A}t} = (1 + t)e^{-t}\mathbf{I} + te^{-t}\mathbf{A}$$

Substitution yields

$$F(\mathbf{A}) = \begin{bmatrix} e^{-t} & te^{-t} \\ 0 & e^{-t} \end{bmatrix}$$

REFERENCES

1. Bellman, R., *Introduction to Matrix Analysis*, New York, McGraw-Hill, 1960.
2. DeRusso, P. M., R. J. Roy, and C. M. Close, *State Variable for Engineers*, New York, Wiley, 1965.
3. Ayres, F., *Theory and Problems of Matrices*, New York, Schaum, 1962.
4. Gere, J. M., and W. Weaver, *Matrix Algebra for Engineers*, Princeton, N.J., D. Van Nostrand, 1965.
5. Hildebrand, F. B., *Introduction to Numerical Analysis*, New York, McGraw-Hill, 1956.
6. Smyth, M. P., *Linear Engineering Systems*, New York, Pergamon, 1972.

Index

TITLES IN THE PERGAMON UNIFIED ENGINEERING SERIES